# EGYPTIAN SOLAR RELIGION IN THE NEW KINGDOM

# EGYPTIAN SOLAR RELIGION IN THE NEW KINGDOM

## RE, AMUN AND THE CRISIS OF POLYTHEISM

JAN ASSMANN

Translated from the German
by Anthony Alcock

Routledge
Taylor & Francis Group
LONDON AND NEW YORK

First published 1995 by Kegan Paul International Limited

2 Park Square, Milton Park, Abingdon, Oxfordshire OX14 4RN
52 Vanderbilt Avenue, New York, NY 10017

*Routledge is an imprint of the Taylor & Francis Group, an informa business*

First issued in paperback 2019



*British Library Cataloguing in Publication Data*
A catalogue record for this book is available from the British Library

ISBN 13: 978-0-7103-0465-0 (hbk)
ISBN 13: 978-0-367-86491-0 (pbk)

**Publisher's Note**

The publisher has gone to great lengths to ensure the quality of this reprint but points out that some imperfections in the original copies may be apparent. The publisher has made every effort to contact original copyright holders and would welcome correspondence from those they have been unable to trace.

*For Erik Hornung*
*(1983/1993)*

CONTENTS

# PREFACE TO THE ENGLISH EDITION

This book is a study of Ancient Egyptian theology, or, more precisely: of the theology of Egyptian texts belonging to a certain period: the New Kingdom. The term "theology" might appear questionable with reference to ancient Egyptian religion. On first view, it seems extremely improbable that something like theology existed in an early or "primary" religion. The application of this term looks like a eurocentristic retroprojection of problems that form the center of our own religion but that by all probability were very remote from ancient Egyptian preoccupations.

The same misgivings apply to the term "polytheism". This notion seems quite inappropriate to describe primary religions, for two reasons. First, because it is formed from the point of view of monotheism and does not serve as an element of self-definition for the religions that are classified as "polytheistic". These religions are not concerned with the plurality of gods in the same way as monotheism is concerned with the oneness of the divine. Second, because in primary religions, questions of religious pragmatics, of sacrifice, ritual and taboo, normally have priority over questions of "-theism", of the conceptions of god and of religious semantics. Theology, however, belongs within the context of religions that are primarily concerned with the conception of god, i.e. monotheistic religions.

An extreme concept of theology even wants to reserve theology for the Christian religion as the only religion that worships God as "logos". Theology, in this view, is correlative to what could be called Christian "logotheism". In this extreme sense, the term "theology" is, of course, inapplicable for anything else than Christian theology. But the term is also used in the broader sense of a logically and argumentatively organized knowledge and discourse on the divine ("lehrhaft entfaltete Rede von Gott"), and in this broader sense it is frequently seen as an exclusive phenomenon of those "secondary" religions that have given up sacrifice and ritual as the center and fundament of religious life and have based themselves on the word, in the form of sacred scripture and oral exegesis.

It is indeed extremely plausible that theology in the sense of "knowledge and discourse of the divine" emerges along with secondary religions and their shift from ritual practice to semantics, to verbal expression and communication. Nevertheless, and inspite of all its intrinsic plausibility, this presumption is false. As improbable and implausible as this fact might appear: there are many hundreds of ancient Egyptian texts (representing only a very small portion of the original literature) that expound a "discourse on the divine" which, as far as terminological differentiation and conceptual complexity is concerned, has no equivalent in the Old Testament.

We are dealing here - as has been shown, among others, by Jack Goody and Philippe Derchain - with a specifically "literate" phenomenon: with an evolutionary process that is based on the specific possibilities of writing, i.e. of critical reference to preceding positions. In view of the structural literacy of this discourse, one should perhaps speak of "theo*graphy*" rather than "theology", "writing of god" rather than "speaking of god", in the same sense as we speak of historio*graphy*, writing of history, because in this case, too, the phenomenon seems inseparably linked to writing and its discursive potentials and possibilties. On these possibilities of intertextual reference is based, what I propose to call the "Theological Discourse" and what this book attempts to analyse and to reconstruct in its evolutionary stages.

Such an intensity of intertextual reference is typical of a highly literate state of culture which, in Egypt, has been reached only in the New Kingdom, especially during the Ramesside period. But it would be a reductionist fallacy to explain the emergence and unfolding of the Theological Discourse by the rise of literacy alone. Literacy here is a necessary but not as a sufficient condition. Behind the rise of the Theological Discourse there can be discerned a fundamental "crisis of polytheism". It is this crisis whose intellectual and spiritual "processing" (Verarbeitung) produces the discourse.

Israel, in its earlier, prophetic stages, is beyond this crisis and less literate. It is simply unconcerned with questions of the One and the Many that preoccupy the minds of the Egyptian priests, sages and *litterati*. For the prophetic discourse, the many do not exist. Radical monotheism means a radical reduction of complexity. The statement, at first sight so strikingly implausible, that Egyptian theology (or theography) is in some respect superior to the Biblical one, thus finds a very simple explanation. The Theological Discourse of the New Kingdom, moreover, is a phenomenon of universal significance. Its results form the fundaments not only of the temple inscriptions of the Greco-Roman period, but also of other Greco-Egyptian religious and philosophical literature including the Magical papyri and the Corpus Hermeticum, and it might be argued that the pan- or "cosmotheistic" monotheism of certain philosophical trends in antiquity ultimately derive from Ramesside theology.

The crisis of polytheism is primarily concerned with the conception of god, with questions of unity and plurality that are pushed - long before the rise of monotheistic religions in the proper sense - to the extremes of radical and revolutionary monotheism. It would again be a reductionist fallacy to see in this conflict nothing but the expression of political and economical tensions. The intellectual dimension of this conflict is revealed by the texts and the Theological Discourse they expound.

These short remarks seemed necessary to explain to an English speaking audience an undertaking that, for whatever reasons, appears somewhat less extravagant in the German context, where the term "theology" has been in use among egyptologists since the days of Richard Lepsius.

The original German version has been revised and enlarged for the English edition in the following points:

- Many texts, the knowledge or easy accessibility of which has been presupposed in the German version, are here included in translation. The book can therefore be used independently of my edition of the Theban hymns (*STG*).

- All texts or quotations are given also in translation (in the German version many of the shorter quotations are rendered in transcription only).

- New texts have been included, especially the "evening" part of the cult-theological treatise ed. C.M.Betrò, the Pap. Leiden J 344 vso. ed. J.Zandee and the inscriptions of the newly discovered Theban tomb No. -162- ed. F.Kampp.

- New literature has been taken notice of as far as possible.

- The over-long chapter 5 has been split in three separate chapters and has been enlarged in several parts.

Anthony Alcock did much more than just a translation of the German text. In many places he helped to avoid errors, proposed better readings and renderings and clarified the line of argumentation. Alan Lloyd read the whole manuscript and contributed many improvements. Martin Bommas invested a great amount of care, intelligence and perseverance in the preparation of the indexes. Thanks are also due to Kaori O'Connor who patiently and efficiently accompanied the project through its different and sometimes difficult stages of realisation.

Heidelberg, August 1994 Jan Assmann

# INTRODUCTION

The golden age of Egyptian solar hymns, the three centuries from c.1500 to 1200 B.C. which have provided us with many hundreds of examples of them, is a unique phenomenon. No other period of Egyptian history, indeed no other culture, has produced such an abundance of poetry in praise of the sun god. There can be no doubt that the sheer volume of this poetry is connected with the institution of the tomb. Once the custom of recording sun hymns in the tomb had become established, it was quite natural that many of these inscriptions should have been preserved for us. Unlike the inscriptions usually categorised under the heading "Personal Piety",[1] which were recorded as a result of individual religious experience, the recording of sun hymns in tombs, it might be argued, was mere routine, the fulfilment of a prescribed norm: they are not to be understood as an expression of living (i.e contemporary) theological discourse, any more than the biographical inscriptions, which are far more numerous and cover a much longer historical period, are to be understood as an expression of contemporary anthropological discourse, i.e the on-going intellectual debate about the problems of "I" and "society", "man" and "the cosmos" and so on; "in fact" (the argument might continue), we are simply dealing with the use of a traditional stock of predetermined formulae and clichés.

Whatever the case with the biographical inscriptions (which, apart from those of the Late Period,[2] still await analysis on the level of intellectual history), I believe that the sun hymns of the tombs can be judged in quite a multi-faceted way. There is

1 Personal Piety is a unique phenomenon that will be dealt with in this book only insofar as it appears within the framework of Amun-Re theology. For a more comprehensive assessment see my articles "Weisheit, Loyalismus und Frömmigkeit", in E. Hornung und O. Keel (ed.), *Studien zu altägyptischen Lebenslehren* (*OBO* 28, 1979), 11-72 and *RdE* 30 (1978), 22-50. I should perhaps explain here the method of quotation adopted in the present work. Since this book represents the product of twenty years of research that has already appeared in a variety of publications, it is unfortunately impossible to avoid referring the reader to these publications for details. In such cases the author has not been cited. These are not, of course, the only works on the subject of Personal Piety. On the contrary, the literature is considerable. Especially important are the early works of A. Erman, *Denksteine aus der thebanischen Gräberstadt* (SBAW 1911) and B. Gunn, "The Religion of the Poor in Ancient Egypt", *JEA* 3 (1916), 81-94, the fundamental essay of H. Brunner on the religious assessment of poverty in ancient Egypt ("Die religiöse Wertung der Armut im alten Ägypten", *Saeculum* 12 (1961), 319-344), the monograph of G. Fecht on the literary evidence for Personal Piety (*Literarische Zeugnisse zur «Persönlichen Frömmigkeit» in Ägypten*, [AHAW 1965]) and the pioneering work of G. Posener, "La piété personelle avant l'âge amarnien", *RdE* 27 (1975), 195-210, which assigns an early date to the phenomenon, and many others, cf. the literature cited in H. Brunner, "Persönliche Frömmigkeit", *LÄ* IV, 951-963. For recent literature on "Personal Piety" cf. A.I. Sadek, *Popular Religion in Ancient Egypt (HÄB* 27, 1987); J. Baines, "Practical Religion and Piety", *JEA* 73 (1987), 79-98; id., "Society, Morality, and Religious Practice", in B.E. Shafer (ed.), *Religion in Ancient Egypt* (London, 1991), 123-200.

2 E. Otto, *Die biographischen Inschriften der ägyptischen Spätzeit* (Probleme der Ägyptologie 2, 1954). Regrettably Otto has not published the texts. For the biographical inscriptions of Dyn. 22 see now K. Jansen-Winkeln, *Ägyptische Biographien der 22. und 23. Dynastie*, 2 vols., ÄAT 8 (Wiesbaden, 1985).

indeed a lot of "routine", the fulfilling of a prescribed norm, in the New Kingdom sun hymns. This is the case with hymns from a small group of "standard texts", where repeated copying indicates a "seal of approval". I have dealt with these in my book *Liturgische Lieder*.[3] But, even if one leaves aside the hymns (in excess of 200) based on just a few exemplars,[4] which can be shown to belong to the cult,[5] there remains an astonishing abundance of hymns that have an individual character and, like the Personal Piety inscriptions, represent the textual expression of a spiritual-religious movement. Even if they are not, like the Personal Piety texts, a spontaneous expression of religious experience (which, of course, even in the case of Personal Piety, can be formulated and recorded only within an institutionalised framework and makes use of a corresponding set of formulae), but arise from a collective debate about the problems and phenomena relating to Egyptian solar religion, they are nevertheless historical, i.e. they can be dated as stages of a spiritual process. As a literary phenomenon, the extant texts represent what might be called the Golden Age of the Egyptian solar hymn. The spiritual movement that is embedded in and expressed by them might be described as the struggle to articulate a concept of the unity of the divine, i.e. the One God.

The uniqueness or oneness of god is the central theological problem of the New Kingdom. The Amarna period, where an attempt was made in the form of revolution from above to encompass and change all aspects of Egyptian culture and to adopt the doctrine of One God by the forceable removal of traditional polytheism, is striking proof of the historical explosiveness of this problem.[6] It is less well known that the problem was by no means solved with the failure of Amarna religion. It may be said that "monotheism" did not succeed because it reduced cosmology to a juxtaposition of "above" and "below", i.e. god and the world, which in no way did justice to the Egyptian experience of reality.[7] In a later age, "monotheism" gave way to the "pantheistic" solution, according to which a transcendentally supreme god was theologically "reconciled" with the cosmic polytheistic world of gods reflecting his naturally concealed unity. It must be understood that I am using concepts like "monotheism" and "pantheism" merely to clarify the problem for which the solution is being sought. The essay contained in the following chapters of this book deliberately avoids using such "labels". The discomfort now rightly felt by Egyptologists in employing these terms, especially after the thorough dismantling of such models by Erik Hornung in *Der Eine und die Vielen* (1971),[8] should not blind us to the vital significance of the attempt to articulate concepts of the unity of god and to harness this conception (or experience) with the ultimately indispensable reality of polytheism in Egyptian religion during these centuries. This problem does not arise from our own "monotheistic" position, which makes it difficult for us to understand polytheistic

3 There are now more than 50 recorded instances of *LL* III 1.

4 Index A in *LL* 373-377 lists 205 "texts" on 160 "monuments", which are to be understood as recorded instances of the 17 exemplars annotated in this study.

5 Cf. chap.1 note 2.

6 Cf. "Akhanyati's Theology of Light and Time", *Proceedings of the Israel Academy of Sciences and Humanities,* VII 4 (Jerusalem, 1992), 143-176.

7 Cf. chap.3 §§ 2.2-2.4 and 5.

8 Eng. tr. *Conceptions of God in Ancient Egypt* (1982).

cosmology, but confronts us in the texts themselves: it is explicit, central and cannot be ignored. It is the dominant theme of the theological discourse which establishes the contours of Egyptian cosmology at the same time as determining the nature of the divine.

The texts in which this discourse manifests itself are sun hymns. For the purposes of this introduction it is sufficient to summarise aspects of the phenomenon differentiated in the two halves of this book and presented relatively independently under the concept "sun religion". The question of one god has been posed within this religion: it is expressed in sun hymns. Not all of these sun hymns (in the broad sense of embracing the composites Re-Harakhty and Amun-Re) are found in the tombs. The longest and most important are preserved in literary and liturgical papyri and on the walls of the temple of Darius I in Hibis. The "tomb-hymns" serve not merely to round off the picture that emerges from the other sources, but rather, and most importantly, provide this picture with a historical dimension. It is thanks to the abundance of inscriptions that we are able to study the temporal, spatial and sociological aspects of the religious tradition. Only in the many precisely dated inscriptions can one see the development of the ideas of the deity, distinguish local traditions and determine the body of knowledge that belonged exclusively to the higher priesthood and ideas of the deity entertained by the broad mass of the population. Only differentiation of this sort makes it possible to understand (i.e. reconstruct the underlying problem posed by these texts) the questions to which they provide the answer. The confusion in which Egyptian theology[9] usually appears in the texts produces a degree of complexity that precludes comprehensive understanding of it. The sun hymns of the tomb inscriptions, which reveal the theological process of solar religion in its temporal, spatial and sociological dimensions, provide us with a means of access, perhaps unique and certainly the first of its kind, to understanding a period and aspect of Egyptian religion.

In this book I shall attempt to follow that path. The book itself is a direct sequel to the annotated edition of all sun hymns from Theban tombs that were accessible to me between 1963 and 1977. It presents a view of these hymns that has taken shape as a result of two decades of studying these texts.[10]

One might ask what value a fully developed exegesis has in a discipline where the edition of primary sources still ranks as "first priority".[11] What students of theology, classical studies and modern literature take for granted is considered by Egyptologists to be a luxury, if not indeed merely idle speculation. Would it therefore not be more sensible to edit new texts instead of trying to present an

---

9 For an explanation and justification of this term with regard to Ancient Egyptian religion cf. "Arbeit am Polytheismus. Die Idee der Einheit Gottes und die Entfaltung des theologischen Diskurses in Ägypten", in H.v. Stietencron (ed.), *Theologen und Theologien in verschiedenen Kulturkreisen* (Düsseldorf, 1986), 46-69.

10 The texts have been edited and translated in *Sonnenhymnen in thebanischen Gräbern* (STG), published in 1983. These texts are cited here as, e.g. *STG* No. 149 (c). My source-book translation *Ägyptische Hymnen und Gebete*, cited as *ÄHG* followed by a number, provides the reader with all necessary bibliographical details.

11 The suggestion made by Posener at the 1st International Egyptology Conference (Cairo 1976), published in Acts of ICE pp.519-522, describes the situation exactly.

interpretation that must still remain subjective? It might be argued, for example, that Sethe, after producing his superb edition of the Pyramid Texts, would have been better advised to devote his attention to the edition of Pyramid Texts on Middle Kingdom coffins instead of yielding to the temptation of sketching "his" view of prehistory and its religion. In the case of New Kingdom sun hymns, however, the chances of understanding are incomparably better than in the case of the Pyramid Texts. The texts are so numerous and varied that, unlike other Egyptian texts, they can withstand the arbitrariness and subjectivity of interpretation, thus presenting a conceivably solid basis for the reconstruction of their conceptual world and message. One should therefore make use of such an opportunity. It is obvious that attempts to understand become outdated more rapidly than the textual editions on which they are based: "understanding" succumbs more easily to the ravages of time than "editing".

What then is the basis of the much-vaunted "intelligibility" of the sun hymns? It is more than simply a question of the abundant textual material. There are, for example, hundreds of copies of the BD, which come from various periods, places and social strata. But there is scarcely a chapter in this corpus of texts, least of all the much studied 17th,[12] where I feel that my understanding is as securely based as it is in the case of the sun hymns. The decisive point of difference between the two is the form in which they have been transmitted: that of the sun hymns is for the most part "dynamically" active, whereas that of the BD is "statically" reproductive. In the case of the sun hymns this productivity makes understanding possible, while the reproductive mode of transmission of the BD makes understanding difficult or impossible. I shall explain the difference in the following paragraphs.[13]

The reproductive tradition is one where the sole function is to copy. Typical examples of this tradition, apart from the BD, are the so-called "classics" of Egyptian literature.[14] In order to analyse the historical dimension of these texts, one has to try to reconstruct the productive stage of their tradition. Our conception of the Heracleopolitan period, for example, has been formed by such a reconstruction of literature that has recently been much criticised.[15] The difficulty of reconstructing a productive phase for BD texts and regaining their historical dimension appears for the moment to be insuperable. Sethe's ingenious attempt to unravel the complexity of the conceptual world revealed in the Pyramid Texts by tracing it back to the "kingdoms" of prehistory strikes us now as almost recherché.[16]

---

12 U. Rössler-Köhler, *Kapitel 17 des ägyptischen Totenbuches* (GOF IV.10, 1979).

13 Cf. also *ÄHG* 91-94

14 Cf. "Gibt es eine Klassik in der ägyptischen Literaturgeschichte?", in *XXII. Deutscher Orientalistentag, Suppl. ZDMG* 1985, 35- 52.

15 W. Schenkel, "Repères chronologiques de l'histoire redactionelle des Coffin Texts", in W. Westendorf (ed.), *Göttinger Totenbuchstudien. Beiträge zum 17. Kapitel* (GOF IV.3 1975), especially pp.29-31. I agree with Schenkel that the "Heracleopolitan Period" is a "fiction", but think that "fictions" of this sort belong to the legitimate and unavoidable, if constantly improvable, arsenal of the historian. If we were to banish all fictions from our statements about Egyptian culture, we should be reduced to silence. The question is whether there are things like "illegitimate" fictions. I do not know of any set of criteria that would make such a distinction possible; cf. the following note.

16 K. Sethe, *Urgeschichte und älteste Religion der Ägypter*, (Beiheft ZMDG 1930). Even this cannot be described as an "illegitimate" fiction, as H. Kees (though he takes the opposite point of view) points

Religious tradition, by its very nature, tends towards reproductivity, i.e. the process of canonisation, which transfers the "holiness" of an object to the discourse that has grown up around that object. This process has taken place in the case of the sun hymns. The three forms within whose institutionalised framework the peculiar phenomenon of the funerary sun hymns developed throughout the New Kingdom are:

1. hymns at the tomb entrance, later also doorways to internal chambers and tomb facade;[17]
2. hymns on stelae and (stelophorous) statues placed in the tomb;[18]
3. hymns with which post-Amarna copies of the BD tend to open.[19]

The three forms survive into the Late Period, but the texts undergo a process of sclerosis and canonisation:

1. hymns in Saite tombs reproduce old models. More use is made of cult texts from the "mysteries" that were still secret in the New Kingdom, especially the Hour Ritual, which had always belonged to the realm of reproductive tradition;
2. typical funerary stelae of the Late Period[20] contain either a text from chap.15 of the BD (see below) or the pair of hymns to the rising and setting sun that are mistakenly referred to as BD A 4/B 5,[21] but in fact have nothing to do with the BD;
3. the sun hymns no longer serve as a preface to the BD in any arrangement, but are integrated in fixed form as "chapter 15".[22] This chapter is thus retrospectively a canonical composite of individual texts, which together reveal a history going back to the 18th Dynasty.[23]

The productive phase of the tradition reproduced in these sources (apart from the "mystery" texts, which will be partly older) is the 18th/19th Dynasty and does need to be reconstructed, but is clear from an abundance of inscriptional material. Even the 20th/21st Dynasty is still productive[24] in terms of sun hymns. But these sun

---

out in his complimentary assessment of Sethe's argument in the Foreword to his book *Der Götterglaube im alten Ägypten*. Even the fiction of prehistoric "kingdoms" has a certain value, inasmuch as "all the layers are removed with surgical or mathematical precision, so that the most diverse influences become clearly recognisable" (p.iv). Sethe too wanted to disentangle complexity, but considered the temporal dimension as the only one valid.

17 Cf. *STG* Introduction §2.

18 On the stelophorous statues cf. the monograph (unfortunately difficult to obtain) of Claire Lalouette, *Fidèles du soleil* (Faculté des Lettres et Sciences Humaines de Paris, Groupes d'Etudes Egyptologiques I 1963) and H. M. Stewart in *JEA* 53(1967), 37ff.

19 The description of these hymns as "chapter 15" of the BD has caused the most unfortunate confusion. These hymns are outside the corpus of canonical spells that had still not been fixed in the New Kingdom. They have been prefixed to this corpus and are associated with the ideas of "entrance" or rather "exit" (*prt m hrww*), rather like the hymns of the tomb entrance or exit. It was only later, in the course of a canonisation process, that these hymns were incorporated into the corpus as "chapter 15".

20 P. Munro, *Die spätägyptischen Totenstelen* (ÄgFo 25, 1973).

21 T.G. Allen, "Some Egyptian sun hymns", *JNES* 8(1949), 349-356; cf. *LL*, 73ff. n.144 and 291 n.43.

22 E. Lefebure, *Traduction comparée des hymnes au soleil composant le XVe chapitre du rituel funéraire égyptien* (1868); T.G. Allen, *The Egyptian Book of the Dead* (Chicago, 1960).

23 H.M. Stewart, "Traditional Egyptian Sun Hymns of the New Kingdom", *BIA London* 6(1967), 42 n.96.

24 On the 21st Dynasty cf. Heerma van Voss "Die Totenliteratur der 21.Dynastie", *JEOL* 24(1975-76), 48ff.

hymns are not reproduced in later periods. The "archaism" of the Late Period[25] does not reach back to what immediately precedes it, but to what was felt to be "classical" antiquity. It was not until the Late Period that the sun hymns, in the form of chap. 15 of the BD, take on the character of "sacred texts", in which the exact wording is important.

By their very nature, sacred texts belong to the reproductive tradition, which requires a culture of exegesis to prevent its meaning from getting lost in later generations. In contrast to productive tradition, which constantly uses new formulations to accommodate changing historical reality, the text of the reproductive tradition sooner or later loses contact with historical reality: the language changes, words and forms become obsolete or take on other meanings, new horizons of experience and understanding create new meanings and frames of reference, and so on. This process is inevitable, but the consequences of it are to some extent mitigated by the creation of a philological and theological science of hermeneutics, the task of which gradually becomes greater and more difficult as the distance between "text" and "reality" increases. As a result of its canonisation the theological (and *mutatis mutandis* the literary) discourse mobilises specialists, who make themselves familiar not merely with the tradition of these texts but also with the constantly expanding body of knowledge required to continue the tradition: the scribes of the House of Tablets (*e-dub-ba*) in Babylonia, the brahmins in Hinduism, the soferîm in Israel, the rabbis in Judaism, the scribes and lector priests in the House of Life in Egypt. Canonisation of the religious discourse, establishment of an exclusive class of priests and identification of religious knowledge as something separable from the whole cultural system are three interdependent processes.[26] Unlike in Hinduism and Judaism, commentary as a necessary correlate of canonisation in Egyptian religion was kept to the minimum.[27] In Egypt, the efforts of scriptural transmission concentrate more on textual criticism than on interpretation.[28]

Priestly cult religion and popular religion begin to diverge as the religious discourse becomes a distinct entity within the entire system of cultural communication, becoming a corpus of canonical texts and esoteric knowledge in the hands of a few specialists. An abundance of tomb inscriptions makes it eminently

25 H. Brunner "Zum Verständnis der archaisierenden Tendenzen der ägyptischen Spätzeit", *Saeculum* 21(1970), 151-161.

26 Cf. A.&J. Assmann (eds.), *Kanon und Zensur* (Munich, 1987).

27 The best known example of an annotated translation of an ancient text into a later stage of the language is the commentary on the Book of Nut, ed. H.O. Lange and O. Neugebauer, *Papyrus Carlsberg 1* (Kopenhagen, 1940); cf. also S. Schott, *Die Deutung der Geheimnisse des Rituals für die Abwehr des Bösen. Eine altägyptische Übersetzung* (AbhAWL 5, 1954). On the problem of "glossing" chapter 17 of the BD cf. W. Schenkel (n.9 p.69) and U. Rössler-Köhler (n.8 pp.348-350). The problem of these glosses is that they operate on exactly the same level as the "main text". Nothing is "translated" into another language level or conceptual world. Equally, nothing is explained. Only possible references are produced. It is almost like an "initiation examination", which summarises an exclusive body of knowledge in the form not only of a "compendium" (Rößler-Köhler), but also of a "catechism", see "Death and Initiation in the funerary Religion of Ancient Egypt", in W.K. Simpson (ed.), *Religion and Philosophy in Ancient Egypt*, *YES* 2 (1989), 135-159, esp. 143ff.

28 Cf. U. Rößler-Köhler, loc. cit.; D.P. Silverman, "Textual Criticism in the Coffin Texts", in: W.K. Simpson (ed.), *Religion and Philosophy in Ancient Egypt* (*YES* 3) (New Haven, 1989), 29-53.

possible for us to check the extent to which religious knowledge penetrated non-priestly, albeit certainly educated and literate sections of the population. These inscriptions represent "productive" tradition, in which new texts were being produced within the institutionalised framework of genre structures[29] and forms of recording.[30] The normative implications of the recording tradition would have been satisfied by always placing the same text at the tomb entrance (as in the case of the Sun Litany in the Royal Tombs). However, the fact that mostly new texts were displayed here shows that it was not a particular tradition that led to the production of these texts, but rather a religious process of enormous "popularity" that created its own tradition. If the productivity of the genre is a criterion, no area of Egyptian religion in the New Kingdom was even remotely as "popular" (i.e. represented in so many individual texts in tombs belonging to different cemeteries and different social strata) as solar religion (in the broader sense that also encompasses Amun-Re). Second in "popularity" by a long way is Osiris, in whose worship the reproductive tradition plays an incomparably greater role.

As for sun hymns, three groups may be distinguished on the basis of formal transmission.

*1. Texts of an esoteric body of knowledge.* In the (reproductive) tradition of these canonical texts Saite tombs are of major importance. Like the underworld books, the wisdom of which was closely guarded in the New Kingdom by royal prerogative, it was not until the Saite period that these hymns became available for use in non-royal tombs. The most valuable document is, in fact, not a sun hymn, but appears occasionally in connection with sun hymns and explains with exceptional clarity how the cult worship of the sun god is possible and thus how the "esoteric" side of the sun cult understands itself.[31] This text provides a bridge between the "esoteric" hymns in the cult and the underworld books, i.e. the equally esoteric cosmographical "gnosis" literature of the royal tombs; it shows clearly that both texts belong with the same mode of discourse. Like the Amduat and the Hour Ritual, it might belong to a tradition that predates the New Kingdom.[32]

Royalty was not satisfied indefinitely with the repetitive tradition of the Amduat for its tombs. After the Amarna period compositions such as the Book of Gates, the Book of Caves, the "Book of the Earth" began to make their appearance. There is

---

29 Cf. *ÄHG*, 6-94 (Introduction).

30 "Recording", in the case of monumental tomb decoration, means more than just a medium of storage. It implies the idea of monumental representation and immortalisation with regard to certain aspects of the tomb-owner's identity and reality. For the concept of "Aufzeichnungsform" cf. my article in *Fragen an die altägyptische Literatur* (Gedenkschrift Otto) (Wiesbaden 1977), 59-65.

31 *Der König als Sonnenpriester*, 24ff.; Maria Carmela Betrò, *I Testi solari del Portale di Pascerientaisu* (BN2), Università degli Studi di Pisa, Missioni Archeologiche in Egitto, Sakkara III (Pisa, 1990).

32 On the dating of the Cult-Theogical Treatise about the king as sun-priest to the Middle Kingdom cf. p.5 n.1 of my edition. The same dating is suggested by H. Altenmüller in *JEOL* 20 (1968), 27-42 for the Amduat, which is closely associated with this treatise. Hornung supports an early 18th Dynasty date, understanding it as a "guide to the underworld". i.e. a funerary text. In fact, the difference between it and the Book of the Two Ways, thought to be its predecessor in the same genre, is so great that they might belong to different epochs. I assign both texts to different genres: the Book of the Two Ways is a funerary text, whereas the Amduat is a cosmography from the Heliopolitan solar cult.

no clearer indication of the intensity of the movement experienced by solar religion in the 18th/19th Dynasty than these changes, which affected even the domain of inaccessible and esoteric traditions of knowledge, though this was far removed from all "popular" currents. Thus one may also imagine that the canon of sun hymns, which form part of the body of priestly-royal knowledge, increased considerably during the New Kingdom. This undoubtedly meant changes in the daily ritual. Nevertheless, it is much more difficult to arrange these texts historically than those generated by the productive tradition on this side of the invisible demarcation line that separated the secret knowledge of the "mysteries" of the sun-cult from the aspect of solar religion that looked outward and embraced increasingly wider circles, constantly gaining greater authority and significance.

2. *Standard texts.* By "standard texts" I mean the liturgical sun hymns used as models by tomb owners who were not in a position to generate new texts of their own. They originate in the cult, but are not secret or esoteric. The sun cult must have had an exoteric side that enabled the lay person to participate in it. Certain people, therefore, would have known these texts; their presence in tombs points more to an oral (i.e. from memory) tradition than to the use of written models.[33] The term "standard text" differs from the category identified by H.M.Stewart as the "traditional sun hymns". The only criterion used by Stewart for classifying a text as "traditional" is that it occurs more than once. Accordingly, texts such as the clearly innovatory hymn of Suty and Hor are categorised as traditional.[34] In my view, a "standard text" is one that occurs not only more than once but in more than one tradition.[35] Analysis of these special "standard texts" reveals a conceptual world that is also apparent in an abundance of other documents that bear witness to the sun cult, especially the numerous vignettes of the BD and tomb scenes of the journey of the sun. Accordingly, I regard all texts based on this conceptual world as traditional, whether they occur once or more than once. In my terms, therefore, all "standard texts" are traditional, but not all traditional texts are standard.

3. *Individual hymns.* By "individual hymns" I mean those that are significantly distant from that which can be identified in the first two groups as the traditional conceptual world. In other words, hymns in which another conceptual world is expressed. There are enough texts for us to identify not only the evolution of new thought in all its different stages but also different traditions within new thought. Accordingly I make a distinction on the one hand between "new solar theology", which is consciously different from traditional solar theology, and on the other hand the two successive expressions of the Theban Amun-Re theology: one that flourished in the time of Hatshepsut-Amenophis II, the other in the 13th BC.

These hymns represent an important stage in the great religious-historical process of these centuries. They are datable not only as inscriptions but also as texts, as statements in a discourse. The topics of this discourse are to be regarded as the central issues of this period. The abundance, variety, scope and theological niveau of those texts bear witness to the intensity with which these issues were debated. Matters that had fully occupied the human mind in a continuous social discourse for centuries now began to move and change in a historical process of development,

33 *STG* Introduction §3.

34 H.M. Stewart n.28 pp.53ff.

35 On the question of its transmission cf. *LL* pp.2ff. and n.4.

elaboration and differentiation. The tradition emerging from such circumstances is always productive.

The initial formulation of all Egyptian texts is rooted in a phase of productive tradition, within which they articulate a specific position in an area of discourse. The forms and contexts in which they have reached us are usually quite a long way from this formative phase and rarely allow us to reconstruct their original meaning and function. The philologist has to be content with elucidating details and producing order at individual points in a pattern of which he is unable to get an overview as a whole. The sun hymns of the New Kingdom offer a better starting point, for they allow us to trace their development. The historical dimension of the discourse manifested in them, the distribution of statements according to the temporal, spatial and social levels of historical reality, is not a matter of tiresome or indeed superfluous reconstruction, but can be read directly from the inscriptions themselves. This opens up a way that promises to take us more deeply into Egyptian thought than is usually possible and to "understand" that thought. By "understanding" I do not mean empathy or "tuning into", which may deceive one into thinking that one has reached the destination without having realised that a journey is either possible or necessary. Rather I mean analysing and sorting the material that has been transmitted to us, so that by reducing its complexity we may uncover meaningful and, as such, intelligible contexts. Thus, we are still a long way from our destination, but we have embarked on a path that will take us nearer to it.

The transmitted material, which I classify in this book, consists of over 500 texts from the New Kingdom that reflect solar and Amun theology. The analysis will be made, as I have already said, according to time, space and social stratum, and I shall use the terms (borrowed from linguistics) "diachronic", "diatopic" and "diastratic" when discussing these criteria. The first two criteria are self-explanatory: the diachronic criterion derives from the productive tradition, i.e. the recording of new texts, in which the date of recording and the date of composition will be quite close to each other; the diatopic criterion derives partly from the spatial distribution of the inscriptions, i.e. predominantly Sakkara and Thebes, but it must be remembered that in the reproductive tradition, where written models were copied exactly, the place of origin might be quite different from the location when copied. The centre of solar religion was Heliopolis. It is therefore reasonable to suppose that Heliopolitan texts were being recorded at least in the reproductive tradition. It can be shown that all texts based on the reproductive tradition are free from elements of Theban Amun theology and are based on traditional solar theoloy. One is therefore justified in looking to Heliopolis as the source of both groups of texts: the "mystery" and "standard" texts, which share the historical-traditional criterion of reproductivity and the content criterion of pure and traditional solar theology.

The distinction between "traditional" and "new solar theology" is based on diachronic differences. "New solar theology" seems to be a universal Egyptian phenomenon: it appears in Theban (Suty and Hor) and Memphite texts.[36] It does

36 Cf. *MDIK* 21,1 (1971), 1-20 and, later on, chap 3. One of the most important texts of the "new solar theology" is located in the tomb of the Ramesseum administrator Haremhab, where one would not expect it. Only very small fragments survive, but these can be supplemented from the Ptah hymn in P. Berlin 3048 (*ÄHG* 143); cf. J. Quibbell, *Excavations at Sakkara IV* (1908-1910), pl. 73.3 and K. Kitchen, *RI III*,188ff.

not, however, appear before the reign of Amenophis III.[37] Scholars used to consider these texts as forerunners of Amarna religion and later versions (of which only a few were known) as echoes of the same. However, the new Theban material makes it clear that we are dealing with a "new solar theology" that is quite independent of Amarna and would have developed without the upheaval caused by Akhenaten. The post-Amarna and Ramesside texts continue uninterruptedly the position developed in the pre-Amarna texts. This would be inconceivable if that position had been understood and discredited as "Atenism".

The distinction beween an "early phase" (Hatshepsut to Amenophis II) and a Ramesside phase of Amun theology (Theban) is based on diachronic differences. The texts expressing these phases of Theban theology are all individual, i.e. they are based on productive tradition and do not appear outside Thebes.[38] There is an additional criterion: Amun occurs in them not only as an occasional extension of the divine name Re-Harakhty (which means nothing at all in Theban inscriptions[39]), but displays in these texts important aspects of his theology:

a. primordial god theology
b. the concept of personal god, related to
c. ethical dimension, alien to pure solar religion
d. distinct emphasis on the uniqueness of god, represented in the early phase as "primacy", in the Ramesside phase as "transcendence".[40]

Unlike the new solar theology, which had considerable influence on Amarna religion but was not itself influenced by Amarna, Theban Amun theology was heavily influenced by Amarna. The specifically "pantheistic" character of Ramesside Amun theology[41] is not evident in its early form and can only be understood as a response to the religion of Amarna: it was an attempt to associate the idea of one god with the polytheistic concept of divinity and multiplicity within the cosmos.

Finally, the diastratic criterion refers to the exclusive nature of the "mysteries": they were texts from a body of knowledge not available to everyone. The books of the underworld and heaven in the royal tombs and the Osireion at Abydos belong to this corpus. One would not be far wrong in making Heliopolis the home of these texts. The Heliopolitan cult was a re-enactment of the course of the sun in the upper and lower worlds[42] and thus a celebration of time that is maintained as the

---

37 *MDIK* 27,1, 1ff. and TT 76.

38 Apart from the parallel to TT 68 in the tomb of Paheri at El Kab (*Urk*. iv, 111) and the pure "Theban" Onuris eulogy of Satepihu at This (Urk. iv, 518). Even the so-called Tura Hymn is a Theban text; the peculiar circumstances surrounding the location of this hymn can probably be explained by the persecution of Amun religion in the Amarna period, cf. chap. 6 §1.3.1.

39 For example pBerlin 3050 I. That it is a pure sun hymn is clear from the title, but the name of Amun is inserted into the invocation. This was reason enough for A. Barucq and F. Daumas to put it among the "hymnes à Amon".

40 Cf. "Primat und Transzendenz" in W. Westendorf (ed.), *Aspekte der altägyptischen Religion* (GOF IV.9, 1979), 7-42.

41 By "pantheism" I understand the cult and theology of a deity praised as "pantheos", i.e. encompassing and incorporating all the other gods. I cannot see why this criterion should not apply to certain Egyptian texts, pace Hornung, *Conceptions*, 128.

42 On the crypt of Heliopolitan temples as cultic representation of the underworld cf. Text 158 (n) and chap.2 and n.144.

continuation of reality.[43] Time is also understood here as the life-cycle of the divine cosmos, the abundance of time and life of the cosmos into which the deceased hopes to enter. For this reason they are recorded as funerary texts for the king in his tomb. The diastratic dimension of social stratum, therefore, is used here to mean a distinction in terms of the sociology of knowledge: access to certain texts that constitute a body of knowledge is limited. As far as I can tell, this category has been hitherto entirely neglected. We shall have to ask ourselves how far the conceptual world of the books of the heavens and the underworld now available to us in the superb editions and commentaries of Alexander Piankoff and Erik Hornung reflect Egyptian cosmology and not simply the arcane knowledge of a small elite that has little or nothing to do with the questions that so profoundly affected Egyptian intellectual history in the centuries dealt with in this book.[44] Some disagreements between the respected friend and colleague to whom this book is dedicated and myself arise from the fact that our material is taken from different bodies of knowledge. Hornung concentrates his attention on royal underworld books, though he is familiar with the abundant non-royal inscriptional material. My own view, despite intensive study of the underworld books, is based more on non-royal inscriptions. Analysis of the Egyptian tradition in terms of the sociology of knowledge points the way that may enable us to resolve the debate and achieve an understanding of the historical reality that does justice to both approaches and at the same time is more satisfactory.

---

43 Cf. "Magische Weisheit im altägyptischen Kosmotheismus", in A. Assmann (ed.), *Weisheit* (München, 1991), 241-258.

44 E. Hornung, *Ägyptische Unterweltsbücher*, 17ff. gives a history of this genre that reflects the changes of Egyptian solar religion.

## Appendix

The following seven texts are the "standard texts" referred to in the Introduction.

### Text A: Sunrise[45]

The most common sun hymn of the New Kingdom, it consists of 14 lines divided into two stanzas, of which the first (6 lines) deals with sunrise and the second (8 lines) with journey. The standard version declines in popularity by the Ramesside period. It occurs also in a short version, in combination with other hymns and in a long version with a third stanza.

| | |
|---|---|
| *jnḏ-ḥr=k Rꜥw m wbn=k* | Hail to you, Re, at your rising |
| *Jtmw m ḥtp=k nfr* | Atum, at your beautiful setting |
| *ẖꜥj=k psḏ=k ḥr psḏ mwt=k* | You appear and shine on the back of your mother |
| *ẖꜥj.tj m njswt psḏt* | appearing as King of the Ennead |
| *jrj Nwt njnj n-ḥr=k* | Nut greets you with *njnj* |
| *ḥtp tw Mꜣꜥt r trwj* | Maat embraces you at all times |
| *nmj=k ḥrt jb=k ꜣwjw* | You cross the sky with dilated heart |
| *mr nẖꜣwj ẖprw m ḥtpw* | The Two Knives Lake is now at peace |
| *sbj ẖrw ꜥwj=fj qꜣsw* | The enemy is fallen, his arms bound |
| *ḥsq.n dmt ṯzwt=f* | The knife has cut through his spine |
| *wnn Rꜥw m mꜣꜥw nfr* | Re is in a fair wind |
| *Msktt sk.n.s pḥ sj* | The *Msktt* boat has destroyed its attacker |
| *sṯꜣ tw rsjw mḥtjw* | The southerners and northeners tow you |
| *jmntjw jꜣbtjw ḥr dwꜣ=k* | The easterners and westerners worship you |

### Text B: Sunset[46]

The full text of the standard version occurs in TT 192, where it stands opposite Text A on the right hand side of the tomb entrance In addition to it there are three short versions and a liturgical copy in a Ramesside ritual for Amenophis I

| | |
|---|---|
| *jnḏ-ḥr=k Rꜥw* | Hail to you, Re |
| *ḥtp=k m ꜥnẖ* | When you set in life |
| *ẖnm.n=k ꜣẖt nt pt* | After you have joined the horizon of heaven |
| *jw=k ẖꜥj.tj m gs jmntj* | You have appeared on the west side |
| *m Jtmw jmj mšrw* | as Atum in the sunset, |
| *jj.tj m sẖm=k nn rqj=k* | Having come in your power, none opposing you |
| *ḥqꜣ.n=k ḥrt m Rꜥw* | You have conquered heaven as Re |
| *sꜣḥ=k ptj=kj m nḏm-jb* | You reach your two heavens in heartfelt pleasure |
| *ẖsr.n=k ḥꜣt šnjt* | After clearing away clouds and storms |
| *hꜣ.n=k m ẖt mwt=k Nnt* | Having descended in the body of your mother Naunet |
| *jtj=k Nnw ḥr jrt njnj* | You are greeted by your father Nun |
| *nṯrw Mꜣnw m hnw* | The gods of Manu are joyous |
| *jmjw dꜣt m ḥꜥꜥwt* | Those in the underworld rejoice |
| *mꜣꜣ=sn nb=sn pḏ nmtt* | When they see their lord with broad stride |
| *Jmn Rꜥw nb tmmw* | Amun Re lord of mankind |

---

45 *Liturgische Lieder*, 263ff. text III 1; *STG*, xxf. text A.

46 *Liturgische Lieder*, 228ff. text II 3; *STG*, xxiif. text B.

## Text C: Sunrise[47]

Texts C and D occur in TT 102 on the left (sunset) and right (sunrise) hand sides of the entrance: the position of the texts is due to the fact that the orientation of the tomb has been been reversed by 180°. The standard version of C contains 21 verses of hymn and 9 verses of concluding prayer. There are numerous short versions.

| | |
|---|---|
| *jnḏ-ḥr=k Rꜥw m wbn=k* | Hail to you, Re, at your rising |
| *Jmn sḫm nṯrw* | Amun, power of the gods |
| *wbn=k sḥḏ.n=k tꜣwj* | You rise and have illuminated the Two Lands |
| *ḏꜣj=k ḥrt m ḥtpw* | You cross the sky in peace |
| *jb=k ꜣwjw m Mꜥnḏt* | Your heart dilated in the *Mꜥnḏt* boat |
| *swꜣ=k ḥr ṯzt n mr nḫꜣwj* | You pass by the sandbank of the Two Knives Lake |
| *sḫrw ḫftjw=k* | Your enemies having fallen |
| *jw=k ḫꜥj.tj m ḥwt Šw* | You have appeared in the house of Shu |
| *ḥtp.tj m ꜣḫt jmntt* | And set in the western horizon |
| *šzp.n ḥm=k jmꜣḫ* | Your Majesty has received venerableness |
| *ꜥwj mwt=k m-sꜣ ḥꜣ=k* | The arms of your mother protecting you |
| *m-ḫrt hrww nt rꜥw nb* | Daily, every day |
| *mꜣꜣ=j tw m ḥꜣb=k nfr* | May I see you in your beautiful festival |
| *m ḫnt=k nt ḏsr-ḏsrw* | As you row to Deir el Bahri |
| *ḫpr jꜣḫw=k ḥr šnbt=j* | May your radiance be upon my breast |
| *dwꜣ=j tw nfrw=k m ḥr=j* | May I worship you, your beauty in my eyes |
| *dj=k ḥtp=j m ḥwt jrt.n=j* | May you allow me to rest in the house I have built |
| *m ḥzwt nt nṯr nfr* | In the favour of the good god |
| *dj=k wn=j m-m šmsw=k* | May you allow me to be among your followers |
| *ḥtp=j ḥrt nt dd=k* | And rest in the tomb granted by you |
| *mj jrrwt n mꜣꜥtj tpj-tꜣ* | As is done for the righteous on earth |

## Text C': Sunrise[48]

This hymn overlaps with C, probably as the result of transmission by memory.

| | |
|---|---|
| *jnḏ-ḥr=k Rꜥw m wbn=k* | Hail to you, Re, at your rising |
| *Jtmw Ḥrw ꜣḫtj* | Atum Harakhte |
| *dwꜣ=j tw nfrw=k m jrtj=j* | I worship you, your beauty in my eyes |
| *ḫpr jꜣḫw=k ḥr šnbt=j* | May your radiance be upon my breast |
| *wḏꜣ=k ḥtp=k m Msktt* | You proceed and set in the *Msktt* boat |
| *jb=k ꜣwjw m Mꜥnḏt* | Your heart dilated in the *Mꜥnḏt* boat |
| *nmj=k ḥrt m ḥtpw* | You cross the sky in peace |
| *sḫrw ḫftjw=k nbw* | All your enemies having fallen |
| *hnw n=k jḫmw-wrḏ* | The Indefatigable praise you |
| *dwꜣ tw jḫmw-sk* | The Indestructible worship you |
| *ḥtp=k m ꜣḫt Mꜣnw* | You set in the horizon of Manu |
| *nfr.tj m Rꜥw rꜥw nb* | Being complete as Re, every day |
| *ꜥnḫ.tj ḏd.tj m nb=j* | Living and enduring as my lord |
| *Rꜥw mꜣꜥ-ḫrw* | Re justified. |

47 *Liturgische Lieder*, 281ff. text III 2 version B; *STG*, xxivf. text C.
48 *Liturgische Lieder*, 281ff. text III 2 version A; *STG*, xxf. text C'.

## Text D: Sunset[49]

The standard version contains 20 verses: a hymn of 12 and a concluding prayer of 8 verses

| | |
|---|---|
| *jnḏ-ḥr=k ḥrj-tp nḥḥ* | Hail to you, master of endless repetition |
| *Jtmw wr ḏt* | Atum great one of endless duration |
| *jj.tj m ḥtp* | You have come in peace |
| *sꜣḥ.n=k tꜣ ẖnm.n=k ꜥwj Mꜣnw* | You have reached land and joined the arms of Manu |
| *šzp.n ḥm=k jmꜣḫ* | Your Majesty has received venerableness |
| *mnj.tj r ꜥ=k n sf* | Moored at your place of yesterday |
| *ꜥwj mwt=k m-sꜣ ḥꜣ=k* | The arms of your mother protect you |
| *sbjj ḥr sẖrt ḫftjw=k* | *šbjj* slays your enemies |
| *sṯꜣ tw bꜣw jmntjw* | The western ba's tow you |
| *r wꜣt nbt jmjt tꜣ ḏsr* | On every path in the Holy Land |
| *sḥḏ=k ḥr n jrjw dꜣt* | That you may illuminate the face of those in the underworld |
| *sṯz=k ntj nmꜥw* | And resurrect those who are prostrate |
| *dj=k n=j ꜣḫ m šmsw=k* | May you give me transfiguration in your retinue |
| *šzp ꜥqw nw msktt mnj mꜥnḏt* | To take the tow rope of the *Msktt* boat and the landing rope of the *Mꜥnḏt* boat |
| *jj.n=j ẖr=k ꜥwj=j ẖr Mꜣꜥt* | I have come to you with my arms full of Maat |
| *jw Mꜣꜥt zš.tj ḥr ḏbꜥwj* | Maat spread out on my fingers |
| *jw ẖnn=j ḥm n spꜣ* | I have rowed the Majesty of the Thousand Feet |
| *jw jr.n=j sꜣḫw ḥr sḥ* | I have performed the transfiguration in the tent |
| *m ẖrt hrww nt rꜥw nb* | Daily, every day. |

## Text E: Sunrise[50]

The standard version contains a hymn of 16 verses and a concluding prayer of 6 verses. There seems to have been no standardised short version.

| | |
|---|---|
| *jnḏ-ḥr=k wbnw m nnw* | Hail to you, who rises in the Primeval Waters |
| *sḥḏw tꜣwj m-ḫt prt=f* | Who illuminates the Two Lands after his going forth |
| *ḥknw tw psḏt tmmtj* | The assembled Ennead praise you |
| *rnn tw nbtj Mrtj* | The Two Ladies, the Mrtj, nurture you |
| *ḥwn nfr nj mrwt* | Beautiful youth of love, |
| *wbn=f ꜥnḫ rḫjjt* | At whose rising people live |
| *ḥꜥꜥw psḏt n mꜣꜣ=f* | At whose sight the Ennead rejoices |
| *hnw n=f bꜣw Jwnw* | To whom the ba's of Heliopolis pay homage |
| *sqꜣ sw bꜣw P Nḫn* | Whom the ba's of Buto and Nekhen exalt |
| *>snsw n=k< jn httw* | "Praise to you", say the sun apes |
| *>dwꜣw n=k< (jn) ꜥwt nbt* | "Worship to you", say all creatures |
| *sbjj=k ḥr sẖrt ḫftjw=k* | Your *šbjj* slays your enemies |
| *ḥꜥꜥ=k ḥr wjꜣ=k* | You rejoice on your boat |
| *jzt=k m ḥtpw* | Your crew is in peace |
| *ẖnm.n tw Mꜥnḏt jb=k ꜣwjw* | Your *Mꜥnḏt* boat has received you, your heart dilated |
| *nb nṯrw qmꜣ.n=k* | Lord of the gods, whom you created, |

49 *STG*, xxvi text D.

50 *Liturgische Lieder*, 314ff. text III 4; *STG*, xxviif. text E.

| | |
|---|---|
| *dj=sn n=k jꜣw* | They give you praise |
| *Nwt ẖsbḏ.tj r-gs=k* | Nut glistens like lapis lazuli beside you |
| *jbẖ.n=k Nnw m stwt=f** | You have permeated Nun with "his" (read: your) rays |
| *sḥḏ=k n=j mꜣꜣ=j nfrw=k* | May you shine for me that I may see your beauty |
| *jnk wḏꜣ tp-tꜣ* | I am one whole on earth |
| *dj=j jꜣw n ḥr=k nfr* | May I praise your beautiful face |
| *wbn=k m ꜣẖt nt pt* | When you rise in the horizon of heaven |
| *swꜣš=j jtn ḥtp=f* | May I worship the sun disk when it sets |
| *ḥr ḏw pfj n ꜥnẖ tꜣwj* | Over that mountain of Ankh Tawy |

## Text F: Sunrise[51]

The standard version contains 28 verses, devoted equally to sunrise and sunset, and is found only in papyri of dynasties 21 and 22 and the Hibis temple. A short version attested in the Ramesside period is based on the first 14 verses.[52] It is the only standard text whose liturgical origin is certain: not only is it attested in three liturgical sources, but it also displays elements of a "ritual style".

| | |
|---|---|
| *rs=k nfr/(jnḏ-ḥr=k)* | May you awake in beauty/(Hail to you) |
| *Jmn-Rꜥw ḥr ꜣẖtj* | Amun-Re Harakhty |
| *Jtmw ḫprj* | Atum Chepry |
| *ḥrw ḏꜣjw pt* | Horus who crosses the sky |
| *bjk ꜥꜣ sḥꜣb šnbt* | Great falcon, adorned of breast |
| *nfr ḥr m šwtj wrtj* | Beautiful of face with the great double feather |
| *rs=k nfr ḥr tp dwꜣjjt* | May you awake in beauty at dawn |
| *m ḏd n=k psḏt tmmtj* | At what the assembled Ennead says to you |
| *hjj hnw n=k m mšrw* | Joy resounds for you at evening |
| *swꜣš tw Knmt* | Kenmut praises you |
| *sḏr jwrt ḥḏ tꜣ r mst=k* | Who spends the night being carried in pregnancy, the earth becomes bright at your birth |
| *ẖnm tw mwt=k rꜥw nb* | Your mother protects you every day |
| *ꜥnẖ Rꜥw mwt njk* | May Re live and the enemy die |
| *jw=k mn.tj rqjj=k ẖrw* | While you endure, your enemy falls |
| *ḏꜣj=k ḥrt m ꜥnẖ wꜣs* | You cross the sky in life and health |
| *sḥꜣb=k pt m mꜥnḏt* | You adorn the sky in the *Mꜥnḏt* boat |
| *wrš=k m wjꜣ=k jb=k nḏmw* | You spend the day in your boat with pleasant heart |
| *jw Mꜣꜥt ẖꜥj.tj r ḥꜣt=k* | Maat has appeared on your forehead |
| *wbn Rꜥw* | Rise, Re |
| *psḏ m ꜣẖtj* | Shine as Akhty |
| *Knmtj ḥꜣjj ẖprw* | Dark one with radiant face |
| *jzt Rꜥw m jhjj* | The crew of Re is jubilant |
| *pt tꜣ m ršrš* | The sky and earth are joyful |
| *psḏt ꜥꜣt ḥr jrt n=k hnw* | The Great Ennead pay homage to you |
| *Jmn-Rꜥw ḥrw ꜣẖtj prjw m mꜣꜥ-ẖrw zp 4* | Amun-Re Harakhty has gone forth in triumph. Repeat 4 times |

---

51 *Liturgische Lieder*, 168ff. text II 1; *STG*, xxixf. text F.

52 For fragmentary examples of the long version on Ramesside stelae cf. J. Assmann, "Fragmente von Steininschriften", in: E. Feucht, *Das Grab des Nefersecheru* (Mainz 1985), 148f.

# CHAPTER ONE

# THE MYSTERIES OF THE SUN CULT

Egyptian solar religion in the New Kingdom appears in tripartite form:

(1) as a closely guarded secret cosmology, depicted in royal tombs as "underworld books" for the use of the king in the afterlife. The relationship of this cosmology to the sun cult, especially the Hour Ritual, is made clear in the Treatise on the King as Sun-Priest discussed below (see p.17ff.); its secret character can be deducted from its exclusive mode of transmission;

(2) as a set of hymns located in countless non-royal tombs, which praise the solar journey in its polytheistic form as a joint operation between the sun god and a "personal sphere" (*Sphäre des Seinigen*, i.e. a group so intimately related to the god that it forms an integral part of his personality) and are based principally on a few much copied and varied "standard texts";

(3) as a sort of monotheism that regards the sun as the natural manifestation of the uniqueness of god and even precipitates a violent revolution in the form of Amarna religion. The first three chapters of this book will be devoted to unravelling this complicated state of affairs. I shall begin with the "mysteries". This means that I shall merely touch upon the books of the underworld and heaven and confine myself to the liturgical texts and accompanying treatises which feature in non-royal tomb inscriptions, rarely in the New Kingdom and much more frequently in Saite tombs.

## 1. Preliminary Considerations

The simplest explanation for the "standard texts", in the sense of models used in various contexts, is that they originate in the temple cult. This thesis, first formulated by Stewart[1] and the basis of my *Liturgische Lieder*, is not only likely in terms of genre, but has been vindicated in terms of transmission[2] in a large enough number of cases to be regarded as a secure basis for further consideration. It does, however, imply a concept of the sun-cult that does not entirely agree with what we know of cult and priesthood in Egypt. There was no congregation in Egypt to sing these hymns, as a church congregation today sings hymns. The cult was organised and performed by a professional priesthood subject to strict purity regulations in the most secret part of the temple and, except for processions, with no members of the

1 H.M.Stewart,"Some pre-Amarnah Sun Hymns", *JEA* 46(1960), 83.

2 E.g. the origin of the texts cited in *Liturgische Lieder an den Sonnengott* (MÄS 19) (Berlin,1969) I 2 from the Hour Ritual, of II 1 from the Amun Ritual, of II 2 from the sun cult of Karnak and of II 3 from the ritual for Amenophis I.

public present. Nevertheless, hymns did find their way out of this cult into the wider non-priestly circles of the population.

This paradox obliges us to make a distinction. The Egyptian sun-cult was probably unique in having both a normal "inner aspect", common to all cults, and an "outer aspect", from which wider circles were not excluded and which was not simply identical with the festival cult. This much is clear from the existence of "standard texts". It is difficult to reconcile the widespread occurrence of these texts in non-royal inscriptions with our picture of normal Egyptian cult performance. The sun-cult did, however, have its professional "inner aspect". The texts that belong to this "inner aspect" are much less widespread than the "standard texts". Their relative infrequency reveals clearly the restrictions of access to which all such texts were subject.

The Egyptian expression for the "inner aspect" of the cult is *sštȝw* (lit. that which has been made inaccessible). If we translate this by the word "mysteries", we have to dispense with some of the meanings of the Greek, e.g. initiation and anticipation of death and apotheosis of the initiate, and confine ourselves to the following two aspects:

1. the "secret", the limited access associated with the mysteries and the *sštȝw*;
2. the totality of "knowing", "speaking" and "acting" that is conveyed by the term "mystery".

The "inner aspect" of the Egyptian sun-cult, its mysteries, is constituted by a tradition that specifies what must be known, said and done during the enactment of it. The representatives of this tradition are a small circle of professional priests and scholars. They are in no sense identical nor should they be confused with the larger circle of sun-worshippers, which in the New Kingdom almost took on the character of a "movement". Only in the most exceptional cases does one of the non-royal tomb owners discussed in this book belong to the more restricted circle.

## 2. Knowing

We are fortunate in having a treatise that deals with cult-theology and provides us with an exceptionally clear and detailed picture of the field and significance of knowledge.[3] This document, originating probably in the Middle Kingdom, first occurs in the Temple of Hatshepsut at Deir el Bahri on the east wall of the sun chapel. It reproduces faithfully the same model used in the southern part of the Luxor Temple of Amenophis III.[4] The latter version is obscure (the lines have been

3 = Text 37 in tomb 33 (Petamenophis), cf. the list there of the variants that have since come to light and the literature. Since Goyon too in his edition of the Taharqa version speaks of a "hymn" and identifies it as a "complete version of chapter 15B of the Book of the Dead" (Parker *et al.*, *The Edifice of Taharqa by the Sacred Lake at Karnak* (Providence, 1979), 38 and n.15), I wish to make it clear once again that, while this text treats the king as worshipper of the sun god, it is not itself a hymn. The fact that this text has strayed into the sun hymns of the BD can be explained by its owner's having been a chief royal archivist. But this does not make it a funerary text. Cf. also my article "Dekorationsprogramm der königlichen Sonnenheiligtümer des Neuen Reiches", *ZÄS* 110 (1983), 91-98.

4 This supposition has since been confirmed by the reconstruction work of the Polish team, cf. J. Karkowski,"Deir el Bahri 1974-75", *Études et Travaux* 9 (1979), 217-219.

copied in the wrong order), perhaps intentionally in view of the special conditions of restricted access surrounding the text, which could not adequately be guaranteed in a place like the Luxor Temple.[5] The text also occurs later on similar royal monuments: the sun chapel at Medinet Habu[6] and the Taharqa building at Karnak[7], as well as on two royal coffins of the 25th dynasty from Nuri.[8] In the tombs of the Saite period, which reveal a certain predilection for exclusive texts of great antiquity, the text occurs three times.[9] In the New Kingdom it occurs only in a much abbreviated version in the tomb of Tjanefer, a third priest of Amun. Since this tomb also contains an extract from the Book of Gates, it is exceptional.[10] The only copy of the BD from the New Kingdom that contains the text belongs to a chief royal archivist.[11] The exclusive or esoteric nature of the text, i.e. the fact that it belongs to a body of knowledge that, like the underworld books of the royal tombs, was subject to restricted access, becomes clear in the history of its tradition.

The text deals with the king as sun-priest, i.e. the role[12] of the sun priest as a function of Egyptian sacred kingship, which was then delegated by the king to local priesthoods of the sun god. The passage dealing with the knowledge of the sun priest (its 20 verses make it the longest) constitutes the central portion of the tripartite text A.[13] It takes the form of a list, in which the word *rḫ* "know(ing)" occurs eight times. It enumerates the objects of knowledge and is arranged as follows:

1. the community of worshippers of the "personal sphere" of the sun god;[14]
   1.1. the eastern ba's;
      1.1.1. words and actions of the eastern ba's;
         1.1.1.1. music of joy at sunrise;
         1.1.1.2. opening of the gates of heaven;
      1.1.2. nature of the eastern ba's;
         1.1.2.1. their *bz* (true form) and *ḫprw* (manifestation as baboons);
         1.1.2.2. their "home" and "position" during the solar journey;
   1.2. the "boat crews" on the solar journey: their words;
2. the arcana of the solar journey;
   2.1 the morning appearance of the sun god;
      2.1.1. as "birth";

5 H. Brunner, *Die südlichen Räume des Tempels von Luxor* (Mainz, 1977), pl.65 and pp.42, 80-82.

6 *Medinet Habu* VI: *The Temple Proper* (Chicago, 1963) 424C.

7 R. Parker *et al.*, *Edifice*, pl. 18B and pp.31-33, 38-40.

8 These excellently preserved variants are cited by Goyon in Parker *et al.*, *Edifice*, pl. 31-33.

9 Petamenophis: Text 37. For tomb 27 mentioned by A. Roccati "I Libri dei Morti di Sesonq" in *Or. Ant.* 15 (1976), 234 n.4. At Saqqara the text is distributed on two pillars at the entrance to the tomb of *P3-šrj-n-t3-jsw* (E. Bresciani " *Egitto e Vicino Oriente*, 1 (1978), pl. 18), see now Maria Carmela Betrò, *I Testi solari del Portale di Pascerientaisu* (Pisa, 1990)

10 K. Seele, *The Tomb of Tjanefer at Thebes* (Chicago, 1959), pl. 32, 35-37.

11 p.BM 9953B (in A. W.Shorter, *Catalogue of Egyptian Religious Papyri in the B.M.*(London, 1935), 3, 66-67).

12 The use of the verb form *jw.f sḏm.f* makes it clear that the text is speaking of a general role and not a current act of worship. On the function of this form als "generalis" cf. Schenkel, "Thesen zum ägyptischen Sprachunterricht", *GM* 40(1980), 85-87.

13 According to the metrical analysis by G. Fecht. On the interpretation of the text structure cf. *König als Sonnenpriester* (ADAIK 7) (Glückstadt, 1970), 69ff.

14 Cf. *LL*, 342-352 ("personal sphere"), 344f. ("community of worshippers").

2.1.2 as "spontaneous genesis";
2.2. the "secret" door of heaven;
2.3. the sun boats;
2.3.1. the manning of the day boat;
2.3.2. the night sun as "great image" in the night boat;
2.4. the landing place and *ḥpwt*[15] of the sun god.

*A: the Morning Text*

1 King N.N.
2 worships Re at dawn
3 at his appearance, when he opens his ball
4 and flies up to heaven as Khepry,
5 entering at the mouth
6 and coming out from the thighs
7 at his birth in the eastern part of the sky
8 His father Osiris raises him on high,
9 the arms of Huh and Hauhet receive him,
10 he takes his place in the Day Boat.

11 King N.N. says,
12 that secret speech, spoken by the eastern ba's,
13 when they make jubilant music for Re,
14 when he rises and appears on the eastern horizon;
15 they open for him the double doors
16 of the gates of the eastern horizon,
17 so that he can travel forth on the ways of heaven.

18 He knows their appearance and incarnations
19 and their cities in the land of god
20 He knows the place where they stand,
21 when he embarks upon his journey.
22 He knows the words
23 spoken by the two crews when they drag the boat of the one who lives in the horizon.
24 He knows how Re is born
25 and his metamorphoses in the flood.
26 He knows that secret gate through which the Great God comes out
27 He knows the one in the Day Boat
28 and the great image in the Night Boat.
29 He knows your landing places in the eastern horizon
30 and your travels in the goddess of heaven.

31 Re has installed the King N.N.
32 on the earth of the living
33 for endless repetition and invariable duration,

15 "Steering instruments" or "runnings".

34 to administer justice to human beings and satisfy the gods,
35 to fulfil Maat and annihilate injustice.
36 He gives food-offerings to the gods
37 and funeral offerings to the transfigured.

38 The name of the King N.N.
39 is in heaven like that of Re.
40 He lives with expanded heart
41 like Re-Harakhty.
42 The *pʿt* people rejoice when they see him,
43 the *rḫjjt* people applaud him
44 in his manifestation as a child.

45 The Coming Forth of Re as Khepry.

### *B: The Evening Text.*[16]

1 King N.N. worships Re,
2 he pacifies him with what he loves,
3 when Re appears in the Night Boat
4 and Horus is satisfied with his left eye,
5 the double doors opening in the Western horizon
6 and Re settles in the west.

7 The rays of Re are in the earth,
8 the inhabitants of the underworld receive them in joy.[17]
9 The ways with secret things are opened for the Great Ba,[18]
10 that he may settle in the land of life.
11 It is caused that the gods go to rest in the earth
12 through the secret speech in his mouth.

13 "O sacred one in the Night Boat,
14 Lord of Life in the West!"
15 Holiness and divineness are given
16 to the Great Ba (through) the words of god.
17 He appears with his one eye,
18 to the Lady at the Prow of the Two Boats,
19 in accordance with the songs of praise sung to him by those in the western sky in their manifestations:

---

16 As far as possible my translation follows the Luxor version as reconstructed by M.C. Betrò *Testi*, 91 fig.6 and therefore varies from her translation on pp.53-56, which naturally follows the text of P.

17 Betrò refers (*Testi*,60 (9)) to the parallels in BD 15 i ("your rays, they penetrate into the earth") and, especially, in BD 15 B ("your rays penetrate into the earth, the inhabitants of Dat receive you").

18 The sun god is always called this in the Amduat (E.Hornung, *Das Amduat* (ÄA 8 and 13) (Wiesbaden 1963 and 1967) I, 4,5; 37,4; 88,2).

20 "The one who is equipped with his forms, who spends millions of years,
21 May Re rest, may he rest in the bowels of the earth," they sing for you,[19]
22 "The one who is equipped with his Divine Eye,
23 the image of the falcon in the Night Boat,
24 the Lord of Holiness in the western horizon!"
25 People come to life when they see him,
26 and gods rejoice when they see his beauty.

27 Rejoice,[20] O Re, over the praises of the king,
28 when he honours Re with hymns.
29 Those living in the east approach you.[21]
30 He travels forth[22] to the western passage,
31 where the "pillar"[23] in its function arises for him;
32 He travels forth[24] to the eastern passage,
33 where the "image of power on his standard"[25] arises for him
34 His name is spread through the East[26] by the cries of the lands.
35 His jackals help him to overcome his enemy,[27]
36 when he reaches the sandbank [of Apophis(?)][28]
37 The images[29] in heaven are announced to the gods of Re,
38 who worship him as he travels forth behind his jackals,
39 serving him as members of his crew with dilated heart.[30]
40 The heart of the Westerners is at ease[31] concerning Re-Harakhty,[32]
41 the heart of the gods is honoured.
42 Re is in the sun disk,
43 as he moves along in the Night Boat.[33]
44 The flood surges.[34]

---

19 *(s)hnw.sn n.k*; occurs only in L.
20 L, T: *jj ḥꜥꜥ*; P: *jw ḥꜥꜥ* "there is rejoicing...".
21 According to: *zn n.k jmj<w> ꜣḫt*. P reads : "He approaches you, Re-Osiris, he gives you the inhabitants of the horizon".
22 P reads *m nꜥ.n.k* "when you travel forth".
23 L: *Jwn [m j]rw.f*; *jwn* probably refers to the moon, cf. the commentary of Betrò. P reads *Jwn-Mwt <.f>* "the pillar of his mother", a priestly title.
24 P: *m nꜥ.n.k* " when you travel forth".
25 Wepwawet? The military character of this god is well suited to the corresponding connotations of the eastern horizon.
26 According to L; P reads: *zšš n jtn m ꜣḫt* "free passage for the sun disk in the horizon".
27 A reference to the Wepwawet aspect of the jackal.
28 According to L; P reads: *spr.f r ṯz m wjꜣ.k* "when he arrives at the setting up of your boat" or something like this. Cf.the discussion by Betrò, *Testi*, 75 (55).
29 According to L: *zr twtw* [...]; P reads: *zr sbꜣw n dꜣt* "the gates of the underworld are announced".
30 *m ꜣwt-jb* according to P; L reads *ꜥꜣ m-ḫnw nbwt.f* "The Great One in his Basket Lands", which I do not understand.
31 Read: *wꜣḥ-jb*; or perhaps one should understand a miscopying of *nḏm*: "the westerners rejoice" (*nḏm jb*)?.
32 P: *Wsjr Rꜥw-Ḥrw-ꜣḫtj.*
33 P: Re, he ascends in the Night Boat.
34 *ḥḥ nwjjt*, only in L.

The tomb of Pasherientaisu was discovered in Sakkara by an archaeological team from the University of Pisa in 1975; its "solar texts", brilliantly edited and analysed by M.C. Betrò[35], contain the section of the Cult-Theological Treatise dealing with the sunset and night that is so confused or so badly preserved in the Luxor Temple[36] and in the Taharqa building[37] that a reconstruction is not possible. The translation is still doubtful in places, but the Evening Text can now be understood in broad outline. It is a text of almost, probably even exactly the same size as the Morning Text,[38] which it complements. Since the objects of royal knowledge enumerated in the Morning Text also refer to the Night Phase,[39] they are not repeated in the Evening Text. The important motif of the secret words, which are spoken in the divine world and which the king joins in as he performs his cultic recitation, also plays an important role in the Evening Text. The phrase "secret words in his mouth" (B 12) clearly refers to the words directed at the inhabitants of the underworld by the sun god, whereas the "divine words" in verse 16 must refer to the words directed by the underworld gods at the sun god passing over. This corresponds perfectly with the idea of language as an animating force, which is characteristic of the underworld books.[40] Like food, the speech of the sun god makes the inhabitants of the underworld "live"; like life-giving air, his words make them "breathe". The songs of praise, mentioned in B 19, belong to the subject of divine speech. Unlike the Morning Text, however, the Evening Text is clearly divided into two sections, not three. The first describes the entry of the sun god into the Night Phase (indicated by phrases such as "Night Boat", "left eye", "gate of the west", "bowels of the earth", "ways with secret things") and thus corresponds to the first stanza of the Morning Text (A 1-10). The second part again adopts the interpersonal form and, using the 2nd p. sing., is addressed to the sun god. The subject of it is support for the god: from the king and his recitation, two creatures that arise for him at the "eastern" and "western passage" and the jackals that drag him through the underworld and kill his enemies for him. As Ba's of the west the jackals correspond to the baboons or "eastern Ba's" of the Morning Text.

Particularly important among these objects of knowledge are the words spoken by the members of the divine "personal sphere" of the sun god on various occasions during his journey. This is because the cult performed in the temple is understood as a replica of events that take place in the divine world.[41] In particular, the words spoken there are understood as divine speeches[42] made by someone performing the role of a god or as the earthly repetition of words spoken in the divine world. One characteristic of Egyptian cult is that it celebrates the communication between gods, not the communication between god and man.[43] Thus, the worship of the sun god on

35 Betrò, *Testi*.

36 Ed. H.Brunner, *Die südlichen Räume*, pl. 41.

37 Ed. J.C. Goyon, in Parker *et al.*, *Edifice*, pl. 20, p.42.

38 The discrepancy between the texts of a single verse only is possibly due to a missing preposition or some equally minimal portion of text.

39 Betrò, *Testi*, 127f.

40 Cf. *Ma'at*, 78-80.

41 Cf. F. Junge, "Wirklichkeit und Abbild" in G. Wiessner (ed.) *Synkretismusforschung. Theorie und Praxis* (GÖF IV, Wiesbaden,1979), 102-104, 108.

42 Cf. "Die Verborgenheit des Mythos", *GM* 25 (1977), 15ff. Cf. the text of Nedjemet, op.cit. p.52.

43 *Ägyptische Hymnen und Gebete* (Zurich, 1975) 11f.,85; *GM* 25 (1977). Especially to the sun-hymns:

earth, according to its own understanding, merely joins in a hymn of praise offered to the god in his "personal sphere" and proves to be an extract of divine speech:

> Hail to you with what your eye says to you,
> Which opens up for you the Way of Eternity.[44]
> Hail to you with what your sun disk says to you.
> When it causes to come up to you those who are in fear of you
> Hail to you with what the *Msktt* boat says to you
> When it sails there [in a favourable wind].[45]
> Hail to you with what its companion, the *Mꜥndt* boat says to you
> When its sister boat moors.[46]
> Hail to you with what your staff says to you
> When it joins your fist.
> Hail to you with what your crew says to you
> When the falcon brings forth its images.[47]
> Hail to you with what the inhabitants of the east say to you,
> The guardians of the banks of heaven.
> Hail to you with what the towers say to you,
> Those who grasp the end of the tow rope.
> Hail to you with what the underworld inhabitants say to you
> When they accompany both your boats on their four ways.[48]

This hymn to the setting sun, which comes from the same cycle of texts as the treatise (it occurs with it in Medinet Habu and the Taharqa building[49]), joins in the speech addressed to the sun god by his "personal sphere" and thus provides a very detailed and informative description of this specifically evening "personal sphere":

1. the most intimate constellation: "your eye/your disk";[50]
2. the two boats;
3. the occupants of the boats: constellations of those assisting: "your staff" and "your crew";
4. the most remote constellation: the witnesses of the solar journey: the inhabitants of the horizon, jackals (which as "western ba's"[51] correspond to the baboons as "eastern ba's") and inhabitants of the underworld.

---

*LL*, 73, 174, 344f.

44 In the Nedjmet version, which is otherwise poorer than the Medinet Habu text. J.C. Goyon translates, following Medinet Habu, "when thou darkenest the way of eternity". Cf. BD 15A IV (= *ÄHG* no.43,20).

45 Suggested reading by Goyon.

46 After Medinet Habu, cf. Goyon 44 n.39.

47 *ms bjk ꜥḫmw.sn.* Goyon translates "whose hawk makes the image", but this is difficult to reconcile with the text.

48 *Medinet Habu* VI 422A, 36ff.; for the 4 ways cf. Goyon, 44 n.44.

49 I.e. within the framework of the same decoration programme, but not in immediate context, for the Treatise (or at least the part we can understand) refers to the morning worship of the sun god, while this hymn refers to his evening worship.

50 The constellation of the god with the eye that "surrounds" him and the disk "in which" he finds himself characterises the sunset; cf. *LL*, 39 and 49-52, and treatise, B 4.

51 Cf. T. DuQuesne, *Anubis and the Spirits of the West* (Oxford, 1990).

The hymn therefore presupposes and translates into action the knowledge stated by the accompanying treatise: knowledge of the words spoken to the sun god by those belonging to his "personal sphere". The knowledge ascribed to the king in the text as coming from the "eastern ba's" and the crews dragging the boat of the sun god through the underworld extends not only to their words but also to the circumstances of their life, in the sense that allusion is made to the same items of information that are contained in a cryptographically written section of the Book of the Day.[52]

The "eastern ba's", which play such a dominant role in the treatise on the worship of the morning sun, are the well-known "apes of the sun". Their importance lies in the fact that they represent the divine community of worshippers of the sun god, whose ranks the sun priest joins with his hymn. By praying to the sun he becomes one of them:

> I have sung hymns to the sun
> I have joined the ranks of the sun apes
> and am one of them[53]

The treatise is accompanied by a representation of a baboon in Deir el Bahri, Luxor, Medinet Habu and the Taharqa building.[54] This representation is amplified by a cosmographical text that is intimately connected with the treatise and, on the coffin of Aspelta, is recorded with it:

> The baboons, who announce Re,
> When this great god is born
> At the sixth hour in the underworld.
> They appear for him only[55] after they have taken on their form[56]
> They are at both sides of this god
> And appear to him[57] until he takes his place in heaven[58]
> They dance for him and leap in the air
> They sing for him, make music and create "joyful sound"
> When this great god appears in the eyes of the *rḫjjt*-people and the "people of heaven"[59]

---

52 Cf. *König als Sonnenpriester*, 50ff.

53 BD 100. An impressive pictorial representation of this idea may be found on a 26th dynasty pyramidion in Glasgow, where the worshipper is seen with a praying baboon on his shoulder; cf. H. de Meulenaere, *JEOL* 20 (1968), 3 and pl.I.

54 Deir el Bahri; cf. J. Karkowski in *Études et Travaux*, IX, 70f. fig.3.

55 Emphatic form: "that they appear for him is...".

56 In the version of Taharqa and Aspelta. There are also traces of the suffix *.sn* in Deir el Bahri. In Medinet Habu *ḫpr* is written throughout, as if *ḫprw* "transformations" were meant. The reference is to the form assumed by the "eastern ba's" at sunrise, and this form is one of the things the sun priest knows about them (Treatise v.18)

57 According to Karkowski's reconstruction of the Deir el Bahri text. Taharqa and Aspelta omit the redundant *ḫʿj.sn n.f.*

58 On *ḥtp* in connection with the sunrise cf. *König als Sonnenpriester*, 28.

59 Cf. Book of the Day: *ḫʿjt.f m jrtj ḥnmmt* "his appearance in the eyes of humankind". Similarly Amduat I 196,6-7. For further examples cf. *LL*,41.

They hear the words of joy of Wetjenet[60]
They are the ones who announce Re
In heaven and on earth.[61]

This is the mythical, i.e. divine model and prototype of the sun worship performed in the cult on earth. Only those who know the baboons can join them as sun worshippers and become one of them. The second part of the objects of knowledge proper to king-priests, as enumerated in the treatise, concerns the solar journey itself, attended by the "eastern ba's" and the sun priest: the "birth" and "emergence" of the sun god, described fully in the first ten verses of the treatise, the "secret door"[62] and the "landing places" between which, and the two boats in which, the celestial voyage takes place.[63] The style of this list is somewhat allusive; it does not go into detail. The knowledge discussed here is stated, but not communicated. This distinction is most obvious from a comparison between the first ten verses describing the sun rise and the couplet in vv. A 24-25 that states knowledge of these events. The first ten verses use the language of "cosmography" and occur almost word for word in the underworld books that deal with sunrise.[64] In the underworld books of the New Kingdom we have part of those texts in which the body of knowledge associated with the sun cult (its "inner aspect") has been transmitted. This is very clear from the title of the Amduat, which refers in a similar form to the same body of knowledge as that envisaged by the treatise:

to know the underworld ba's
to know the secret ba's
to know the gates and the ways on which the great god travels
to know what is done
to know what is in the hours and their gods
to know the course of the hours and their gods
to know their transfigurations for Re
to know what he calls to them
to know those who flourish and those who have been destroyed.[65]

This catalogue arranges its objects of knowledge according to the same categories as the treatise:

1. the divine creatures of the "personal sphere" of the sun god, their nature, acts and words;

---

60 *LL*, 206, 96.

61 *LL*, 208f.; *König als Sonnenpriester*, 28f.; Karkowski, *Études et Travaux*. 9, 70-72; J.C. Goyon, *Edifice*, 46f., pl. 38 (Medinet Habu, Taharqa, Aspelta).

62 Cf. Betrò, *Testi*, 33 (30), who refers to the representation of the "Great secret door of the Dat" in TT 335 (B. Bruyere, *Deir el Medina* (Cairo, 1924-25), 142) and to its occurences in CT 38, 107, 159, 341; BD 17, 109.

63 Cf. *König als Sonnenpriester*, 53-55. J.C. Goyon translates *ḥpwt* not as "rudders", but as "runnings", which is perhaps better. On *ḥpt* as a description of the solar journey cf. *LL*, 218 note 143.

64 *König als Sonnenpriester*, 47

65 Translation: E.Hornung, *Altägyptische Unterweltsbücher* (Zurich,1972), 59.

2. the stations of the solar journey ("gate", "ways" etc.).

The Cult-Theological Treatise establishes what kind of knowledge is presupposed by the sun cult. The Amduat serves to codify and transmit the appropriate knowledge inasmuch as it relates to the Night Phase of the solar journey. Hitherto, these underworld books have been regarded as merely royal funerary literature, the Pyramid Texts, as it were, of the New Kingdom. But the discovery of the Treatise has established for certain that the sun cult and the "mysteries" of the solar journey are their real and original meaning and purpose. We must distinguish here between forms in which they were recorded and situations in which they were originally used.[66] The king takes those texts with him into the tomb, which in its decoration and architectural lay-out copies the nocturnal journey of the sun through the underworld,[67] to be united with the sun god as "one who knows the initiation (*bzw*) into the mysteries of the underworld, having penetrated the holiness of the mysteries".[68]

Now, it would be too much to suppose that the Amduat or its Heliopolitan model was enacted in the cult: it does not belong to what is said or done, but (and the title makes this clear) what is known. The form in which knowledge necessary for the sun cult is codified, stored and transmitted is cosmography. We are now better informed about the relationship between cosmography (=what is known) and liturgy (=what is said and done) in the sun cult since the discovery of the Hour Ritual.[69] The 12 hymns that accompany the 12 hours of the day constitute the liturgical part of this ritual, and the cosmographic part (known as the Book of the Day) describes the stages of the solar journey and what happens during the hours of the day. It is significant that only the cosmographic part of this ritual was taken over into the decorative scheme of royal tombs. In his tomb the king receives only the body of knowledge belonging to the sun cult, while the cult itself is performed in the sun chapel of his mortuary temple. Thus, the cosmographic part of the sun mysteries belongs in the tomb, the liturgical part in the temple.

The 12 hours of the Hour Ritual[70] present an extremely clear impression of what one has to imagine as a "secret" (esoteric or exclusive) sun hymn, compared with the "ordinary" cult hymns as represented in the standard texts. A special knowledge is expressed, for example, in the frequent references to creatures in the vicinity of the sun god, knowledge of which is so important in the cosmography. The following are invoked:

1. Seven uraei
4. Four fire snakes; vanguard and retinue
10. uraeus snake

66 I have introduced this distinction on the basis of the Song of the Harper cf. "Fest des Augenblicks", *Fs. Otto* (Wiesbaden, 1977).

67 E. Hornung, "Auf den Spuren der Sonne. Gang durch ein ägyptisches Königsgrab", *Eranos Jb.* 1981 (1982), 431-475.; H. Brunner, "Die Unterweltsbücher in den ägyptischen Königsgräbern", in G. Stephenson (ed.), *Leben und Tod in den Religionen. Symbol und Wirklichkeit* (Darmstadt 1980), 215-228; F. Abitz, *Die Bedeutung der sogenannten Grabräuberschächte in den ägyptischen Königsgräbern der 18.-20.Dynastie* (ÄA 26) (Wiesbaden, 1978), 19); K.J. Seyfried, "Zweiter Vorbericht", *MDIK* 40 (1984), 270-73.

68 Litany of the Sun, cf. *LL*, 30 with references to similar passages.

69 *LL*, 113-163; *ÄHG* No.1-12. E. Graefe is preparing an edition of all known versions.

70 The recitations accompanying the Hours of Night are extracts from chapters of the BD.

11. vanguard and retinue
12. western gods.

The following are mentioned:

2. encircling snake; eye; uraei; crowns
3. inhabitants of the outer edges of the world
8. Chonsu; gods around the cabin
9. gods of turquoise; inhabitants of the western desert
11. gods of the west; those who tow.

Characteristically, it further appears that a series of hymns (those grouped around the midday hours) begin not with an invocation, but with the words "Re appears" in the form of a proclamation:[71]

5. "Re appears, the gold of the gods".
6. "Re appears, he has taken up his throne".
7a "Re appears, the power of heaven".
8. "Re appears, the bull of Maat".

We shall find similar characteristics in other hymns, which clearly have their origin in the same cult area, the Heliopolitan "mysteries".

The occurrences of the Hour Ritual correspond rather closely to those of the Cult-Theological Treatise:[72]

1. mortuary temples of the 18th dynasty: Hatshepsut and Thutmosis III;
2. (only the cosmographic part): royal tombs (Ramesses VI);
3. a short version of the liturgical part (only Hours 1 and 2) in a Ramesside non-royal tomb: TT 183;
4. numerous examples in Saite tombs:
   (a) in extenso version of the liturgical part: TT 27, 34, 37, 196, 297; Saqqara: Bakenrenef;
   (b) short version of the liturgical part: TT 128; Hours 1 and 12 only: Amenirdis;
   (c) individual hymns: TT 27 (no.2), TT 33 (nos. 2 and 5), TT 34 (no.7), TT 36 (no.1);
   (d) short version of the cosmographic part: TT 132.[73]

TT 183 therefore constitutes an exception, as TT 158 does for the Cult-Theological Treatise. Even in TT 183 knowledge of the secret text can be explained by the position of the tomb owner: Nebsumenu was *jt-nṯr* of Re-Atum in the *pr-ᶜnḫ*. The cult in the *pr-ᶜnḫ* served to prolong time and life and to protect the king.[74] The Hour

71 *LL*, 122; 261f.

72 For bibliographical details see *LL*, 15-17.

73 A.Piankoff,"Livre du Jour dans la tombe no.132 de Ramose" *ASAE* 41 (1942), 151ff. I owe this reference to E. Graefe.

74 Cf. Ph. Derchain, *Le Pap.Salt 825 (B.M.10051), rituel pour la conservation de la vie en Égypte* (Brussels,1965), I, 13ff and "Le role du roi d'Égypte dans le maintien de l'ordre cosmique" in L.de Heusch (ed.), *Le pouvoir et le sacré* (Brussels,1962), 61-73. Cf. *Zeit und Ewigkeit*, 28-30.

Ritual, which refers in numerous intercessions to the protection of the king,[75] may well have belonged to the liturgies performed there. The tomb of Nebsumenu contains another fragmentary variant of the spell for the Ma'at offering, which likewise derives from the inner aspect of the cult.[76] Particularly informative for the sources used by Nebsumenu for his sun hymns is the text which, together with the hymn of the 1st Hour of the day, is inscribed on the southern entrance (*STG* No.173). It is quite explicit on the subject of special knowledge about the secrets of the solar journey: "I know the *ḫprw* of Re when he rises ... I know the boat of Khepry". Further on in this very fragmentary text, which incidentally begins like the midday hymns of the Hour Ritual with the proclamation of an event ("Re shines in the eastern part of the heaven" - it is not quite certain whether this verse constitutes the beginning of the text), the most secret arcanum known to the mysteries of the solar journey is mentioned: the nocturnal union of Re and Osiris.[77] To know the *ḫprw* of Re likewise is one of the subjects of cosmographic literature[78] (but not attested until the Late Period).

Moreover, the first stanza of the 1st Hour of the day occurs on a Theban stelophore in Brooklyn, dating from the early 18th dynasty, whereas the hymn to the 12th Hour occurs in an extended version in some copies of the BD from the 18th dynasty and later and, in a short version based on this extended version, was even taken up in the canonical Late Period recension as chapter 15h.[79] We must therefore not imagine the secrecy surrounding esoteric cult literature as too impenetrable. Indeed, the BD itself is secret literature and, as part of the funerary equipment, inaccessible. In addition, this text, unlike all other sun hymns, was given a title rubric that describes it as "the secrets of the underworld, an initiation into the mysteries of the kingdom of death".[80]

If the origin of a tomb inscription can be proved to come from the secret body of knowledge of the sun cult, it seems clear that the owner of the tomb has also drawn upon other texts from this source. In the tomb of Tjanefer, for example, there is a short version of the Treatise and a section from the Book of Gates; in the tomb of Nebsumenu the other sun-texts (as shown earlier) reveal characteristics of the cult and the arcane. It is therefore methodologically desirable to pay close attention to the Saite tombs in which the Hour Ritual and/or Cult-Theological Treatise occur. In this respect it is worth considering the tomb of the chief lector priest Petamenophis, who had an entire collection of sun hymns together with the treatise recorded on the east wall of the first columned hall:

75 5,18-19; 6,25-26; 7A,18-19; 8,16-18; 9,15-19; 10,15-21; 11,19-20; 12,28-29.

76 *STG* No. 175b, cf. *STG* No. 62 and commentary for further references.

77 *LL*, 101-105; ch.2.

78 Cf. A. Gasse, "Litanie des douze noms de Re-Harakhty", *BIFAO* 84 (1984), 190-227; R. Merkelbach, M. Totti (eds.), *Abrasax. Ausgewählte Papyri religiösen und magischen Inhalts* 2 (Opladen, 1991), 2-17.

79 Cf. *LL*, 21-23.

80 Cf. *LL*, 19f., 28-36, esp. 29-31, 70-76.

| *STG* no. | position | type |
|---|---|---|
| 31 | entrance | BD 15 a&b |
| 32 | entrance:left | BD 15 (c)-e |
| 33 | entrance:left:inside jamb | Hour Ritual (2nd Hour) |
| 34 | east wall:north section ll.1-16 | cult hymn, attested in Medinet Habu |
| 35 | ibid. ll.17-18 (?) | Hour Ritual (1st Hour) |
| 36 | ibid. ll.19(?)ff. | cult hymn=*STG* No.83 |
| 37 | east wall: south section ll.1-9 | Treatise |
| 38 | east wall: south section ll.10-17 | hymn in the Hour Ritual style |
| 39 | east wall south section ll.18-21 | Hour Ritual (5th Hour) |
| 40 | east wall south section ll.22-25 | cult hymn=BD 15A4. |

The "exoteric" sun hymns of BD 15 are outside on the entrance wall, the "esoteric" cult hymns inside. In the case of four out of eight texts recorded here, the origin is already known: three hymns from the Hour Ritual, and the Treatise. In the case of the other four we need to check the origin. No. 34 is attested as an inscription in the sun chapel of Medinet Habu and in the copy of the BD belonging to Queen Nedjmet, in which the hymns are all of liturgical origin.[81] There is hardly another sun hymn in which the proclamation of specific knowledge is as prominent as in this text, which deals with knowledge of the 7 ba's and 14 ka's of the sun god. Equally specific are the ideas expressed by the text in connection with actions, which will be dealt with in part three of this chapter. No. 36 is clearly a late Ramesside cult hymn, of which the liturgical origin is suggested only by the history of its transmission. Since it cannot be assumed that Petamenophis copied the text in the tomb of Imiseba (TT 65 Ramesses IX), one must postulate a common source accessible to both, the most obvious being a text from the Theban sun cult. No. 38 is a hymn that exhibits all the characteristics of hymn belonging to the Hour Ritual:

| verse | cf. Hour Ritual |
|---|---|
| 5: *nb ḫᶜw* | 4,6;7a,3;8,2;9,4 |
| 6: *jmj mḥn(t).f* | 2,1;3,3 |
| 19: uraei | 1,16-17;2,13;4,6.10-12.16;5,3; 10,3-6,15;12,4 |
| 12: eye | 2,14;3,12;4,13;5,8;6,2.17.19;7a,15;7b,11; |

81 Lines 1ff.= *Medinet Habu* VI 420 B 1-3 + 424 B 4-11;18ff.= *Edfou* III 221 Hour Ritual, 7th Hour; 25ff. = *LL*, II 1; 51ff. = *Medinet Habu* VI 422 A 36ff. = Taharqa ed. Goyon, 44-46; 29-31 = Apophis Litany cf. *LL*, 200; 47-50, cf. *ÄHG* Nr.19.

12,5-9.

In v.16 the "those four shining faces of yours" is a reference to the environment; cf. the four fire serpents in text 4 of the Hour Ritual. Compare vv.34-35 "He tells you what is in the Night Boat. He announces to you what is in the Day Boat" with vv.27-28 of the Treatise (text 37) "He knows the one who is in the Day Boat and the Great Image in the Night Boat". Finally, text 40 is a variant of the text known as BD 15 A4.[82] This text has nothing whatever to do with the BD. It occurs only on Late Period stelae juxtaposed with solar worship, where it (right) stands as a morning hymn opposite an evening hymn (left: "BD 15B 5"[83]). It is the connection with acting rather than knowing that makes it a cult text, albeit one that belongs to the Late Period.

Tomb 27, which has copies of the Treatise[84] and the Hour Ritual, also seems to have derived its sun hymns from similar sources. I shall deal with text *STG* 28c in connection with the acts implied specifically in the cult. Text 27 propagates a specific knowledge that goes beyond the same implied acts: it refers to the "7 uraei" by name, which are also mentioned in the Hour Ritual (1st Hour), even if not by name. All these hymns belong to the Hour Ritual in the broadest sense, reveal evidence of the same conceptual world and derive from the same inner aspect of the sun cult, a body of knowledge that before the Saite period was protected because access to it was strictly limited.

## 3. Acting

We are very well informed about what has to be *known* in the solar mysteries from the Cult-Theological Treatise and the light it throws on the original purpose of the royal underworld books. The Treatise, however, says nothing about what has to be *done*. The final stanza in A about the duty of the king

to give law to the people
to satisfy the gods
to realise Maat
to destroy Isfet
to make offerings to the gods and the dead

does not refer specifically to the solar mysteries, like the section about knowledge, but in general to the role of the king. However, there is a frieze-text in the sun chapel of Medinet Habu that stresses the active side of the royal solar priesthood:[85]

82 Cf. T.G. Allen,"Some Egyptian Sun Hymns", *JNES* 8 (1954), 349-355; A.Barucq and F.Daumas, *Hymnes et Prières de l'Ancien Égypte* (Paris, 1980), 149f. No. 45.
83 = *STG* No. 137 in TT 132; cf. *LL*, 291 n.43; *ÄHG* Nr.23.
84 Cf. Roccati, *OrAnt* 15, 234 n.4.
85 *Medinet Habu* VI 422-23.

The god present lives, clever (*jp*) as Re
and alert (*wḥ*ᶜ *jb*) as the Hermopolitan,
the enlightened (*sbꜣq*) son who came forth from Atum,
the supporter (*nḏtj*) of Harakhty
who defeats the sun's enemies by the "radiant strength" of his utterance,
who causes the boat to travel where it will.

The first three verses of this predication refer to the knowledge of the king as sun priest, the last three to his actions. They represent his actions, however, as speech. It is not by the strength of his arm, but by the "radiant power", the magical efficacy of his utterance,[86] that the king overcomes the enemies of the sun god. The "dromenon" (what is done) does not entirely coincide with the "legomenon" (what is said): the constant references to the "fire" and "burning" in the hymns of the Hour Ritual and related texts[87] clearly point to concomitant burnt offerings, and occasionally even a milk offering is mentioned.[88] However, these actions are of an accompanying nature and the decisive effects (destruction of enemies and achievement of an unimpeded journey for the sun boat) are achieved by reciting the hymns.

We have already considered in detail the knowledge required by the solar mysteries. Let us now consider the actions implied in those same mysteries. To do so we must consider how the hymns express the ambitious concept that mere recital can achieve cosmic effects, such as the overthrow of the sun god's enemy, which go beyond simply worshipping the sun god. The form in which the texts make such implications explicit is the "closing statement" (*Schlußtext*): at the end of his hymn, which has strictly excluded every reference to the speaker and the context in which he speaks,[89] the speaker now appears in his cult role, draws the attention of the god to himself and the speech act being offered to the god and asks the god to grant him a favourable *quid pro quo*.[90] Apart from this request, which represents another speech act, the closing statement is what linguistic speech act theory calls a "meta-communicative hyper-sentence". In the same way that a promise is prefaced by the sentence "I hereby promise you ...", a cult hymn concludes with the statement "I have hereby overcome for you your enemy". Like a promise, wish, curse, judgement etc., the cult sun hymn is construed by a meta-communicative hyper-sentence of this sort as a "performative" speech act, a form of "doing things with words",[91] and the type of action is specified. The shortest of all closing statements known to me says: "... on behalf of Senenmut the Chief Courtier; I have overcome your enemies" (*STG* No. 240). The hymn to which Senenmut appends this statement is stylistically close to the Hour Ritual hymns and appears also to originate from the sphere of the

86 On the use *ꜣḫw tpjw rꜣ* cf. *LL*, 210 and 365 note 90. On the concept of cultic language and its "sacramental" or "magical" power (*ꜣḫw*) cf. *Ägypten - Theologie und Frömmigkeit* (Stuttgart, 1984), ch. 4.

87 2,13f.; 4,4.6.10-12; Text 163, 20f., 25f.; Text 27 passim.

88 Text *STG* 38, 23-24; cf. Text 254, 28-30?

89 *LL*, 360-63, 368-71; *ÄHG* 85f.

90 A. Barucq, *L'expression de la louange divine*, (BE 33, 1962), 364ff. ("présentation de soi"); *LL*, 217ff.; for an especially expressively example cf.*ÄHG* Nr.144 C, 105-158.

91 J.L. Austin, *How to do Things with Words* (Oxford,1962); *LL*, 13, 363-372; *ÄHG*, 87-90.

"mysteries". Senenmut also had it inscribed in an inaccessible place.

When we examine the closing statements of most extant sun hymns, we begin to see that we are dealing with the same small group of texts which have been identified as sun hymns under the heading "Knowing". The closing statement in the form of a meta-communicative hyper-sentence is a distinctly cultic form, because it presupposes a cult role and authorisation. This idea is quite inappropriate to the situation of the non-royal "deceased", because he appears before the sun god "representing" himself and not in a cult role. The most he says of himself is something like: "I am one who was whole on earth".[92] Let us now consider more closely the closing statements that have a bearing on the implied acts of cult

| Text | Verse | Content | Type of Action |
|---|---|---|---|
| Hour | 13-15 | NN causes Maat to rise up to Re | Causing Maat to rise |
| Ritual | | and embark on the boat of Re | |
| 1st | | to be united with the seat | |
| | 21-24 | NN opens the way of the green heron | Way Opening |
| | | leads the bodyguard on the solar way | Protection |
| 2nd | 15-17 | NN drives away the clouds on the solar way | Way Opening |
| | | he gives your boats and your followers "Elevation" | "elevation" |
| 4th | 13-18 | (NN pays homage to the divine retinue) | Worship |
| | | so that you may be victorious over your enemies | Support |
| | | and his ba and shadow be destroyed | Destruction of enemy |
| 8th | 14-15 | NN has opened for you your way | Opening |
| | | he has joined in the rejoicing | |
| 9th | 13-14 | NN kills all your enemies | Support |
| | | he worships your beauty, punishes your enemy | "Dual Intention"[93] |
| 10th | 13-14 | (Worship and Conciliation) | |
| 11th | 16-18 | NN unites with Re in life | Protection ? |
| 12th | 25ff. | (Conciliation) | |
| 38 | 19-29 | NN brings you the sweet milk of your mother Isis | Milk Offering |
| | | NN has protected you | Protection |
| | | he has killed all your enemies for you | Support |
| | | he worships you in your ba's, your rank, your body | |
| | | (Knowing): he tells you what is in the night boat | |
| | | he tells you what is in the day boat[94] | |
| 40 | 6ff. | NN has recited to you the 77 book rolls | Recitation |
| | | about the slaughter house of Apophis every day | |
| | | His ba is given up to the fire, his body to the flames | Destruction of Enemy |
| | | his magic to the Horus Eye. His memory is expunged | |
| | | NN has performed the Apophis Ritual as slaughter every day | |
| | | He has caused you to conquer your enemies | Support |
| 28c | 26ff. | NN causes the boat of the pilot | Free Passage |
| | | justifies you against your | |
| | | enemies | |
| 34 | title | Praising his ba, Pacifying his ka (Knowing) | |

92 *STG* No. 52, 65; *LL*, III 4 = *ÄHG* Nr.27, 21.

93 Cf. *LL*, 182 n.71; 201 (35); 222.

94 In this end statement the contrast between "acting" and "knowing" is very clearly expressed.

| Text | Verse | Content | Type of Action |
|---|---|---|---|
| | | Causing the sun-boat to have free passage | Free Passage |
| | | according to his call | |
| | 4-5 | (Knowing): NN knows you and your name, the names of your ba's | |
| | 16 | (Knowing): NN knows the names of your ka's | |
| | 23-24 | (Knowing): NN has pacifyed you with your beautiful name. | |
| | | He has pacifyed your ba and your ka | |
| | 41ff. | (Cult Divine Roles): | |
| | | He is Isis, when she makes fast your crowns. | Crowning |
| | | He is Huh, when he carries you[95] | Lift-Off |
| | 43ff. | NN has entered the "pure canal" to see the god | |
| | | in the primeval waters and pacify the flood. | Looking |
| | | He has conquered the enemies for Re | |
| | | He has destroyed his enemies at their | Support |
| | | place of execution | |
| 41 | 133f. | Causing the 7 ka's to rise by Maat(?)[96] | |
| | | Opening the ways in heaven and the underworld | Way Opening |
| | | Opening of eyes and ears | |
| | | "NN has come to you to speak to you: | |
| | | it is he who loves you (var. whom you love) among men" | |
| | | He has chewed myrrh on the banks of the | Cult Purity |
| | | Two Knives Lake | |
| | | It is he who says Maat to Re | Causing Maat to Rise |
| | | It is he who announces Maat to Atum | |
| | | who praises the sun god with her | |
| | | (further in Nedjmet) Re is justified | Support |
| | | against his enemies | |
| 50 | | Presenting Maat[97] | Maat |
| 77 | | Presenting Maat | Maat |
| 109 | | I have come to you, my arms full of Maat | |
| | | Maat spread out on my fingers | |
| | | I have rowed (..) | |
| | | (I have) ... the Majesty of the Thousand Foot... | |
| | | I have performed the transfiguration in the tent | Transfiguration |
| 162 | | He protects you and repels your enemies | Protection |
| | | secures your place in your boat | Support |
| 173 | | NN with pure arms, when he worships Akhty | Purity |
| | | who provides protection for the one in the palace | Protection |
| 219 | | I have provided free passage for the Great Boat | Free Passage |
| | | I have deflected the anger of Neha-her | Support |
| | | The journey of the Mesktet boat is successful daily | |
| 240 | | I have put down your enemy | Support |
| 254 | | NN has come to worship you with pure arms | Purity |
| | | He gives you your two eyes, your two sisters | Crowning |
| | | who have come forth from your head, | Animation |
| | | so that you may live | |
| | | Maat is brought to him | Maat |
| P. Berlin | | NN makes the solar journey safe, repels the rebels, | Free Passage |

95 Allusion to the picture of sun child "on the arms of Huh and Hauhet"; cf. *STG*, Text 233(b) and *König als Sonnenpriester*, 42 note 2.

96 Nedjmet has "your daughter", Montemhet "your mother". Clearly Maat is meant.

97 Cf. *LL*, 154-57; 162; *Ma'at*, 192-195.

| Text | Verse | Content | Type of Action |
|---|---|---|---|
| 3050/*LL* | | drives all enemies back Transfers the "eye", | Support |
| 2 "E" | | causes the two eyes to show the way to their owner | Crowning (?) |
| | | Causes the light eye to rise | Maat (?) |
| | | Opens the ways Opens the ways in Rosetau | Way Opening |
| Hour Ritual | | Worshipping Re. Praising his ba. Causing him to be seen | |
| 9th. Title | | Destroying his enemies | Support |
| *LL*, 160 n.5 | | Causing free passage for his boat | Free Passage |
| Cop.A 70 | | I have come to you.to make you triumph | Support |
| | | over your enemies | |
| ÄHG 52 | | to pacify you and praise you | |
| Stelophore | | I have come to you to worship your beauty | |
| of *Nfr-Mnw* | | to praise your Majesty at all times | |
| Moscow[98] | | I have given free passage to your boat | Free Passage |
| | | You have appeared as king of the gods | |
| | | My arms bear Maat, I present her, | Maat |
| | | so that I may cause you to be united with the Mesktet boat | |
| | | Re sails on with a favourable wind (*m-r3-ʿ*) every day | |
| BD Ani | | I beat the donkey. I punish the rebels | |
| *ÄHG* no.30 | | I have destroyed Apophis in his attack | Support |
| | | I have seen the abdu-fish as its case occurred | |
| | | I have seen the inet-fish in its changes | Looking |
| | | when he guided the boat on its canal. | |
| | | I have seen Horus at the rudder, Thoth, Maat on his arms | |
| | | forward tow rope in the night boat | |
| | | and the after tow rope in the day boat | |
| Urk.VI,97 | | I have hampered Apophis in his attack | Support |
| | | caused the enemy to spit out what he swallowed[99] | |
| | | I have steered the *Msktt* boat past the sandbank | Free Passage |
| | | of the Two Knives Lake in a favourable wind[100] | |
| Stela RIV Abydos | | I have brought down Apophis or you | Support |
| BIFAO 45, 159 | | I have caused your boat to sail | Free Passage |
| | | on the sandbank of Apophis on the great voyage | |
| Nauri | | The duty (of the sun priest-hood) in this temple, when | |
| | | they praise the Horizon One in his rising: | |
| | | they praise the (gods) in heaven | Dual Intention |
| | | to slay the enemy on his way | |
| | | by giving Khepry a good wind | Free Passage |
| | | and by putting his boat on this *ḫntš* | Elevation |
| | | and by making the crew rejoice, | |
| | | their hearts blessed with Maat | Maat |

While "causing Maat to ascend" is certainly a rather general paraphrase for the form of worship (perhaps especially morning)[101] peculiar to the sun cult, the motifs

98 S. Hodjash and O. Berlev, *The Egyptian Reliefs and Stelae in the Pushkin Museum of Fine Arts* (Moscow-Leningrad, 1982), No. 53.

99 Cf. *LL*, 198f.

100 Cf. *LL*, 295ff.

101 The First Hour of the Day "raises itself for" Maat. In the accompanying hymn the offering of Maat plays a particular role: for details cf. *LL*, note 72.

of support (destruction of enemies/protection) and clearing a path (way-opening/sandbank) emphasise the "apotropaic" functions associated with the king as sun priest and the mysteries of the sun chapel. I have already explained elsewhere in detail the "dual intention" of this speech, which simultaneously "praises the uraeus snakes and spits at Apophis" (Amenemope[102]), and the stylistic peculiarities of the texts that belong to it (e.g. imperative, *sḏm.f* forms in the enemy theme, while the stative form is used to present a "crisis overcome") as an indication of their magical nature, which demonstrates their proximity to texts such as the Apophis Book and ultimately to that literature described by the Egyptians as *b3w Rʿw* (manifestations of Re's power).[103] The hymns that have come to light since then, especially the hymns of the first few hours of the Hour Ritual, have confirmed this analysis, with the result that we can now confidently describe this type of "apotropaic" sun hymn as a special sub-genre of Egyptian sun hymns: they belong to the mysteries of the sun cult, the most intimate and royal sphere of the sun cult, whose performance is associated with the concept of cosmic maintenance, a directly supportive intervention in the events of the solar journey.

The magical nature of the Hour Ritual hymns is evident, for example, in their numerous imperatives (1,1; 2,4-9; 3,1; 5,6,18; 6,24; 7a,10.11.13; 7b,1; 8,4-6; 9,1.3). Their apotropaic nature is evident in the dominant role of the uraeus snakes and crowns with their flames (Uraei: 1,16-17; 2,13; 4,6.10-12.16; 5,3; 10,3-6; 12,4. Eyes: 2,14; 3,12; 4,13; 5,8; 6,2.17.19; 7a,15; 7b,11; 12,5-9. Crowns: 2,8-9; 3.7; 4,5; 6,2-3). The same criteria are also evident in the other texts that have been assigned, together with the Hour Ritual, to the "mysteries" of the sun cult: 27 (Uraei v. 10-24); 28c (Flames v. 5), 38 (Encircling Snake v. 6 and 19. Uraei v. 19. Flames of Your Eyes v 12), 163 (Re-Apophis contrast v. 8-9.[104] Direct Re-Apophis Confrontation v. 7.20.25. Eye Flames v. 20-21), 240 (Direct Confrontation v. 11[105]). Other examples of apotropaic hymns are Nedjmet (ll.29-31 Re-Apophis Confrontation[106]) and a hymn in the Medinet Habu sun chapel, of whose title the words "Causing the boat to have free passage ...... Apophis."[107] have been preserved.

The last part of this hymn may be translated:

> (...) Re in his boat,
> when he crosses the heaven in the Day Boat
> the flame of his eyes on his head.
> O great one, lady of the flame,
> who is in her basket, first of the Ennead,
> (...)
> who drives off the rebel in his hour,
> and burns the enemies of Re.
> May you give the boat elevation,
> May you give free passage to that boat of Re.
> May you cause the slaughter of Apophis,

102 pBM 10474, X, 19-20, cf. *LL*, 182 n.71.
103 *LL*, 181f., 220-224.
104 *LL*, 200f.
105 *LL*, 221f.
106 *LL*, 200.
107 *Medinet Habu* VI 421B.

May you defeat him (...)

By means of hymns like this the "king as sun priest" intervenes in the solar journey in the capacity of "assistant to Harakhty" (as expressed in the above-mentioned frieze-text *Medinet Habu* VI 422-23), by strengthening the defences of the sun god and weakening the enemy powers. A similar description of the meeting between Re and Apophis in the divine sphere is given in the Amduat: "It does not come to a real struggle at all. Rather Isis and Seth immediately set about "bewitching" (*Hkȝ*) the enemy, with Re himself also taking part. Apophis is paralysed by the magic power of their spells and robbed of his strength (*pḥtj*)..."[108]

The "performative" function of the sun hymn, as described in the closing statements and expressed in the style and subject matter of the hymns (giving elevation and free motion and clearing the way for the boats, support for the god, destruction of the enemy) can now be confined (much more clearly than was possible when I wrote *Liturgische Lieder*) to that sphere of the sun cult which I have here called the "solar mysteries". The solar mysteries were closely associated with the role of the king as sun priest and took place in the sun chapels and probably also in the House of Life. Their function was to keep the solar journey going, which was the same as preserving both cosmic order and the life of the king and mankind. Only the king was authorised to perform them, but in practice he delegated the authority to a priesthood.

It is no accident that this basic idea of kingship is reminiscent of African rainmaker kings, and it undoubtedly goes back to prehistoric levels of Egyptian culture,[109] but it must also be borne in mind that the role of the king in the complex cosmic event of the solar journey is less of a "doer" than that of "participant". All the acts to be performed by the sun priest/king (providing "elevation" and clearing the way for the boat, "causing Maat to rise", fighting Apophis, opening the ways etc.) are also performed by the gods. The enemy is kept at bay by Isis and Seth (sometimes replaced by Thoth[110]). Gods have the task of "giving the boat elevation",[111] sailing, rowing and towing it. The task of the king as lord of the solar mysteries and sun chapels was therefore not to keep the solar journey going, but to incorporate mankind into the solar journey by taking part in it himself, strengthening and confirming it by means of his recitations. What he keeps going is the total interconnection of cosmos and society, that idea of "continuity" which is so characteristic of Egyptian thought about time.[112] This connection between knowledge and participation is expressed very clearly in the caption to the vignette accompanying c. 15 of the Queen Nedjmet BD (ed. A. Shorter, *Catalogue* p.77):

---

108 E. Hornung, *Amduat* II, 139f.

109 W. Westendorf, in his research on the panther goddess *Mȝfdt*, has come across various ideas connected with the problem of solar kinetics that are clearly of great antiquity: Maʿat as "steering goddess" ("Ursprung und Wesen der Maat", in *Festschrift für Walter Will* (Cologne, 1966) and Ka as lifting force (*Festschrift pour W.Vycichl*,[ =*Bulletin de la Société Égyptologique de Geneve*. 4 (1980)], 99-102). For a general treatment cf.W. Westendorf, *Altägyptische Darstellungen des Sonnenlaufes auf der abschüssigen Himmelsbahn*, (MÄS 10) (Berlin, 1966).

110 *LL*, 308f.

111 Cf.A. Piankoff, *Livre du Jour et de la Nuit*, (BE 13) (Cairo,1942).

112 Cf. *Zeit und Ewigkeit im alten Ägypten* (AHAW 1) (Heidelberg, 1975), 28-30.

Osiris Nedjemet, justified, knows
those words spoken by the eastern ba's.
Osiris Nedjmet is in the midst of your council,
Osiris, and enters the crew of Re, every day.

This knowledge, however, becomes at the same time an ideal item of funerary equipment, because it guarantees the dead king participation in the solar journey even after death. The way in which his worshipping figure is depicted in the cosmographic representations of the solar journey makes this wish very obvious. Here too the accompanying inscription says:[113]

Worshipping Re when he sets in life by Ramesses VI.
He causes the two boats of Re to travel in peace.

In the afterlife he himself belongs to the divine "personal sphere", a position which he has simulated on earth in his cult role.

In their own way the mysteries of the sun cult certainly share in the astonishing rise of solar religion in the 18th and 19th dynasties, as can be seen from the development of underworld books.[114] The numerous sun hymns of the period are in part not far removed from the basic idea of the mysteries, as is clear from the importance of the enemy motif (cf. chapter 2). But it seems to me very important to distinguish carefully between these two phenomena. The mysteries are undoubtedly much older than the golden age of the sun hymn and they outlasted this period by many centuries. It is clear from the Hour Ritual in Edfu that they were still being performed in Late Period temples. They were probably quite far removed from the *Zeitgeist* of the 18th and 19th dynasties. Thus, there are two reasons why they do not appear in non-royal tombs before the Saite period. The first reason, which can be explained in terms of the sociology of knowledge, is that they belonged in the New Kingdom to a protected body of knowledge restricted to a small circle of initiates; the second reason is that the 18th and 19th dynasties had an ample supply of religious texts that were much more suitable to the religious consciousness of the period. The golden age of the sun hymn was long past by the Saite period, and it therefore seemed an obvious step to reach back to the cult texts of the sun chapels, sanctified as they were by antiquity.

113 Cf. Piankoff, *Livre du jour*, pl 4, p.14.
114 Cf. E. Hornung, *Unterweltsbücher*, 17-23.

# CHAPTER TWO

# THE ICONOGRAPHY OF THE SOLAR JOURNEY

## 1. "Icon" and "Constellation"

Contrary to what the reader might expect from the title, this chapter proposes to deal with linguistic, not visual representations of the solar journey.[1] Instead of the term "iconography" I could equally (and perhaps less misleadingly) have used the term "imagery". However, I use the term "icon" in the technical sense as an expression or articulation of content that can be realised in both language and image. In my article "Verborgenheit des Mythos in Ägypten"[2] I argued that myth, in the strict sense of a narrative form, is strikingly rare in Egyptian religious texts. Using the term "icon", I shall try to focus on the specifically non-narrative form in which myth appears in Egyptian texts.[3] The expression "iconography", therefore, is the exact equivalent of what is usually known as the "mythology" of the solar journey. It is a view of cosmic events as acts in the divine world, including boats and their crews, "sun apes" and jackals, Isis and Seth, Horus and Thoth, and Apophis, the enemy of the sun god.

Tales of actions that take place in the divine world are known as myths.[4] The "solar journey"[5] too appears, in the representational form that interests us, as an act or complex of acts in the divine world. But they are not being "told", because they lack the specifically narrative coherence of a story. Stories derive their specific

1 I realise, of course, that inclusion of the profuse visual material would considerably support and clarify the thesis presented in this chapter. Such an investigation, as attractive as it is necessary, would not only have to deal with the well-known "vignettes", first attested in the post-Amarna period (cf. H. Schäfer, *Ägyptische und heutige Kunst und Weltgebäude der Alten Ägypter* (Leipzig 1928); K. Sethe, *Altägyptische Vorstellungen vom Lauf der Sonne* (Berlin 1914); H. Schäfer, *ZÄS* 71(1935), but would also take us back into the Middle Kingdom via objects such as pectorals (cf. Erika Feucht-Putz, *Die königlichen Pektorale* (Bamberg 1967). Erik Hornung is preparing a work on solar journey representations; cf. Hornung, "Die Tragweite der Bilder", *Eranos Jb. 1979* (1981), 183-237 and "Schlussszenen der Unterweltsbücher", *MDIK* 37 (1981), 217-226.

2 "Die Verborgenheit des Mythos", *GM* 25 (1977), 7-43.

3 I borrow the term "icon" from H. Blumenberg, *Arbeit am Mythos* (Frankfurt, 1979), 165ff. Cf. also "Die Zeugung des Sohnes" and *Ägypten - Theologie und Frömmigkeit* (Stuttgart 1984), 135, where the relationship between iconicity and narrativity in Egyptian mythology is treated in more detail.

4 This is the usual understanding among Egyptologists; cf. S. Schott, *Mythen und Mythenbildung im alten Ägypten* (Leipzig, 1945).

5 By "solar journey" I mean the apparent course of the sun around the earth and by "movement" the apparent movement of the sun. The expression "solar journey" does not mean a particular Egyptian idea of this apparent movement, as "course" (*ḥpt*). The expression is used here to refer always to the cosmic phenemenon in its "natural" appearance, not to a particular "iconic" illustration.

coherence and dynamic as a result of overcoming an initial state of deficiency.[6] The story of Osiris, which does not begin with his kingship on earth (Plutarch is the first to mention it), but with his murder and dismemberment, may be regarded as paradigmatic. This narrative core of overcoming a state of deficiency unfolds in a series of episodes, which are teleologically interrelated.[7] The final episode, for example, the "Triumph of Horus", brings the chain of events into a sphere where a final state is achieved and describes the world as it is now and, through the ritual realisation of the myth, is to remain forever.[8]

The "icons", which express the Egyptian idea of the solar journey, form a cycle, in which the beginning and end are constantly crossing over into each other. There is never a transition to a final state. The cycle of icons does not belong to the historical time of human beings on earth, in which stories take place (even when the protagonists are gods), but to the time of the cosmos that circles within itself, in which the acts are repeated "day by day" for all eternity. In this way the icons structure, indeed "ornament" time as a model of constantly self-repeating movements.[9]

Nevertheless, the icons of the solar journey are also interrelated in a kind of coherence that does not dispense with logic. They are connected, not by a logic of purpose, but by a logic of analogy. According to this logic, the cosmic and anthropological levels are related to each other in that idea of the solar journey which I propose to investigate. This gives rise to the four-phase structure of the solar journey:

Rising-Birth-Child
Crossing-Rule-Man
Setting-Dying-Old Man
Night Journey-"Transfiguration"-Deceased.[10]

This scheme sounds perhaps more artificial than it appeared to the Egyptians, for whom the tripartite division of the day and the quadripartite division of the entire

---

6 W. Burkert, *Structure and History in Greek Mythology and Ritual*, 14-18 and Assmann, cit. in note 3.

7 Cf. "Das ägyptische Zweibrüdermärchen", in *ZÄS* 104 (1977), 1-25.

8 For an analysis of the myth of Osiris in 5 basic scenes or episodes cf. *Ägypten*, 149-176.

9 For the concept of "ornamentalisation of time by ritual" cf. "Die Verborgenheit des Mythos", *GM* 25 (1977), 27f.; *Stein und Zeit*, 55f.

10 In the iconic structure of the Solar Phases Hymn (cf. §2,1) the third and fourth phases, landing and night journey, are brought together in one image. The corresponding theory of the *ḫprw* of Re distinguishes 3 *ḫprw*:

| | |
|---|---|
| Khepry | Sunrise |
| Re | Crossing |
| Atum | Landing and Night Journey |

It is thus also possible to speak of a three-phase structure, as I did in *LL*, 333-339 and *ÄHG*, 48, but such a structure conceals the deliberate blurring of a demarcation line and the deliberate "seeing-in-one" of two existential forms, viz. old age and being dead. Other observations also make it necessary to keep the landing and the night journey apart: the landing is interpreted as union with the mother goddess, while the night journey culminates in the union with the father (cf. §2.2.3)

cycle must have been "naturally" evident.[11] On the other hand, the 24 "icons" division is artificial. Here the solar journey unfolds in the mysteries of the sun cult according to a division of hours and the hourly celebration of the appropriate rituals. These icons cannot be related by the logic of analogy to anything that is as naturally obvious as age and are often related to each other only in a complementary way, as equally "true" images for the same basic idea.[12] It is not necessary to examine this special iconography in detail here.[13] The "icons" belong in the context of a cosmology that is strictly polytheistic. By this I mean that the gods can be seen only in relation to and dependence on each other and that no god is conceivable without the others, i.e. without certain others. If one were to try to separate Osiris from Isis and Horus, Seth, Nephthys, Anubis and Geb, not a great deal of him would remain. Osiris would then appear like Death to whom

> all that lives on earth belongs.
> The whole world comes equally to you
> You are the Lord. There is no-one beside you.
> All of this belongs to you".[14]

In representations of this sort, which incidentally show that the crisis of polytheistic cosmology was not exclusively a feature of solar religion, the "mythical dimension" of the development of his nature is not considered.[15] In the mythical dimension the nature of a god unfolds in constellations, in which he forms a relationship with other gods both actively and passively. These gods become such an intrinsic part of his active (and passive) character development or "self-realisation" that they form a quite indispensable aspect of his person in the guise of a "personal sphere".[16] This is not the place to examine the very obvious correspondences on the anthropological level. The so-called "family sense" of the Egyptian is merely one way of expressing a concept of the person which understands the person as (a) a multiplicity of integrated parts or aspects, such as ka, ba, heart and shadow[17] and (b) as part of a whole that encompasses human society and its meaning centre (the king) beyond the immediate "personal sphere".[18] Polytheistic cosmology has an anthropological basis, which for Egyptian thought gives it a sort of necessity. It

11 Cf. *LL*, 333ff.; On the relationship of the solar phases/age to the riddle of the Sphinx cf. W. B. Kristensen, *The Meaning of Religion* (Leiden, 1960), 68.

12 The complementary character of the icons of the 12 hours in the Amduat which do not represent a part of the nocturnal journey but an aspect of the whole, has been emphasized by W.B.Kristensen, *Het leven uit den dood* (Haarlem, 1926), 26ff., but his interpretation of all hours as complementary aspects of the entire night journey is somewhat extreme.

13 Cf. the "Book of the Twelve Names of Re-Harakhty": A. Gasse, "Litanie des douze noms de Re-Harakhty", in *BIFAO* 84(1984), 190-227; R. Merkelbach, M. Totti (eds.), *Abrasax. Ausgewählte Papyri religiösen und magischen Inhalts* 2 (Opladen, 1991), 2-17.

14 *ÄHG* no.219, 36-39.

15 Cf. *LÄ* II, 769-771; *Ägypten*, Chapter 4 and 5.

16 *LL*, 339ff.

17 Cf. "Harfnerlied und Horussöhne", *JEA* 65(1979), 70-72, 75-77; E. Brunner-Traut, *Gelebte Mythen* (Darmstadt, 1981), 64-67; A. Rupp, *Vergehen und Bleiben. Religionsgesch.Studien zum Personenverständnis in Ägypten und im Alten Testament* (Saarbrücken, 1976).

18 Cf. "Vaterbild", 21-29, esp.27 (repr. in *Stein und Zeit*) and "Persönlichkeits-begriff und -bewusstsein", in *LÄ* IV, 963-978.

determines that aspect of the Egyptian concept of god which I call the "mythical dimension of the divine world".[19]

In the theology of the solar journey the "mythical dimension" does not develop into a mythology of stories that tell of the sun god[20], but an "iconography" of images, which represent the constellations of acts belonging to each phase of the cosmic cycle. They are "mythical images", which at any time can develop into stories.[21] In their totality they form the mythical dimension of solar theology in exactly the same way as the multitude of Osiris-Isis-Horus-Seth stories form a totality to express the mythical dimension of Osiris. From a theological point of view the icons of the solar journey have precisely the same function for the sun god as the myths have for Osiris: they unfold the nature of the god in a "personal sphere". It therefore seems legitimate to produce a more general, non-narrative concept of myth that encompasses both: the icons as "mythical images" and the stories as "mythical episodes". The anthropological basis of myth relates it to human fate and the understanding of existence. Human institutions find in myth their prototype and basis. This is the more fundamental reason for the principle of analogy, which gives the icons of the solar journey, as we have already seen, their coherence.

In the mythical dimension the gods appear as "persons", i.e. role-bearers in constellations of acts. Their decisive characteristic is personality, "active" and "passive". Numina and natural phenomena are not capable of.i. action. Thus the concept of action assumes a decisive theological significance. Actions are always communicative, i.e. they have a meaning which can be realised only in relation to the participant(s). Accordingly, the concept of constellation is implied in the concept of action. It is impossible to think of the god as an actor without relating him to beings that give his actions meaning and purpose. Those who deny the polytheistic divine world but cling to the notion of god as an actor burden mankind with the entire weight of being constellation partners, as is the case with Hebrew monotheism.[22]

---

19 I call the other dimensions of the divine world or the polytheistic concept of god characteristic of Egypt the "cosmic" and the "cultic" (or "local/political"). In principle every genuine god appears in all three dimensions: each one has (a) a cosmic manifestation or *modus operandi*, (b) a cult place, in which he/she is worshipped as local deity (or as "guest") and (c) a nature that can be articulated linguistically, as a name or with a genealogy and, in certain cases, a mythology; cf. *Ägypten*, ch.4. Chapter 7 deals with the emergence of a fourth dimension during the New Kingdom: time, fate and history.

20 Examples of myths in which the sun god is protagonist are the Book of the Celestial Cow edited by E.Hornung, *Buch von der Himmelskuh* (OBO 46) (Fribourg, 1982), or the Cunning of Isis, translated by J.F.Borghouts, *Ancient Egyptian Magical Texts* (Leiden, 1978), 51ff. no. 84: these stories have nothing to do with the "iconography of the solar journey".

21 The Book of Overcoming Apophis (in R.O. Faulkner, *P.Bremner Rhind*, (Bibliotheca Aegyptiaca 3) (Brussels, 1933) §§22.1-33.18) offers several examples of attempts at such narrative expansion of the enemy-icon, e.g. in *ÄHG* no.18, 35, where reference is made to the "pre-history" of the confrontation, viz. the conspiracy of the enemy against the solar god who has appeared as ruler; cf. also *ÄHG*, 49-54. The question of "iconicity" and "narrativity" has recently been discussed by J. Zeidler, "Zur Frage der Spätentstehung des Mythos in Ägypten", *GM* 132(1993), 85-109.

22 Cf. O. Keel.(ed.), *Monotheismus im alten Israel und seiner Umwelt* (Bibl.Beitr.14) (Stuttgart,1980)), 11-30. For this notion of "action" cf. H. Arendt, in H. Lenk (ed.), *Handlungstheorien - interdisziplinär*, vol. 2.1 (Munich, 1978), 13-87. More specific is the concept of Habermas, *Theorie des kommunikativen Handelns* (Frankfurt, 1981).

These very general and basic considerations are quite important for us, because they reveal the internal cohesion of phenomena against which the profound religious change of dynasties 18 and 19 can be seen. The "new solar theology", which will be described in Chapter 3, discards the traditional icons, i.e. the constellations of actions, and attempts to achieve, by means of this "demythification", a concept of god based purely on the phenomenology of cosmic events. The resulting isolation of the sun god on his celestial journey has the anthropocentrism we have described as its logical consequence.

## 2. The icons of the solar journey as reflected by the traditional Solar Phases Hymn

### *2.1 Preliminary observations on the category of the Solar Phases Hymn*

I use the term Solar Phases Hymn ("Tageszeitenlied") to denote the type of sun hymn in which the content corresponds to the four phases of the 24 hour period viz. morning, noon, .i.evening, night. It may be that only two or three phases of the cycle are represented in a particular hymn. The hymn refers always, even in its "demythified" form, to the solar journey and not to the sun god. The "verbal form" is therefore just as indispensable to the hymn to represent events and actions as the "nominal form" is to the eulogy to represent atemporal characteristics.[23] The Solar Phases Hymn in the form of "transfiguration" or sacramental interpretation refers to an event, whereas the eulogy in the form of a "name" refers to an essence or identity. By "sacramental interpretation" I mean correlating the semantic levels: the level of "cultic acts" ("human world") and the level of "mythical meaning" ("divine world"). This sort of correlation and reciprocal clarification of the one sphere vis-à-vis the other happens verbally in that speech act which I call "transfiguration" (Verklärung, the same term used by Siegfried Schott) and which is closely associated with the Egyptian concept of the magical power of words as *ꜣḫw tpjw rꜣ*,[24] even if it does not perhaps correspond exactly to the Egyptian *sꜣḫw* "transfiguration". The different semantic levels correlated by the Solar Phases Hymn in its original function as "transfiguration" of the solar journey are (if it is permissible to summarise the results of extensive research into sun hymns and mortuary texts in one sentence): (a) the cosmic level of the events summarised in the concept "solar journey", (b) the kingship level and (c) the funerary belief level. The meaning content of the acts that represent the solar journey in the mythic-iconic mode of thought can be fully understood by the reader only when those actions are related to these three semantic levels. Take, for example, the act of "overcoming": on the cosmic level it refers to overcoming resistance, personified in the solar enemy Apophis as standstill, clouds, darkness; on the kingship level, it means overcoming

23 On "naming" and "transfiguring" (*Nennen und Verklären*) as basic forms of hymnic speech in Egypt cf. *ÄHG*, p. 26-45. On the "verbal style" of the traditional sun hymn as distinct from the "nominal style" of the eulogy cf. also *LL*, 4ff.; *LÄ* II, 40-46 s.v. "Eulogie" and III, 106f. s.v. "Hymnus".

24 *LL*, 364ff. with n.90; *GM* 25, 15-23; *Ägypten*, 108-117.

external and internal enemies and embodying the triumphant rule of justice;[25] on the funerary belief level, it means overcoming death. The icon sees all three levels as one and relates them to each other. Cosmos, kingship and funerary belief in the Solar Phases Hymn form three semantic levels that refer to and explain each other. Thus, the solar journey appears as the prototype of rule and eternal life. In the defeat of the enemy and of death, which takes place anew every day, the Egyptian sees that his own continued existence is guaranteed both on the personal and political level.

### *2.2 Phases of the Sun*

The vast majority of visual representations of the solar journey in tombs, Book of the Dead papyri and coffins are structured in a B-A-B scheme.[26] The central position A represents the act of the sun god, his rising,[27] and the gods who participate in this act, mostly Osiris as the djed-pillar and Nut as heaven.[28] Position B represents the worshippers attending this event in prayer: the baboons are always there, often accompanied by other divine beings and the deceased in ba-form. The cosmographies of the royal tombs are structured in the same way, but horizontally. "Each hour of the night is divided into three registers: in the middle register the sun boat with its attendants, while in the other two registers creatures and phenomena encountered by the sun god on his nocturnal voyage are enumerated and described."[29] But strict symmetry in the case of position B, indicated by the vignettes, is not observed.

Corresponding exactly to this principle of visual composition, the hymn divides the event of solar journey into positions A and B. They are not arranged cyclically, but alternate in A-B sequence: position A represents the act of the sun god, position B the responses of the "congregation" witnessing this act. This structure is common to all phases of the sun.

25 Cf. *Ma'at*, chapter 6.

26 Because "A", the action of the god, theoretically has precedence over "B", the action of the gods who react to "A", I use the scheme B-A-B, which in fact corresponds to the A-B-A scheme used by Westendorf as a symbol of the solar cycle in his *Ägyptische Darstellungen des Sonnenlaufs*, index p. 99 s.v. Schema, A-B-A.

27 In the Schäfer/Sethe controversy over the meaning of these images both are right: Schäfer sees them as a representation of the whole cycle, whereas Sethe regards them as referring exclusively to the sunrise, i.e. the action of the sun god. I too see in them an upward movement from the underworld (=Osiris as djed pillar) to heaven and agree with Sethe in identifying the solar motion as "rising" from the netherworld (=Djed pillar = Osiris) to the sky, but I agree also with Schäfer in interpreting this representation of the rising sun as a *pars pro toto* symbolisation of the whole circuit.

28 For references cf. *König als Sonnenpriester*, 45 n.2; a particularly beautiful example is given by E. Feucht, *Das Grab des Nefersecheru (TT 296)* (Mainz, 1985), 77ff. scene no. 25.

29 Cf. Hornung, *Unterweltsbücher*, 18.

| | | |
|---|---|---|
| Morning | A: Appearance<br>(transformed<br>into address) | Hail to you, Re, lord of commands<br>Khepry, father of the gods,<br>who illuminates both lands with his eye<br>Atum, who sets in the evening.<br><br>May you shine in my face in the morning<br>until your setting in life |
| | B: Reception | The sun apes worship you.<br>They announce you at the gate of the horizon<br>They dance and sing before you |
| Midday | A: Act of the god.<br>Passage,<br>Victory | You take your place in the day boat,<br>Manned by the "indestructibles"<br>You go forth from there with heart expanded, your enemies destroyed<br>The impious one has fallen at your knife, his ... having been cut. |
| | B: Response<br>of the retinue | The crew of Re is jubilant<br>and rejoices over the fate of the enemy of their lord. |
| Evening | A: Act of the god.<br>Setting,<br>Night Journey | Re sets in the night boat,<br>Manned by the "inexhaustible ones"<br>The jackals assembled at the tow rope,<br>they pull you, your heart dilated,<br>to your setting on the horizon of the western mountain |
| | B: Reception | The transfigured and the "western ba's"<br>rejoice as Your Majesty approaches<br>They see you coming in peace<br>in your rank of "ba" in heaven[30] |

### *2.2.1 Morning*

A: the act of the god.

As an act the solar journey has three aspects: passive (the sun being born to the sky goddess Nut), intransitive (the appearance of the god) and transitive (illuminating the earth). The passive aspect emphasises the semantic level of funerary belief as rebirth. It is therefore almost more common in funerary texts than in sun hymns[31] and is so important, especially in the pictorial representations of the morning icon,[32] which represent the sunrise as a symbol of resurrection from death.[33] The Cult-

30 Berlin 7316 = *ÄHG* no. 61

31 Some references, which could easily be multiplied, may be found in: *LL*, 119.

32 These images do not usually represent the birth process (which rather belongs to the realm of the "mysteries" cf. A. Piankoff, *Livre du Jour*, pl.1 and 8), but the sun god in passive form, "raised on high" and "received" by the arms of his "constellation partner". .

33 This seems to be reason why the morning phase functions as a representation of the whole cycle;

Theological Treatise also devotes, like the cosmographic descriptions of sunrise in general,[34] as much space to the passive aspect of sunrise as to the intransitive aspect, while the transitive aspect is missing completely:

| | |
|---|---|
| | at his appearance, |
| | when he opens his ball |
| intransitive (*ḫpr*) | and flies up to heaven as Khepry |
| | by entering at the mouth |
| | and comes out at the thighs |
| | at his birth on the east side of heaven |
| passive (*msj*) | His father Osiris lifted him on high |
| | the arms of Hu and Hauhet received him |
| | He takes his place in the Morning Boat |

In the same way the event of birth is also described in the sun chapels.[35]

In the sun hymns the passive aspect of sunrise, the birth motif, plays a significantly less important role.[36] But here the sun child "on the arms of Isis and Nephthys" is the typical morning icon, which appears in Ptolemaic epigraphy as a hieroglyph for *dwꜣw* "morning".[37] I have collected several linguistic parallels for this picture in *Liturgische Lieder*, pp.197ff. and 202ff. They come mostly from hymns that belong to the esoteric sphere of the "mysteries".[38] A particular icon of the morning sun is the sun-child on the lotus, which first appears in the Amarna-Tutankhamun period.[39] The hymn of the Nakhtamun BD (P.Berlin 3002) comes from the post-Amarna period:[40]

Greetings, boy from the womb
Child, who ascends in the lotus flower
Beautiful youth, who comes from the land of light
And illuminates the [Two Lands] with his light

The motif of the maternal rebirth or rejuvenation of the sun-god as a child symbolises time in its cyclical or reversible aspect, which the Egyptians called

---

ideas of resurrection are conveyed by the djed pillar and the life-sign.

34 See *KaS*, 46f. with the synopsis on p. 47.

35 Cf. e.g. *Medinet Habu* VI pl. 420 B.

36 E.g. BD Ani *ÄHG* no.38, 3: *ms ṯw mwt=k ḥr ḏrt.s* "your mother gives birth to you on her hand"; cf. *LL*,120f.

37 *Wb* V 422.

38 This applies with certainty to pBerlin 3050, as well as to the hymns in the papyrus of queen Nedjemet (ch.1, p.XXX), but less to the funerary pap. of Nakht, *LL*, 202 (28) citation2.

39 cf. H.A. Schlögl, *Der Sonnengott auf der Blüte* (AH 5)(Geneva, 1977); cf. also M.L. Ryhiner, *L'offrande du lotus dans les temples égyptiens de l'époque tardive* (Brussels, 1986).

40 *ÄHG* no. 43; the sun god is called "child of the morning" (*ẖjj n dwꜣt*) on a pyramidion of Amenophis in Cairo (after Photo Heidelberg 99a34) and P.Louvre 3292=*ÄHG* No. 48,5; "child in the east" (*ẖjj jmj Bꜣẖw*): *STG* text 45 (TT 36), 2; "Ihii of the ennead": *STG* text 129; "child (*ẖjj*) of the flame with sparkling rays": O.Cairo 25206; "he is a child (*ẖjj*) that becomes young again at his time, suckled (*ꜣṯ*) by Nut 'at both times' (*r trwj*)": P.Berlin 3056,VIII, 7-8; "perfect child (*sfj*) that came forth from the primeval waters": P.Berlin 3055=ÄHG No. 126, 11. All these texts are Ramesside and later.

Neheh as opposed to time as duration and quasi-spatial expansion, which they called Djet.[41]

Apart from birth, which relates the sun god to the sky as mother in a constellation, the passive aspect of sunrise also includes rearing by the mother herself (*LL*, II,1) or the nurses Isis and Nephthys (*LL*, II,2) or the two Crown Goddesses (*LL*, III,4). The motif of rearing the child places the cosmic event in a particularly clear relationship to funerary belief[42] and especially to kingship, where the "rearing for kingship" (*rnn r njswt*) by the Crown Goddesses and the "creation of beauty" (*qmꜣ nfrw*) by the mother goddesses have central importance.[43]

The typical form in which sunrise is represented in the hymn, however, is the brief, mostly two-line alternation of intransitive and transitive aspects:

> he rises in the eastern part of the sky
> and illuminates the Two Lands with gold.[44]

This couplet forms a "thought couplet",[45] which follows the stylistic form of the theophany description in its antithetic combination of intransitive and transitive.[46] The meaning of this stylistic form is based to some extent on the temporal-deictic categories of the verb forms involved, as can be seen from the following diagram:

---

41 A very comprehensive collection of references to the idea of solar rejuvenation and the symbolisation of cyclical time is given J. Zandee, *Amunshymnus* (Leiden, 1992), 176-185.

42 *CT* VI 395 provides an example that may be regarded as typical:
Nut the Great One raises you on high in your beauty
She embraces you in her arms
The Two Ladies of Buto suckle (*ꜣṯ*) you,
Like Horus the son of Isis.

43 *rnn r njswt*: cf. Leclant, in *Mél.Mar.*, 264 n.3, 275 n.3; *qmꜣ nfrw* see M. Münster, *Untersuchungen zur Göttin Isis*, (MÄS 11) (Munich, 1978), 143ff.; Zandee, *Amunshymnus*, 16f. By distinguishing 3 sucklings (post-natal, post-coronation and post-mortem) Leclant dismantles the semantic levels brought together in one image by the complex icon of suckling.

44 *Theban Necropolis*, pl.7. For this and many other examples cf. *LL*, 293ff., esp. n.50. F. Junge explains the form grammatically as "co-ordinate sentence" ("Wechselsatz"): "when you rise you have illuminated"; cf. *Syntax der mittelägyptischen Literatursprache* (Mainz, 1978), 177ff. This explanation is plausible for the only one-verse example of this motif that I have (perhaps unwisely) taken as the starting point for my excursus about this stylistic form, since this is probably linked to the distich form of the "thought couplet": *wbn=k sḥḏ.n=k tꜣwj*, especially since the variant *sḥḏ=k* also occurs several times. The relationship with other obvious "Wechselsätze", such as *wbn=k ꜥnḫ rḫjjt*, is clear. I should still prefer to call this stylistic co-ordination (not grammatical subordination) of two sentences. Stylistics, as has often been observed, goes beyond what can be described by sentence grammar of the transformational-generative sort taken as a model by Junge. On the co-ordination of *sḏm=f* and *sḏm.n=f* cf. P. Vernus, "Études de philologie et linguistique", *RdÉ* *32*(1980), 117-121 and L. Žabkar,"Hymn to Osiris Pantocrator", ZÄS 108(1981), 145-165.

45 J.L. Foster, *JNES* 34(1975), 1ff., *JNES* 39(1980), 89-117 and *Thought Couplets and Clause Sequences in a literary Text: The Maxims of Ptah-hotep* (Chicago,1977); cf. *LÄ* IV, 900-910 ("Parallelismus membrorum").

46 *LL*, 294f.

| Verb | | |
|---|---|---|
| | Resultative[47] | |
| Tense- and Aspect-neutral "event in itself" | intrans. state of subject | trans. state of object |
| *sḏm=f* | PsP | *sḏm.n=f* |
| *wbn=k* | *ḫꜥj.tj* | *sḥḏ.n=k* |
| *nfr-wj tw* | *wbn.tj* | *tꜣwj* |

The stylistic form thus contrasts event and act in concise and complex antithesis: the appearance of the god and effect caused by his appearance. When the stylistic form is applied to sunrise as theophany, it achieves the contrast of heaven (place of appearance)/earth (place of effect caused by appearance) and god/world (since the whole world is filled with omnipresent light[48]).

B: greeting the god.

On the B side of the morning stanza we find first and foremost the baboons (*jꜥnw*) or "sun-apes" (*jmjw-htt*), which as "eastern ba's" in the cosmography appear as morning worshippers of the sun.[49] The previously quoted hymn of Berlin stela 7306 is typical (other examples are given in *LL*, pp.189 and 208ff.) The "Ennead" is often mentioned as witness and worshipper of the sunrise:[50]

The Ennead praise you
Because they live from your rays.
They touch the earth when you come near
When they see the strength of Your Majesty as noble and great power
They say to you, when you appear,
Their arms bent before your power:
"Welcome ! Welcome ! Lord of the gods,
Atum Harakhty".

This subject is particularly important in hymns, clearly for the same reason why the "eastern ba's" play such an important role in the Book of the Day and the Cult-Theological Treatise: because the praise of the divine "communities" represents the prototype of sun worship by mankind and because man, with his praise, joins the heavenly beings and becomes one of them:[51]

The sun apes worship you
The inhabitants of the east rejoice before you

47 "Agyptologie und Linguistik", *GM* 11(1974), 64f. with n.22.
48 See chapter 3, § 2.4.
49 Cf. chapter 1.. *König als Sonnenpriester*, 48-53; *LL*, 207-214.
50 Bologna 1891 = *ÄHG* no.59; Cairo JE 13698; P.Leiden J 344 vso. I,9-10.
51 BD 100; cf. ch.1.

The lying ones (snakes) rise up before you on their tails
The standing ones prostrate themselves before you
The way of *Nḥḥ* is swept clean for you
Those in the southern sky worship you
Those in the northern sky rise up
The Ennead comes to you united
They kiss the earth prostrate before you
They say to you "Welcome, father of the fathers of all the gods".[52]

In Theban tombs and copies of the BD of the post-Amarna period there are many sun hymns where the treatment of this subject reads like an exact description of the accompanying pictorial representations, and, indeed, they begin to appear in the tombs at this time[53]:

The one whom the assembled Ennead praise
Their arms raised
The one at whom the ba's of Buto and Hieraconpolis rejoice
The sun apes worship you
"Praise him", says the whole world.[54]

The assembled Ennead praises you
The Two Ladies and the Merti bring him up
The beautiful and beloved one
When he rises, humankind lives.
The ba's of Heliopolis applaud him
The ba's of Buto and Hieraconpolis raise him up
The sun apes say, "Worship him"
All animals say, "Praise him".[55]

The treatment of this subject in the hymn sung by the underworld gods to greet the sun god in the First Hour of the Amduat is merely a summary pictorial description: "It begins with the baboon groups of the upper and lower register, proceeds (still only with the group title) with the praising goddesses and the shining uraei of the upper and lower registers, followed by the two remaining groups of the upper register (worshipping gods and hour-goddesses). Finally, the gods of the middle registers are enumerated, but only certain gods are named. They are followed by the two remaining groups of the lower register."[56] A genuine pictorial description, therefore, sounds exactly like the subject "greeting" in a sun hymn:

The Ennead in your retinue
The sun apes are in praise when you rise
And appear as Re-Harakhty
The Ennead of the gods rejoice

52 BD 15AIV P.Berlin 3002 = *ÄHG* no.43.
53 The earliest examples, TT 41 and P.Leiden T2, are early post-Amarna.
54 *STG* Text No. 59a (TT 49), 5-10.
55 Standard text E (*LL*, III 4) in the version from P.Leiden T2; see *LL*, 314f., 331-32, 331 n.77 (some indications to parallels of iconic sun-rising- representations).
56 Hornung, *Amduat II*, 40f.

And raise up Khepry".[57]

At the same time this text makes it clear that the morning praise is not simply a greeting of the god, but a participation in the solar journey. The hymns give the morning god (Khepry) "elevation" (*sṯzw*: setting upright. The same expression is used for the resurrection of the deceased "lying on his side" and appears as a parallel to *s3ḫw* "transfiguration" in mortuary spells).[58] In chapter 1 I argued that the cult performed in the sun chapel was also understood as active participation in the solar journey, an idea that is taken up occasionally in tomb hymns.

### *2.2.2 Midday*

A: Acts of the god.

1. The crossing of the sky

The midday stanza of the Solar Phases Hymn emphasises the character of the solar journey as a boat journey. Of course, the entire movement of the sun is conceived as a voyage and is also represented as such in the cosmography. In the hymnic representation of the solar journey this aspect is emphasised only in the midday stanza.[59]

The idea of the solar journey as a boat journey is at the same time the oldest attested[60] and most enduring. It is still used in Greco-Roman temples. The movement of the sun is illustrated in the image of the boat and enacted in the boat processions of the temple festivals by other gods too. The sun boat is not only a symbol of movement, but also and most importantly of royal authority and the judicial power associated with it. The two boats of the sun god (*Msktt* for the night journey and *Mᶜnḏt* for the day journey) correspond to the "two big ships" used by the king in the Old Kingdom to travel through the country to dispense justice and fix taxes.[61] The heavenly journey has the character of such a royal journey and the boats represent more a means of imposing rule than of mere movement.[62]

In the iconography of the sun boats the instrument of justice symbolises judicial power and the falcon standards royal authority.[63] Both symbols distinguish the two

57 *Urk* IV 1673. To "elevate" see ch.1,

58 *Wb* IV 361, 6-7 cf. 5; the translation "praise, magnify with words" is perhaps a little colourless. It means utterances that elevate the recumbent, like the litanies beginning with *wṯz ṯw* (*LL*, 199f.): "The utterances of the ancestors relate true things. Those who hear them are elevated in their places" (S. Schott, *Der Denkstein Sethos' I. in Abydos* (Göttingen,1964), 80).

59 Changing boats in the morning: *ḥtp m Mᶜnḏt* "taking one's place in the Morning Boat", cf. *König als Sonnenpriester*, 28 - occurs, e.g. in the hymn of stela Berlin 7306; *LL*, III 4, p. 326, and Hour Ritual, 8th hour, *LL*, 122f.

60 Ivory Comb of Djet: R. Engelbach, "An alleged Winged Sun Disk of Dynasty 1", *ZÄS* 65(1930), 115f.;W. Westendorf, *Altägyptische Darstellungen des Sonnenlaufs* (MÄS 10) (Berlin, 1966) pl.8 fig.14, p.22-24.

61 O. Firchow, "Königsschiff und Sonnenbarke", in *WZKM* 54(1957), 34-42; R. Anthes, "Sonnenboote in den Pyramidentexten", in *ZÄS* 82(1957), 77-89.

62 Cf. *Ma'at*, chapter 6.

63 In representations of the New Kingdom and later there is often a child sitting on the bow of the Night Boat and a swallow on the Day Boat; cf. Hornung, *Unterweltsbücher*, fig. 113. For the graphic

boats, which are scarcely distinguishable from each other,[64] from other divine vessels. In the royal cosmographies the representations of heaven on the ceiling show an elaborate type. The underworld books on the walls (Amduat and Book of Gates), however, reveal a simplified form without the instrument of rule, falcon standards, mast and mat or "Treibtafel"[65] on the bow. Even the cabin is often replaced by the *mḥn* snake, which encircles the sun god in a protective gesture.

The two boats are symbolic of day and night/east and west, which comprise the total movement of the sun. The sun god travels during the day in the *Mʿnḏt* boat (east-west) and at night in the *Msktt* boat (west-east). The change of vessel takes place in the morning and at night.[66] But in the hymns this detailed conception of solar movement is unimportant. The duality of boats, moreover, stems from the basic structure of Egyptian thinking in polar opposite pairs or "dual units", which expresses an abstract and complex higher concept of "unification" of two concrete and complementary partial concepts.[67] What is expressed in the two boats and all pair symbols relating to the day-night cycle is a concept of periodicity and perpetuity characterising the Egyptian concept of cosmic time as eternal movement circling within itself.[68]

The representation of the solar journey in the Solar Phases Hymn concentrates all ideas associated with the boat journey on the specifically midday manifestation of the sun god as "Re". In this form the sun god appears as ruler and judge, travelling through his domain in the boat as the instrument and symbol of rule in order to enforce law and order (Maat). The sentence that usually begins the midday stanza and contains an introductory "thematic catchword"[69] expresses this

---

distinction between the two see the inscription of the Treasury Scribe Ptahnefer in Cairo JE 12/24/66:

> When I am transfigured for having worshipped the god
> I shall become helmsman in the Boat of Millions
> And shall be transferred from the  to the 
>
> In the retinue of the sun god as he crosses the heavens.

64 E.g. Assmann, *Das Grab der Mutirdis* (Mainz 1990), 91 Abb.41.

65 According to E. Dondelinger, *Die Treibtafel des Herodot am Bug des ägyptischen Nilschiffes* (Graz, 1976) the mat is a nautical device allowing the ship to keep on course while sailing downstream; oars and "Treibtafel" are the only genuinely navigational instruments of a ship that, as it says in the texts, is rowed and sailed. I know of no representation of a Day Boat with mast and sail; but cf. the two boats on the picture of sunset in the Book of Night (Hornung, *Unterweltsbücher*, fig. 114).

66 E. Thomas, "Solar Barks from Prow to Prow", *JEA* 42(1956), 65-79. Firchow derives the duality of sun boat from the duality of the 'Two Lands' (note 64). Anthes regards it as a "difficult problem". Neither considers at all the solution proposed by E. Thomas, which she regards as so obvious that she does not discuss it any further.

67 Cf. E. Otto, "Die Lehre von den beiden Ländern in der ägyptischen Religionsgeschichte" *StudAeg* I (1938), 10ff.; A. Massart, *Mélanges Bibliques* (=Fs. A. Robert) (1957), 38ff. Concerning the term "dual unity" s. *LL*, 380, on "unification" cf. *LL*, 307f. n.33. Cf. E. Otto, in *LÄ* I, 1148-50 (Dualismus) and E. Hornung, *Der Eine und die Vielen* (Darmstadt, 1971), 237 with n.72.

68 For the cycle-symbolism of the sun-boats: *LL*, 274 with n.76, 288-89 (5), 289-90 (7-8), 377 with.note 8a; Zandee, in *JEOL* 18(1964), 257; Derchain, "Perpetuum mobile", in *Orientalia Lovanensia Periodica*, 6/7 (1975/76 =Fs. Vergote), 153ff. On the Egyptian concept of time and continuity: *Zeit und Ewigkeit*, 28-30.

69 *LL*, 387 s. Struktur, thematisches Stichwort.

specifically ruler-like manifestation of the sun god as follows: "You cross the sky with dilated heart" (*ḏ3j=k pt/nmj=k ḥrt m 3wt-jb/jb=k 3wjw*). The "dilated heart" is a specifically royal emotion: the joy of the victor in a triumphal procession.[70] The usual translation "joy" does not manage to convey the full meaning. The heart of the god dilates when the enemy is overcome. The corresponding stanza of a common tomb hymn may be cited here as typical example: [71]

| | |
|---|---|
| *nmj=k ḥrt jb=k 3wjw* | You cross the sky with dilated heart |
| *b3w P Nḫn m z3=k* | The ba's of Buto and Hieraconpolis in your protection |
| *ḏ3j=k pt m ḥᶜᶜw* | You cross the sky in joy |
| *mr nḫ3wj ḫprw m ḥtpw* | The Two Knives Lake is now at peace |
| *ᶜpp ḫrw n šᶜt=f* | Apophis has fallen at his slaying |
| *ḥsq.n dmt ṯzwt=f* | The knife has cut his vertebra |
| *nṯrw m ḥᶜᶜw* | The gods are in joy |
| *wnn Rᶜw m m3ᶜw nfr* | Re sails in favourable wind |
| *Msktt sk.n.s pḥ sj* | The *Msktt* boat has destroyed its attackers |
| *Mᶜnḏt šzp.n.s ršwt* | The *Mᶜnḏt* boat has received joy |
| *wj3 n ḥhw ḥr ršrš* | The boat of millions is in joy |
| *jzt Rᶜw m ḥ3b* | The crew of Re is festival |
| *m33=sn sḫrw sbj* | When they see that the rebel is dead |
| *d3r.n sw Nsrt* | And the Flaming One has subdued him |

## 2. The triumph over Apophis

When the sun god crosses the sky in the hours of midday, he comes up against the sun enemy Apophis.[72] This confrontation is, however, described as such only in the cosmographies. The Book of the Day places the struggle with Apophis in the 6th Hour (the Hour "that rises for Seth") and refers also in the 7th and 8th Hours to the heavenly struggle.[73] The apotropaic hymns, which also belong to the mysteries of the sun cult, refer directly to the struggle as an action of the attendant gods as well as of the sun god himself.[74]

The midday subject of the Solar Phases Hymn is not, however, the struggle, but the triumphal procession of the god, which presupposes the successful outcome of the struggle. The confrontation with the enemy is articulated here only in the form of a "crisis overcome"[75], expressed in the "resultative form":

| | |
|---|---|
| *mr nh3wj ḫprw m ḥtpw* | The Two Knives Lake is now at peace |

70 The king as "lord of *3wt-jb* "lord of dilated heart" and the "dilation of heart" as gift of the gods to the king are such common ideas that examples are unnecessary. A collection of examples for these hymns may be found in *LL*, 277ff. note 75 and Zandee, *Amunshymnus*, 552-555. The 7th Hour of the day, which follows the Hour of the Celestial Struggle, is called *s3wt-jb* "which makes the heart dilate".

71 *TG* Text No. 20 = *ÄHG* no.64. Cf. also *LL*, 276.n.70.

72 Zandee, *Amunshymnus*, 143-168, gives a collection of passages dealing with the combat against Apophis.

73 Piankoff, *Livre*, 16-17; *LL*, 297. In the ninth hour there is the statement that "the lord of the universe lives after the passing this evil sand-bank."

74 *LL*, 221f with references to other treatments of the combat theme.

75 *LL*, 379 see "Behobene Krisis"; on the motif of periodical crisis cf. *Zeit und Ewigkeit, 28f.*

| | |
|---|---|
| *ᶜpp ḫrw n šᶜt=f* (PsP) | Apophis has fallen at his slaying |
| *ḥsq.n dmt ṯzwt=f (sḏm.n=f).* | The knife has cut his vertebra |

It is not the struggle that is represented here, but the state of the enemy defeated and harmony restored. The vignettes of the midday period also represent the sun boat above the enemy who is cut to pieces with knives.[76]

The confrontation with the enemy involves the attendant gods. It is part of the idea of the boat journey as a royal journey that the sun god is surrounded by a "court" (*šnjt*),[77] as is specifically mentioned and addressed in certain sun litanies:[78]

Giving incense, singing for Re, for his disk
for Atum, for his eye, for his hand
for Khepreṛ, for Ru, for Ruty
for Shu, for Tefnut
for Maat at the bow of the sun boat
for Isis
for Hathor
for Hu
for Sia
for Khonsu
for Seth.[79]

According to the description of the 6th Hour in the Book of the Day Isis "with her magic"[80] and Seth[81] play a decisive role in the struggle against Apophis. Although Seth occasionally uses magic (according to other types of texts, e.g. *CT* II 350/1), it is principally his spear that brings down the enemy.[82] The uraeus serpent of the sun god spits fire at the enemy[83]. This icon expresses the experience of the aggressive heat of the sun which at midday reaches its peak, but should also be regarded as "sacramental interpretation" of accompanying sacrifices.[84] Thoth, who

76 Frequently on coffins; cf., e.g., A. de Buck, *De zegepraal van het licht* (Amsterdam 1930), fig.18.

77 *šnw/jjt ḥ3t k3r* "the retinue around the cabin", cf. e.g. *CT* I 391, 390, 386, VII 458; *šnwt k3r* "the retinue of the cabin": IV 178k. Cf. also Zandee, *Amunshymnus*; 26f., 558 with n. 162.

78 Ritual for Amenophis I, P.Chester Beatty IX rto 6,3-10 and P.Cairo+Turin C 8,7 - T 19,8; A.H. Gardiner, *Hieratic Papyri in the BM*, 3rd ser.I, 88f. (London, 1938) pl.52-53; Nelson, *JNES* 8, 231 ep.33; *LL*,351 n.61 with parallels and related litanies. Cf. also *LÄ* III, 1064.

79 In P.Chester Beatty and "Opening of the Mouth" sc.59: Thoth. Thoth as deputy of Seth: Otto, in *Orientalia* 7(1938), 69ff.

80 Piankoff, *Livre*, 16; cf. BD 100: "I made myself the companion of Isis and strengthened her magic power".

81 Isis and Seth are also deities who fight against Apophis in the netherworld, cf. Hornung, *Amduat II*, 130ff.

82 On the "30 cubits spear" see *STG* Text No. 52, 25 and Pyr 1212a; cf.T. Säve-Söderbergh, *On Egyptian Representations of Hippopotamus Hunting* (Uppsala, 1953), 33. Seth in the sun-boat: Piankoff, *Livre*, 16 n.2 with lit.

83 References: *LL*, 275 n.64; 130f. (4); for the role of the goddess Maat as *Nsrt* "raging justice" see *Ma'at*, 180-84. See also Zandee, *Amunshymnus*, 535, 538-549.

84 Cf. P.Bremner Rhind xxxiii, 1-18 = *ÄHG* no.18, 41f.:
Apophis has died in the flames
The impious one has been sacrificed in the fire.

occasionally replaces Seth on the bow of the boat, cuts him to pieces with a knife.[85] The sun god himself, according to the Solar Phases Hymn, does not fight: the enemy is despatched not by him, but "for him".[86]

The victory over Apophis is less a manifestation of strength than of law and order, i.e. Maat, which as a result of the victory "appears before Re."[87] The struggle takes on the nature of a judgement that has been enforced, the confrontation between the sun god and the enemy is like an act of jurisdiction.[88] Re travels through the sky "justified".[89] Apophis therefore not only embodies cosmic opposition to light and movement, but also the principle of evil (*ḏw qd*). But there are also images of mere violence without any legal connotations. Most prominent among them is the icon of the sun god as a predatory bird, esp. a hawk (*bjk, gmḥsw*), a form that embodies the aggressive, annihilating aspect of the sun in the moment of its most intense heat and radiance.[90] The same aspect is also embodied in *Nsrt*, the "flaming goddess", the cobra diadem of the god, who casts her fiery breath against the enemies of the sun. But she is also a form of Maat, which relates her to the sphere of justice.

Defeat of the enemy takes place when the sun is at its zenith in a place described as "Two Knives Lake",[91] "Sandbank of Two Knives Lake",[92] "Sandbank of Apophis"[93] or simply "(that) Sandbank".[94] In the cosmographic description of the hours of day in the Book of the Day "this sandbank" is mentioned in Hours 6 to 8 and is successfully negotiated only in the 9th Hour:

> The heaven is in beauty
> The earth is in harmony.[95]
> The gods have grasped the end of the rope
> Those around the cabin, their heart is dilated.
> The lord of all lives after passing (*znt*) this sandbank
> He has slain the enemies of Re.[96]

The Egyptian word for "midday" means literally "standstill" (*ᶜḥᶜw*). Thus, the midday period was probably genuinely felt as time standing still, when the sun at its

---

85 Cf. the hymn of Thoth *Urk* IV 2092f.; *ÄHG* no.222, 33-36 and *ÄHG* no.43, 37-38.

86 *LL*, 89 (13) etc.

87 *LL*, 177-179; *Ma'at*, 177-195.

88 For this reason the combat is usually referred to as *sswn* "punishment, to punish", e.g. *LL*. 301,11: *ÄHG* No. 87G, 182; P.Greenfield XXIX, III:
> Apophis has perished in the flame,
> his destruction is complete, you have punished him,
> he has been consumed by the flame of the Eye of Horus."

89 *STG* Text No. 58, 16; Text 74, 6; Text 165, 9; Text 182, 17; *ÄHG* no.56, 4; *LL*,181f.; Zandee, *Amunshymnus*, 562-66.

90 Cf. Zandee, *Amunshymnus*, 106-114.

91 *LL*, 271f.; for the reading: Altenmüller, *ZÄS* 92(1966), 86-95.

92 *Urk* VI 123.

93 *BIFAO* 45, 159 l.25; BD 7; Amduat 7th hour; Vandier, *Moᶜalla* (Cairo, 1942) 220; Hornung, *Amduat III*, 65 ad p.132; P.Chester Beatty VII rto V, 4-5.

94 The Book of the Day qualifies the sand-bank as *qsn* "evil", cf. also BD 7.

95 For the stylistic form of the festival song which is used here, cf. *LL*, 250ff.; below, "B".

96 Piankoff, *Livre*, 18f.; *LL*, 297.

zenith between rising and setting pauses for a while. For a visual mind thinking pictorially this becomes the enemy of the sun, which as a turtle[97] or snake drinks up so much of the heavenly ocean that the sun boat runs aground on the "sandbank of Apophis" as a result of low water. It can proceed only after Seth has stabbed the enemy with his spear and compelled him to "regurgitate what he has swallowed".[98] The widespread occurrence of this expression as a proverb is evidence of the general intelligibility of this icon and at the same time of the diversity of the semantic levels in which it was important.[99] The same is true of the "sandbank of Apophis", an expression used in the inscriptions of the First Intermediate Period to indicate drought and famine.[100]

The midday pause of the sun boat does not therefore denote the concept of a purely cosmic crisis, to which one ought after some time to have become accustomed on a daily basis. Rather it denotes a danger that threatens life on all its semantic levels and can attack at any time and in any form (famine, disease, sickness, snake bite, uprising, war etc.) the life of the individual and the community and, by disturbing order on one of its semantic levels, can bring the solar journey, time and life to a standstill. This "sympathetic" connection between cosmos and society, solar journey and human order, is particularly evident in later sources. The magical healing spells of the Metternich stela represent an accident on the individual-human level (e.g. scorpion bite) as a disturbance of the general order of things, which results in the immediate stopping of the sun boat and, with it, life, in order to mobilise the gods the gods to intervene.[101] The spells against Seth (*Urk.*VI) depict the cosmic catastrophes that will ensue if the enemy of the gods interferes with the order of the country and desecrates the secrets of the cult.[102] Here too the emphasis is: "so that the sun does not become dark on the Sandbank of the Two Knives Lake".[103]

P. Jumilhac depicts the consequences of a general abandonment of the cult in terms of such a global catastrophe.[104] These are not specifically Late Period conceptions, but very old and very real anxieties based on multifarious historical and personal experiences (famine, epidemic, revolution, foreign rule etc.). The persistence of this theme in quite diverse areas of Egyptian literature reveals the obsessional nature of these anxieties.[105]

The icon of the sun god in the boat, sailing over the defeated enemy and his sandbank "with a fair wind", expresses hope or rather confidence in overcoming the

---

97 Turtle as enemy of gods: cf. B. v.d.Walle, *La Nouvelle Clio* 5, 180; T. Säve-Söderbergh, *MDIK* 14, 175ff.; J. Vandier, *Le Pap. Jumilhac*,(Paris, 1960) 201f. (616); H.G. Fischer, *Ancient Egyptian Representations of Turtles* (New York,1968).

98 *LL*, 198f.; *Edfou* V, 121.11-12; *Urk* VI 97.8-10; Zandee, *Amunshymnus*, 543-45.

99 Cf. occurrences such as Israel stela and BM 566.

100 J. Vandier, *La famine dans l'Égypte ancienne*, (RAPH) 7 (Cairo, 1936), 74ff.; W. Schenkel, *Die Bewässerungsrevolution im Alten Ägypten* (Glückstadt, 1978), 50f.; Vandier, *Mo*ᶜ*alla*, 220; *LL*, 295-298.

101 A. Klasens, *A Magical Statue Base* (Leiden,1952), 31-32, 96. Cf. *Stein und Zeit*, 283f.

102 *Urk* VI 122-128.

103 *Urk* VI 123.

104 J. Vandier, *Le Papyrus Jumilhac*, 129ff. § xxvi col. xvii,15-xviii, 21.

105 S. Schott, "Altägyptische Vorstellungen vom Weltende", in *Analecta Biblica* 12(1959), 319-330; P. Derchain, *Le Pap.Salt 825*, I, 24-28; *Zeit und Ewigkeit*, 26-30; *Stein und Zeit*, 259-287.

crisis and averting the catastrophe in all its manifestations. It is the symbol and embodiment of "welfare" in the broadest sense.[106] The example of this icon shows most clearly what this pictorial thought as a way of constituting reality is about and what constitutes the essential truth of these icons, for it is this essential truth that explains their incredible durability. They are not meant to explain, but to make sense of cosmic phenomena. The icon integrates them into a cosmology, in which one semantic level refers to another.

B: the victory celebration of the retinue.

With the victory of the sun god the hymns celebrate the successful management of a crisis threatening all life. Thus, the relief expressed in the jubilation of the gods reflects the fact that everybody is affected by the crisis. "Celebrating" is an appropriate word in many ways both for the subject of this passage of the midday stanza and the form in which it is treated. The representational form of the victory jubilation follows the pattern of the cult festival hymn. I have examined the connection between the two in great detail in *LL*[107] and will therefore merely summarise the position here. Among the characteristics of a genre of hymns sung by a chorus that celebrate the appearance of the divinity in festival processions[108] are:

(a) the description of the general jubilation, always starting with heaven and earth, which the sun hymns modify with regard to the specific "communities" of the solar journey, and always in verb forms and sentence types denoting a state;

(b) the subsequent naming of the appearance of the god as the cause of jubilation, for which the sun hymns in appropriate places use statements like: "when they see that the rebel has fallen";[109]

(c) the form, without address or dialogue, which describes the effect of the appearing god, without addressing him. This characteristic is also taken over by the sun hymns. Since they refer in almost every verse to the one being addressed, this change of interpersonal form is the most infallible sign that the speech here is another form, viz. that of a festival hymn.

Whereas the B-theme of the morning stanza represents an act, viz. the greeting of the sun god by his "communities", the B-theme of the midday stanza represents a condition in which the communities are placed. This contrast is quite clear from the difference in sentence form and interpersonal form in the two stanzas. *STG* Text No. 20 may be regarded as a typical example:

106 Cf. *Eloquent Peasant*, B1 55; *Amenemope* x,11; *Urk* IV 944,2; Zandee, *Amunshymnus*, 566f.

107 *LL*, 246-262, cf. *LÄ* III, 853f.; cf. also Zandee, *Amunshymnus*, 163-68.

108 *LL*, 250-52.

109 *LL*, 237-39.

| Morning | Verb Form | Address |
|---|---|---|
| *jrjj n=k mwt=k Nwt* | *sḏm=f* | + |
| *šzp tw jmjw M3nw* | *sḏm=f* | + |
| *dw3 tw Nbtj* | *sḏm=f* | + |
| *sw3š=sn nfrw ḥm=k* | *sḏm=f* | + |
| *sḥtp tw Gb Nwt* | *sḏm=f* | + |
| *jrjj n=k msw=sn hnw* | *sḏm=f* | + |
| *dw3 tw jmjw htt* | *sḏm=f* | + |
| *jb3 n=k ʿwt qm3.n=k* | *sḏm=f* | + + |

Your mother Nut acts for you
the inhabitants of Manu receive you,
the two Ladies worship you,
they praise the beauty of Your Majesty,
Geb and Nut pacify you,
their children give you acclamations,
the sun apes adore you,
the cattle which you have created dance for you.

| Midday | Verb Form | Address |
|---|---|---|
| *mr nẖ3wj ẖprw m ḥtpw* | N *m* + N | - |
| *ʿpp ẖrw n šʿt=f* | N PsP | - |
| *ḥsq dmt ṯzwt=f* | *sḏm* N N | - |
| *nṯrw m ḥʿʿw* | N *m* + N | - |
| *wnn Rʿw m m3ʿw nfr* | *wnn* N m + N | - |
| *Msktt sk.n.s pḥ sj* | N *sḏm.n=f* | - |
| *Mʿnḏt šzp.n.s ršwt* | N *sḏm.n=f* | - |
| *wj3 n ḥḥw ḥr ršrš* | N *ḥr* + Inf. | - |
| *jzt Rʿw m ḥ3b* | N *m* + N | - |

The Two Knives Lake has become peaceful
Apophis is fallen to his slaughter,
the knife has cut through his spine.
The gods jubilate,
Re endures in a fair wind,
the *Msktt* boat has destroyed its attacker,
the boat of Millions is in joy,
the crew of Re is in festival

The thematic contrast seems to me indisputable, and this helps to clarify the meaning of the verb form and sentence types used. The sentences with verb-subject sequence are used to describe the act, while sentences with subject-verb sequence (where the position of the verb may also be filled by the construction m + N, e.g. "in jubilation") refer to states. These are not grammatical rules, but a description of the syntactic expression of the thematic contrast in the sun hymns. The decisive point concerning this contrast is the festive nature of the heavenly journey in the Solar Phases Hymn. In the Nedjmet copy of the BD a hymn devoted exclusively to the midday event begins like a festival hymn with the word "festival": *hrw nfr* "beautiful day". The text is cited here *in extenso*:

Your day is beautiful, boat of Re
In this beautiful hour of the day
Your rising is beautiful, sun (7 times).
The prow of the boat
Is turned to the west on the sandbank
The son of Nut holds his spear
He has killed the tortoise, slain the gazelle and trampled on the enemy
Tilapia is joyful
The abdu fish is in festival
The gods of heaven jubilantly beat the drum
Re is happy
The illuminator of the Two Lands is joyful.
The great praised one, Osiris Nedjmet, justified,
Is saved from that enemy.[110]

Overcoming the obstacle of the sandbank means the salvation of Nedjmet.

### *2.2.3 Evening and Night*

Evening and night are not iconically distinguished like morning and midday, but seen together in one image. In this phase the sun god appears as Atum, the "complete" and pre-existent god of the beginning, to whom every cycle returns in order to be able to begin truly anew.[111]

A: act of the god.

The act of the god has a twofold aspect: visible and hidden, an outer and inner aspect. The god appears to the dead in the underworld and himself assumes temporarily the existence of a "transfigured being" (*jm3ḫjj*). With his descent into the underworld he not only wakes up the dead from their sleep, but also shows them that death can be overcome. The oldest text that deals with the subject of the underworld journey of the sun (*CT* 1068) alludes to this double aspect:

| | |
|---|---|
| *CT* VII 329a | *jnḏ-ḥr=k Rᶜw* |
| b | *sḥtp=k n=j ḥr n Wsjr*[112] |
| c | *dw3 tw jmjw jmḥt* |
| 330a | *s3ḫ tw jmjw d3t* |
| b | *dj=sn n=k j3w* |
| c | *jj=k m ḥtp* |
| d | *dj=k ḥtpw n wrw* |
| | *w3ḫw n šrrw* |
| 331a | *dj=k n=j ḥtpw* |
| b | *zbjj r jm3ḫ* |
| | *mj Rᶜw rᶜw nb* |

Hail to you, Re!
May you pacify the face of Osiris for me.

110 *ÄHG* no.19.
111 *Zeit und Ewigkeit,* 44 n.155, 47 w.n.161; *König als Sonnenpriester*, 44 w.n.2 and 9.
112 Var. *sḥtp=k ḥr n Wsjr* NN.

The inhabitants of the deep worship you,
The inhabitants of the underworld transfigure you,
They praise you,
When you come in peace,
To give offerings to the great
And prosperity to the small.
May you give me offerings
And promotion to venerableness
Like Re every day.

The "venerableness" of Re, which the dead wish for themselves in this text, is frequently the subject of New Kingdom hymns, especially in the widely used standard text "D" (e.g. *STG* Text No. 180b):

Welcome in peace, you have reached earth,
The arms of the western mountain have embraced you.
Your Majesty has received venerableness,
By landing at your place of yesterday.
The arms of your mother protect you,
*Sjb* slays your enemies.
The western ba's pull you
On the path in the sacred land.
You illuminate the face of the those in the underworld,
you listen to the call of one in the coffin.

In this representation of the night-icon five typical components emerge:

(a) the "landing" (*s3ḥ t3)* in the west, as entering the "arms" of the western mountain;

(b) the "mooring" (*mnj*) as the end of the cycle and entering the underworld existence form of *jm3ḫjj*;

(c) embracing by the mother;

(d) dragging the boat by the western ba's;

(e) the revitalising provision of light and encouragement for the dead.

Let us examine these components in sequence.

(a) The spatial-cosmic aspect of the event, the sun entering the western mountain, is described in this couplet as in pictorial representations of sunset, where a pair of arms emerge from the western mountain to embrace the setting sun.[113] The nature of the event as an appearance of the god in the underworld is expressed in the "welcome" address. It is the typical address of the god in the evening, because, unlike at sunrise, sunset is interpreted as "arrival".[114] The god appears to those on earth in the morning only to remove himself from them and place an immeasurable distance between heaven and earth, i.e. himself and mankind[115], whereas he comes in person to those in the underworld and speaks to them.

(b) The inner personal aspect of this event is the transformation of the god into the underworld existence form as *jm3ḫjj*, in which humans too hope to "repeat" their

113 *LL*, 232 n.9; cf. 61 n.97.
114 *LL*, 46-48; *STG* Text No. 17, n. (a).; *STG* Text No. 52 (h), (m); Zandee, *Amunshymnus*, 513f.
115 *LL*, 302-306 cf. below, ch.3 §2.2-2.3.

life. The sun god "receives" this honour. This event, therefore, has something of the passive. In the text of *LL* I,2 occurs the statement: "To you is given 'venerableness' in the presence of Osiris".[116] It is the passivity of death that is being expressed. The expression *jm3ḫ* refers both to the provision of tomb, cult and rites for the "tomb owner" to guarantee his continued existence and to the veneration implied in such a provision.[117] The sun god also appears as "one provided for", who survives the passage into the underworld as a member of protective and life-giving constellations:

> The protection of Re keeps you safe,
> The magic of Thoth is with you,
> The healing power of Isis permeates your limbs.

This sentence does not come from a funerary text, but from a hymn to the setting sun.[118]

(c) The physical embodiment of the life-giving and protective constellation, within which death proves to be a passage to a new life, is the embrace by the mother goddess and the sky goddess.[119] In the description provided by the cosmographies the sun god does not enter the embrace, but the mouth of the sky goddess in order to re-appear in the morning from her vagina.[120] But this is practically never mentioned in sun hymns.[121] The icons of sun hymns illustrate the cosmic events in such a way that they become intelligible on other semantic levels. Here this method is particularly clear. With the image of the sun being embraced by the sky goddess the Solar Phases Hymn gives sunset the same sacramental interpretation as funerary spells ("transfigurations") give to the funeral. Indeed, the formulations are so identical that it would be impossible to decide from isolated quotations who is intended: the sun god or the deceased.[122] The meaning of this constellation is to be found in the union with the mother and death is to be interpreted as a return to the source.[123] It is interesting, however, that in the iconic illustration this union takes on the form of an embrace and not re-entry into the womb. The iconic formulation follows the laws of what can be represented pictorially and what can be celebrated ritually.[124]

---

116 Cf. *LL*, 63f. for further references (Amduat; *LL*, I 3, 77, 8a).

117 Cf. *Ma'at*, 99ff. for the meaning of the term *jm3ḫjj* as "tomb-owner".

118 Florence 1603, Schiaparelli, *Cat.Gen ... Firenze* (Rome 1887) I, 337; W. B. Berend, *Musée Égyptien de Florence* (Paris 1882), 98-99; Barucq-Daumas, *Hymnes et prières* (Paris 1980), No. 43. This text is of interest because it equates Osiris and the nocturnal sun god in a mysterious way:

> The lords of the underworld rejoice
> They worship you when you visit them
> In your face of Osiris.

Cf. BD 181, s. *LL*, 97 w.n.23.

119 *LL*, 146 n.34; *LÄ* IV, 266-71.

120 *KaS*, 26f., 42f.

121 Cf. *STG* Text No. 233; *ÄHG* no. 129, 110 (Hibis 32, 23).

122 A collection of funerary texts is given by A. Rusch, *Die Entwicklung der Himmelsgöttin Nut zu einer Totengottheit*, (MVÄG 27) (1922).

123 *LL*, 382 s.v. "Heimkehr"; *LÄ* IV, 267-269.

124 This constellation is represented pictorially by the representation of Nut on the inside of the coffin; cf. the description of this image in I Rhind XI, 5, which constitutes a particularly fine example of

(d) The western ba's are the jackals that belong to sunset, just as the eastern ba's (baboons) belong to sunrise.[125] It is their function to drag the sun boat through the underworld, and this is represented in the Book of the Night and boat scenes in the sun chapels,[126] but not, curiously enough, in the underworld books.[127] The icon of the sun boat being dragged through the underworld can similarly be understood from funerary belief. It is one of the central wishes of the deceased "to take hold of the front tow rope of the Night Boat".[128] This means that he wishes to identify himself with those creatures called "jackals", "western Ba's", "western gods"[129] or "gods of the underworld"[130] in the same way that the baboons of the sunrise represent the figures with which the worshippers wish to identify themselves.

(e) The life-giving welfare extended by the sun god to the inhabitants of the underworld consists of "giving light" and "hearing". The deceased aroused by his rays present their petitions to him:

> They all tell you their requests
> After you have shone for them.[131]
>
> They tell you what they have in their heart
> After you have let them see you again.[132]
>
> The living ba's wake up on their seats
> After they have looked upon the lord of the gods.[133]

Curiously enough, the linguistic communication of the sun god with those in the underworld, which is referred to throughout, next to seeing the light, as a life-giving act and is obviously considered to be just as important, is expressed not only as hearing and granting, but also as giving the breath of life:

---

the interrelationship between image and word in iconic thought:

> My arms are extended to embrace your divine body
> That I may shield your body and protect your mummy
> And animate your ba forever.

125 Cf. *STG* Text No. 61 n.(a); *LL*, 54f.; cf. also part B of the Cult-Theological Treatise. For the *bꜣw jmntt* and their role in the solar journey cf. also T. DuQuesne, *Anubis and the Spirits of the West*, (Oxford, 1990), who is working on a major study of the *bꜣw jmntt*.

126 *Medinet Habu* VI 422C etc.; cf Parker *et al.*, *The Edifice of Taharqa*, 42 n.17.; *ZÄS* 110(1983), 91-98.

127 In the Book of Gates the sun boat is also towed, but by the "underworld gods", which are represented as humans not jackals (H). There the jackals appear in another function as guardians of the "Lake of Life" (218ff.)

128 E.g. *CT* VI 313 q; VII 14 o; Text 52, 71 etc.; cf. W. Barta, *Aufbau und Bedeutung der altägyptischen Opferformel* (Munich, 1968), 159, 245. In *ÄHG* no.44, 31 the deceased drags the sun boat through the underworld too.

129 E.g. Hour Ritual. 12th.Hour, 10.15; *Medinet Habu* VI 422C.

130 *passim* in the Book of Gates.

131 BD 15 B II *ÄHG* no.44, 23.

132 O.Cairo 25106 = *ÄHG* no.191, 27-28.

133 *Edfou* V 131-132.

You give air to the one who calls in the underworld,
They are saved[134] when they see you.[135]

You listen to the prayers of the one in the coffin,
You drive away their sorrow and their misfortune
you give the breath of air to their noses.[136]

You lead your sun disk to the caves
And your light irradiates the corpses.
The one who was stifled can breathe.
Air is in the nostrils.[137]

You listen to the prayers of the one in the coffin,
You have raised up the one lying on his side.
You give Maat to eat to the one who possesses it,
You rejuvenate the nostrils with what is in them.[138]

That this giving of breath really means a sort of life-giving utterance of the god is clear from the detailed representation of these events and actions in the underworld books. The words used by the sun god to address the deceased, judge them and allocate their livelihood[139] are the breath that gives them life. "They breathe from hearing his voice."[140]

The union with the mother is a typically "iconic" formulation of the night phases, which is unimportant in the underworld books, since these books do not give a "sacramental interpretation", but a cosmographic description of the solar journey. They do, however, reveal another aspect of the underworld journey, which is likewise based on an anthropological analogy: "The entire night journey of the sun is sometimes portrayed as if the sun god were descending in his ba form from the sky into the world below 'for the sake of his dead body'".[141] In the Book of Caves the analogy with human fate is made explicit: "I cause the ba's to alight on their corpses. I have alighted on my corpse."[142] This nocturnal visit (*sjp*)[143] of the sun god to his underworld corpse is already known from the *CT*.[144] At the same time the

134 *wḥ*ᶜ cf. Mariette, *Abydos I*, 52: "You (Re) deliver him (Osiris), you make his nostrils breathe".
135 P.Berlin 3048,7,6 = *ÄHG* no.143, 141f.
136 BD 15 B II = *ÄHG* no.44, 28-30.
137 G. Vittmann,"Die Hymne O. Wien 6155 und O.Kairo CG 2521", *WZKM* 72(1980), 2 pls.2-3.
138 Cf. P.Leiden I 344 vso IV.3 = *STG* Text No. 180b (TT 192), Zandee, *Amunshymnus*, 280-299.
139 On provision and jurisdiction as the dominant aspects of the sun god's care for the dead see *LL*, 145f. with n. 29-30.
140 *LL*, 144f. with n. 26.; *Ma'at*, 78-82.
141 Hornung, *Unterweltsbücher*, 36 (for the closing text of the 2th hour of the Amduat); Zandee, *Amunshymnus*, 121
142 Hornung, *Uunterweltsbücher*, 317: Book of Caves, I, 3rd Reg.
143 Cf. Zandee, *Amunshymnus*, 253-261.
144 Cf. *STG* Text No. 158 note (n). According to this and many other passages Heliopolis is the place where the underworld corpse of the sun god is concealed:
*CT* VII 19h: "My limbs are Re, when he descends to Heliopolis to mourn his corpse"
*CT* IV 64c: "I see my father, the lord of the sunset
I kiss my *ḏt*-body in Heliopolis"
*CT* I 184-85: "You travel upstream in the *Msktt* Boat

corresponding anthropological idea of the nocturnal union of ba and body is formulated.[145] The hymns also mention it sometimes.[146] One has the impression, however, that these things already belong to the "mysteries".

One definite element of the mysteries of the solar journey is the interpretation of this event as the union of Re and Osiris:

> Whoever reveals this will die a violent death
> Because it is a great mystery.
> It is Re and Osiris.[147]

The antagonism between Re and Osiris embodies on the highest level of abstraction that "dual unity" which expresses the Egyptian concept of reality (all that exists - *wnnt nbt*): *nḥḥ* and *ḏt*.[148] The nocturnal union of these complementary aspects of time gives rise to the "continuity of time", i.e. the continuity of life which is realised in time.[149] It is, however, especially important for the understanding of this constellation that in the embrace of Re and Osiris ("tomorrow" and "yesterday"/ *nḥḥ* and *ḏt*) it is not ba and corpse that unite, but son ("tomorrow") and father ("yesterday").[150] This constellation thus appears as important on various semantic levels: it is thought that when father and son embrace, the ka is transferred.[151] Occasionally, Tatenen appears in the role of embracing father,[152] just as Isis (instead of Nut) can appear as the embracing mother.[153] The decisive point for the meaning of constellations is the immutability of the role, not its occupant.

B: worship and jubilation of the underworld inhabitants.

Comparison of the verb forms and sentence types used to present the B-side of the event in the morning and at midday has made it possible to distinguish clearly between worship as an act and jubilation as a state. We may therefore also ask, with respect to the night stanzas, whether the responses of the underworld inhabitants are expressed as worship or jubilation, i.e. act or state. There does indeed seem to be a stylistic change. In the earlier hymns and the Amduat the response of the underworld inhabitants are regularly presented as an act: as a greeting of the type made in the morning on earth. In Ramesside hymns, however, most verb forms are durative or stative:

---

> You travel downstream in the *Mʿnḏt* Boat;
> your Ba has been transferred to the upper heaven
> Your flesh and corpse are in Heliopolis

145 Cf. W. Barta, *Das Gespräch eines Mannes mit seinem Ba* (MÄS 18) (Munich 1969).

146 Zandee, *Amunshymnus*, 189f. gives a collection of references to Ba-corpse dichotomy in solar theology.

147 P. Salt 825, 18, 1-2; cf. R. Lanzone, *Papyrus du Lac Moeris* (Turin,1896), pl. VI. *LL*,101-105.

148 *CT* IV 198ff.; cf. Hornung, "Zum ägyptischen Ewigkeitsbegriff",in *FuF* 39(1965), 334-336; *Der Eine und die Vielen*, 178; *Stein und Zeit*, 32-58.

149 *Zeit und Ewigkeit*, 28-30 with references to the interpretation of P.Salt 825 (P. Derchain).

150 *LL*, 103-105; *König als Sonnenpriester*, 43f. n.4; *Zeit und Ewigkeit*, 44.

151 Frankfort, *Kingship and the Gods* (Chicago 1947), 32f., 66, 122, 132ff.;P. Kaplony, *LÄ* III, 275

152 *LL*, 60-63.

153 *LL*, 56-60.

## Example 1: *LL*, I 2

| | Address | Verb Form |
|---|---|---|
| *jw n=k jtrtj m ks* | + | *sḏm=f* |
| *dj=sn n=k jꜣw rꜥw nb* | + | *sḏm=f* |
| *ḥꜥꜥ nṯrw jmntjw m nfrw=k* | + | *sḏm=f* |
| *dwꜣ ṯw štꜣw-st* | + | *sḏm=f* |
| *jꜥb n=k wrw* | + | *sḏm=f* |
| *qmꜣ=sn n=k zꜣ-tꜣ* | + | *sḏm=f* |
| *ẖnn ṯw jmjw ꜣẖt* | + | *sḏm=f* |
| *sqdd ṯw jmjw Msktt* | + | *sḏm=f* |
| *sns ṯw bꜣw jmntt* | + | *sḏm=f* |
| *dd=sn n=k m ẖsf ḥm=k* | + + | *sḏm=f* |
| *jꜣw jꜣw spr.tj m ḥtp* | + + | *sḏm=f* |

The chapels of the Two Lands come to you in obeisance
They give you praise every day
The western gods rejoice over your beauty
Those whose places are secret worship you
The great ones join you
They intone "beware, earth!"
The horizon dwellers row you
Those in the Night Boat ferry you
The western Ba's praise you
They say to you as Your Majesty approaches:
"Welcome, welcome in peace".

## Example 2: Amduat I 20

| | | |
|---|---|---|
| *sns tw snsjjwt=k* | + + | *sḏm=f* |
| *sḥḏ n=k ꜣẖw=k kkw* | + + | *sḏm=f* |
| *dwꜣ tw nṯrw=k Rꜥw* | + + + | *sḏm=f* |
| *ssm tw wnwt jmjwt=k* | + + | *sḏm=f* |
| *stꜣ tw zꜣtj=k m bꜣw=k* | + + + | *sḏm=f* |

Your praising ones praise you,
Your uraeus snakes illuminate for you the darkness.
Your gods worship you, Re.
The hour (goddess), in which you are, accompanies you,
Your two daughters drag you in your boat

## Example 3: P. Louvre 3292 "M"

| | | |
|---|---|---|
| *ẖrw jj m rꜣ n jtrtj* | - | N+*m*+N |
| *mk-sw mk-sw m jꜣwt* | - | "S"+*m*+N |
| *dꜣtjw <ḥr> dwꜣ* | - | N+*ḥr*+Inf. |
| *jmntjw <ḥr> hkn* | - | N+*ḥr*+Inf. |
| *ꜥbꜥb m st sqr* | - | N+*m*+N |
| *sḏrjjw <ḥr> sqd* | - | N+*ḥr*+Inf. |
| *ꜣẖw <ḥr> ftft*[154] | - | N+*ḥr*+Inf. |
| *wrḏ-jb ẖrw <ḥr> nmꜥ* | - | N+PsP |

154 *ftft* "hop" is a word frequently used to describe the reaction of the rising dead to the sunlight, cf. exx. 4 and 6 and *LL*, pp.249.

| | | |
|---|---|---|
| *nꜥt mwtw r šzp bšw=sn* | - | Inf? + N |
| *z nb <ḥr> wnm šnst=f* | - | N + *ḥr* + Inf. |
| *nṯrw dꜣt ḥr smj n ḥm=k* | + | N + *ḥr* + Inf. |
| *jj=k m ḥtp ḫnm.n nfrw=k* | + + | *sḏm=f* |

Praise resounds in the mouth of the chapels of the Two Lands
"Here he is, here he is", cry the places
Those in the underworld worship
The westerners praise
Rejoicing is heard in place of silence
The sleeping are ferried [*sqd*?]
The transfigured leap
The 'weary one' has fallen on the bier [?]
The dead come forward to receive their rations
Everyone eats his food
The gods of the underworld announce to Your Majesty:
"Welcome in peace! We have united ourselves with your beauty".

## Example 4: Černý-Gardiner *HO* 30

| | | |
|---|---|---|
| *wjꜣ Mꜥnḏt pḥ=f jmntt* | - | N + *sḏm=f* |
| *tꜣ-tmm m jhh* | - | N + *m* + N |
| *jmjw-dꜣt m dwꜣw ḫft=f* | - | N + *m* + N |
| *jmntjw m ksw* | - | N + *m* + N |
| *sḏrjjw ftft r jrt=f* | - | N + *sḏm* |
| *ḫnm=sn ṯḥṯḥ* | - | *sḏm=f* |

The *Mꜥnḏt* Boat has reached the west
People are exultant
Those in the underworld worship you
The westerners are united
The sleeping leap before his eye and are seized with jubilation

## Example 5: BD 15B II

| | | |
|---|---|---|
| *nbw qrst m tpḥwt=sn* | - | N |
| *ꜥwj=sn m jꜣwt n kꜣ=k* | + | N + *m* + N |
| *ḏd=sn n=k sprwt=sn nbwt* | + | *sḏm=f* |
| *m-ḫt jr=k psḏ <=k> n=sn* | + + | *sḏm=f* |
| *nbw dꜣt jbw=sn nḏmw* | - | N + PsP |
| *sḥḏ.n jꜣmt=k jmntt* | + | *sḏm.n=f* |
| *jrtj=sn zšw n mꜣꜣ=k* | + | N + PsP |
| *hꜥꜥ jbw=sn mꜣꜣ=sn tw* | + | *sḏm=f* |

The cave dwellers in their caves
Their arms are stretched forth in worship of your ka
They tell you all their concerns after you have shone forth for them
The lords of the underworld, their hearts rejoice
Your radiance has illuminated the west
Their eyes are open to see you
Their hearts rejoice when they see you (*ÄHG* no.44).

Example 6: *STG* Text No. 244 (TT 359)

| | | |
|---|---|---|
| *jrjj jmntt j3w n-ḥ3t=k* | + | *sḏm=f* |
| *n3 sḏrw sn-t3 n ḥr=k* | + | N + PsP |
| *n3 qrrtjw ḥr ftft* | - | N + *ḥr* + Inf. |
| *jḫmw-sk nhmw ḥr=k* | + | N + PsP |
| *ᶜprw d3t m nwḥw=k* | + | N + *m* + N |

The west praises your face
The sleeping kiss the earth before you
The cave-dwellers leap
The indestructible ones rejoice with you
The underworld is equipped with your tow-ropes

Examples 1 and 2 present the description of an act in its purest form, while examples 3 and 4 contain the description of a state. In both types, especially example 3, the change of sentence type is accompanied by a change of interpersonal form: acts are related (to the constellation partners) as communicative acts, but states are not. Examples 5 and 6 contain a mixture of both types, and this is the most common.

The description of how the sun god is received in the underworld reflects the hope of the deceased for a similar fate. Here too the funerary texts can read like a sun hymn and vice-versa:

Cries of joy resound in the kingdom of the dead
the inhabitants of the underworld cry "Welcome",
they say to this N.
Those in their tombs, their hearts expand because of this N:
"You are the great god, the heavenly one among the gods.[155]

The arms of your father Geb receive you,
your mother Mut embraces you.
The gods, who lead through the underworld,
rejoice from love of you.
They receive you in peace: 'Welcome, welcome'[156], they say to you
after you have arrived in peace
and reached your house of eternity
your tomb of permanence."[157]

## *2.3 Conclusion*

Two observations have been made throughout the detailed study presented in this chapter and they may be repeated here:

(a) image and language are equivalent, in the sense that either can be used to express "thought", i.e. to formulate content;

155 *CT* IV 97.

156 Literally "praise, praise!". For the equivalence of *jjwj jjwj* and *j3w j3w* as a greeting of welcome cf. *LL*, 46-48.

157 CG 29301 ed.Maspero, *Sarcophages de l'époque persane et ptolémaique*, 45.

(b) several semantic levels can be brought into a relationship of mutual reference: they can be woven together in one icon and various spheres can consciously be "seen in one". In this way the icon allows human beings to participate in events that take place in the divine world. They can transpose themselves into the icon, e.g. by becoming a baboon in the morning, overcoming Apophis at midday (BD 39) and "taking the tow rope" at night.

Both are intrinsic elements of polytheistic cosmology, which structures its divine world in "constellations". These constellations are the principle by which the divine world can be represented pictorially. Without them the divine world cannot be represented "iconically": the "icons" represent the constellations. They also embody the principle of identification, enabling human beings to participate in the acts of the divine world, in the sense that, as priests in the cult and deceased in the underworld, they can function within constellations. In this way they enter into contact with the god and and participate in divine life.

In this respect, Amarna religion was a form of "iconoclasm". I shall examine this in the next chapter. But the question that presents itself here is: did this attempt at a radical discarding of iconic polytheism unleash as a reaction the flood of images that, gradually at first and increasing steadily until the 21st dynasty, filled the tombs, sarcophagi and copies of the BD, so that in the 21st dynasty the image became self-contained and, in "mythological papyri" and on sarcophagi, became the only means of expressing the content? This question cannot be dealt with here, but the relationship seems clear enough to me.

# CHAPTER THREE

# THE PHENOMENOLOGY OF THE SOLAR JOURNEY

## 1. Historical aspects: the discarded image

The previous two chapters have presented an entirely ahistorical picture of Egyptian solar religion and have examined neither the historical place of its origin nor the changes it underwent in the course of centuries or even millenia. This procedure seems justifiable to me in the sense that I have consciously limited myself to basic structures, which can in fact be properly treated within Egyptian history in a meta-historical way. As far as the inner aspect of this religion (the "mysteries") and the outer aspect (the "icons") are concerned, their origin is unknown to us and changes are not identifiable.

In the following chapters I should like to compare these basic structures with two ideas that can be located precisely both in terms of their origin and historical changes. The Theban tomb hymns, whose chronology and social history can both be determined, are the first documents that enable us to understand these ideas as historical phenomena. One of these ideas, the subject of this chapter, is a new solar theology, which is not simply "different" from everything that has preceded it but which represents the polar opposite and most radical negation of all that has been said in the previous two chapters: the blurring of "icons", the dismantling of "constellations", the denial of participation through knowledge and identification, and the replacement of the "mythic" by the "cosmic" dimension.

By this I mean not only Amarna theology, but a new solar theology that took root before Amarna (it can be traced back to Amenophis III) and carried on without interruption after it. The religion of Amarna is based on this theology, but is in no way identical with it, otherwise it would have disintegrated with Amarna. On the contrary, the most important hymns of this theological tendency come from the tombs of the post-Amarna and Ramesside periods. It is quite impossible to argue that a basically discredited tradition has been able to survive (for however long), according to some "law of inertia", or to talk of "echoes" of the Amarna period. Hymns of this tendency have been discovered in the tombs of the vizier Paser and the high priests Parennefer-Wennefer[1] and Nebwenenef, who may be reckoned among the leading lights of the intellectual and religious revival after Amarna. The new solar theology, even after the catastrophic experience of Amarna, lost none of its relevance and was quite clearly felt to be different from Amarna religion.

On the other hand, it is not only difficult but also pointless to look for differences between the new solar theology and the solar theology of Amarna texts.

1 Recently discovered by Friederike Kampp, dating from the time of Tutankhamun/Haremhab, and assigned the provisional no. TT - 162 -.

Such differences are in fact "nuances",[2] and some of them will be dealt with later. There can, however, be no doubt that Amarna religion grew out of this movement and represents a radical variant of it. The following account of the phenomenon will therefore include Amarna texts. Thus, it is clearly not the solar theologyitself of Amarna religion that was branded as heretical, but rather the radical and intolerant nature of its enforcement. In particular, the second pillar of its theological structure, viz. the theology of kingship, must have been regarded as intolerable.[3]

We learn from new Theban texts (principally *STG*, nos. 76, 113, 151, 161, 253, 254) not simply to equate this movement with Amarna religion. It proves to be an expression of an epoch-making crisis of polytheistic cosmology. This crisis by no means came to an end with the collapse of Amarna religion. These texts provide us with a new picture of the epoch, which cannot be understood merely as a "return to orthodoxy".[4]

## 2. Theological aspects

### *2.1 Aloneness and Uniqueness*

The aloneness of god is a concept that is not opposed to polytheism, but is opposed to "embeddedness", viz. in a constellation. Aloneness, written with the "bad bird" in hieroglyphic writing, was associated with deficiency.[5] In terms of the concept of a person that understands the self as part of a whole, it is a *summum malum*, indicative of a stage of deficiency, which existed in the divine world only as a primeval condition and which, incapable of being sustained, led to creation. As Erik Hornung has convincingly demonstrated, aloneness is a category of non-being and death.[6] Life is always "constellative" or "embedded". It is important to be aware of this in order to understand the first lesson of the new solar theology as an idea completely opposed to traditional cosmology: "The sun is alone on its journey." Sometimes this is stated explicitly,[7] but otherwise it forms the basic presupposition

---

2 Cf. here the studies of Piankoff and Aldred, cited in "Die 'Häresie'", *Saeculum* 23(1972), 110. It should be noted that the differences, which amount to no more than "nuances", affect only the solar theology of "natural philosophy" of Amarna religion on the one hand and the "new solar theology" on the other, i.e. neither Amarna religion nor solar theology as a whole. On Amarna religion cf. also E. Hornung, in O. Keel (ed.), *Monotheismus im alten Israel und seiner Umwelt* (Bibl.Beitr.14) (Stuttgart, 1980), 83-97 ; J.P. Allen, "The Natural Philosophy of Akhenaten" in W.K. Simpson (ed.), *Religion and Philosophy in Ancient Egypt*, (YES 3) (New Haven,1989), 89-102. and my article "Akhanyati's Theology of Light and Time", *The Israel Academy of Sciences and Humanities: Proceedings* VII.4(1992), 143-176.

3 Cf. in detail my essay "Die loyalistische Lehre Echnatons", *SAK* 8 (1980), 1-32.; cf. also "State and Religion", 66-68.

4 *pace ÄHG*, 64-77; "Primat und Transzendenz", in W. Westendorf (ed.), *Aspekte der spätägyptischen Religion* (Göttingen, 1979)26f.; *LÄ* I 528 with note 32.

5 In the formula *wᶜ wᶜjw* the word *wᶜjw* in the CT and the Cairo Amun Hymn has the "bad bird" determinative; cf. also Chapter 5.

6 *Der Eine und die Vielen* (Darmstadt,1961), 180-181, 171f.

7 Cf. for example *ÄHG* no.90, 7: "You have shown yourself in heaven, you being alone". Cf. also

of its image of god, since other gods are never mentioned as participating in any way in the solar journey.

In the context of the monotheism debate the meaning of this statement is apt to get lost. It is first and foremost not a matter of importance whether there are other gods besides this solitary god of the solar journey, but rather that he can be thought of and described as acting without reference to other gods. In polytheistic thought, as we have seen, a god as actor is inconceivable without certain other gods, who make up an "action-constellation" with him. But in his action (and the solar journey is still considered as such) this god is alone. It certainly makes a difference whether a concept of god independent of other gods is possible or whether it excludes the existence of other gods. It is this difference that sets Amarna religion apart. The difference was more important in the practice of religion than in the texts, because there is scarcely any mention of other gods in the new sun hymns, either in Amarna or Thebes. If they do appear, it is as a variety of creatures and living things next to human beings and animals, but not as constellation partners of the god.

The aloneness of the sun god is the theological interpretation of a cosmic phenomenon, viz. the uniqueness of the sun, which is occasionally also emphasised: (*STG* Text No. 253) *jtn=k wꜥjw stwt=f m ḥr*, "your sun disk is alone, its rays are in the face". An expression like "your sun disk" is inconceivable in Amarna texts and it is one of the differences between the new solar theology and its Amarna form. In Amarna the god is the sun itself, at most its "incarnation" (*ḫprw*).[8] In the other texts (non-Amarna), the sun is his *ḥꜥw*-body[9] or *ḏt*-body.[10] This too expresses a much tighter relationship between god and heavenly bodies than in the traditional conception, where the sun is regarded as "eye", head-dress, uraeus, attribute of the god.[11] The god of the new solar theology is in the truest sense of the word "heliomorphic" or "sun-shaped". The forces assembled around him by polytheistic thought in the form of a sphere of attendant gods are now described in their cosmic character as effects of the sun. The fire of the uraeus serpent becomes "scorching heat",[12] the power of Seth becomes a radiant energy that "subdues"[13] everything. By absorbing, as it were, the "personal sphere", taking it into himself, the god is the only actor. His action is, however, strictly "heliomorphic". The only action ascribed to him is that which theological interpretation of cosmic phenomena understands as the effect of the sunlight.

In contrast, polytheistic religion has represented the solar journey as a complex pattern of actions, in which the sun god was certainly the protagonist, but by no means the only actor. He is born, suckled, reared and worshipped. The enemy is

---

P.Leiden I 344 vso X, 9 ed. J. Zandee, *Amunshymnus*, 974ff.: "You are the unique one of heaven, the earth is founded below you. There is no one beside you."

8 M.Sandman, *Texts from the Time of Akhenaten* (Bib.Aeg. 3) (Brussels, 1938), 76.5; 76.8-9; 95, cf. 91;"Zwei Sonnenhymnen", *MDIK* 27.1, 17 n.40a.

9 *STG*, text 181a. 50.

10 *Urk* IV 2178 etc., cf."Zwei Sonnenhymnen", *MDIK* 27.1, 17 n.40a.

11 *LL*, 114 (2).

12 Cf. Suty-Hor (*ÄHG* no.89,57): "he becomes hot when he wishes, and cold when he wants. He causes bodies to sleep when he surrounds them". Amarna Great Hymn (*ÄHG* no.92,107-109): "... hot, so that they feel you".

13 Cf. *wꜥf* "subjugate" to describe the effect of the sun god's rays on foreign lands: Amarna Great Hymn (*ÄHG* no.92,24).

destroyed for him. He is received in the underworld by the arms of his mother. These are just a few of the specifically passive aspects of the complex pattern of actions of the solar journey. In this way the description of these actions becomes a hymnal characteristic of his "status".[14] The semantic categories of these actions, in which the traditional "iconic" representations describe the solar journey, may be summarised as follows: LIGHT/MOVEMENT/LIFE/RULE.[15] They are also the semantic categories of the theological interpretation, which the cosmic phenomena of the solar journey receive as the ONE action of the ONE god in the new solar theology. Because the cosmic is prevalent in the new theology, light and movement are dominant; life and rule are subordinate to them. The world is animated and ruled by the god in his light and through his movement.[16] It is therefore most impressive how everything becomes accessible to this new view that concentrates on cosmic phenomena as the effect of light and solar movement. The individual examples will be considered later. It is easy to see how just one more step was required to attribute everything to this one actor and proclaim his aloneness as uniqueness.

### *2.2 Remoteness and Hiddenness*

(1) He has withdrawn on high, nobody knows his form.[17]

(2) You have settled[18] very remote and very far
you have revealed yourself in heaven, you being alone.[19]

(3) You made heaven remote for his sake, very far and very remote.[20]

(4) High one, who cannot be reached.[21]
(...) Lord of throne, who keeps secret what he has hidden
(...) Hidden one, whose appearance is unknown.[22]

(5) High one, whose journey is unknown
how mysterious your forms are
Great power, first one of the east
high one, who cannot be reached.[23]

14 On the semantic or "inner" form of the traditional sun hymn as "status characteristic" cf. *ÄHG* nos.33-45
15 Cf. with more details *ÄHG*, 35-63.
16 Cf. *ÄHG*, 54-63; cf. *Zeit und Ewigkeit*, 49-54.
17 BM 706, Kitchen, *Ramesside Inscriptions*, III 330.
18 Or even: "you have departed", cf. Zandee, *Amunshymnus*, 197 n. 502, who derives *smn* not from *mn* "to remain, to endure" but from *mn* "to move (away)".
19 Leiden V 70 = *ÄHG* no.90; Leiden K 12 = Kitchen, *RI* III, 175, 3-4.
20 P.Berlin 3048 = *ÄHG* no.143, 81-83.
21 *jwtj pḥ=f*: P.Leiden I 344 vso. III,2 cf. Zandee, *Amunshymnus*, 239f.; cf. ex. 5 and P.Berlin 3050, viii, 9 = *ÄHG* no.22D, 25-30: "who traverses the sky, who cannot be reached."
22 Ibid., 206-214 without refrain.
23 O.C 25207 = *ÄHG* no.192, 5-8.

(6) You who have created heaven in order to elevate the forms of your appearance,
to conceal the place where you dwell
you have made it remote to entrust your image to it.[24]

(7) You have withdrawn as the 'remote' one over them.[25]

(8) When you are in heaven, your surroundings do not recognise you
your retinue does not understand you at all
the Ennead does not come near you.[26]

(9) He has surrounded his place with fire
and withdrawn high over every god
very far and very remote, too secret to be reached
but his rays penetrate into the earth.[27]

The subject of the remoteness and hiddenness of the sun god, illustrated in the preceding examples, is peculiar to the new solar theology. It is not mentioned in the "iconic" representations of the solar journey. This difference can be explained by the fact that the aspect of the remoteness and hiddeness of the sun god develops only from the perspective of human beings, which was consciously excluded from the iconic representation. This distinction can be related to what Emma Brunner-Traut calls "aspective" and "perspective"[28] (though it should be borne in mind that "aspective" has nothing to do with "aspect", since the spectator is not considered here at all). The problem with these terms is that they express an opposition that is related to the viewpoint of a spectator. In fact, the "aspective" categorically excludes the spectator. It does not form a "view", but illustrates a purely conceptual articulation of the content. In this sense, the term "conceptual" ("vorstellig"), used by Schäfer, is more appropriate.

The "iconic" representation of the solar journey in the traditional hymns, as analysed in Chapter 2, in this sense is "conceptual". Man as the reference point is categorically excluded.[29] Things are described which the human eye has never seen. New solar theology takes the opposite view: it limits itself to what is visible to the human eye. The forms in which the nature and activity of the god are visible to the human eye become the sole basis of what can be known and said about that god. The "mythic dimension" of the god, the dimension of the linguistic unfolding and representation of his nature (in short, his "name"),is equated with his cosmic visibility. The human eye becomes the only reference point of the theology, which states about god only what appears to the gazing eye and interpreting "heart". This process of a theological interpretation of the visible phenomena of nature may be called the "phenomenology" of the solar journey. It is quite different from the "iconography", where the imagery is conceptual and arises from "analogical

24 *STG* Text No. 161 = 253.
25 P.Louvre 3292 section "M" = *ÄHG* no.47, 5.
26 Ibd., section "T", = *ÄHG* no.48, 21-23.
27 Hibis 32,4-5 = *ÄHG* no.129, 18-21.
28 "Die Aspektive", epilogue to H. Schäfer, *Von Ägyptischer Kunst* (Berlin, 1963 4th edn.); cf. *LÄ* I, 474-488.
29 Cf. also the "absence of reference to the speaker", which characterises the "interpersonal form" of the cult sun hymn in *ÄHG*, pp. 85ff. and *LL*, pp. 359ff.

imagination".

What is described here in relation to the theme of "remoteness" as "perspective" (the relation of the representation of divine nature to the human eye as the reference point) is the same structure that will be presented in another context as "anthropocentric" (§.2.5). With the discarding of the polytheistic constellations man is made the only reference point of divine acts. This will be dealt with later on in detail. In the present context it is significant that human beings in their role as reference point for divine acts are often indicated by expressions such as "all faces" and "all eyes". Through the eye, which "owes its existence to light",[30] the creatures of light participate in the nature of divinity.

But they see only the radiating and overwhelming external side of the divine appearance. The internal side of his nature is concealed from them. "You are in their face, but nobody knows your movement."[31] "You who appear to us, we do not know your image. You reveal yourself to our gaze, but we do not know your body (*ḏt*)".[32] "Who conceals his image while being in front of mankind".[33] This sort of statement, which is attested in many forms before,[34] during[35] and after the Amarna period,[36] may be regarded as a *Leitmotiv* of the new solar theology, to serve as a criterion for classifying a text of this sort.[37]

### *2.3 Remoteness and Nearness*

1. You have made heaven remote, so that you can ascend to it
to see everything that you have created, you who are a unique one.[38]

2. You have withdrawn as the remote one over them
to be able to watch over them every day.[39]

3. You are remote, but your rays are on the earth
you are visible to them, but your movement is not known.[40]

---

30 J.W. v. Goethe, *Einleitung zur Farbenlehre* (Hamburger Ausgabe XIII, 323); cf. "Akhanyati's Theology of Light and Time", 157f.

31 Sandman, *Texts*, 93.16-17; *ÄHG* no.92, 26.

32 P. Berlin 3050, viii, 9 = *ÄHG* no.22D, 29-30.

33 Thebes, tomb of Parennefer-Wennefer (to be published by F. Kampp) provisional no. -162-, Text 2. Cf. *STG* Text No. 54, 6; P.Leiden I 344 vso, i,4 ("who conceals his image in the body of Nut", Zandee, *Amunshymnus*, 27ff.) and viii.7 ("who conceals his image in his heaven", Zandee, *Amunshymnus*, 733-740). On the motif of contrasting heavenly presence and hiddenness cf. also Zandee, *Amunshymnus*, 129f.

34 STG, text 76 in tomb 57 (Chaemhet).

35 Cf. Sandman, *Texts*, 89, 14-15.

36 *STG* Texts No. 54, 161, 253, 42a etc.; Zandee, *Amunshymnus*, 29f. gives many pertinent passages, partly from Edfu texts, but mixed up with passages referring to quite different conceptions and belonging to different traditions.

37 Cf. "Zwei Sonnenhymnen", *MDIK* 27.1 (1971), 8-12 with all references known to me.

38 Amarna, *ÄHG* no.91, 53-54; no.92, 110-111.

39 P.Louvre 3292 = *ÄHG* no.47, 5-6.

40 Amarna, *ÄHG* no.92, 25-26.

4. You remote one in the east,
your rays touch the faces.[41]

5. You have appeared, radiant
you are remote and near (at the same time).[42]

6. Remote one and (at the same time) near one, who cannot be known.[43]

7. Your sun is alone, but your rays are visible
the earth is heavy, but you penetrate to the end of it (...)
You have withdrawn and yet you are near, and nobody can know you
you move over all that you have made
you alone, and you consider them, you being alone.[44]

8. Very remote one, too secret to be reached
his rays nevertheless penetrate into the earth.[45]

9. He withdrew to heaven and looked at creation
his sight is the sight of all.
He is remote in the brilliance of light and (at the same time) as in this land (present),
his two eyes penetrate as far as the desert valley (i.e. the necropolis).[46]

10 His Ba is in heaven, far from humankind,
but his rays touch the underworld caves.[47]

It is clear that this subject is inextricably linked with the previous one. To some extent the same texts and even the same passages will be used now and again for the purpose of illustration.[48] Like "aloneness" and "remoteness", the idea of "nearness" is based on the theological interpretation of a natural phenomenon, viz. the sunlight. The light is now recognised for what it is: the radiation of the sun. It is thus an act in which the god turns to earth, "comes", "touches the face" (ex. 4),[49] causes hearts to live,[50] floods the earth with his presence,[51] even plunges down into the depths of the

41 N. de G. Davies, *The Temple of Hibis* (New York,1950) pl.16 below on the left (entrance to E).

42 *ÄHG* no.92, 113-114.

43 J.E. Quibell, *Excavations at Saqqara* IV (Cairo,1908-10) , pl.73.3 = P.Berlin 3048 *ÄHG* no.143, 17.

44 *STG*, texts 161 = 253.

45 Davies, *Hibis* 32,4-5 = *ÄHG* no.129, 20f. cf. n.25.

46 Davies, *Hibis* 32,20-21(=*ÄHG* no.129,96-99). Cf. Sobek-Re II,24 (=*ÄHG* no.144A,54-55): *ḥrjw-tw [r ḥrt r wnb jm.s/ r] m33 š3ᶜ.n=k* "You have ascended [to heaven to rise in it /in order to ] see what you have begun".

47 *STG* Text No. 17, 13-15 cf. P.Leiden I 344 vso. V, 8-9: "You travel across heaven and open the firmament, but your rays touch the caves of the underworld", cf. Zandee, *Amunshymnus*, 444-454.

48 Cf. n.22 with n.42, n. 25 with n.43, n.23 with n.37.

49 On the motif of "coming", which connects the "iconography of the solar journey" with the night (*LL* pp.46-48), with reference to the sunrise cf. "Zwei Sonnenhymnen" *MDIK* 27.1, 26 n.58. On the motif of "touching the faces" cf. *ÄHG* no.91,13 and G. Lefebvre, *Le Tombeau de Petosiris* II (Cairo, 1914) text no. 60, 14-15: "Remote one, shining in heaven, who touches the face with his rays".

50 This phrase first occurs in the Hymn to the Inundation (*ÄHG* no.242,92), later in Amarna (Sandman, *Texts* nos. 11 and 12=*ÄHG* no.91,31); cf. also *STG*, text 60,13, *ÄHG* no.200,22 and *STG*, text 189,25; P.Leiden I 344 vso. I.9: "their hearts live when they see him", cf. Zandee,

ocean[52] and the underworld, into the "crypts" of the dead.[53]

> 1. He who approaches the face, even when he is remote
> for every face is opposite him.
> One spends the day looking at him and is still not sated with him.[54]
>
> 2. Every eye sees you before it
> when you appear high over the earth as the diurnal sun.[55]
>
> 3. When Your Majesty approaches the southern part of the earth,
> you are opposite what is in the north of the earth
> west and east, you are visible to them.[56]
>
> 4. [He ascends to the hea]ven as this Ba who is in the sun-disk,
> he removes himself as Harakhty,
> who illuminates the Two Lands with his radiating eyes.[57]

It is precisely the remoteness of god, in which he raises himself above the entire world, that makes him simultaneously visible to all. The immeasurable distance that separates god from the created world is at the same time the condition necessary for the relationship that binds the two most closely. Remoteness is the condition of his visibility. The radiant brilliance that veils him is the condition of his *parousia*.

*Parousia* is the physical presence of the divinity. I associate this concept with the Egyptian word *nfrw*, which we (not inappropriately ) translate as "beauty", because it indicates the quality corresponding to the emotion *mrwt* "love". It is what Rudolf Otto has called the *mysterium fascinans* of the sacred.[58] The Amarna texts use the words *nfrw* and *mrwt* as synonyms of *stwt* "rays".[59] This usage, which remains

---

*Amunshymnus*, 45-49.

51 *STG* Text No. 17, 4.

52 *ÄHG* no.92, 58.

53 *STG* Text No. 151, 36; No. 17, 15 (p). Cf. n.45.

54 *STG*, text 83, 8-11.

55 *ÄHG* no.92, 118-119.

56 *STG*, No.161 = 253, 30-32.

57 P.Leiden I 344 vso. III, 3-4; cf. Zandee, *Amunshymnus*, 186-207.

58 Rudolf Otto, *Das Heilige* (Reinbeck, 1963), p.42. Cf. *LL*,65 (and note 108);A. de Buck, *Godsdiensten der Wereld* II (Leiden,1943) 36; J. Zandee, *De Hymnen aan Amon van Papyrus Leiden J 350* (OMRO 28) (Amsterdam, 1947), 7-8. The Egyptian concept of divine beauty and the love it induces is expressed most clearly, in my opinion, in the following section of the Cairo Amun Hymn (*ÄHG* no.87D, 97-106):

> Love of you is diffused throughout the Two Lands
> Your rays appear in the eyes
> Human beings are beautified by your rising
> Animals grow tired when you shine (at midday)
> Love of you fills the southern sky
> Desire for you the northern sky
> Hearts are seized by your beauty
> Arms are made weak by love of you
> Hands grow limp from your beautiful form
> The senses are confused by the mere sight of you.

59 *LÄ* I, 532.

generally characteristic of the new solar theology,[60] reflects the theological interpretation of light as a form of the physical presence of god, in which he reveals his "beauty" and releases the feeling of "love", the enraptured fascination[61] with which "every eye" is fixed on him.

> "Every eye rests on beauty until you go down."[62]
>
> "All faces, their eyes are fixed on you."[63]
>
> "All work is done through the eye's resting on him."[64]
>
> "All eyes see through you. They can do nothing when Your Majesty goes down."[65]
>
> "Wild animals and beasts of the field turn to you,
> the plants grow according to your beauty,
> and there is no life for that which does not see you."[66]
>
> "His image is constantly perfect in the eyes."[67]

All eyes are fixed on their creator, who for his part looks down on his creation. It is for this reason alone that he made the sky so remote and raised himself so high. Light is merely the gaze that god, in the aloneness of his heavenly remoteness, directs at the endless teeming abundance of his creation. For its part, creation is unable to avert its gaze from him and lives by the mere sight of him:

> Beautiful One, who comes down from heaven
> To see what he created on earth.[68]

Light is the medium of communication between creator and creation. The gaze of the created at the sun is met in turn by the gaze of the creator, who animates their hearts and fills them with joy.

---

60 "Beauty" : cf. §2.4, references 14,15,16,17,19,20,22; "love": 21.

61 "Drunkenness", cf.*STG*, text 26,5 (a).

62 *ÄHG* no.92, 129.

63 P.Leiden J 350 II, 20; Zandee, *Hymnen*, 34.

64 P.Berlin 3056, 8, 8; *LL*,176 w.n.44.

65 Suty-Hor *ÄHG* no.89, 25-26. Cf. P.Leiden I 344 vso. V,9: *jw=k dd ꜥwj=kj n ntj nb/ḥtp=sn ẖft ḥtp=k/nn m33=sn m ḥrw=sn/dgg=sn* <*m*> *nṯrwtj-kj* "You give your hand to everyone; they rest when you rest. They cannot see with their faces; they look <with> your divine eyes". The dependence of the capacity of seeing on the (divine) light serves as a symbol of the dependence of creation on the creator. Cf. Zandee, *Amunshymnus*, 456-460.

66 P. Ch. Beatty IV (*ÄHG* no.195,235-237); cf. also Cairo CG 42208 (*ÄHG* no.200,13-15):
Every face lives from the sight of your beauty
all seed grows when you shine on it
there is no one who can live without you.

67 P.Leiden I 344 vso, iii.11; cf. Zandee, *Amunshymnus*, 239-245.

68 J. Lipinska "Excavations in the area of Tuthmosis III at Deir el Bahri", *ASAE* 60 (1968), 167 pl.9 fig.17.

## *2.4 Omnipresence of the Light: God-Filled World*

(1) Every way is full of your light.[69]

(2) Every way is full of love for me
there is no deficiency in this country.[70]

(3) The one who uncovers the millions with his beautiful face
no way on earth is free of him (when he shines.)[71]

(4) Light on every way.[72]

(5) It is he who leads the faces on all ways.[73]

(6) Are you not the leader on all ways?[74]

(7) The ways are innumerable under his leadership.[75]

(8) Who leads millions with his rays.[76]

(9) No land can do without his gaze,
which makes possible coming and going on all ways
and reaches the ends of the earth in one day.[77]

(10) You reach the ends of the earth with your rays.[78]

(11) Who reaches the ends of the earth when he considers those who move upon it.[79]

(12) The one who sees much, whose movement knows no limits.[80]

(13) There are no limits to the field of his vision
and no place hidden to his ka.[81]

(14) Your rays penetrate into the caves,
no place is untouched by his beauty.[82]

---

69 P.Berlin 3050, *LL*, 206 (32) with more references; P.Leiden I 344 vso II,8, cf. Zandee, *Amunshymnus*, 118f.; on the motif of the "ways" cf. also Zandee, *Amunshymnus*, 41-42.
70 P.Leiden J 347,8,4.
71 P.Leiden J 350 II, 18; Zandee, *Hymnen*, 31f.
72 P.Leiden,J 350 II, 19.
73 P.Leiden J 350, V, 20f.
74 P.Chester Beatty IV rto 3,7 *ÄHG* 195,8.
75 Suty-Hor *ÄHG* no.89, 12; cf. *STG*, text 212 (i).
76 *STG*, text 113 (q); Neschons *ÄHG* no.131, 57.
77 G. Lefevbre, *Petosiris*, text 60, 9-10.
78 *STG* Text 54;parallel: TT -162- text no.4.
79 Suty-Hor *ÄHG* no.89, 53.
80 P.Berlin 3049,17,6 = *ÄHG* no.127B, 209-210.
81 P.Louvre 3292 "H" = *ÄHG* no.45, 5-6.
82 P.Anastasi II, 5-6 (to the king).

(15) Heaven and earth are pervaded by your beauty.[83]

(16) Heaven and earth are subject to his beauty,
inundated with gold.[84]

(17) You distribute your beauty throughout the lands.[85]

(18) No place is without his light.[86]

(19) You have illuminated the two banks with your eyes,
the ocean is subject to your beauty.[87]

(20) The one who pervades heaven, earth and the hills with his beauty.[88]

(21) He has given his rays,
his uraeus has illuminated the globe
all lands are full of love for him.[89]

(22) Every city is full of love for you, Amun,
all lands are subject to your beauty.[90]

This tedious and by no means exhaustive collection of passages may illustrate the central meaning of this subject in the new solar theology. The concept of a god-filled world is again merely the theological interpretation of the cosmic phenomenon of the omnipresence of light. God himself is present in the light. The synonomous use of terms like "rays", "beauty" and "love" emerges very clearly from this phraseology; cf., for example, 2,21 (love), 14-17, 19-20, 22 (beauty).

The light opens up the world and makes it inhabitable. This is what the many metaphors of the "way" are intended to convey.[91] The light creates order and orientation among human beings:

(23) He who raised heaven on high for the circuit of his two eyes,
created earth to diffuse his brilliance,
to enable everyone to know his neighbour.[92]

(24) How beautiful you are when you rise, Re
You force the thief to steal away,
one eye sees the other
and all eyes are distraught (when you set).[93]

83 Sobek-Re IV, 21-22 = *ÄHG* 144C, 75; Neschons, 18 = *ÄHG* no.131, 47.
84 Ritual for Amenophis I P.Chester Beatty IX rto 13 = P.Berlin 3056,7,1-7; *LL*,248.
85 Quibell, *Excavations at Saqqara* (1908-10), pl.70.
86 *STG*, Text 151.
87 P.Chester Beatty IV rto 9, 4-5 = *ÄHG* no.195, 187-188, cf. 244.
88 Davies, *Hibis* , pl.9.
89 Stela Ramesses IV; cf. W..Helck,"Ramessidische Inschriften aus Karnak", *ZÄS* 82, 14.
90 O. Wilson = O.IFAO inv.2181; cf. G.Posener, "Amon, juge du pauvre" in *Fs.Ricke* (Wiesbaden,1971), 61 and pl.15B.
91 Cf. *LL*, 206f.; Zandee, *Amunshymnus*, 41-43.
92 BD 15 B II = *ÄHG* no.44, 6-8.
93 P.Chester Beatty IV rto 11,15-12,1 = *ÄHG* no.195, 304-306 (diverse). Cf. Tura-Hymnus = *ÄHG*

(25) When you are united with the east,
no eye can see the other
all reptiles (come to life) on earth
They sleep, until you irradiate them,
and wake them up, so that they can see your beauty.
When you appear, they see,
they recognise through you, when you give them your rays.[94]

(26) You are the light, which rises for humankind;
the sun, which brings clarity,
so that gods and humans can be recognised and distinguished
when you reveal yourself.
Every face lives from seeing your beauty,
all seed germinates when touched by your rays,
and there is no-one who can live without you.
You lead everyone, because they have a duty to their work.
You have given form to their life, by becoming visible.[95]

(27) When it rises, it brings light to the world,
so that all can distinguish themselves from each other.[96]

(28) The morning sun, which enables one to know all things.[97]

(29) He lets everybody know his way where to go,
their hearts live when they see him.[98]

The light creates the inhabitable world, the distinctive contours of things, the order of reality, in which human beings can find their way. In the light god "seizes" the world as far as its furthest boundaries:

(30) You have taken possession of heaven with its two horizons,
shining over its.i. air space.
The earth is under your control to its furthest boundaries.

---

no.88, 42.

94 *ÄHG* no.94, 13-19.

95 Cairo CG 42208 (*ÄHG* no.200). The following is a transcription of the important text:
*...ntk Šw wbnw n ḥnmmt*
*jtn ddw ḥḏḏwt*
*r djt sjꜣ.tw wḏꜥ.tw*
*nṯrw rmṯw ḫft dj=k tw*
*ꜥnḫ ḥr nb n mꜣꜣ nfrw=k*
*sḫpr prt nbt mꜣwj=k r=sn*
*n-wn ntj ꜥnḫ m ḫmt=k*
*sšm.n=k [ḥr] nb ḥnw ḥr kꜣt=sn*
*jr.n=k qj n ꜥnḫ=sn m-ḫt mꜣꜣ=k*
Cf. also E. Otto, *Die biographischen Inschriften der ägyptischen Spätzeit* (Leiden,1954),139-142.

96 Sauneron, *Esna V*, 151 text no.331, 10.

97 E. Iversen, *P.Carlsberg VIII*, (Copenhagen, 1939), 16ff. (Thoth: I.5, I.6).

98 P.Leiden I 350, IV, 8 (ÄHG no. 136, 24-25), Zandee, *Hymnen*, 66 cf. P.Leiden I 344 vso, I, 8-9, Zandee, *Amunshymnus*, 42.

You have taken hold of it.[99]

In the Book of Nut and its demotic commentary (P. Carlsberg I C II 14-16) this event is described in the sober language of cosmography as follows:

(31) Thus the form of its appearance becomes great (dem.: the form of its appearance becomes great: that is, its flame)
Thus it emerges in the lands (dem.: he causes it to emerge in the lands, viz. the flame in its circuit. One cannot name the place where he does not cause it to emerge).[100]

This is what the Book of the Celestial Cow also refers to when it speaks of the "ba" of Re: "it pervades the land".[101] This omnipresence of light is also referred in the hymns to human beings as a reference point:

(32) The bodies are full of your beauty,
the eyes, they see through you,
their hearts are turned to you.
You are beautiful at every hour.
Humankind lives from your sight (...)
Your sweetness is in all hearts,
no body is without your beauty.[102]

(33) Great in height, in heaven and on earth,
every body is full of your beauty.[103]

(34) No body here is free from love for him.[104]

(35) Love of him floods like the Nile
and permeates all bodies.[105]

These passages go a step further in the theological interpretation of the omnipresence of light: with his rays god fills not only all lands, but also "all bodies". The radiant energy of god penetrates into the inmost heart through the eye, which in seeing "incorporates" the beauty of god. Nobody can escape the sensual experience of the presence of god in the light. The entire being,[106] as well as the entire human race, is seized by loving submission to the beauty of god.

---

99 *STG*, text 158; cf. *LL*,302f.

100 H.Lange and O.Neugebauer, *P. Carlsberg I* (Copenhagen, 1940), 23.

101 C. Maystre, "Livre de la vache céleste", *BIFAO* 40 (1940), 103; E. Hornung, *Der ägyptische Mythos von der Himmelskuh* (Fribourg,1982) 26f., 47.

102 P.Chester Beatty IV rto 9,4-5; *ÄHG* no.195,126-131, 136-137.

103 *STG*, text 188, 5 (b) with more references.

104 O.Michaelidis 15 vso.

105 O.IFAO 1038.

106 The Egyptian term *ḫt*, unlike our term "body", often refers also to the "inner spirit", memory, consciousness, "interiority"; cf. *LL*, 196 note 22

### *2.5 Life (Creatio Continua)*

The central concept of Amarna theology is "life". Rather than quote all the passages concerned, I shall simply remind the reader that the concept of "life", added to the word *jtn* "sun" in the form of *ᶜnḫ* "living", is an integral part of the name of the god. It is only by adding the decisive word that the name (*jtn ᶜnḫ* "living sun") is distinguished from the normal word for the heavenly body, which even in Amarna texts means simply "sun".[107] The god of Amarna is called "life": he is the sun as the source and condition of life. He embodies in the purest form the model of a "life-god", the germ of whose theology was the origin and basis of life, just as the question of the origin of the world is at the core of the theology of the creator god.[108]

The Shu theology of the Middle Kingdom, as far as it can be reconstructed from the CT spells 75-80, distinguished between cosmogony and biogony, creator-god and life-god. Atum was the creator of the world and life according to this theology, but the task of life-giving and developing both fell to his two children, Shu and Tefnut. In this capacity Shu received the name *ᶜnḫ* "life" and was called *nḥḥ* "endless time", while Tefnut was called *mȝᶜt* "truth/justice/order" and *ḏt* "invariable permanence". Life, truth and time were the energies that perpetuated the world created by Atum.[109] Akhenaten must have known about this theology. It offers the only example of a triad with the structure 1:2 (father/two children), which is otherwise always 2:1 (two parents/child). In this latter type the divine child usually represents the king. In Amarna theology, however, the 2:1 structure refers to Akhenaten and Nefertiti, assuming the roles of Shu and Tefnut,[110] opposite a god (*jtn ᶜnḫ*). This explains the striking role of Nefertiti as a member of the official "Triad of Amarna"[111] and also the links between Amarna theology and the Shu theology of the Middle Kingdom. I shall examine this connection in the context of the theology of Amun-Re, who also represents the category of "life-god". In these points Amarna religion goes beyond the framework of the new solar theology and makes use of other traditions. In the present context theological reflection about the origin and basis of life is important, inasmuch as it arises from the interpretation of the natural phenomena of the solar journey.

The theological interpretation given to the cosmic phenomena of light and movement in the new solar theology and Amarna religion does not distinguish between creating and life-giving. The formative and life-giving, productive and preserving energy is exactly the same energy which manifests itself in the rays and movement of the sun. Creation is regarded only as *creatio continua*. The Great Hymn of Amarna devotes a passage of 46 lines to the theme of creation, which in Egyptian terms is tantamount to a treatise. The first part of the treatise contains a

---

107 Cf. *LÄ* I,526.

108 Cf. "Akhanyati's Theology of Light and Time". *Proceedings of the Israel Academy of Sciences and Humanities*, 7 (1992), 143-176.

109 Shu theology in the MK: A. de Buck, *Plaats en betekenis van Sjoe in de egyptische theologie* (Mededeelingen der koninklijke nederlandsche akademie van wetenschappen, Afd. letterkunde, N.R. 10.9) (Leiden,1947); "Primat und Transzendenz", 24f.; *Ma'at*, ch. 6; here Chapter 6.

110 Cf. Mohammad Hassan Abd-ur-Rahman, "The Four-Feathered Crown of Akhenaten", *ASAE* 56(1959), 247-249.

111 *JNES* 31(1972), 152-154.

unique embryological text, which presents an (ontogenetic) biogony instead of the traditional cosmogony: the origin of life in the maternal womb.[112] The second part praises the world order, whose division into peoples of different skin colour, language,[113] and living conditions (some having a Nile in the sky,[114] others a Nile under the earth), is attributed to the wisdom of the creator, and thus also refers to the present state. This treatise is pure Amarna theology, but we will also find traces and basic ideas in Theban texts.

The life-giving effect of sunlight is clear and is expressed hundreds of times in the texts. Moreover, the importance of seeing as the life-impulse par excellence and the link between seeing and life as living from the sight of god[115] and the created world's springing into life at sunrise require no documentation (which would, in any case, fill many pages[116]). The most profound and informative formulations make it clear that.i. air and time are more fundamental conditions of life than light:

> You have made heaven remote, so that you can ascend to it
> and see all that you have created, you who are a unique one,
> but millions of lives are in you for you to animate them,
> for the breath of life to their nostrils is the sight of your rays.[117]

Air, not light, is the element of life par excellence for the Egyptian. As light is equated with beauty and love, air is equated with life. It is for this reason that Shu, the air-god, also had the role of life-god in the above-mentioned Middle Kingdom theology.[118] Nevertheless, there was no strict distinction between "light" and "air". The god (and cosmological concept) Shu refers to "luminous air", light-filled living space. Like other people, the Egyptians did not necessarily regard the light as dependent on the sun.[119] On the other hand, the idea has been expressed from time to time that it is not only light, but also air (as warmth = "hot breath") that emanates from the sun.[120] There were probably various contradictory ideas about this, but one may reasonably argue that the new solar theology helped to make the view that the light was dependent on the sun the only valid one. It was a view whose significance for contemporary cosmology cannot be underestimated; a view that was expressed

---

112 Cf. "Theology of Light and Time", *Proceedings*, 152-154.

113 Differentiation of language is possibly a subject that appears first in the Amarna period, but later becomes more widespread; cf. *ÄHG* no.42, 37ff.; no.58, 74; 129, 85f. cf. before Amarna no.87C, 67f. ("qualities"). J. Černý, "Thoth as creator of languages", *JEA* 34, 121-122; S. Sauneron,"Différenciation des langues". *BIFAO* 60 (1960), 31ff. and D. Müller, *Ägypten und die griechischen Isis-Aretalogien* (Berlin,1961), 54-57.

114 The current topic; cf. *ÄHG* no.127B, 45-46; 195, 166; 144C, 39; 214, 29-32; especially no.143, 164f., 100 and 46; Zandee, *Amunshymnus*, 747-761.

115 Cf. example (25a) with P.Chester Beatty IV *ÄHG* no.195, 237; STG, text 156, 15 (h);.Sandman, *Texts*, 23.5.

116 Cf. the formula "mankind lives, when he rises", *LL*, 321f.; Zandee, *Amunshymnus*, 47-49.

117 Amarna, Short Hymn *ÄHG* no.91, 53-56.

118 A. de Buck, *Plaats*, 11ff.

119 A. de Buck, *Plaats*, 33f.

120 *CT* IV 296/7; *STG*, text 52, 18-19 (e); P.Leiden 344 vso v 10: *ṯ3w=k r fnḏw tmw/ẖnm=sn m hh r3=k/prj=k r ḥrt ꜥnḫ.tw ẖr wḏ=k* "your breath reaches the noses of mankind, they breathe from the warm breath of your mouth; you ascend to the sky and life is at your command", see Zandee, *Amunshymnus*, 460ff.

in so many ways in the texts that the importance attributed to it cannot be questioned.[121]

The "shorter" hymn, quoted above, interprets the sun rays not in the sense of the old syncretism of light and air as cosmic elements, but as animating "breath of life". The god contains within himself "millions of lives",[122] which enter his creatures in the form of rays. The sunlight is interpreted as the form of this "emanation". The other passage that speaks of the "millions" of emanations of the god makes it certain that creation and preservation, formation and life-giving are here one and the same thing. The light does not fill a given form with life, but produces this form itself:

> You create millions of personifications from yourself, the unique one,
> cities and villages,
> field, road and river.[123]

The whole light-filled, ordered and "inhabitable" world emanates from the One as multiple transformations and fills itself with the million "lives", which irradiate human beings with the endless supply of divine abundance.

It is not only the sunlight that is interpreted as producing (*msj/ḫpr*) and preserving (*sᶜnḫ*) life, but also the other cosmic manifestation of the sun, viz. movement:

> The earth emerges at your hand, as you have created it;
> when you arise, they live;
> when you set, they die.
> You are the time of life itself, through you life is possible.[124]

The movement of the sun (expressed in the texts by the verbs *wbn* and *ḥtp*) give rise to time, in which all life unfolds. By his movement the sun god not only divides time into measurable units,[125] but also sets "deadlines" for the embryo in the womb,

---

121 e. *g. LL*, 318f.

122 On the notion of "million" cf. *STG* Text No. 149 note (c); Zandee, *Amunshymnus*, 168-176; 557-560.

123 Great Hymn *ÄHG* no.92, 115-117.

124 Ibd., 125-128.

125 Here too we come across the equation between "differentiation" and "creation", as in the widespread mythologoumenon about the separation of earth from heaven (W. Staudacher, *Die Trennung von Himmel und Erde* (Tübingen 1942)): by dividing the continuum of time into measurable units the sun god creates time. "I am the one who divides the years and creates the seasons": Pleyte-Rossi, *Papyrus de Turin* (Leiden, 1869-76) 133.9 = P.Chester Beatty XI rto 3.5. According to G. Posener, "Notes de transcription", *RdE* 28, 147ff this predication already occurs in P. Ramesseum IX 3, 7 in the Middle Kingdom, which means that it is not an original achievement, but rather a re-worked generalisation of the "new solar theology". On the concept *wp trw* "dividing times" cf. A. Klasens, *A Magical Statue Base* (Leiden,1952) 96 to f 24. Cf. also P.Leiden I 344 vso, iii, 10-11:

> *jrj hrww sḫpr wnwwt*
> *jp.tw r st nmtt=f*
> *wp rnpwt [ȝbdw] km(t)*
> *ḫft sqdd=f (...) m pt*
> Who creates the days and brings the hours into existence,

the chick in the egg and human beings on earth.[126]

Time, required by all life to realise itself (*ḫpr*), and the breath of life (*ṯȝw n ꜥnḫ*), which animates everything with the force of life, stream from the sun through its rays and movement into the created world, continually bringing it forth and keeping it alive. As the source of time, the god is named *Nḥḥ* (endless time):[127] as the source of the breath of life he is named the "living (sun)". Already in the Shu theology of the Middle Kingdom these two epithets indicate the function of the life god, being the two aspects in which reality is understood as the result of the unceasing action of a god acting on the world.[128] What is specifically Amarna theology about this conception and what belongs to the more comprehensive question of the "phenomenology of the solar journey", which forms the basis of the new solar theology ? The question calls for a comparison between the Amarna conception and the Theban hymns. What is found in them may be used as the basis for the new solar theology.

The hymn of the architects Suty and Hor, in exactly the same way as the Great Hymn of Amarna, adds a second hymn to the sun hymn in the form of a Solar Phases Hymn, whose theme is expressed by the invocation in the form of a heading:

> Greetings, sun of the day,[129]
> creator of mankind, who creates their life.

This formula, attested elsewhere in the texts close to the new solar theology,[130] expresses the concept of a god who is both creator and life god in concise form. But whereas the Amarna Hymn expounds this concept of god, in the form of a didactic treatise, by means of theological interpretation of a whole range of natural phenomena, the Suty-Hor hymn condenses, in the form of the eulogy,[131] the massive creative operations into "names", which are used to praise the god:

> The one who fashioned the earth and created the soil,
> Khnum and Amun of humankind.
> The one who seizes the Two Lands from the big to the small,
> benevolent mother of gods and men.
> Craftsman with patient heart,
> who has worked tirelessly at incalculable creation,
> strong shepherd, who drives his flock,
> their shelter, who creates their life.[132]

The entire stanza refers to the earth-related operations of the god and

---

> so that they are counted according to his movement,
> who divides the years and months,
> so that they are complete while he travels (...) in the sky.

Cf. Zandee, *Amunshymnus*, 234-239.

126 On the period spent in the womb cf. *ÄHG* nos.92, 71-74 and 145A, 16 and 145B, 13ff.

127 "Zwei Sonnenhymnen", *MDIK* 27, 27 esp. n.65; *Zeit und Ewigkeit*, 56.

128 De Buck, *Plaats*, 23; *LÄ* II, 50 III.b.2.

129 On this appellation cf. *STG*, text 114, 21 (i).

130 Cf. *STG*, text 232 (h).

131 Chapter 6; *LÄ* II, 40-46.

132 *ÄHG* no.89, 39-46.

corresponds to a previous stanza, which praised his heavenly appearance.[133] Hence the naming of earth-creation in the first verse, where the whole of visible reality (*pars pro toto*) is, of course, meant. The second verse contains the essence of the embryological question posed in the Great Hymn: Khnum and Amun form a pair only in one single thematic context, which is unmistakeably evoked here, viz. the royal birth. The generative, formative and animating principle, which they embody in respect to the royal child, is ascribed here to the sun god with regard to the whole of humanity.[134] In the third verse we recognise the theme, dealt with earlier, of the omnipresence of light and the god-filled world, which appears here in the personal form: as "seizing" of everything that lives and receives light from the sun.

Khnum and Amun are aspects of fatherhood: they bodily form and spiritually animate the child, but they do not give birth to it. This explains the statement of the following verse, which would be very unusual without this connection. Here too, the god, as elsewhere in this theology, is praised as "mother and father".[135] The "father" aspect is expressed in verse 2:

> Khnum and Mut, who gives birth to the gods,
> who creates every eye and every life.[136]

"Mother and father": this metaphor expresses the inner relationship between god and the created world in both their aspects, the procreation/production and the taking care/preservation:

> (1) Mother of the earth, father of humankind,
> who illuminates the earth with his love.[137]
>
> (2) You are mother and father of those whom you have created,
> their eyes, when you rise, see through you.[138]
>
> (3) You are the one who gave birth to humankind,
> mother and father of all eyes.
> You rise for them every day, to create their life for them,
> unique shepherd, who protects his flock.
> Who leads millions with his light.[139]
>
> (4) You are mother and father of every eye,
> you rise for them every day, to create their life for them.[140]

---

133 On this arrangement and interpretation cf. G. Fecht,"Zur Frühform der Amarna Theologie", *ZÄS* 94(1967), 36-42.

134 F. Daumas, *Les mammisis de Dendera* (Cairo,1959) 403ff., esp.412/13; Zandee, *Amunshymnus*, 91f.

135 On this motif cf. Zandee, *Amunshymnus*, 67-70.

136 P.Berlin 3048, 3, 6 = ÄHG no.143, 36-37.

137 Louvre C 67.

138 Amarna *ÄHG* no.91, 21. Alternative translation: "You are mother and father for those whose eyes you have created; when you rise, they see through you".

139 *STG*, text 113, 32-35; cf. also *STG*, text 255,6.

140 STG, text 225, 23-24. This sentence occurs also on the stela BM 706, Kitchen, *RI* I, 330.

The widespread occurrence of this formula shows that we are dealing with a concept common to the new solar theology and Amarna religion.[141] The important thing is to see creation and preservation as one, the theological interpretation of solar phenomena as *creatio continua*. Equally important is the anthropocentricity of this concept, for it interprets not only the sun rays and movement as parental care and love, but also, and more importantly, man is raised to the status of divine child, the object of parental attention from the god.[142] As such, human beings are in the same group as all other creatures, "everything that has an eye".[143] to which, according to Suty-Hor, the gods too belong. This shows how irrelevant the monotheism question is with regard to the new solar theology (as opposed to Amarna religion). The concept of the aloneness and uniqueness of god, which removes him from all divine constellations and confronts him with the world, leaves the world its gods and sees them, together with human beings, as the children of god, for whom the sun god lovingly cares as "mother and father" from the remoteness of his solitary journey.

The "artistry" or "craftsmanship" of god is likewise one of the leading motifs common to the new solar theology and Amarna religion. In the other texts this idea is regularly expressed in the form of an admiring exclamation, which is as important for its cognitive meaning as it is for the emotional attitude that gives expression to this meaning. Two aspects of divine creativity especially provoke this exclamation from the spectator: the incalculable abundance of what is produced and the wisdom that is able to support such variety:

> What an artist you are in everything you have created.[144]
> How great is your creation, not visible [Incalculability].
> How effective your plans are,
> lord of endless time[Wisdom].[145]

The first exclamation, which occurs also in Psalm 104,[146] refers to the abundance and variety of creation. The second refers to the wonderful arrangement of the "twofold Nile", i.e. the one that sustains some as rain from heaven, others as a stream from the depths of the earth:

> What an artist you are in what you create.
> Do you not create millions and give birth to them. [Incalculability]
> The creatures you create in the water, they live,
> breathing in the midst of the river

141 Note the important difference from *STG*, text 165, 23, where Amun is called: "Father and mother (in this sequence !) for those who put him in their hearts". Cf. also Chapter 4 §§2 and 4.

142 On the problem of the divine filiality of man, which is dealt with very clearly in the *Teaching for Merikare*, but is never explicitly stated, cf. E. Otto, "Der Mensch als Geschöpf" in H.W. Wolff (ed.) *Probleme Biblischer Theologie*, Fs. von Rad (Munich,1971), 335-348, esp.341f.

143 Cf. n.135. This is the significance of the formula *jrt nbt*.

144 *STG* Text No. 76.

145 Amarna, Great Hymn *ÄHG* no.92, 76f. and 100.

146 Ps. 104, 24. On the relationship between Ps. 104 and the Great Hymn of Amarna cf. F. Crüsemann, *Studien zur Formengeschichte von Hymnus und Danklied in Israel* (Stuttgart,1969), 286-288; "Die 'Häresie'", *Saeculum* 23, 122 n.51 and especially P. Auffret, *Hymnes d'Égypte et d'Israel*, (OBO 34) (Fribourg,1981), 279-310; "Akhanyati's Theology of Light and Time", *Proceedings*, 166-171.

The creatures of the land, you provide fodder for them. [Wisdom]
There has been no end to your creation since its beginning. [Permanence].[147]

The Suty-Hor hymn emphasises the incalculable abundance (*nn tnw=sn*), but also makes it clear, especially with the "patience" (*w3ḥ-jb*) and "effort" (*ʿ3-wrḏ*) of this divine artistry, that is a matter of the continuity of a creative process that repeats itself every day (*creatio continua*).

Finally, one may compare the passage from the previously quoted hymn of the vizier Paser with the shepherd motif of the last couplet:

You unique shepherd, who protects his flock,
who leads millions with his light.[148]

Just as the parent-image declares the creatures to be children of god, the shepherd motif declares them to be the herd of god. Both metaphors of the god-man relationship occur in the Instruction for Merikare and determine the divine image of the Middle Kingdom that is defined in the predications, not of the god himself, but of his earthly representative, the king. The metaphor of "refuge", which Suty-Hor uses to complement the shepherd-image, clearly points back to the royal image of the Middle Kingdom.[149] Because the Amun-Re theology is based on this divine and royal image, it will be necessary to examine them in more detail. Both concepts have in common an anthropocentric cosmology, which worships a supreme being outside all constellations of the polytheistic world. Even the image of god as shepherd, whose caring actions extend to "small cattle":

(1) which he created
for humankind, which came forth from his eye.[150]

(2) who created all that exists and brought forth all that is
for the small creatures that came forth from his eye.[151]

(3) who spends the night watchfully, when all are asleep,
looking for what will benefit his creatures.[152]

(4) shepherd, who protects his flock.[153]

makes human beings the reference point of creation and all divine actions.

147 *STG* Text No. 54. On the concept of differentiation between life conditions for Egyptians and foreigners cf. also P.Leiden I 344 vso viii, 8-9, Zandee, *Amunshymnus*, 747-761: "Nun and Nut give nourishment divided in two halves, one for the sand-dweller and one for Egypt."

148 Text *STG* 113, 33-34 (p), (q); cf. also P.Leiden I 344 vso, ii,4: "shepherd, vigilant of his creation", Zandee, *Amunshymnus*, 94-100.

149 J.M.A. Janssen, "De Farao als goede Herde", *Mens en Dier* (Amsterdam, 1954), 71-79; D. Müller,"Der Gute Hirte", *ZÄS* 86 (1961), 126-144.

150 Cairo JE 28569; cf. W.M. Müller, *Egyptological Researches* (Berlin,1906) I pl.14-15; F. Hintze, "Menschen als Kleinvieh", *ZÄS* 78 (1942), 55f.; G. Gaballa, "Three acephalous stelae" *JEA* 63 (1977), pl. 22.

151 Berlin 7317 = *ÄHG* 62, 5.

152 *ÄHG* no.87E, 123-124.

153 P.Berlin 3053,143.

The creation theology of the new solar theology understands creation as *creatio continua*. Creation and preservation of the world take place in the simultaneous mother-father attentiveness of god, and it is in this way that the solar journey is interpreted theologically in the abundance of natural phenomena.

## 2.6 The Mystery of Participation

If the eye did not partake of the sun
How could it gaze on the light?
If we did not share in the power of God
In the godly we could not delight.

It would be difficult to find a more beautiful or appropriate expression of the new solar theology philosophy concerning human participation in the divine nature than this passage of Goethe, which paraphrases Plotinus and ultimately Plato.[154] "You are the eyes themselves," according to *STG* Text No. 151, "one sees through you". As Ptah is the heart and tongue in every body, according to the Memphite Theology,[155] the sun god is, in the form of eyes, "leader in every body".[156] In the same context Goethe writes: "The light calls for an organ of the body that resembles itself, and so the eye was made by the light for the light, in order that the inner light might face the outer light."[157] As creatures of the light, living creatures are described in the new solar theology as "all faces" or "all eyes". God created living creatures as receptacles for his light, partners of his gaze. Human beings participate in the nature of god, not only because they have been created by god, but also because of their ability to see, which allows the life-giving power of god to flow into them in a continuous stream.

In the "iconography of the solar journey", as generally in traditional polytheistic cosmology, the mystery of participation was based on the principle of identification, which enabled human beings to enter divine constellations both in the performance of ritual and after death. In a sort of mystical identification human beings take part in the life of the divinity. This concept of divine life is re-interpreted as an act of vivification in which god is subject and man object. This asymmetry of participation in life categorically excludes identification. In its place we find a relationship between creator and created that can scarcely be more intimate: the created is a child and image of god.[158]

The nature of human beings is determined in the cosmology of the new solar theology as a form of creatureliness, which proceeds from the concept of a *creatio continua*. This "being created" is not a unique event, but a continual process that happens every day with the sunrise. It is the consciousness of this creatureliness, this "creature feeling", that is at the root of the hymns of the new solar theology,

154 C.F. von Weizsäcker (ed.), *J.W. v.Goethe*: *Sämtliche Werke*, (Hamburg,1963) XIII, 324, together with 323 and 550ff. (commentary and citations of ancient sources (to which may be added Plato, *Republic* VI 508f.); cf. also "Akhanyati's Theology of Light and Time",*Proceedings*, 157.

155 H. Junker, *Die Götterlehre von Memphis*, (APAW) (Berlin,1939) Nr.23 (1940), 48-54.

156 P.Chester Beatty IV = *ÄHG* no.195, 250.

157 *Sämtliche Werke* XIII, 323.

158 Cf., however, n.139.

expresses itself in them and determines their internal form. In place of the "status-characteristics" of the sun god, which praise his "inclusion" or "embeddedness" in the divine constellations,[159] the hymn of thanks has been introduced: human beings use the hymn to respond to the acts of the god ( as the reference point of which they regard themselves) and creation uses it to praise the creator.

This new self-understanding of the hymns is expressed in those verses that speak of praising the sun god. In the sun hymns of the older type, worship and jubilation were mentioned as having been offered to the sun god by his multifarious divine "congregations", viz. the eastern and western ba's, the boat crews, the ba's of Nekhen and Buto etc., whose ranks human beings join with their hymn, on the principle of identification, as "members of the group". In the new sun hymns, however, the sun god is not praised by distinct "communities", but by the "whole world", "all faces", "every eye". Their praise is presented in sentences of the stative type, and these make clear the nature of this praise as "creaturely responsion". It is important, however, that this praise is not, as in the festival hymn, described as a mere condition of jubilation and celebration brought to the world by god, but that the god is named here as the cause and recipient of this jubilation in every verse. Let us first consider a few typical examples of this theme in Amarna hymns:

(1) All faces, they come to life when they see you,
the whole land is assembled when you appear,
their arms are held up in praise when you rise.[160]

(2) Welcome in peace.[161] The whole land is assembled when you appear,
their arms held up in praise when you rise
They kiss the earth, because you shine on them,
they rejoice up to heaven,
seized by joy and jubilation,
they rejoice when they see Your Majesty.[162]

(3) Their arms are held up in praise of your ka,
you have animated their hearts with your beauty.
People come to life, when you project your rays,
every land is in festival.[163]

(4) All eyes see through you,
and rejoice when you shine.
Their arms are in jubilation for your ka.
You are the god who has created their bodies,

---

159 For the term "inclusion" cf. *LL*, 339ff.; "status characteristics" cf. *ÄHG*, 33ff.

160 Sandman, *Texts*, 23 cf. 28:
"When you rise, every face comes to life
their arms give you praise
the entire land assembles when you appear".

161 Cf. note 47. In the traditional sun hymns the typical form of address to the evening-night sun god is "welcome", because it implies the idea of bodily presence. It is also the same concept that links the light theology of Amarna religion, and to some extent the new solar theology, with the sunrise: the god "comes" down to earth in the form of light.

162 Sandman, *Texts*, 33.

163 Sandman, *Texts*, 13 = *ÄHG* no.91, 30-33.

they come to life, when your rays are on the earth.[164]

(5) The one who rises in heaven, to flood their hearts,
every land is in festival when he appears.
Their hearts are glad with jubilation.
Their lord and creator has risen over them.[165]

(6) Humankind rejoices at the sight of you,
and gives praise to its creator,
kisses the earth before the one who brought it forth.[166]

The character of the hymn as a hymn of thanks to the creator and the feeling of gratitude from the creator is clearly expressed in exx. 4-6. "They pray to you, as you created them".[167] This motif occurs in the Cairo Amun Hymn, where, according to the detailed description of the power of god who creates and preserves everything and is conceived of here as creator and life god, the song of praise of the created is cited here in direct speech:

Praise to you with what they all say to you:
"May rejoicing resound in your ears, since you have taken pains with us.
May the earth be kissed before you, since you have created us".[168]

The gods too join in this song of praise:

"We worship your power, as you have created us,
we sing you hymns of praise, because you have brought us forth,
we sing you hymns of praise, because you have taken pains with us."[169]

The Tura Hymn, which gives a narrative account of creation, likewise concludes with the hymn of thanks of the created:

they worship you, as you have created them
they kiss the earth, as you have created them.[170]

Particularly characteristic of how Amarna religion understands the meaning of praising god are those descriptions of the morning sun worship, according to which this worship appears as the pure life impulse and human beings, in the same way as animals and plants, react to the life-giving effects of the sunlight:

(7) Plants and trees move at the sight of you,
fish in the water leap at your appearance,
'every eye' raises himself on his place;
they purify their bodies and put on white garments,

164 Sandman, *Texts*, 142.
165 Sandman, *Texts*, 91.
166 Sandman, *Texts*, 46.
167 Sandman, *Texts*, 73.
168 *ÄHG* no.87E, 127-129. On the topic of the thanks of creatures for the creation *LL*, 326-7.
169 *ÄHG* no.87E, 142-144.
170 *ÄHG* no.88, 45-46.

every creature goes to his work.[171]

(8) All living plants that grow on the earth,
thrive at your rising,
having drunk from the sight of you.[172]
All creatures of the wild dance on their feet;
the birds that were in their nests fly into the air for joy;
their wings, which were folded,
open in praise
of the living sun, their creator.[173]

(9) You drive away the darkness, you project your rays,
the Two Lands are in festival every day.
What has feet awakes; you have set them upright.
They purify their bodies and put on white linen garments;
their arms are held up in praise at your appearance,
the whole land does its work.
All animals browse contentedly,
trees and plants grow.
Birds fly up out of their nests,
their wings outstretched in praise of your ka.
All creatures of the wild dance on their feet,
all creatures that fly up and come down again,
they live when you rise for them.
Ships sail downstream
and upstream with equal ease.
Every way is opened at your appearance.
Fish in the river
leap at the sight of you;
your rays penetrate to the middle of the ocean.[174]

These texts are not dealing with worship in the ordinary sense. It is not a question of a particular ritual act, but rather the ordinary life impulse of nature awakening which is interpreted as a single hymn of praise offered up by the light-created world to the creative power of light: waking up, rising, washing, dressing, going to work by human beings, whose arms are spread out in praise, exactly like the wings of birds,[175] the life impulse of animals, the growth and movement of plants, everything praises the life-giving creator in its natural response to the sunlight. In this extreme form it is pure Amarna religion, which limits the possibility of a personal approach to god and has basically reduced human beings to a state of pure receptiveness, the state of receiving his rays.[176] I would therefore like to offer,

171 Sandman, *Texts*, 76.

172 Cf. *STG*, text 26 (a). On the motif of drunkenness cf. *Instruction of Ani*, III, 7-9 (Gardiner, "Didactic passage" *JEA* 45 (1959), 12ff.); *LL*, 161 n.9.

173 Sandman, *Texts*, 15 = *ÄHG* no.91, 57-65.

174 Sandman, *Texts*, 94 = *ÄHG* no.92, 40-58.

175 Cf. example (9), line 5 and line 10 (as well as (8), 7-8); Cf. n.191.

176 Cf. "Die 'Häresie'", *Saeculum* 23 (1972), 121ff (esp. note 52). The concept of a purely receptive position vis-a-vis the divine has something mystical about it, like the following hymn written by G. Tersteegen (an 18th century German itinerant preacher), "God is Present":

You pervade everything.

by way of comparison, several descriptions of morning worship and the responses of the created from Ramesside texts:

> (10) Those, whose eyes were dim, he made it bright for them,
> to make their faces shine in a new form.
> Their eyes gleam, their ears are open.
> Every body is clothed with the brilliance of his rays.
>
> The heaven is gold, Nun is lapis lazuli
> the earth is covered with turquoise when he rises.
> The gods look, their temples are open
> human beings are astonished to see him.[177]
>
> All trees sway from side to side
> they turn to see his One Eye, their leaves unfolded
> Fish leap in the water
> they come out of their waters eagerly to him.
>
> All creatures of the wild dance before him
> the birds beat their wings
> They know him in his beautiful hour
> They come to life when they see him every day.[178]
>
> (11) Your rays announce you
> in the eyes of those on the mainland and in the islands
> Those in the underworld surround you with praises
> the living bow down when you rise
> those in heaven dance for you at the sight of you,
> people high and low worship you
> creatures wild and tame turn to you
> all plants direct themselves to your beauty
> There is no life for that which does not see you.[179]

Both of these texts come from literary hymns and deal with the subject in more

---

> Lord, let your beautiful light
> touch my face
> As the tender flowers readily unfold
> and stand still before the sun,
> let me quietly and joyously
> receive your rays
> and feel your influence".

The sunlight is for Tersteegen, of course, a metaphor for the presence of god and the "heliotropic" ability of plants to receive light a metaphor for the receptive nature of true piety. However, everything in Amarna religion is meant quite literally: god is really present in the light and the movements of nature are real praise of the creator, in which human beings join. But in the theological interpretation of natural phenomena Amarna religion is concerned with the presence of god. This explains the remarkable similarity in the expressions. See also "Akhanyati's Theology of Light and Time", *Proceedings*, 7 (1992), 151f.

177 Cf. Hour Ritual. 1st Hour 6, *LL*,151ff.; Sandman, *Texts*, 49 = *ÄHG* no.94, 17-19.

178 P.Leiden J 350 II,2-10; Zandee, *Hymnen*, 18-25; *ÄHG* no.132.

179 P.Chester Beatty IV rto *ÄHG* no.195, 229-237.

detail than, on the whole, is usual for much shorter tomb hymns. Take, for example, the hymn of Nebwenenef:

> (12) You are the one who has formed all that exists
> they come to life when you shine
> They turn to you when you shine for them
> they are transfigured when your rays are diffused over their limbs
> no place is without your light(...)
>
> The breath of your mouth comes to all nostrils
> you are the eyes themselves, sight is possible only through you
> Your light wakes up the faces
> and rouses everyone who was asleep.[180]

This text too interprets the life impulses of nature awakening as praise of the creator. The underworld also seems to be included in the omnipresence of the light: "transfigured", "lie down" are clear allusions to the dead, whose "awakening" in sunlight is mentioned even in the traditional hymns. Of crucial importance is the idea that the worship of the sun god is taking place in the life impulses of nature awakening and that this morning awakening is an act of creation, to which the revival of creation corresponds as thanksgiving. This connection is particularly expressed in the quotation from *STG* Text No. 151.

It is the semantic categories LIFE and RULE that are expressed in this description of worship as the response of the created. The rule exercised by the creator over his creation manifests itself in the.i. dependence of all life on its one origin. The 9th hymn of the Leiden Amun Hymn, for example, continues after the passage cited in example (10):

> they are in his hand, made fast by his seal
> no god can open them except His Majesty
> No one can do anything without him
> the great god, the life of the Ennead.[181]

Creation and rule belong together in Egyptian thought.[182] The creature belongs to the creator. This creaturely belonging can be seen in the dependence that, in the context of such a radically conceived *creatio continua*, a daily "re-creation", reaches almost the point of "absolute dependence".[183]

180 *STG* Text No. 151, 12-15 and 24-28 and on the motif of "awakening" cf. section (t). Here too, as in the motif of "arrival", a complex of ideas originally referring to the underworld appearances of the god has been transferred to the morning. Just as the dead awake from their "sleeping beauty" sleep (cf. Hornung, *Unterweltsbücher*, pp.38-42) with the arrival of the sun god, the sleeping awake to new life once again with the sunrise and not only put on new clothes (exx. 7 and 9), but even a new personality (ex. 10, cf. the interpretation of Zandee to this passage).

181 P.Leiden J 350, II, 9-10, Zandee, *Amunshymnus*, 23-25.

182 Cf. *STG* Text No. 158 (d).

183 "Schlechthinnige Abhängigkeit" in the sense of F.Schleiermacher, see "Die 'Häresie'", *Saeculum* 23 (1972), 122.

## 3. Stylistic Aspects: The Transformation of the Solar Phases Hymn

Although the icons which in the traditional hymns were used to represent the solar phases also become invalid with the constellations of the traditional polytheism, the new sun hymns nevertheless retain the external form of the Solar Phases Hymn. But it is natural for the new "aniconic" forms of representation, which limit themselves strictly to the visible natural phenomena and their theological interpretation, that the contours of phases should become blurred and that certain subjects cannot be made to correspond regularly to certain times of the day, as was the case with the "icons" of the traditional sun hymns. The new view of the divisions of the day may be seen in the Great Hymn of Amarna, which presents the clearest example of the new type. Examples from other sun hymns will be added for comparison.

### *3.1 Morning*

You appear beautiful<br>
in the eastern part of the sky<br>
you living sun, who assigns life.[184]<br>
You have risen in the east<br>
and filled all lands with your beauty.

The short stanza is confined to what has been described in the "iconography of the solar journey" as the "A-side" of the process: the action of the god. This can be explained by the cyclical structure of the whole hymn, which leads back from midday and night to morning. This is followed by the description of nature awakening and the responses of creation as the "B-side" in 21 verses (cf.above example (9)). The stanza places the semantic categories LIGHT and LIFE in the foreground as keywords and in cyclical arrangement:

1 beautiful<br>
2 [LIGHT] lightland<br>
3 [LIFE] living, life<br>
4 [LIGHT] lightland<br>
5 beauty

The presence ("beauty") of the divine abundance of life in the light is the subject of this stanza, which develops entirely from the old stylistic form of the description of the theophany:

Intransitive aspect: appearance in heaven (a) event= *ḥʿʿ=k* [*sḏm=f*][185] and (b) state = *jw=k wbn.tj* [PsP].<br>
Transitive aspect: effect on the earth (c) act = *mḥ.n=k* [*sḏm.n=f*]

184 The usual translation, "the one who first lived", is based on a reading of Bouriant (*šȝʿ*), which is not supported by parallel examples of this invocation (where *šȝjw* "who determines, assigns" has to be read). Since the primeval period rather typically plays no part in Amarna religion, *šȝjw* also makes more sense. Cf. *LÄ* I, 539 n.113. "Theology of Light and Time", 148 with n.20.

185 Emphatic form: "Beautiful it is how you rise".

The morning stanza of the Shorter Hymn is somewhat more explicit:

(a) You appear beautiful,
You living sun, lord of Endless Time,
are sparkling, beautiful and strong,
Love of you is great and powerful.
Your rays touch every face
(var. they create eyes for everything produced by you)
Your radiant skin animates hearts.
(c) You have filled the Two Lands with love of yourself.[186]

This longer stanza also develops from the stylistic form of the theophany. But the intransitive is expanded here:

| | | | |
|---|---|---|---|
| (b) state | (1) state of the subject | PsP | *ṯḥn.tj ꜥn.tj wsr.tj*[187] |
| | | | *mrwt=k wr.tj ꜥꜣ.tj* |
| | (2) durative action | N+ *sḏm=f* | *stwt=k tks=sn...*[188] |
| | | *ḥr*+Inf | *jnm=k .. ḥr sꜥnḫ...* |

This series of adjective verbs in the pseudo-participle (i.e. the intransitive form of the resultative, which expresses the state of the subject[189] is a characteristic form of Egyptian hymns, which becomes especially appropriate in the new solar theology.[190] The examples of the new and traditional types have been collected in *LL* 114ff. It is worth noting that the new types use verbs expressing visible qualities of appearance, such as beauty, luminosity, greatness and height, while the traditional types combine, in a finely adjusted balance, visible and invisible qualities, such as mightiness, "transfiguredness", animatedness etc. Fondness for these forms in the late 18th dynasty can thus be connected with the interpretation of light as *parousia* (physical presence = "beauty") of the god. The same explanation is also true of the striking predilection for sentences of type (c), viz- *sḏm.n=f*+dir.obj., in hymns of the new type. These sentences, which refer formally to the "state of the object" and indeed of the earth, nevertheless express in a distinctly clear and concise form the idea of the "god-filled world", as a theological interpretation of its illumination.

The Suty-Hor hymn contains the following version of the morning stanza:

Your rays are in the face, but they cannot be known.
White gold is not the equal of your brilliance.
You are a Ptah, you cast your body from gold,

186 Note the repetition of the keyword *mrwt=k* in vv.4 and 7, exactly as the word *nfr* is repeated in the Great Hymn. *nfrw* "beauty" refers to the eye, while *mrwt* refers to the heart. It is no coincidence that the motif of causing hearts to live occurs several times in this text; cf. *ÄHG* no.91, 14, 24 and 31.

187 Variant: *wbḫ.tj* "you are radiating".

188 Var. *stwt=k r jrt jrtj n qmꜣ.n=k nb* cf. also *STG* Text No. 188 (c).

189 Cf. supra, p. 47 with n. 47.

190 On this form cf. also Zandee, *Amunshymnus*, 437-39 and 972-74.

One who gives birth,
But is not born.
Unique one, who traverses endless time,
Who is on the ways with millions under his command.
The brilliance of heaven is like your brilliance,
Your colour shines more brilliantly than its skin.[191]

The idea expressed in verse 1 occurs again in a different formulation in the midday stanza. It belongs to those aspects of the solar journey which cannot be assigned to one of its phases and in which the contours of the solar phases are blurred in the revolutionary view which the new solar theology takes of natural phenomena. In the same way, motif "b(1)" of the morning stanza, as it occurs in the Shorter Hymn, has intruded into the midday stanza also in the Great Hymn. "White gold" is the symbol of the beauty and luminosity of the god[192] and belongs thematically with the last two verses. Ptah as the goldsmith is the symbol of self-creation of god. This verse and the next one formulate the total "autarky" of the god, who stands outside all constellations, encompasses all power and natural abundance and, independently of maternal and paternal powers, completes his life-cycle by himself. Closely associated with it is the subject of the next couplet. The "continuous flow of *Nḥḥ*" refers to the endless time of the life-cycle, which *Nḥḥ* completes alone, i.e. outside the constellations, and independently of a "personal sphere". The contrast between "individual" and "millions", in a certain sense, prefigures the passage in the Shorter Hymn to the Aten, where the "million lives in you, the One" are spoken of and the passage in the Great Hymn, which says: "you create millions of incarnations from yourself, the One".[193] The "ways" motif refers, as already shown, to the idea of the omnipresence of light and the god-filled "inhabitable" world. The fact that the Suty-Hor hymn confines itself to the "A-side" of the event (the act of the god) is certainly significant and is connected with the idea of his "autarky", which is here in the centre. This limitation, however, is not an integral part of the new solar theology. Compare, for example, the following example from Memphis-Saqqara:

You have settled very remote,
very far away
you have revealed yourself in heaven in your aloneness
Every god on earth
their arms are held out in praise at your rising
You shine, and they see

191 This stanza differs quite substantially from the model text, which can be reconstructed from Saite texts ("Zwei Sonnenhymnen", *MDIK* 27.1, 6-7). The first four verses there are an appendix to the "midday stanza" and as such refer not to the morning, but to the entire cycle. The model text is not based on the structure of the Solar Phases Hymn. The last four lines are an addition that is not present in any other version.

192 Cf. F. Daumas, *RHR* 149 (1956), 1-17; *LL*,129f. One of the hymns on the pillars in the tomb of Ptahmose (Leiden K 11; Kitchen, *RI* III, 175,2) has the following version: *pꜣ nbjw sw nn nbw jm=f* "The one who casts himself in gold, but is not of gold himself" (but of a much more brilliant and inscrutable material).

193 *STG* Text No. 149 (c); *STG*, text 253 (2); chapter 5.

they raise themselves, their arms bent in respect before your display of power.[194]

Remoteness and aloneness of the sun god, creaturely responses of the gods (the typical formula: "their arms in praise"[195]), whose life impulse here represents the whole of creation.

### *3.2 Midday*

You are beautiful, powerful and shining
You are high over every land
Your rays, they embrace the lands of the earth as far as the end of your whole creation
As Re you penetrate to its limits
And subject them to your beloved son
You are remote, but your rays are on earth
You are in their face, but your movement is not known.

The first two verses, as I have already indicated, have been inserted into the midday stanza out of their original context (the morning theophany) to express the concept of the height and maximum radiance with which the god "embraces" the earth as he descends from his zenith. As in traditional sun hymns, the theme RULE prevails in the midday stanza, in which the god also appears "as Re" (*jw=k m Rᶜw*). In the verb *wᶜf* "subjugate" there is even a hint of the old theme of overcoming the enemy, which includes the semantic level of the political, in which this theme appears here. The concluding couplet, therefore, connects the idea of the omnipresence of light with the motif of remoteness, concealment and inscrutability of god. The typical paradox that the god is physically present in the light and at the same time immeasurably distant represents one of the leading motifs of the new solar theology (cf.2.3). The second stanza of the Shorter Hymn is no less than a "midday stanza" :

You elevated god, who formed himself
who created every land and brought forth what is in them
human beings and animals, domestic and wild
and all trees that grow on the earth
they live when you rise for them
You are father and mother of those whom you have created
Their eyes, when you rise, see through you
Your rays have made bright the entire land
every heart rejoices at the sight of you
you have appeared as their lord.

The relationship of this stanza to RULE, characteristic of the idea of the midday epiphany of the god, is revealed only by way of the connection between creation and rule. The midday stanza of the Suty-Hor hymn begins with the traditional thematic keyphrase *ḏ3j=k pt* "you cross over heaven" and carries on in a

194 Leiden V 70 = *ÄHG* no.90; Leiden K 11 = Kitchen, *RI* III, 175, 2-5.
195 Cf. "Die 'Häresie'",*Saeculum* 23, 122f.n.52. References: *LL*, 208 n.90.

way that quite clearly transposes the traditional theme of "overcoming" from the mythic-iconic (overcoming the enemy) to the cosmic. This is the *locus classicus* for the subsequently widespread interpretation of solar movement as creator of time:[196]

> You cross the heaven and every face sees you
> but your movement is concealed from their face
> You reveal yourself in the morning every day
> your journey is steady under Your Majesty
> The day is short, your journey is long
> millions and hundreds of thousands of miles
> Every day that you bring is a moment;
> it passes, when you set
> You have completed the hours of night in similar fashion
> and divided them. Your work never ceases.

This text has already been subjected to so much commentary that it needs no further explanation.[197] The same subject is dealt with, similarly in the form of a Midday Stanza under the keyword *ḏ3j* "pass over", in the 20th canto of the Leiden Amun Hymn.

> How 'passing over' you are, Harakhty
> completing your task of yesterday every day
> The one who creates the years and joins together the days and months
> days and nights
> the hours correspond to his stride.
> You are newer today than yesterday
> while passing the night, you are already set upon the day
> Unique watchman, who loathes sleep,
> everyone sleeps, but his eyes are watchful
> The one who shines upon millions with his beautiful face
> no way on earth is devoid of him when he shines
> Swift of stride while shooting rays
> who circumnavigates the earth in a moment, all being accessible to him
> who crosses heaven and passes through the underworld
> light on every way
> Who circulates in the faces.
> every face, their faces are turned to him,
> men and gods, saying, "Welcome".[198]

The omnipresence of light making space accessible and the periodicity of movement making time accessible constitute the dominant theme of this treatment. The theme of periodicity, which has also to some extent been the subject of traditional sun

196 With more details *Zeit und Ewigkeit*, 49-54; cf. also P.Leiden I 344 vso, ii, 7-8: *ẖnd t3 pn ḥr fdw=f, spẖr sw m km n wnwt* "who walks the four sides of this earth and circumambulates it in the span of an hour", see Zandee, *Amunshymnus*, 115-118. On the motif of the creation and division of time by the solar movement cf. also Zandee, *Amunshymnus*, 234-239.

197 "Zwei Sonnenhymnen", *MDIK* 27.1, 8-10; *Zeit und Ewigkeit*, 51-54; G. Fecht, "Zur Frühform", *ZÄS* 94, 25ff; Baruq-Daumas, *Hymnes et prières*, No.68.

198 P.Leiden J 350 II, 15-20; Zandee, *Hymnen*, 29-34; *ÄHG* no.133; "Zwei Sonnenhymnen", *MDIK* 27.1, 18f.; *Zeit und Ewigkeit*, 49f.

hymns,[199] appears in the hymns of the new type often in expressions like "you appear in your place of yesterday" (or "in your condition of yesterday").[200]

> (1) You sit on the stern of your boat
> and take your place of yesterday.[201]
>
> (2) You set and rise again in the morning
> you have shown yourself in your place of yesterday.[202]
>
> (3) The earth becomes light at his birth every day
> he has reached his place of yesterday.[203]
>
> (4) The earth becomes light when he shows himself at his place.[204]
>
> (5) The earth becomes light when you show yourself at your place.[205]
>
> (6) The earth becomes light on his horizon of yesterday.[206]
>
> (7) He ages and is rejuvenated in the morning,
> the one who gives light to his place of yesterday.[207]
>
> (8) The one who circumnavigates the earth on a single day
> who reveals himself on his throne of yesterday.[208]

and very often:

> (9) The earth becomes light in its place of yesterday.[209]

Continuous time is divided up (*wpj*) into discontinuous time units by this periodicity, and it is the natural phenomenon that is theologically interpreted as the creation of time in the sense of a life-giving act:

> You have crossed over the sky in order to create time (*ᶜḥᶜw*)
> and keep human beings and gods alive.[210]
>
> Who makes the days and creates the hours,
> one reckons <time> following his movements;

199 Cf. *LL*, 118ff.; here ch.4; Derchain, "Perpetuum mobile", in *Orientalia Lovanensia Periodica* 5/6 (1975/76), 153ff.

200 Zandee, "Prayers to the sun god from Theban tombs", *JEOL* 16 (1959), 48; *Hymnen*, 4; *Amunshymnus*, 940-43.

201 BD 101.

202 *STG* Text No.76.

203 BD Ani = *ÄHG* no.30, 26-27; cf. BD Leiden T 2 = *ÄHG* no.28, 3.

204 *STG*, text No.29, 24; cf. *STG*, text 232, 45 (1); O.Cairo 25208 = *ÄHG* no.193, 11.

205 *STG*, text 232, 45.

206 *LL*, 229 "R", line 16; cf.241 (14).

207 P.Chester Beatty VIII, 11 (5).

208 Lefebvre, *Petosiris II*, 33, 10.

209 References: *LL*, 241 n.69.

210 *ÄHG* no.50, 8-9.

who divides the years, the months are complete
when he sails [the sunboat] in the sky.[211]

"Work"[212], "task"[213], "effort"[214] are typical designations for this interpretation of the heavenly journey as an act of god that gives life in the form of temporal development.

### *3.3 Night*

When you set in the western horizon
the earth is in darkness
in the condition of death.
The sleepers in the chamber, their heads are covered
no eye sees the other
Their belongings are stolen from under their heads and they do not notice
Every wild animal comes forth from his hole
all reptiles bite.
Darkness is a tomb[215]
the earth lies in silence[216]
its creator has set in his horizon.

The underworld journey of the god has been replaced by a description of his absence, which means an absence of life, a cosmic "death-strickenness"[217] and a relapse into "the world before creation", as every new sunrise represents a new creation.

You rise up - they live
You set - they die.

Or, as it says in the King James version of Psalm 104,

Thou hidest thy face: they are troubled;
thou takest away 'their ' (read: thy)[218] breath: they die and return to their dust;
thou sendest forth thy breath: they are created
and thou renewest the face of the earth.

---

211 P.Leiden I 344 vso. III, 10-11, Zandee, *Amunshymnus*, 234-239.
212 *STG*, text 54, 9 (f); Suty-Hor *ÄHG* no.89, 6.
213 Zandee, *Hymnen*, 30; *Zeit und Ewigkeit*, 49f. n.2.
214 *STG*, text 76; STG, text 54; Neschons *ÄHG* no.131, 49 cf. 19; Suty-Hor *ÄHG* no.89, 44 cf.6.
215 Read *ḫ3t* "tomb" but cf. now Westendorf...
216 H. Grapow, "Die Welt vor der Schöpfung"," *ZÄS* 67 (1931), 34-38; Hornung, *Der Eine und die Vielen*, 169f. Cf. Leiden K 1: "The one who raised his voice when the earth was engulfed in silence" and P.Leiden J 350 IV, 6: "He raised his voice in the midst of silence" and IV, 7-8 "He began to cry out when the earth was still in silence (read *sgr* for *sg3*). Zandee, *Hymnen*, 70f; *ÄHG* no.172, 32; *RdE* 30, 32 (v) w.n.44.
217 P.Seibert, *Die Charakteristik* (Wiesbaden, 1971), 42f.
218 See "Theology of Light and Time", *Proceedings*, 170 n.101.

This passage, which contains the idea of life issuing from god at regular intervals, may provide something like a "missing link" between the conceptual world of the new solar theology and Psalm 104.[219] Letter no.147 of Abimilki of Tyre contains a poem that might easily have been inspired by, if not translated from, an Egyptian original.[220] Albright translates the relevant passage as:

> "The one who gives life through his sweet breath
> whose absence diminishes life
> The one who brings peace to the whole earth by his power".[221]

Unfortunately, Albright's reading rests on rather insecure foundations. Moran, in his new translation of the El Amarna letters, basing himself on an article by C. Grave,[222] renders the passage as:

> qui accorde la vie par son doux souffle
> et revient avec son vent du nord.[223]

But, with or without the mediation via Tyre, it seems to me evident that the idea of God's intermittent introjection of life into the world is common both to the Psalm and to the Egyptian hymn.

Outside Amarna this theological interpretation of night as the absence of god and proof of his power *ex negativo* occurs, as far as I know, in only two texts: (a) the Suty-Hor hymn and (b) Leiden Stela V 70.

(a) All eyes see through you,
They can do nothing when Your Majesty sets.
You awake early, to rise in the morning.
Your light opens the eyes of the cattle.
When you set, they sleep like the dead.

(b) When you set in your land of light,
The earth lies in profound darkness[224]
No eye sees the other.
Everyone's face is blinded.[225]

In view of the scarcity of the examples it is hard to decide whether this interpretation of the night belongs exclusively to Amarna theology ( in which case

---

219 But see now C. Uehlinger "Leviathan und die Schiffe in Ps. 104,25-26", *Biblica*, 71(1990), 503-6.

220 Cf. W. Albright, "The Egyptian correspondence of Abimilki", *JEA* 23 (1937), 198f.

221 ša i-ba-li-it i-na še-ḫi-šu tabi
ù i-ZA-ḪAR i-na sa-pa-ni-šu

222 C. Grave, "Northwest Semitic sapanu in a Break-up of an Egyptian Stereotype Phrase in *EA* 147", *Orientalia* NS 51 (1982), 161-182.

223 W.L. Moran, *Les lettres d'El-Amarna* (Paris, 1987), 378. The rendering of i-ZA-ḪAR as "revient" is a mere guess. Albright reads i-ša-ḫir "who diminishes", scil. life. His rendering makes better sense if the passage relates to the sun god, whereas Grave's translation seems preferable with reference to the king.

224 This too is a form in which pre-world chaos appears, cf. Hornung,"Chaotische Berichte in der geordneten Welt", *ZÄS* 81 (1956), 29ff.

225 *ÄHG* no.90, 12-15.

the Suty-Hor and Leiden texts would then be closer to Amarna theology than the other sun hymns of the new type) or whether it is common property of the new solar theology and simply by accident does not occur more frequently. The former seems more likely. The Amarna treatment of the night is consistent with a "phenomenology of the solar journey" that confines itself to theological interpretation of visible phenomena. From here there is no way to the traditional concept of the underworld journey, which follows the sun god into what cannot be seen or experienced. Nevertheless it looks as though the new solar theology clung to this concept or at least returned to it after Amarna.[226]

226 Cf. *STG*, text 113 (clearly a new solar theology text),69 and *STG*, text 151, which at least alludes to the underworld journey.

# CHAPTER FOUR

# AMUN THEOLOGY OF THE EARLY PERIOD

## Eulogies from tombs: Hatshepsut to Amenophis II

### 1. Eulogistic extensions of the Offering Formula

The earliest solar hymns in Theban tombs date from the time of Hatshepsut and Tuthmosis III and are connected with the establishment of solar chapels that had a regular cult both in the mortuary temple of Hatshepsut at Deir el Bahri[1] and the temple complex of Amun-Re at Karnak.[2] To this period also belongs a quite remarkable phenomenon in the history of the Offering Formula (*ḥtp dj njswt*).[3] The offering formulae of stelae,[4] less frequently the frieze texts,[5] are occasionally extended by a eulogy. Epithets are attached to the names of the gods (Amun-Re on the stelae, Re-Harakhty on the ceiling texts) and specify the nature of the god. Without exception this takes the form of predication in the nominal style, for which the term "eulogy" has been proposed.[6]

The form of the eulogy is derived from the Egyptian concept of the name, which not only identifies but also characterises its owner.[7] The ten names used by the sun god in the well-known story The Cunning of Isis[8] to deceive Isis and deflect her from the question of his real name contain a basic core of solar theology and, taken

1 R. Stadelmann, "*šwt-Rᶜw* als Kultstätte des Sonnengottes", *MDIK* 25 (1969), 166-67.

2 H. Kees, *Orientalia* 18 (1949), 427-442; J. Leclant, *Enquètes sur les sacerdoces* (Cairo, 1954 ).47 n.1; P. Barguet, *Le temple d'Amon-Re à Karnak* (Paris, 1962), 291ff; B. Bruyere, "Nouvelles familles de prêtres à Deir el Bahri", *ASAE* 54 (1956), 17 and 22; Abd el Qader Mohammed, "Two Theban tombs", *ASAE* 59 (1966), 153 and pl. 21; P. Anus and R. Sa'ad, "Fouilles aux abords de l'enceinte occidentale de Karnak", *Kemi* 19 (1969) p.220 fig.1; S. Pernigotti, *Studi Classici ed Orientali* 21 (1962), 310-11; J. C. Goyon, in Parker *et al.*, *The Edifice of Taharqa*, 21 n.3.

3 For a general discussion of the Offering Formula see W. Barta, *Aufbau und Bedeutung der altägyptischen Opferformel* (ÄF 24) (Glückstadt, 1968). The phenomenon dealt with here seems to have escaped the attention of Barta (see the brief remarks on pp. 87 and 289).

4 *STG* nos. 68, 127, 130 and 164. In general see A. Hermann, *Die Stelen der Thebanischen Felsgräber der 18.Dyn.* ÄF 11 (Glückstadt, 1940). On the "by no means isolated invocations in the hymn in the prayer for the dead" see especially pp.102-106.

5 *STG* nos. 81, 92, 105, 108 and 136.

6 For a summary see *LÄ* II, 40-46.

7 I have discussed the connection between the Egyptian structure of names and the style of the eulogy in *ÄHG* pp.26-33. On the name see also E. Brunner-Traut, in *LÄ* I, 281-291; P. Vernus, in *LÄ* IV, 320-26; H. Brunner, "Name und Namenlosigkeit Gottes in Ägypten", in H. v. Stietencron (ed.), *Der Name Gottes* (1975), 33-49.

8 P. Turin Pleyte-Rossi p.113; pCh. Beatty XI rto 3. Translation by E. Brunner-Traut, in *Altägyptische Märchen* (Munich, 1976), 115-120.

together, make up a eulogy.[9] The best-known example of the descriptive function of the name is that of the five royal "names", which together make up the "Great Name". They proclaim a political-theological programme,[10] that is, the name indicates an extratemporal nature or ability that will be realised in acts that take place within time. The official royal inscriptions extend the royal name sequence by additional predicates to a eulogy that can include more than 30 verses.[11] This form is probably the model for the corresponding extension of the divine name in the stelae of the early 18th dynasty.

### *1.1 Type A: extensions of the name Amun-Re*

These eulogies follow the same scheme and use the same phraseology, even to some extent the same concretely formulated models. They are not confined to Thebes, but are known also from El Kab[12] and This.[13] The stela of Satepihu from This, which extends the name of Onuris with the predicates typical of the Amun-Re eulogy, is so similar to the Theban texts that it may be quoted here:

| | |
|---|---|
| *ḥtp dj njswt Jnḥrt nṯr nṯrw* | An offering to Onuris, the most divine of gods |
| *njswt pt ḥqꜣ tꜣwj* | king of heaven, lord of the Two Lands(a) |
| *nb-r-ḏr m st=f nbt* | universal lord in all his places(b) |
| *nṯr ʿꜣ ḫprw ḏs=f* | great god, who created himself (c) |
| *pꜣwtj msjw pꜣwtjw* | primeval god, who brought the primeval ones into the world(d) |
| *sḫm spd prjw m Nnw* | power equipped that came from Nun |
| *djw sšp n ḥnmmt* | and gave light to the people of heaven (e) |
| *sḥḏw jꜣḫw=f n psḏt=f* | his radiance causes there to be light for his Ennead |
| *ʿnḫ=sn mꜣꜣ=sn jm=f* | they come to life when they see through him |

The basic scheme is as follows:
I. Rule
II.Primeval God.
III. Preserver/ Light.

The following brief commentary, which aims to show that this text makes use of the same sources as the Theban texts, employs Roman numerals for parallel passages to indicate not only the stanza from which they come, but also the themes listed above. Thus, "I" means "stanza I" and the theme "RULE", since they go together. The other eulogies develop theme II mostly in the aspects (a) primeval god and (b) creator.

(a) *STG* no. 127 (TT 123) I: *njswt n pt ḥqꜣ n tꜣ* "king of heaven, ruler of the earth" *STG* no. 92 (TT 67) only I: *nb pt nb tꜣ* "lord of heaven and earth".

9 This form of "I am" statement has come to be known among Egyptologists as an aretalogy; cf. *LÄ* I pp.425-434 for many more examples.
10 According to the interpretation of E. Hornung in *Saeculum* 22(1971), 48-58.
11 Exx. in *LÄ* II, 40-41 n.18-30.
12 *Urk* IV p.111 (Paheri). It uses the same model as *STG* no. 68.
13 Stela of *Zꜣ-tp-jḥw* in *Urk* IV p.518.

(b) *STG* no. 127 I: ditto; *STG*, text no. 164 (TT 164) as conclusion of the whole eulogy. The same epithet on the Turin Stela *ÄHG* no.72,4

(c) *STG* no. 68 (TT 53) *nṯr nṯrj ḫpr ḏs=f* "divine god who originated by himself" (at the end); in *STG* no. 164 developed into an entire stanza (in II). *STG* no. 136 (TT 131) II: *ḫpr ḏs=f jwtj mst=f* "self-originated, unborn".

(d) *STG* no. 68 (TT 53) II = Paheri (Urk.IV 111) II: *pꜣwtj jwtj mst=f* "primeval one, unborn"; *STG* no. 136 (131) II *pꜣwtj tꜣ n zp tpj* "primeval one of the land, unborn", cf. Turin Stele *ÄHG* no.72,2 *pꜣwtj n zp tpj* "primeval one of the beginning"; *STG* no. 164 (TT 164) II *pꜣwtj [jrjw ntt qmꜣw] wnnt* "primeval one, who makes what is and creates what exists".

(e) *STG* no.68 III: *tkꜣ ꜥnḫ prjw m NNw/jrjw sšp n ḥnmmt* "living fire that came forth from Nun, who makes light for the heavenly people". Parallel text Paheri (Urk. IV 111) reads *djw* ("who gives") instead of *jrjw* ("who makes"). *STG* no.130 (TT 127) III: *tkꜣ ꜥnḫ prjw m Nnw/ddw zš n jrt nbt. tkꜣ ꜥnḫ*, "living fire that came forth from Nun, who gives light to every eye". "Living fire" is a name for the sun and does not occur outside these eulogies (as far as I know[14]). *sḫm* "power(ful image)" is also a common name for the sun[15]. In *STG* no.164, which makes III into a long stanza, it is called *sḫm špss ḫꜥjw m ꜣḫt* "noble power that appears in the light-land". Very similar to the formula of our text is the beginning of the hymn on the 7th Hour, e.g. *STG* no.41 vv.1-2 cf. note (a).

(f) The last couplet has no parallel in the eulogies of the offering formulae, but there are similar statements in contemporary hymns, e.g. P. Cairo CG 53038 (*ÄHG* no.87C,80-81) *ḥꜥw nṯrw m nfrw=f/ ꜥnḫ jbw=sn mꜣꜣ=sn sw* "the gods jubilate at your sight/ their hearts live when they see him"; Tura Hymn 6 (*ÄHG* no.88,15) *ꜥnḫ psḏt mꜣꜣ=sn sw* "the Ennead lives when they see him"; P. Berlin 3055 17,9 (*ÄHG* no.123,26) *ꜥnḫ psḏt mꜣꜣ=sn tw* "the Ennead lives when they see you"; O. IFAO inv. 2139 [...] *n psḏt/ ꜥnḫ=sn n mꜣꜣ=f* "the Ennead ... they live at his sight".

Apart from this group of texts the individual formulations and theological concepts expressed in them are for the most part attested elsewhere until the Late Period. Peculiar to the early Theban offering text-eulogies is this characteristic grouping of the three aspects Rule (I), Primeval God and Creator (II) and Preserver (III), which are always arranged in the same way.

On the basis of the numerous similarities we can draw up the following scheme in the form of a phraseology that identifies each aspect of the god:

1. The nature of the god is presented in the three aspects: (I) Rule, (II) Primeval God and Creator, (III) Preserver or Sun.

2. The aspect "rule" includes

(a) the insignia of rule

| | | |
|---|---|---|
| *nb šwtj wrtj* | "lord of the double plumes" | *STG* no.68, Paheri |
| *nfr-ḥr m šwtj wrtj* | "Beautiful of face with the double plumes" | *STG* no.105[16] |
| *nfr-ḥr m sšd šwtj* | "Beautiful of face with diademe and plumes" | *STG* no.164 |

14 Cf. Pyr §237a: *sḏt prt m Nnw* "flame that came forth from Nun", Sethe, *Übersetzung und Kommentar* I, 209.

15 Cf "Zwei Sonnenhymnen", *MDIK* 27.1, 25f.; Zandee, *Amunshymnus*, 54f.

16 Cf. *LL*, 172-174; 173 n.20.

| | | |
|---|---|---|
| *twt jrw qꜣ šdḥ* | "Perfect of form, high with diademe" | *STG* Nos. 164, 105 |
| *nṯr ꜥꜣ ḥrj st wrt* | "Great god on the great throne" | *STG nos.* 105, 100 |

(b) title of the divine primate

| | | |
|---|---|---|
| *nṯr nṯrw* | "divine god" | Urk IV 518 |
| *jtjj nṯrw nbw* | "ruler of all gods" | *STG* no.130 |
| only *jtjj* | "ruler" | *STG* no.68, Paheri |
| *ḥrj-tp nṯrw* | "chief of the gods" | *STG* no.92 |
| *njswt nḥḥ nb ḏt* | "king of eternity, lord of everlastingness" | *STG* no.68, Paheri |

(c) world rule.

| | | |
|---|---|---|
| *njswt pt ḥqꜣ tꜣwj* | "king of heaven, ruler of the two lands" | Urk IV 518; sim. *STG* no.127. |
| *njswt tꜣwj* | "king of the two lands" | *STG* no.108b |
| *ḥqꜣ Jwnw* | "ruler of Heliopolis" | *STG* no.92 |
| *Nb-r-ḏr* | "universal lord" | Urk IV 518; *STG* no.164; Turin Stele *ÄHG* No. 72 |

3. The aspect "primeval god/creator" includes
(a) primevality

| | | |
|---|---|---|
| *pꜣwtj* | "primeval one" | *STG* no.68; Paheri; Urk IV 518 |
| *pꜣwtj tꜣ n zp tpj* | "chthonic primeval one of the beginning" | *STG* no.164 |

(b) uniqueness[17]

| | | |
|---|---|---|
| *jwtj snnw=f* | "without his equal" | *STG* no.68; 130; 164; Paheri |
| *wꜥ ḥr ẖw=f* | "unique in his kind" | *STG* no.164; 102,2. |
| *nṯr wꜥ* | "unique god" | *STG* no.108b |
| *wꜥw* | "unique one" | *STG* no.130 |
| *wꜥw jmj bꜣḥ* | "unique one in the beginning" | *STG* no.68; Paheri |

17 On the concept of uniqueness, which applies to every Egyptian deity, cf. Hornung, *Der Eine*, 180f. The concept of "Oneness" does not, however, necessarily imply monotheism in the strict sense (this is the opinion of Hornung, who for this reason rejects the concept for Egyptian religion with the sole exception of Amarna theology), but is characteristic of the conception of a deity whose nature is not dependent on "constellations" with other deities, but is essentially single and independent. This necessary singleness or "Oneness" is in Egyptian mythology and theology typical of the concepts of creator god, life god, ruler god (a god bearing the title "king of the gods") and (with the exception of the doctrine of the 8 primeval gods) primeval god as a personification of pre-existence.

## (c) superlative expressions[18]

| | | |
|---|---|---|
| *wr wrw* | "greatest of greats" | *STG* no.68; 130; Paheri |
| *jtj jtjw* | "ruler of rulers" | *STG* no.130 |
| *jtj jtjww=sn mwt mwwt=sn* | "father of their fathers, mother of their mothers" | *STG* no.108b |

## (d) self-creation

| | | |
|---|---|---|
| *ḫpr ḏs=f* | "self-created" | Urk IV 518; Turin *ÄHG* No.72.3; *STG* no. 136; cf. *STG* text 164. |

## (e) creator

| | | |
|---|---|---|
| *qmȝw rmṯw nṯrw* | "who created humankind and gods" | *STG* no.68 cf. 164; Paheri |
| *jrjw nṯrw* | "who made the gods" | *STG* no.108b |
| *jrjw ntt qmȝw wnnt*[19] | "who made what is and created what exists" | *STG* nos. 130; 92. |
| *ꜥḫ pt* | "who raised high the sky" | *STG* no.136; TT 179[20] |
| *qdw jrjw jrt nbt* | "builder who made every eye" | *STG* no.136 |

## 4. The aspect "preserver" includes
## (a) the sun as "living flame" and the sun as "image of power"

| | | |
|---|---|---|
| *tkȝ ꜥnḫ prjw m nnw* | "living flame who came forth from Nun" | *STG* No. 68; 130; Paheri; sim. *STG* No. 164. |
| *sḫm spd/špss* | "sharp/noble power | *Urk* IV 518; *STG* No 164; *ÄHG* 72 |

## (b) light for humankind

| | | |
|---|---|---|
| *jrjw ssp/ddw zš* etc.[21] | "who makes light/gives free passage" | Urk IV 518; *STG* Nos. 68; 130; Paheri |

18 Cf. G. Schäfer, *'König der Könige' - 'Lied der Lieder'. Studien zum Paronomastischen Intensitätsgenitiv* (AHAW) (Heidelberg, 1974) (on Egypt: pp. 15-23); Zandee, *Amunshymnus*, 581-603.

19 Formula. Some examples: TT 41 (7); P.Harris I,3,3 *ÄHG* 197, 12; *STG* no.60, 17; Berlin 6764 (Ptah); P.Luynes; Turin 3070; Philae 467, 3239 Leiden, Boeser, *Beschr.* IV, pl.30.

20 The short offering formula in a frieze text from TT 179 has not been included in the collection *STG*:

| | |
|---|---|
| *ḥtp dj njswt [...]* | Offering prayer for [Amun-Re] |
| *ꜥḫw pt sštȝw ȝḫt.s* | who raised the sky and made secret its light-land, |
| *qmȝw tȝ jrjw nwjjt* | who made the earth and created the flood, |
| *nb [ṯȝw] r f[nḏw]* | lord of [breath] for n[oses]. |

21 Cf stelophore BM 29944 ed. Stewart, *JEA* 53, 37:

| | |
|---|---|
| *bjk ꜥȝ zȝb šwt* | Great hawk with colourful feathers |
| *jrjw ssp n ḥnmmt* | who makes light for mankind |

(c) air

| | | |
|---|---|---|
| *nb ṯ3w sšm sw r fnḏw* | "lord of breathe who leads it to the noses" | only STG no.108b; stelophore Chicago ÄHG No. 81, 7-8 |

(d) ethical authority, which plays such an important role in the hymns; it is rather marginal in the offering formulae and seems not to be as phraseologically fixed as the other aspects.[22]

| | |
|---|---|
| *STG* no.68, cf. note (g): | |
| *ḏdw ḫpr ḫprtj* | who speaks and what is to happen happens |
| *qrst nfrt nt wḏ=f* | a good burial of his command |
| *zm3-t3 m ḥrt jmntt* | an interment in the tomb of the west |
| | |
| *STG* no.130: | |
| *ᶜq m t3 ḫft wḏ=f*[23] | to enter the earth according to his command |
| [...] | |
| [*zm3-]t3 m jmntt nfrt* | an interment in the beautiful west |

These texts are more closely interrelated than is normal in texts of the same genre. In addition to the common features of style (eulogy) and theme (Amun-Re) we find (a) a common text structure (compare the model of the Solar Phases Hymn, which is similarly defined through the common text structure within the more comprehensive genre of the solar hymn) and (b) the common phraseological base (which is not the case in the Solar Phases Hymn). Genres usually have a subject and conceptual world in common,[24] but seldom whole phrases. For example, the quite unusual and poetical description of the sun as *tk3 ᶜnḫ prjw m nnw* "living flame that comes forth from the primeval waters".

On the other hand, this is not an isolated example, but is typical of all those sorts of texts to which the phraseological method can profitably be applied: traditional biographical texts,[25] excluding examples such as that of Ahmose son of Ebana,[26] royal inscriptions,[27] excluding e.g. the annals of Tuthmosis III and the narrative parts of Qadesh, certain genres of the Greco-Roman temple texts[28] and various other, hitherto unexamined genres. It might have become clear already from

22 *STG* no. 130 yields the only occurrence of *nb m3ᶜt* in these texts. Compare, on the other hand, the great importance of this predicate in the hymns.

23 See G. Posener, *Enseignement loyaliste* (Geneva, 1976), §7.1 and p.32.

24 *GM* 6(1973), 26ff.

25 J. M. Janssen, *De traditioneele Egyptische Autobiografie voor het Nieuwe Rijk.* 2 vols. (Leiden, 1946); E. Edel, *Untersuchungen zur Phraseologie der ägyptischen Inschriften des Alten Reiches, MDIK* 13 (1944), 1-90.

26 It is worth noting that E. Otto did not use the phraseological method in his *Untersuchung der Spätzeitbiographien.*

27 E. Blumenthal, *Untersuchung zum Königtum des mittleren Reiches I: Die Phraseologie,* (ASAW 61) (Leipzig, 1970). N.C. Grimal, *Les termes de la propagande royale égyptienne de la xix. dynastie à la conquête d'Alexandre* (Paris, 1986).

28 E. Otto, *Gott und Mensch nach den Tempelinschriften der griechisch-römischen Zeit. Eine Untersuchung zur Phraseologie der Tempelinschriften* (AHAW) (Heidelberg, 1964).

this very limited examination that a phraseological analysis also has to take into account possible "text structures" and other genre-specific structures that make up the text as a whole. How it happens that certain texts make use of a common stock of characteristic phrases in addition to the "normal" features of style, theme and conceptual universe and how one is to explain the type of tradition of these phrases can be decided only according to the individual case. The phenomenon under discussion here has probably to be distinguished from the use of a "formula" as a "mnemonic", such as might be found in oral poetry,[29] or from that of proverbs and idioms which are characteristic of an oral tradition.

We are dealing here with a specifically written phenomenon, viz. the codification of priestly knowledge. This knowledge, however, seems to be less traditional than innovative and the result of intellectual or theological labour. The phraseology of the eulogies has to be understood as the result of a conscious conceptual elaboration of certain semantic complexes and problems, such as the "oneness" of the divine, the relationship of the "one" and the "many", the relationship between mythical and historical, celestial and terrestrial kingdom, between creation and preservation and between cosmic and local rule. The formulations expressing aspects of the divine nature and activity are fixed in characteristic form, because they are understood as "names" or "titles" of this divinity and they cannot simply be altered at will. The "phrases" out of which these eulogies are built up function as fixed expressions of theological concepts. In a similar way the phraseology of Middle Kingdom biographies reflects the emergence of a new concept of man, i.e. the discovery (or invention) of an inner universe of virtues.[30] The basic stock of phrases in traditional biographical texts is thus an expression of the attempt to determine the nature of man, even though it is much less obvious who may be considered as the authors of such an enterprise. In the New Kingdom, we are confronted with the emergence of a new concept of god which leads to the beginnings of "explicit theology" and its textual manifestation in the form of new types of hymns and eulogies.[31]

Historical analysis of these eulogies makes it clear that this enterprise was not always in all cases carried out with the same intensity. The new genre of the offering formula extended by the eulogy is intimately connected with Amun-Re. It is rarely attested with other gods.[32] Its emergence and climax occur in the relatively short period between Hatshepsut and Amenophis II. Later eulogies, which on the whole appear much less frequently in offering formulae, sometimes use a new phraseology. An offering formula of the 19th dynasty will serve as a comparison:[33]

29 A.B. Lord, *Singer of Tales* (New York, 1960); G. Wienold, *Formulierungstheorie* (Frankfurt, 1971), 81-94.

30 Cf. *Ma'at*, 109-121.

31 On the distinction between "implicit" and "explicit theology" see *Ägypten: Theologie und Frömmigkeit einer frühen Hochkultur.*

32 An example for Osiris occurs in *Urk*IV pp.544ff.: An offering prayer for Osiris, the First of the Westerners, the Great God of the (Five ?) Gods, the first prince of princes, the king and leading noble since the primeval age, who looks after humankind, Lord of the Living, Chief of the Dead, who determines what is and what is not".

33 Statue of the vizier Paser BM 687; T.G.H. James, *Hieroglyphic Texts* IX (London, 1970), pl.10; Kitchen, *RI* III, 18-19.

| | |
|---|---|
| *ḥtp dj njswt Jmn Rꜥw* | An offering prayer to Amun-Re |
| *Jtmw Ḥrw-3ḫtj* | Atum Harakhty |
| *Ḫprj b3 jmntt [Ḥrw j3btt]* | Khepry, the ba of the west, [Horus of the east][34] |
| *jtjj nṯrw nṯrwt* | sovereign of the gods and goddesses |
| *nb nbw njswt psḏt* | lord of lords, king of the Ennead |
| *jtj jtjw mwt mwwt* | father of fathers, mother of mothers[35] |
| *ḥrj-tp m pt t3 d3t* | leader in heaven, earth and underworld |
| *ꜥḥꜥw dmḏw m ḫfꜥ=k* | Lifetime is gathered together in your fist |
| *dd=k n [mr]n=k* | you give only[36] to those you love |
| *[ṯ3w] mw qrs [r] ḫt=k* | [Air], water and burial are under your command[37] |
| *wdḏt=k ḫprwt nbwt* | Everything that happens has been ordered by you.[38] |

Text structure: stanza I links Amun and the sun in different names; stanza II combines the aspect of rule (I) and primeval god (II); stanza III is devoted to the aspect of preserver (III).

Phraseology: not attested earlier, apart from verse 6. The most decisive modification is that of the preserver aspect: the sun has been replaced by the personal god of fate, the "ethical authority" of the Ramesside period.

The changes of phraseology make it clear that theological work on determining the nature of Amun-Re had not stopped and, during the centuries of the New Kingdom, was constantly achieving new results, culminating in the divine titularies of the 21st dynasty.

### *1.2 Type B: extensions of the divine name Re-Harakhty*

We have already indicated that the eulogistic extensions of the name Amun-Re in the offering formulae of the early New Kingdom cannot be compared with any other eulogies that may be attached from time to time to divine names in offering formulae, either in length or variety. This is also true of the eulogistic extensions of the divine name Re-Harakhty, which are confined to the solar aspect and based on a much less extensive stock of phrases. Accordingly, the similarities between the individual texts are much greater here than in Type A. Except for Cairo CG 1079 and TT 172 all the passages analysed here (of which only a few have been used in *STG* and all have been quoted from my own copies, except for TT 82[39] come from ceiling texts:

1) Type B1: TT 59, 96A, 54, 172, 84, Cairo CG 1079

| | |
|---|---|
| *b3 ꜥnḫ wbnw m Nnw* | living Ba, who rises from Nun[40] |
| *sḥḏw t3wj m ḏ3m* | who illuminates the Two Lands with electrum[41] |

34 Cf. *STG* no. 113 (b).
35 *STG* no. 108b.
36 The "emphatic" form *dd=k* may perhaps include the notion of exclusivity.
37 On this topic s. *STG* no. 59a (m) and ch.5.
38 Cf. *STG* no. 68 (g).
39 N. Davies and A. Gardiner, *The Tomb of Amenemhet* (London, 1915), pl.30, D.
40 Cf. *STG* no. 134 (TT 131).
41 Var. TT 96A: *m j3mw 3ḫt=f* "with the brilliance of his radiant eye"; TT 54: *m j3mw* "with radiance"; TT 172; 84: *m stwt jrtj=fj* "with the rays of his two eyes"; Cairo CG 1079: *m ḥḏḏwt jrtj=fj* "with the

| | |
|---|---|
| *ḫpr ḏs=f jwtj mst=f* | self-created without being born[42] |
| *ṯnw jrw=f r nṯrw* | whose form is distinguished from the gods. |

2) Type B2: TT 96A, 99, 82, 125, 131

| | |
|---|---|
| *bꜣ ʿnḫ ḫpr ḏs=f* | living Ba,[43] self-created |
| *ʿnḫ m mꜣʿt rʿw nb* | who lives on Maat[44] day by day. |

The predicate *bꜣ ʿnḫ wbnw m nbw* "living ba, who appears in gold" is, as far as I know, not attested outside this type of text and can therefore be used as a criterion to determine whether or not a text belongs to this tradition.[45] Thus, the mention of a

| | |
|---|---|
| *bꜣ ʿnḫ wbnw m nbw* | Living Ba, who appears in gold |
| *m ḫrt-hrww nt rʿw nb* | in the course of every day |

on the ceiling of the tomb of Khaemhet (TT 57),[46] from the time of Amenophis III, may be regarded as an isolated instance of the continuation of this tradition. *bꜣ ʿnḫ* also occurs outside this tradition: *STG* no. 205 (b), with three further examples in (c). When this predicate is associated specifically with solar epithets, as for example in a ceiling text of TT 58:

| | |
|---|---|
| *bꜣ ʿnḫ prjw m nnw* | Living Ba who comes forth from Nun |
| *sḥḏw dꜣt m jrt=f*[47] | who illuminates the underworld with his eye |

the early tradition is once again being used. Apart from this tradition, however, there are examples, such as that of the vizier Paser, which link *bꜣ ʿnḫ* with predicates relating to the primeval period that belong to Type A:[48]

| | |
|---|---|
| *bꜣ ʿnḫ šꜣʿw ntj nb* | Living Ba, who started everything that exists |
| *pꜣwtj jrjw nṯrw* | primeval one, who created the gods |

Otherwise the predicates of Types A and B tend not to overlap, except for *ḫpr ḏs=f*, which in Type B refers to the daily self-creation of the sun god and in Type A to the primeval self-creation of the creator god.

Comparison of the two types of eulogistic extension of the offering formula is theologically instructive. The complex character of Amun-Re demands much more comprehensive definition than the relatively simple concept of the sun god, who is

---

light of his two eyes"; sim. stelophore BM 26270 ed. Stewart, in *JEA* 53, 36.

42 Only TT 59. TT 96A: *jrj sšp m wn ḥr=f* "who makes light by opening his eyes" (lit. "face"), see on this motif "Primat und Transzendenz", 10 n.14; Zandee, *Amunshymnus*, 39-41.

43 TT 82: *nṯr ʿnḫ* "living god", id. *STG* no. 114, 10.

44 TT 131: *ḥkn m mꜣʿt* "who is praised with Maat".

45 On the Ba-predication of the sun-god in general cf. Zandee, *Amunshymnus*, 186-192.

46 V. Loret, *Khaemhat* (MMAF I) (Cairo, 1884) 124.

47 Similarly TT 106 (Paser); cf. K. A. Kitchen, *RI* III p.1. As in TT 58 and the texts cited in note 34 the writing of *bꜣ* with the ram is typical of the Ramesside period (cf. *STG* no. 150[a]).

48 S. Sauneron, in *BIFAO* 55 (1956), 110. *Bꜣ ʿnḫ* also in *STG* no. 113 T. Cf. BD 148:
*jnḏ-ḥr=k psḏ m jtn=f* Hail to you who shines with his disk
*bꜣ ʿnḫ pr m jꜣḫw* Living Ba who comes forth from light.

to be understood here simply as the sun. In comparison, the three aspects in which Type A seeks to determine the nature of Amun-Re clearly represent an attempt to combine the natural characteristics of Amun and Re, integrate them and thus reach a theological interpretation of the "syncretistic" formula Amun-Re:

I. Amun: ruler/king of the gods with the insignia of the Theban cult image.

II.Amun and Re: primeval god and creator.

III. Re: preserver as sun.

This problem of theologically integrating Amun and Re forms the central concern of the theology that is revealed in the eulogies of this god and the changes of the phraseology and terminology basic to these eulogies.

## 2. Hymns

Apart from a single exception (*STG* no.240, in an inaccessible place, which derives from the "sun mysteries" tradition[49]), the hymns of the early period fall into the tradition expressed in the offering formulae. They also prefer the nominal style of predication, the form of the eulogy, and partly use the same phraseology, though they use a different text structure. Unfortunately, so little has survived from these hymns that our generalisations are based on very little substance.

The most extensive hymns from this period are those of tomb 84 (*Ꜣmw-nḏḥ*: active during the reign of Tuthmosis III in Heliopolis[50]). The hymn to the left of the entrance, which must have been addressed to the morning sun god, has disappeared. The hymn to the right of the entrance (to Atum) and the hymn on the stela have been preserved. The stela hymn has the unusually (for this period) large number of 34 verses, made by assembling various texts; this method of compilation is also found in other contemporary texts. The first hymn has ten verses. The first stanza (vv.1-4) follows the phraseology of the Type A offering formula/theme II (primeval god/creator) completely:

| | |
|---|---|
| *jnḏ ḥr=k Rꜥw nb nḥḥ* | Hail to you, Re, lord of *nḥḥ*[51] |
| *wꜥw ḥr ẖw=f ḥqꜣ ḏt* | Unique in his kind, ruler of *ḏt*[52] |
| *ḫprw m bꜣḥ nn snnw=f* | who came forth in the beginning without his equal[53] |
| *ꜥẖ pt smn sꜣṯw* | who raised high the heaven and established the |

49 Chapter I, p.31. The eulogistic form of this text is worth noting since the liturgical sun hymns are usually formulated in the verbal style, in keeping with their reference to an event (solar journey) rather than a being (sun god). But the hymns from this same area of the "mysteries", especially the Hour Ritual, use the same formula very freely. This may be a sign of either its antiquity or the special place it occupied in the cult. Cf. Hymns on the 4th Hour 1-7; 5,9-14;6,8-10, 14-17,20-24; 7A 2-5, 15-17;9 4-7.

50 W. Helck, *Materialien zur Wirtschaftsgeschichte* I (Wiesbaden, 1971), 19 124, referring to *Urk*IV p.940, 11.

51 Cf. *Urk* IV 111: *njswt nḥḥ nb ḏt*; id. Cairo CG 34152; cf. BM 2294 (stelophore) ed. Stewart, *JEA* 53, 37: *njswt nḥḥ ḥqꜣ ḏt*. Cf. generally *MDIK* 27.1, 27-28.

52 *STG* no.164: *wꜥw ḥr ẖw=f ... snnw=f*.

53 *STG* no.130: *nb ḥḥw jwtj snnw=f* "Lord of millions without his equal"; *STG* no.68: *wꜥw jmj bꜣḥ* "Unique in the beginning".

earth.[54]

The second stanza, which develops a special set of themes relating to the sun god and his movement, follows a model that has been used in *STG* no.164:

| | |
|---|---|
| *ḥwnw nfr prjw m nnw* | beautiful youth who came forth from Nun |
| *pḥrrw hrw n mswt=f* | circulating on the day of his birth.[55] |
| *bjk špss ḫꜥj m ꜣḫt* | Venerable hawk who appears in the horizon |
| *sḥꜣbw tꜣwj m stwt=f* | who makes festive the Two Lands with his rays |
| *pḫrww kmt dbnw dšrt* | who circumnavigates Egypt and circumambulates the desert |
| *Gmḥsw bnnw pḏt 9* | falcon who encircles(?) the nine bows.[56] |

The eulogistic style is strictly adhered to in the hymn, even when it refers to the solar journey. In contrast to the sun hymns of the traditions dealt with in Chapters 4 and 5, which are always in the verbal style, this eulogy does not refer to the solar journey in its individual phases, but to the sun god as the one who performs this journey (*pḥrrw, pḫrw, dbnw*).[57]

> Hail to you a million times in an hour,
> the one who does not grow tired.
> To you belongs praise. You are so great,
> the limits of your creation are not known.[58]
> May you awake in peace,
> the Great Illuminator, who has emerged from himself,
> who gives free passage to heaven, awake in peace
> may your awakening be peaceful

The second text, a peculiar invocation attested on a stelophore (in the British Museum), calls the god *sḥḏw wr* "great illuminator"[59] and adds to it the well-known predication of the benefactor/preserver *djw zš n ḥnmmt* "who gives free movement to the heavenly people" (cf. *STG* no.68=Paheri;[60] Urk.iv 518;[61] *STG* no.100;[62] *STG* no.130;[63] P. Cairo 58038:4,7[64]).

The third text is a concluding prayer, where the author/tomb owner makes a personal, not a cult statement.[65] It employs a formula used elsewhere, especially in

54 *STG* no.136; *ꜥḫw pt shrw tꜣwj* "who raised high the sky and pacified the two lands"

55 *STG* no.164: *pḥrrw grḥ mj hrw* "circulating by night and by day"; sim. *STG* no.165, 10.

56 *STG* no.164 is almost identical, the only variant being verse 9: *dbn kmt dšrt*, instead of *pḫr kmt dbn dšrt*. For further parallels cf. *STG* no.102 (h); Zandee, *Amunshymnus*, 35 and 115-118.

57 Cf. Hour Ritual 3rd Hour: *dbnw Kmt pḫrw dšrt* "who circumnavigates Egypt and circumambulates the desert".

58 On the motif of limitlessness cf. Zandee, *Amunshymnus*, 120-126.

59 *STG* no.254, 37 (K).

60 *jrjw* (Paheri: *djw*) *sšp n jrt nbt* "who makes (gives) light for every eye."

61 *djw sšp n hnmmt*. "Who gives light to the heavenly people".

62 *jrjw sšp n jrt nbt* = *STG* no.68. Who makes light for every eye".

63 *ddw zš n jrt nbt* "Who gives free movement to every eye".

64 = *STG* no.130. Cf. above n.21 for further exx.

65 On this subject cf. Chapter 1. By a "personal statement" I mean one where the worshipper talks of himself and presents himself to the god as "one who was whole on earth" (cf. n.68), "one whom you have raised on earth" (*ÄHG* no.35,18), "one of those who worship you" (*STG* no.66 q), "one truly

the Osiris hymns of this period, cf. TT 258(4) = Urk.iv 1642ff.:

> I want to give you praise and elevate you
> I want to sing you a song of propitiation in all your names
> Osiris, Khentamenty
> and you gods of the underworld.
>
> Listen to me, for I am calling to you
> turn your heart to my pleading
> There is no god who forgets his creation.
>
> For may your breath of life
> enter my body,
> may your north wind be sweet in my nostrils.
>
> I have come upon the beautiful path of righteousness
> to preserve all my limbs
> May my ba live, my akh be divine
> may my name be excellent in the mouth of people

In this form the concluding prayer is clearly a standard text in widespread use throughout the 18th dynasty. The appeal to be heard[66] recalls in its urgency the prayers that come under the heading of "personal piety". The principle on which this appeal is based can be understood in two ways:

1. there is no god who forgets his creation;[67]
2. there is no god who forgets him who has been active in his service.

TT 258 clearly reproduces the first interpretation, as is indicated by the phrase *jrt.n=f*.[68] The usual writing, without "t", suggests the second interpretation. This sentence, undoubtedly a proverb, is already attested in this form in the Teaching for Merikare[69] as an appeal to mankind/to the king to be active in the service of god. The sentence occurs in New Kingdom royal inscriptions in its first formulation: no father forgets his son.[70] It seems doubtful whether a person in pre-Late Period Egypt could feel himself a creature of god and appeal to god as a creature.[71] But

---

justified" (*ÄHG* 33,52) etc. The role is clearly not a cult role, but a personal one. Cf. also n.71.

66 Cf. also Leiden D 51; Turin Stela 153 and Copenhagen A 70 = *ÄHG* no.52, 12.

67 So I understood this formula in *MDIK* 28 (1972), 66 n.92 and I corrected it in *LÄ* I, 1089 n.13.

68 According to my own collation of the inscription.

69 *Merikare* 130: "God knows (= does not forget) the one who acts on his behalf". Cf. *LÄ* I, 1086 (and n.13); *Ma'at*, 68f.

70 Kadesh Inscription (Kitchen, *RI* II p.34, 92ff.); coffin lid inscription of Merenptah cf. *MDIK* 28 (1972) pp. 55 and 66.

71 E. Otto, "Der Mensch als Geschöpf und Bild Gottes in Ägypten", in *Festschrift G. von Rad. Probleme der biblischen Theologie* (1971), 335-348, *Zeit und Ewigkeit*, 62. In this context the inscription of Stela 75 (5815) in Vienna seems to me extremely important. It may be late 18th Dynasty:

| | |
|---|---|
| *jnḏ ḥr=k Rʿw Jmn* | Hail, Amun-Re. |
| *jnk wʿ m nn jrjw.n=k tp tȝ* | I am one of those whom you have created on earth, |
| *sḫprw.n=k m tȝ* whom you have caused to come into being on earth,, | |
| *jrjw.n=k m stpw rmṯw* | whom you have made among the elite |
| *sšpssw.n=k m-m tȝ mj qd=f* | whom you have ennobled in the whole country". |

then .i."acting for god"; was a royal privilege[72] and the Teaching for Merikare was intended for a king. Nevertheless, the non-royal person who appears before god as the speaker of a hymn has already appropriated for himself one of the royal prerogatives: the ability to act for god. It is undoubtedly this act to which he appeals in the concluding statement:[73] "I have acted for you, by worshipping you. Do not therefore forget me when I ask for something."

*Ꜣmw-nḏḥ* has taken over the form of the first stanza, but changed it in a way that is most instructive for the way he understands his hymn. I have translated the phrase "*ḥsj sḥtp*" as "to sing a song of propitiation". But the expression *sḥtp* also alludes to the setting (*ḥtp*) sun, just as *dwꜣ* "worship" is an allusion to "morning" (*dwꜣw*).[74] The addition "with incense", however, seems to me more important. The use of incense accompanies the "appellation litany",[75] the invocation of a god "in all his names"[76]. The eulogistic hymn can thus also be understood as "incense burning for Re in all his names". It must be imagined (and this is indicated by the occasional use of the instruction "*snṯr ḥr sḏt*", which means "incense on the flame"[77] that, as each name was recited, a ball of incense would be thrown on the flame.

The hymn to the right of the entrance is probably addressed to Atum (cf. the divine names in vv.9 and 21):

> Giving praise to [Amun-Re]
> [Atum], the bull of the body of the [Great] Ennead,
> who generates himself within the egg,
> who fashions human beings and forms[78] the gods,
> the venerable elder in Heliopolis.
>
> Who detaches the earth by his emergence from Nut,
> who illuminates the Two Lands with his right eye,
> who creates light according to Primeval Time.
> You are Atum, the first one on earth,
> who has appeared as [king] of the gods.
>
> You [have] seized heaven and taken possesion of earth,
> you have embraced them both in your arms,
> you have driven away the total darkness as soon as you rose in Naunet.
> The horizon gods come to you
> in joy, for love of you.

---

72 *Zeit und Ewigkeit*, 13.

73 On the function of concluding statements to explain the intention of the hymn cf. *LL*,217-220 and above Chapter 1.

74 Cf. the 18th dynasty text that later became chapter 15a of the BD: TT 57=*ÄHG* no.55A, 9-10 (Sobekmose); W. Hayes, *Scepter of Ancient Egypt vol. II*, 270-71: *dwꜣ=f tw m dwꜣjjt/sḥtp=f tw m msrw*.

75 O. Firchow, *Grundzüge der Stilistik in den altägyptischen Pyramidentexten* (1953), 199.

76 S. Schott, in *Festschrift Hermann Grapow* (1955), 289ff. Cf. also *LL*, 90; *LÄ* III, 1064.

77 A. Calverley and A. Gardiner, *The Temple of Seti I at Abydos* II, pl.5 and 23: a morning hymn to Amun-Re (to Ptah on pl. 23) where every name entered in the formula *rs=k m ḥtp, rs NN m ḥtp* also has an instruction like *snṯr, snṯr ḥr sḏt ꜥr sḏt snṯr*.

78 The verb *ṯz* "to tie, knot" has in its nominal form *ṯzw* "knot" the metaphorical meaning of "utterance" and may thus allude to the creation of the gods by speech.

Great Phoenix on his bank,
shining like Re (?)
who raises his voice without [being visible(?)]
The Great Powers tremble before you,
Jubilation greets him in [Karnak (?)]

Rise, Atum,
You have appeared and are shining,
your beauty [...]

It will have been an ancient ritual hymn. The eulogistic passage (vv.1-10) outlines the theology of the god as a primeval god, creator and sun god without any recognisable use of the phraseology discussed in §1.1. *kꜣ ḫt psḏt, jmj swḥt, nḫḫ špss jmj Jwnw* are specific attributes of Atum.[79] It is easy to imagine that this is a Heliopolitan text, with which the author became acquainted when he was working in Heliopolis. This is not necessarily contradicted by the fact that there are similarities to the first stanza in a later Theban text, an inscription from the funerary temple of Seti I at Gurna. Royal inscriptions are less attached to places than non-royal ones.[80]

The second stanza, which also has ten verses, is in the verbal form in the first part. Accordingly, its theme refers to a phase of the solar journey: sunset. These verses also sound ancient, especially 11-12, which recall PT 728 c-d.[81]

If the two hymns of TT 84 are rather different from the subject matter and phraseology of the offering formula/eulogy, the opposite is true of the other hymns of the period. The two hymns in TT 53 are short, each with only six lines. In four verses the hymn on the left side (*STG* no.66) develops epithets that deal with the solar aspect. The opening line probably does not have a divine name and can be amended to

*jnḏ ḥr=k wbnw m mfkt.* Hail to you who rises in Turquoise.[82]

It is thus a small modification of the phrase *wbnw m nnw*, which is usual in the offering formula tradition (and only here), cf. *STG* no.135. The last two verses deal with the subject of primeval god and rule, using the phraseology of the offering formula/eulogy. *STG* no.67 is more explicit in its final three verses about the aspect of god as benefactor and preserver:

| | |
|---|---|
| *jrjw sšp n ꜥwt nbt* | Who makes light for all cattle |
| *jrjw ꜣḫ n qmꜣ.n=f* | who creates what is useful for his creatures |
| *nb smw swꜣḏ ḫt-n-ꜥnḫ* | lord of pasture who makes the fruit trees grow |

This subject seems to play a greater role in the hymns than in the offering formulae. We find it also, for example, in the short text on the stelophorous statue of *Rꜣjj*:[83]

79 K. Mysliwiec, *Studien zum Gott Atum II: Name, Epitheta, Ikonographie* (Hildesheim, 1979).

80 *jrjw* (Paheri: *djw*) *sšp n jrt nbt* "who makes (gives) light for every eye."

81 See *STG* text 158 (f).

82 On the meaning of "turquoise" in sun hymns cf. Zandee, *Amunshymnus*, 361-364.

83 This stelophore is usually attributed to the owner of TT 255 (Haremhab at the earliest) and for the sake of convenience (but not accuracy) I follow this attribution. It belongs to the early period of

| | |
|---|---|
| *jnḏ ḥr=k nb mꜣꜥt*[84] | Hail to you, lord of Maat, |
| *nb rmṯw jtj nṯrw/* | lord of men, father of the gods, |
| *jrjw ꜣḫt n ḥr nb* | who creates what is useful for every face |

Similarly Berlin 9571

| | |
|---|---|
| *jrjw ꜣḫw n ḥr nb* | The one who performs acts of beneficence for everyone |
| *nb ꜥnḫ swꜣḏ rḫjjt* | the lord of life, who makes people prosper. |

The text of a stelophore in Chicago also belongs in the same tradition:[85]

| | |
|---|---|
| *jj nb=j n nṯrw* | My lord, lord of the gods |
| *Jmn nb nst tꜣwj* | Amun, lord of the Throne of the Two Lands |
| *Ḥrw-ꜣḫtj nṯr wr jrjw jrjjwt*[86] | Harakhty, great god, creator of what is created |
| *wꜥw ḥr ḫw=f* | unique, there is no one of his kind. |
| *nfr jꜣḫw ṯḥn jꜣmw* | Beautiful of rays, shining with light |
| *Rꜥjj nb ḫꜥw* | sun-like one, lord of appearances |
| *ntk js ṯꜣw n fnḏw* | You are the breath of life for nostrils |
| *nšp.tw m dd=k.* | one breathes from what you give |

Vv. 3-4 show traces of the primeval god-creator phraseology of the offering formula/eulogy (*wꜥw ḥr ḫw=f*: *STG* nos. 164 and 102). Vv.5-8 develop the theme of "preserver" in the style typical of Theban hymns, in the sense that the epithets of luminosity[87] as well as the extremely peculiar appellation *Rꜥjj* "Re-like" are contrasted with those of airiness.[88] Light and air are the life-giving elements, which derive from the sun god. CT IV 196-7 and the Amduat attest to the antiquity of this concept.[89] Thus, it seems to me that we are not dealing here with Amun as air god. This aspect of the god is not developed until later in connection with the Ramesside theory of the elements (Chapter 6).

Of particular significance, in my view, is the Song of the Harper in TT 11, with a hymn that is also attested on the Cairo statue CG 921 and thus represents a widespread composition. This text takes a decisive step beyond the usual phraseology

Sunrise: "gold" motif.

World Rule: with "water" as the third region next to heaven and earth.

Creation: with emphasis on plants[90]

the phenomenon we are studying here.

84 = *STG* no.130. Cf. above n.21 for further exx.

85 NHM 88906 = *ÄHG* no.81.

86 Also. on stelophore Cairo JE 11509.

87 *nfr jꜣḫw, ṯḥn jꜣmw, nb ḫꜥw* cf. *STG* no.66: *nb ḫꜥw, ssp ḥḏḏwt, ṯḥn ḥrw.* "lord of appearances, shining with light, with sparkling faces."

88 Cf. *STG* no.108b: *nb ṯꜣw sšm sw r fnḏw* "lord of air who leads it to the noses".

89 *STG* no.54 (e). Many pertinent passages, mixed up, however, with those from different traditions, in Zandee, *Amunshymnus*, 460-470.

90 *Urk* IV p.469: *nb Nprj sḫpr rnpjjwt* "Lord of the corn god, who brings forth the crops".

and makes the theme "benefactor and preserver" personal, i.e. not just anybody can participate in and receive divine benefactions, only the pious:[91]

> Hail to you, who rise in the Primeval Ocean,
> who shine and who inundates the Two Lands with gold,
> Amun, father of the gods.
>
> Lord of heaven, lord of earth, lord of water,
> lord of what exists, who created the plants and made all that exists!

| | |
|---|---|
| *rdjw ṯ3w n dw3w sw* | Who gives the breath of life to those who worship him |
| *smnḫw ʿḥʿw n jrjw ḥr mw=f* | and provides an excellent life for those who act "on his water". |

> Cause this equable prince, who will continue to exist, to be healthy.

This is not an isolated example. The passages which I have assembled and published elsewhere,[92] together with the contemporary prayer ostraca published by Posener,[93] make it possible to speak of a first phase of "personal piety". Particularly close to *STG* no.13 is a stelophore in Brooklyn:[94]

| | |
|---|---|
| *s3ḫ ʿḥʿw n dw3w nfr[w=f]* | who makes glorious the lifetime of the one who worships [his] beauty |

The Turin stela, cited several times for the purpose of comparison, also belongs to this tradition:

| | |
|---|---|
| *ḥtp dj njswt Jmn-Rʿw nb nst t3wj* | An offering prayer to Amun-Re, lord of the Thrones of the Two Lands |
| *p3wtj n zp tpj ḫntj Jpt-swt* | primeval god of the beginning, prince of Karnak |
| *sḫm špss ḫprw ḏs=f* | enlightened image of power, self-created |
| *Nb r ḏr m st=f nbt* | lord of all in all his places |
| *dj=f ʿnḫ n mr.n=f* | He gives life only[95] to those he loves |
| *j3wt n ddw sw m jb=f* | an old age to those who put him in their heart |
| *ṯ3w n r3=f n ntj m ḥswt=f* | the breath of his mouth to those in his favour |
| *n fḫ.n=f ḥr ḏt m33=f* | who never stop looking at him |
| *nṯr jtj t3-tmmw* | God, father of humankind[96] |

91 On the Egyptian concept of piety as a decisive act for god, an active devotion expressed in acting and knowing and on the "pious" as the partner in a reciprocal god-man relationship see the next note.

92 "Weisheit, Loyalismus und Frömmigkeit", in E. Hornung and O. Keel (eds.), *Studien zu altägyptischen Lebenslehren* (1979), 12-72.

93 "La piété personelle avant l'âge Amarnien", *RdÉ* 27 (1975), 195-210.

94 T.G.H. James, *Corpus of Hieroglyphic Inscriptions in the Brooklyn Museum I* (New York, 1964) no.176; LL, 150 no.21.

95 On the "emphatic" character of this construction see "Weisheit" (n.92), 54 n.133.

96 On the predication of god as"father", usually referring to mankind in general and almost always in the sequence "mother and father", see *ÄHG* 545 and *STG* no.75, 23; "Vaterbild", 18 n.25. Cf. also P.Leiden I 344 vso II.1: *Jmn j[tj] mwt nṯr nṯrwt* "Amun, fa[ther] and mother of gods and goddesses" (Zandee, *Amunshymnus*, 67-70). Also ch. 3, § 2.5.

| | |
|---|---|
| *Jmn mn jḫt nbt* | Amun, the enduring possessor of everything.[97] |

The most penetrating formulation regarding a personal god-man relationship occurs in *STG* no.165:

| | |
|---|---|
| *jtj mwt n rdjw sw m jb=f* | Father and mother for those who put him in their hearts |
| *mkḥw wnjw njwt=f* | turning from those who ignore their city. |

The stela of Antef (27vv) is a long text, especially for this early period, when hymnic inscriptions are usually between 6 and 10 verses. Like *STG* no.102, it achieves this length by combining three hymns of the usual length, all introduced by the name and "he says". The same method is also used in the contemporary stelophore Copenhagen A 72, which has a similar hymn to *STG* no.175:[98]

I. Hail, [the one who forms himself] every hour
[who comes forth from his mother] every day
and goes to rest in her when the time is right[99]
You cross both your heavens in triumph[100]
your crew rejoicing in your retinue.

II. Hail, primeval one of the Two Lands
lord of Maat without equal
the one who begat his begetter
who created his mother and brought forth his hand[101]
who comes forth from the horizon
transfigured in the company of his ka.

III. You appear and shine on the back of your mother
you appeared as the king of the Ennead
Nut offers your face the *njnj* greeting
Maat embraces you at all times
in peace, every day.

I corresponds to the first hymn of Antef. The text was also known elsewhere in Thebes, cf. *STG* text no.s 74 and 180c (in TT 57 and 192 respectively: Amenophis III). The peculiar feature of this hymn is the reference to the solar journey in both nominal and verbal form: the eulogy refers to the solar cycle as a whole (*prj/ḥtp*), the verbal form (vv.4-5) only to the phase of "passage".[102] In this the text follows a

97 On this old predicate of Amun see *STG* no.134 (b).

98 H. Stewart, "Traditional Egyptian Sun Hymns", *Bull. Inst. Arch.* (London) 6 (1967), 63 no.xv; *ÄHG* no.51.

99 Formula, see *STG* no.74 (a).

100 Cf. *STG* no.74, 6; 182, 17. The "two skies" of the sun god refer certainly to the southern and northern skies, not to the sky above and below the earth. The distich refers therefore in "iconic" form to the midday phase of the "crossing" (cf. ch. 2 § 2.2.2, pp. 49ff.), not to the entire circuit.

101 On the Heliopolitan conception of the "hand of the god" s. J. Leclant, in *LÄ* II, 813-815.

102 Assuming that my interpretation presented in n.99 is accurate.

rule that is frequently observed.[103]

III = text *LL* III,1 vv.3-6.

II is a eulogy inserted between these two traditional texts and is closely connected with our texts. Here too the subjects are primevality, uniqueness and self-creation, but in phraseologically different forms of expression. The subjects "rule", "creation" and "benefactor" are missing. The solar aspect is expressed in vv.10-11, again using different phraseology. The relationship to Maat, emphasised in v.7, also plays a striking role in *STG* no.165 (vv.14-15).[104]

The strong emphasis on the benefactor-preserver aspect of the divine nature might be peculiar to Theban Amun-Re theology, as it occurs in the eulogies of the early phase of the New Kingdom. The text of Antef (*STG* no. 165), in the two hymns which it associates with I, develops exclusively this benefactor-preserver aspect, which is missing from the Copenhagen text. II explains in the first three verses the adjective *mꜣʿtj*, which corresponds to the *nb Mꜣʿt* of the Copenhagen text (v.7), here as there in connection with the uniqueness (*jwtj snnw=f*). The last two verses interpret the solar movement as an intentional act of the god aimed at preserving his creation:

| | |
|---|---|
| *pẖrw tꜣwj m grḥ mj hrww* | The one who crosses the Two Lands night and day |
| *r sʿnẖ prt m jrt=f* | to keep alive what came forth from his eye. |

Here we have an extremely concise expression of an anthropocentric cosmology, which makes the solar journey take place for the benefit of human beings, since they are the ones who, according to a widespread biogonic myth, have come forth "from the eye" of the creator god.[105]

The earliest and most explicit statement of this anthropocentric interpretation of the solar journey occurs in the well known closing hymn of the Teaching for Merikare:

| | |
|---|---|
| *ḥnw rmṯw ʿwt nt nṯr* | Humans, the livestock of god, are well cared for |
| *jr.n=f pt tꜣ n jb=sn* | he made heaven and earth for their sake |
| *dr.n=f snk n mw* | he pushed the greediness of the waters back |
| *jr.n=f ṯꜣw n-jb ʿnẖ fnḏw=sn* | and created the air so that their nostrils might live. |
| *snnw=f pw prjw m ḥʿw=f* | His images are those that have come forth from his body |
| *wbn=f m pt n-jb=sn* | For their sake he rises to heaven |
| *jr.n=f n=sn smw ʿwt* | it is for them that he has made plants and animals |
| *ꜣpdw rmw <r> snm.st* | birds and fish to nourish them. |
| *smꜣ.n=f ẖftjw=f ḥḏ.n=f msw=f* | He killed his enemies and went against his children |
| *ḥr kꜣt=sn jrt sbj* | because they thought of rebellion. |
| *jrr=f sšp n jb=sn* | For their sake he causes there to be light. |
| *sqdd=f r mꜣꜣ st* | To see them he travels (the heavens). |
| *ṯꜣz.n=f n=f kꜣr ḥꜣ=sn* | He established for himself a chapel at their back |
| *rmj=sn jw=f ḥr sḏm* | When they weep, he hears. |
| *jr.n=f n=sn ḥqꜣw m swḥt* | He created for them rulers in the egg |
| *ṯzw r ṯzt (m) psḏ sꜣ-ʿ* | and commander to strengthen the backbone of the |

103 *LL*, 4-6 and passim.

104 See n.84.

105 See Chapter 6.

| | weak. |
|---|---|
| *jr.n=f n=sn ḥkꜣw r ꜥḥꜣw* | He made for them magic as a weapon |
| *r ẖsf ꜥ n ẖprjjt* | to ward off the blow of fate |
| *rsw ḥr.s grḥ mj hrww* | watching over them night and day |
| *smꜣ.n=f ẖꜣkw-jb m-m* | He thrashed the rebels among them |
| *mj ḥwj z zꜣ=f ḥr sn=f* | as a man beats his son for the sake of his brother. |
| *jw nṯr rḫw rn nb* | God knows every name. |

In Chapter 3 I described how this cosmology, 700 years after the supposed composition of the Teaching for Merikare (but in exactly the same period from which the extant mss. date), emerges in the sun hymns of the new solar theology. There the anthropocentricity of this version is toned down and human beings, together with all other creatures of the sun god (everything that has an eye), are the recipients of the life-giving and preserving care of the sun god. But here too the emphasis is often on human beings as the "herd" or "cattle" of the sun god, which "came forth from his eye", a mythologoumenon not only based on a word play (*rmjt* "tears" and *rmṯ* "human beings"), but also expressing a deep-seated relationship between the god of light and humans as "eye-creatures".

Clearly, quite independent of new solar theology and earlier than in the corresponding sun hymns, this cosmology appears in the Theban Amun-Re eulogies. It does so in connection with the benefactor-preserver aspect of the deity that plays such a central role in these texts, in the hymns more than in the eulogies of the offering formulae.

## 3. P. Cairo 58038 (Boulaq17) = ÄHG no. 87

By bringing out that aspect of deity, which we paraphrase with expressions such as "benefactor", "preserver" and "ethical authority" (i.e. translations of Egyptian phrases such as *jrj ꜣḫt* "to make benefaction",[106] *sꜥnḫ* "to make live/keep alive"[107] and *nb mꜣꜥt* "lord of justice", i.e. "just distribution"[108]), the Theban eulogies of the early New Kingdom are theological attempts to define the nature of the Theban Amun-Re, of which the most elaborate is that in P. Cairo 58038.[109] The text has been preserved in an excellent manuscript from the time of Amenophis II,[110] as well as on several Ramesside ostraca.[111] The first part occurs on a votive statue from Deir el Bahri, which on palaeographical grounds cannot be later than the 17th dynasty and thus

106 E.g. *STG* Texts. 67 and 220, 3; P. Berlin 9571.

107 On god as *sꜥnḫw* cf. the stela of a singer published by C. Kuentz, in *Recueils Champollion*, 601ff.: *nṯr ꜥꜣ sꜥnḫ ḥr nb/mnmnt ꜥꜣt ꜥwt/šwt nšmt jrt nbt gmḥt* "The great god, who keeps everyone alive, animals large and small. "feathers" and "scales" and every eye that looks". The programmatic title of P.Cairo 58038 I 1-2 calls god *rdjw ꜥnḫ n srf nb* "who gives life to all warm things". Very common too is the phrase *jrj ꜥnḫ* "create life" (e.g. as a parallel to *sꜥnḫ* pCairo 58038 VI 4-5, 5-6; cf. VIII 3).

108 On the connection of Maat with care cf. *King as Sun Priest*, 58-65. Cf. also *LL*, 144ff. and E. Otto, *Gott und Mensch*, 24ff.; pLeiden I 344 vso V.4, Zandee, *Amunshymnus*, 395-398.

109 *ÄHG* no.87; Barucq-Daumas, *Hymnes et Prières* no. 69 with bibliography. M. Römer, in *Fs. Fecht* (Wiesbaden, 1987).

110 On the dating (Amenophis II or 17th Dynasty) cf. G. Möller, in *ZÄS* 56 (1920), 34ff.

111 O.IFAO 1224-1226. I am grateful to G. Posener for drawing my attention to O.Chicago 16976 and O.Turin 6358.

represents the earliest version of sections A-C.[112] The beginning of the text also occurs on a stela[113] and in a text of the BD.[114] Several hymns from Deir el Medina (especially *STG*, texts nos. 206 and 212)[115] freely adapt this text, being based on an oral rather than a written version.

The beginning follows the same text structure, only in more detail, as the eulogies of the offering formulae:

### 1. Rule

| | |
|---|---|
| *jnḏ ḥr=k Jmn Rʿw* | Hail, Amun-Re |
| *nb nst tꜣwj ḫntj Jpt swt* | lord of the Throne of the Two lands, prince of Karnak |
| *Kꜣ-mwt=f ḫntj sḥt=f* | Bull of his mother, who stands before his fields |
| *pḏ nmtt ḫntj tꜣ-šmʿ* | who steps widely, first one of Upper Egypt |
| *nb mḏꜣw ḥqꜣ pwnt* | lord of the Medjay and ruler of Punt |
| *wr n pt smsw n tꜣ* | great one of heaven, eldest of the earth[116] |
| *nb ntj mn jḫt nbt* | lord of all that exists, who remains in possession of al things.[117] |

### 2. [Primeval God], Uniqueness, Creator

| | |
|---|---|
| *wʿ ḥr ḫw=f m-m nṯrw* | Unique of his kind among the gods[118] |
| *kꜣ nfr n psḏt ḥrj tp nṯrw nbw* | beautiful bull of the Ennead, chief among all the gods[119] |
| *nb mꜣʿt jtj nṯrw* | lord of Maat, father of the gods[120]) |
| *jrjw rmṯw qmꜣw ʿwt* | creator of humans and maker of animals[121] |
| *nb ntj qmꜣw ḫt-n-ʿnḫ* | lord of what exists, creator of the "wood of life" |
| *jrjw smw sʿnḫw mnmnt* | who makes the fodder[122] that keeps animals alive |

### 3. Preserver as Sun

| | |
|---|---|
| *sḫm nfr jr.n Ptḥ* | Beautiful image of power, whom Ptah created[123] |

---

112 S. Hassan, *Hymnes Religieux du Moyen Empire* (1930), 157ff.; H. Hall, *Hieroglyphic Texts* IV (London, 1935), 50. The fragmentary parallel BM 40959 begins at I.6 and ends at IV.4.

113 Bankes Stela no.4, edited by J. Černý, *Egyptian Stelae of the Bankes Collection*.

114 pBM 9988 in A. Shorter, *Catalogue*, 66.

115 There are also echoes in Musée Guimet (Louvre) Stela C 21 = *ÄHG* p.170.

116 Id. Tura-hymn *ÄHG* no.88, 3-4; *STG* text 236, 3-4, cf.(a). *STG* text 75, 27(j).

117 See *STG* text 134 (f).

118 Cf. *STG* text 102; STG, text 164; Stelophore Chicago *ÄHG* 87; Hornung, *Der Eine und die Vielen*, 180 w.n.142; Otto, *Gott und Mensch*, 12 w.n.4-5.; on *wʿ ḥr ḫw=f* cf. Zandee, *Amunshymnus*, 20f.; 214-216.

119 *ḥrj-tp nṯrw*: *STG* text 92d; Berlin.9571 = *ÄHG* no.82, 2; Cairo CG 34152.

120 Similarly *STG* text 130: *nb mꜣʿt jtjj nṯrw nbw*. *STG* text 211b, 2 has the same version as P.Cairo 58038.

121 Strangely enough, the animals, which play such an important role in P.Cairo 58038, are never mentioned in the offering formulas, and in the hymns only in *STG* text 67, 5 (but there in a metaphorical sense, referring to humankind as "cattle" (*ʿwt*) of god).

122 Cf. *STG* text 67: *nb smw swꜣḏ [ḫt] n ʿnḫ* "lord of fodder, who makes the 'wood of life' grow".

123 On the predication of the sun as *sḫm*, which frequently occurs in the eulogies of the offering

| | |
|---|---|
| *ḥwnw nfr n mrwt* | youth, beautiful of love[124] |
| *ddw n=f j3w* | to whom the gods give praise |
| *jrjw ḥrjw ḫrjw sḥḏ=f t3wj* | who makes those under and those above,[125] when he illuminates the Two Lands |
| *ḏ3wj ḥrt m ḥtpw* | who crosses heaven in peace. |

More striking than the numerous similarities in detail, which have been pointed out in the footnotes, is the fact that the primeval god aspects, viz. the predicates of primevality (*p3wtj, p3wtj t3wj*) originality (*ḫpr ḫr ḥ3t/jmj b3ḥ*) and self-creation (*ḫpr ḏs=f* etc.), which play such an important role in the tomb eulogies, do not occur in the Cairo text, either in the passage cited or any other hymns of the collection. The only motif connected with the primeval god theme of the eulogies, which occurs both in the Cairo papyrus and in the tombs, is the idea of the uniqueness and aloneness of god:

| | | |
|---|---|---|
| 1,5 | *wʿw ḥr ḫw=f m-m nṯrw* | unique of his kind among the gods.[126] |
| 6,2-3 | *twt wʿw jrjw ntj nb*<br>*wʿ wʿw jrjw wnnt* | you are the One who creates all that exists,<br>the One Alone, who creates what is.[127] |
| 6,7 | *jrjw nn r-3w*<br>*wʿ wʿw ʿš3 ʿwj=fj* | who created all this,[128]<br>the One Alone with his many arms.[129] |
| 8,5 | *wʿ wʿw jwtj snnw=f* | the One Alone without his equal.[130] |
| 9,2-3 | *njswt wʿ m-m nṯrw* | the sole king among the gods |

The Cairo Amun Hymn fuses the aspects of creator and preserver and understands under the term "creation" (by eradicating completely the categories of the primeval period) the continuing creation of the world by the "One Alone" (*wʿ wʿw* ), the one source of life:

| | |
|---|---|
| *twt wʿw jrjw ntj nb* | You are the one who created all that exists |
| *wʿ wʿw jrjw wnnt* | the One Alone, who created what is |
| *prr.n rmṯw m jrtj=fj* | from whose eyes human beings came forth |
| *ḫpr.n nṯrw tp r3=f* | from whose utterance the gods emerged |
| *jrjw smw sʿnḫw mnmnt* | creator of pasture that keeps the animals alive |
| *ḫt-n-ʿnḫ n ḥnmmt* | and the "wood of life" for human beings |

formulae (*Urk* IV, 518; *STG* text 164; *ÄHG* No.. 72), see *MDIK* 27.1, 25f. The addition *jr.n Ptḥ* "whom Ptah created" (cf. Haremhab BM 551 = ÄHG No. 58, 46) makes it clear, that *sḫm* really means the sun as an object, a kind of cult image. Cf. also Zandee, *Amunshymnus*, 54-56; 249f.; 319-321; 1025-26.

124 *LL*, 326f.

125 *STG* text 72 (a).

126 Cf. *STG* Texts Nos. 102, 164; Stel. Chicago.

127 Cf. *STG* no.130: *wʿw jrj ntt qm3 wnnt* "the One who creates what is and makes what exists".

128 *STG* no.68, Paheri: *wʿw jmj b3ḥ* "the one in the beginning"; on *jrjw nn r-3w* cf. Zandee, *Amunshymnus*, 61-63.

129 Cf. *STG* no.108b: *nṯr wʿ jrjw nṯrw* "the One god who created the gods".

130 Cf. *STG* no.68, Paheri: *p3wtj jwtj snnw=f* "the primeval one without his equal".

| | |
|---|---|
| *jrjw ꜥnẖ rmw m jtrw* | who makes it possible for the fish in the river to live |
| *ꜣpdw gnẖ pt* | and the birds that populatethe air |
| *rdjw ṯꜣw n ntj m swḥt* | Who gives breath to the one in the egg[131] |
| *sꜥnẖw zꜣ n pnnt* | and keeps alive the young of the snakes |
| *jrjw ꜥnẖ ẖnw jm* | who makes it all possible for the mosquitoes to live |
| *ḏdft pwjw m mjtt jrj* | together with worms and fleas |
| *jrjw ẖrt pnw m bꜣbꜣwt=sn* | Who takes care of the mice in their holes |
| *sꜥnẖ pwjjw m ẖt nbt* | and keeps alive the beetles (?) in every tree. |
| *jnḏ-ḥr=k jrjw nn r-ꜣw* | Hail, one who does all of this |
| *wꜥ wꜥw ꜥšꜣ ꜥwj=fj* | the One Alone with many arms |
| *Jmn mn jẖt nbt* | Amun, remaining in possession of all things |
| *Jtm ḥrw ꜣẖtj* | Atum Harakhty |
| *(...)*[132] | |
| *jtj jtjw n nṯrw nbw* | father of the fathers of all the gods |
| *ꜥẖ pt dr zꜣṯw* | who raised heaven and kept earth down |
| *jrjw ntj qmꜣw wnnt* | who made what is and created that which exists |
| *jtjj ꜥ.w.s. ḥrj-tp nṯrw* | ruler (l.p.h.), chief of the gods (...).[133] |

What the verses show us is a specific variety of the same theology of the life-god that we encounter in the CT (Shu spells) first,[134] then again in the new solar theology, especially in its radical form at Amarna. Along with other varieties of life-god theology, this text also shares the character of a *Naturlehre* or "natural philosophy", a classification of animate creatures according to their living conditions, i.e. how the life god has provided for them.[135] This section of the Cairo Hymn is unique in the way it describes, almost lovingly, the creatures kept alive by the god.

Part of the theology of the life god is the emphasis on uniqueness. The formula *wꜥ wꜥw*, used three times in the Cairo text, translates literally as "one who is alone". This double emphasis on the concept of Being One expresses the idea of a god who is not "embedded", like all the other gods, in the "constellations" of the divine world,[136] but is "alone as the only one" and "persists in the aloneness of his oneness".[137] The formula is an attempt to go beyond the concept of uniqueness, which applies to practically all Egyptian gods and can therefore be reconciled with

131 These verses occur also on the statuette Berlin 6910 *ÄHG* No. 169. Cf. "It is me who makes the grass for the cattle and the 'wood of life' for the sun-folk (*ḥnmmt*). I am the nurse of the suckling who gives breath to the one whose throat is narrow, he being still in the egg. I am the one who provides for humans and for the dwellings of the gods (*jwnnw*). I am the one without equal, sun disk (*jtn*) that will not be repeated", P.Leiden I 347, VIII.9- IX.1 (unpublished, quoted by Zandee, *Amunshymnus*, 78 n.128, 91 n.246.

132 Lines 127-133 contain the gratitude of the creatures.

133 Lines 142-144 contain the gratitude of the gods.

134 "Primat und Transzendenz", 24ff. and Chapter 5.

135 S. Morenz, "Eine Naturlehre in den Sargtexten", *WKZM* 54 (1957), 119ff.; A. de Buck, *Plaats en betekenis van Sjoe in de Egyptische Theologie* (1947), 22ff. On the interpretation of the "Nile Hymn" and the Great Hymn of Amarna as "natural philosophy" see *SAK* 8 (1980), 1-32 and esp. J.P. Allen, "The Natural Philosophy of Akhenaten", cf. also "Theology of Light and Time", 153-55.

136 See Chapter 2 and "Primat und Transzendenz", 23-25.

137 A. Barucq and F. Daumas, *Hymnes et prières*, 197 (z) interpret this formulation of Iamblichus (*De Mysteriis* VIII, 2) correctly (in my opinion) as an exact translation of the Egyptian *wꜥ wꜥw*.

the concept of being a member of a constellation (for the concept of uniqueness relates one god to another) and achieve a concept of oneness that defines the relationship of the god to the world or being as a whole. The life god is not only "unique", but "one", because it is the basic proposition of this theology that all life proceeds from only one source. This has nothing to do with monotheism, because the Cairo text throughout speaks of the "gods". They do not occur individually by name, which would imply the concept of constellations,[138] but as a group of living creatures, along with human beings and animals. The life god is a "supreme being" and, as such, "one". The idea of transcendence is alien to the Cairo text, and it is left to later theological speculation to place the supreme being outside the divine world in a position of transcendence (Chapter 5). This early stage of life god theology still talks about the supreme being in terms of primacy. It is to this primacy that the frequent predicates of oneness refer:

| | | |
|---|---|---|
| 1.5 | *wᶜ ḥr ḫw=f m-m nṯrw* | unique of his kind among the gods |
| 2.3 | *ṯnw sḫrw=f r nṯr nb* | distinct in his essence from every god |
| 9.2-3 | *nswt wᶜ m-m nṯrw* | sole king among the gods |

The god is unique as ruler of the gods, i.e. in his specific relationship to the divine world. As life god he is the only one capable of sustaining the entire abundance of created life.[139]

So far, the theology of the life god, inasmuch as it can be understood in the Cairo text, is probably based on the ancient tradition of solar theology, which is very likely to be the inspiration of that theory of nature represented pictorially in the 5th dynasty sun temples. In this tradition are the sources common to the CT, our hymn and, later, the new solar theology and Amarna religion. The Cairo text also expresses another aspect of the deity, which is alien to the usual characteristics of life god theology and whose absence from Amarna hymns is especially renoticeable: the aspect of "ethical authority".[140] Pure life god theology draws the line at dealing with the problem of ethics.

Apart from a formula in section B (*ddw ᶜwj=fj n mrr=f* "the one who gives his arms to those he loves"),[141] the personal aspect of the god as ethical authority is expressed in section C, and confirmation of the antiquity of this text is provided by the London parallel:

| | |
|---|---|
| *jnḏ ḥr=k Rᶜw nb mȝᶜt* | Hail, Re, lord of Maat |
| *jmn kȝr=f nb nṯrw* | whose chapel is hidden, lord of the gods |
| *ḫprj ḥrj-jb wjȝ=f* | Khepry in his boat |

138 The only exceptions are *jr.n Ptḥ* in v.18 (note 101) and Hymn G, which belongs to the tradition of "Solar Journey Iconography" (Chapter 2) and in which only Thoth is mentioned among the supporting gods (v.172).

139 *Pace* E. Hornung, *Conceptions of God* (pp. 184ff.), who allows the concept of uniqueness only for the creator.

140 On the absence of "ethical authority" in Amarna Hymns see *SAK* 8 (1980), 31ff. and *Zeit und Ewigkeit*, 54-61.

141 *ÄHG* no.87B, 57; cf. P.Leiden I 344 vso v.1 *dd ᶜwj=fj n ntj m jtnw=f* "who gives his arms to him who is in his bondage"; V.9: *dd ᶜwj=fj n ntj nb* "who gives his arms to everybody".

| | |
|---|---|
| *wḏ mdw ḫpr nṯrw* | at whose command the gods emerge[142] |
| *Jtmw jrjw rḫjjt* | Atum, creator of human beings |
| *ṯnw qd=sn jrjw ꜥnḫ=sn* | who differentiates them and makes them live |
| *wpjw jnw=sn wꜥ r snnw=f* | who distinguishes people by the colour of their skin |
| *sḏmw snmḥw n ntj m btnw* | Who hears the prayers of those in distress |
| *jꜣm-jb ḫft njs n=f* | and is well disposed to those who call on him |
| *nḥm sndw m-ꜥ sḫm-jb* | who rescues the fearful from the overbearing |
| *wpjw mꜣr hnꜥ wsr* | who judges between rich and poor |
| *nb sjꜣ ḥw tp rꜣ=f* | Lord of perception, on whose lips is the creative utterance |
| | |
| *jj.n ḥꜥpj n mrwt=f* | it is for his sake that Hapi has come |
| *nb bnrt ꜥꜣ mrwt* | lord of sweetness, great of love |
| *jw.n=f sꜥnḫ rḫjjt* | it is to make people live that he has come |
| *ddw zš n jrt nbt* | He gives free way to every eye[143] |
| *jr.tj m Nnw* | it being made in Nun (?) |
| *sḫpr.n jꜣmw=f ḥḏḏwt* | whose radiance has caused there to be light |
| *ḥꜥꜥw nṯrw m nfrw=f* | at whose beauty the gods rejoice |
| *ꜥnḫ jbw=sn mꜣꜣ=sn sw* | their hearts live when they see him. |

The first stanza addresses the god in the three names of the classical Trimorphic Theology,[144] but does not link them, as usual, with the three manifestations of the sun as morning/midday/evening sun, but three theological aspects: Re (ethical authority), Khepry (heaven/creator of the gods) and Atum (earth/creator of human beings). The epithet *jmn kꜣr=f* is to be understood in the light of the above-mentioned passage from Merikare: *ṯꜣz.n=f n=f kꜣr ḥꜣ=sn, rmj=sn jw=f ḥr sḏm* (he established for himself a chapel behind them. When they cry, he listens." The "hidden chapel" is a symbol of the hidden omnipresence of the listening Lord of Justice. The second stanza expounds this passage in more detail.The first couplet refers to the "listening", which is also mentioned in Merikare; the second to the "judging", which is similarly expressed in CT 1130:

| | |
|---|---|
| *wḏꜥ=j mꜣr m-ꜥ wsr* | I judge between the poor and the rich |
| *jrjj=j mjtt r jsftjw* | I do the same against wrongdoers |
| *jw n=j ꜥnḫ jnk nb=f* | Life is mine. I am the owner of it |
| *n nḥmm wꜣs m ḏrt=j* | the sceptre will not be taken from my hand.[145] |

"Listening" and "judging" are the two ways in which the Lord of Justice functions, and from remote antiquity they have been associated with the sun god.[146] The hymns of the early 18th dynasty go beyond the Amun Hymn by adding to this picture a decidedly new feature: the concept of piety as an active submission of

142 Cf. stelophore Cairo JE 11509, infra, p. 126f.: *ḏd mdw ḫpr nṯrw* "who speaks and the gods come into being". Vv. 64-65 occur also in a caption text in TT 3 according to WbZ ( = unpublished slips of the *Wörterbuch*) <1743> .

143 Cf. supra, n.

144 Chapter 2; *LL*, 339-352.

145 On this text cf. E. Otto, in *Gedenkschrift Otto* (1977), 1-19, esp.11.. For similar formulations cf. Zandee, *Amunshymnus*, 387-394.

146 Cf. Spiegel, "Der Sonnengott in der Barke als Richter", *MDIK* 8 (1939), 201-206; B. Janowski, *Rettungsgewissheit*, 112-179.

human beings to gods. *STG* no.165 speaks of *rdj m jb* "putting into the heart"; *STG* no.13 of *jrj ḥr mw* "loyalty to god", and god rewards both with his personal attention: *STG* no.165 calls god "father and mother"; *STG* no.13 speaks of "guaranteeing completed life span". This concept of piety, which is absent from the Cairo text, forms the basis of a new divine-human relationship, which might represent what is new and peculiar about Theban Amun-Re worship.

On the aspect of god as ethical authority I should also like to quote the quite unusual divine title of an offering formula. It occurs in a ceiling text from the tomb of the Theban Mayor Sennefer (TT 96A. Amenophis III):[147]

| | |
|---|---|
| *ḥtp dj njswt...* | An offering prayer to (Amun-Re...) |
| *k3 pt sḫm jmj* | the bull of heaven (a), the image of power in it (b) |
| *ḥmw nfr jwtj sb=f* | the good rudder, that does not fail (c) |
| *wḏ<sup>c</sup> rjjt m sb3 nfr sḥḏw t3wj* | judge ...(d) who illuminates the Two Lands. |
| *dgg.tw=f ḫpr zp nfr* | When he is looked at, something good happens (e) |
| ... | |

(a) *k3 pt*: cf. Cairo CG 42120 (Tuthmosis III)[148]

| | |
|---|---|
| *jnḏ ḥr=k R<sup>c</sup>w k3 pt* | Hail, Re, bull of heaven |
| *Jmn ḥrj-tp nṯrw* | Amun, chief of the gods |
| *sḥḏw stwt=f m prw=f nw hrww* | whose rays make light when he goes forth by day |

(b) On the *sḫm*-predication of the sun cf. *MDIK* 27.1, 25f.

(c) On this and other passages cf. *STG*, text no. 187 (t);

(d) *Sic*: *m* *nfr* "as good star"?. On the basis of the parallel text in Paheri it should probably be emended : *wḏ<sup>c</sup> rjjt m pt m t3 sb3 nfr sḥḏw t3wj* "judge in heaven and earth, beautiful star that illumines the Two Lands".[149]

(e) *ḫpr zp nfr*: cf. also *Sinuhe* B 160 and W. Westendorf, in *Fs. Schott*, 125-131. His interpretation of this phrase as "death" does not, of course, fit the context here (cf. also *RdE* 30, 30) A similar statement occurs in Tomb 11 (*Urk*. IV 445): *[dg3].tw=f ḫpr zp nfr*]

Throughout its association with the judicial title *wḏ<sup>c</sup> rjjt* (otherwise unknown to me in hymns), the predicate *ḥmw nfr*, quite in keeping with the later topos of personal piety, can only refer to guiding activity in the human world.[150] Thus, despite its extremely unusual formulations, this passage also fits in with the general picture of these Theban eulogies, which place the aspect of god as preserver, benefactor and ethical authority in the forefront.

Two contrasting examples seem to me to illustrate quite well the basic form of the early Theban eulogies in various ways. Both are hymns on stelophorous statues,

---

147 This unpublished text in a now inaccessible tomb is cited from the copy in Davies Notebook 3/33, kindly supplied by the Griffith Institute, Oxford. I am grateful to G.P.F van den Boorn for the reference to J.J. Tylor and F.Ll. Griffith *The Tomb of Paheri* (London, 1895) pl.1, where vv.3-5 of this text occur in a hymn to a goddess, not to Amun. Cf. G.P.F. v.d.Boorn, *JNES* 42 (1983).

148 G. Legrain, *ASAE* 4 (1904), 182.

149 On the predication of the sun god as *sb3* "star" cf. Hornung, *Sonnenlitanei* (Aeg.Helv. 3), 120, 121 n.188; Zandee, *Amunshymnus*, 355f.

150 Cf. "Gespräch im Goldhaus", in *Fs. Brunner-Traut* (Tübingen, 1992).

a type of monument that appears simultaneously with the emergence of solar hymns and is undoubtedly connected with them.[151] The main interest of the first text is that it abandons the eulogistic form in favour of the verbal of the solar hymns, but typically emphasises the benefactor aspect of the god:[152]

| | |
|---|---|
| *jnḏ ḥr=k jrjw jrjjwt* | Hail, creator of the created (a) |
| *ḏd mdw ḫpr nṯrw* | at whose utterance the gods emerge (b) |
| *wbn=k m ꜣḫt nt pt* | You rise in the horizon of heaven |
| *ḫᶜ.tj m jrtj rḫjjt* | and appear in the eyes of human beings (c) |
| *dj=k zš n jrt nbt* | You give free passage to every eye (d) |
| *n ᶜwt nbt jmjt tꜣ* | and all animals on earth |
| *dwꜣ=sn tw m jrt=k [sn]* | They worship you, because you created them |
| *jꜣw n=k ḥr s[ḫpr=k] st* | Praise to you for creating them (e) |

(a) cf. the Chicago stelophore *ÄHG* no.81,3; and above p.

(b) cf.P. Cairo 53038 IV 2: *wḏ mdw ḫpr nṯrw* "who commands and the gods emerge".

(c) cf. *LL* 41ff. and Zandee, *Amunshymnus*, 39.

(d) P. Cairo 58038 IV 6-7: *ddw zš n jrt* nbt "who gives free passage to every eye"..

This brief commentary, with its reference to the Cairo Amun Hymn, may already have made it clear that the text belongs to the corpus of early Theban solar hymns. For the first time, apart from the Amun Hymn, we come across the novel motif of the hymn as a song of thanksgiving from the creature to the creator, which was to play a central role later in connection with the new solar theology (Chapter 3).

The polar opposite of this is the text of a stelophore (in the British Museum), which comes from the same period but is based on a different tradition:[153]

*jj.n=j* (a) *ḫr=k nṯr ṯꜣjj nṯrw*
*Jmn* (b) *pꜣwtj tꜣwtj ḏsr-ᶜ* (c)
*nb šwtj wrrt tpt=k* (d)
*njswt nṯrw ḫntj* (e) *Jpt-swt*
*twt Jmn mn jḫt* (f) *nbt*
*m rn=k pn* (g) *n Jmn*
*sḫm ᶜꜣ* (h) *n nṯrw nbw*
*n-ḥm [psḏ.s]n jr=k*
*m rn=sn n psḏt* (i)

B = P. Berlin 3055 6,3ff.

(a) B: *Pr-ᶜꜣ* "Pharaoh" (b) om. (c) B adds *Jmn-Rᶜw* (d) B: *ḥr tp=k* (e) B *ḥrj-jb* (f) B *m jḫt nbt* (g) B omits (h) B: *sḫm tw r* (i) supplemented from (?) B.

151 On this type see Claire Lalouettte, *Fidèles du Soleil* (1963) and H.M. Stewart, *JEA* 53 (1967), 34-38 for further references.

152 Cairo JE 11509. My own copy.

153 BM 1735; cf. I.E.S. Edwards, *Hieroglyphic Texts* VIII, 51 pl. 43; Stewart, "Traditional Egyptian Sun Hymns", *Bull. Inst. Arch* 6 (1967) 67; parallel texts are P.Berlin 3055, 6, 3ff; W.C. Hayes, *Ostraca and Name-Stones*, no.48-49. *ÄHG* no.119.

(a) B: *Pr-ʿ3* "Pharaoh" (b) om. (c) B adds *Jmn-Rʿw* (d) B: *ḥr tp=k* (e) B *ḥrj-jb* (f) B *m jḫt nbt* (g) B omits (h) B: *sḫm tw r* (i) supplemented from (?) B.

I have come to you, god, most virile of gods
Amun, primeval god of the Two Lands, who raises his arm[154]
lord of the Double Feather and the *Wrrt*-crown, which is on your head
king of the gods, prince of Karnak.
You are Amun, remaining in possession of all things
in this your name "Amun"
you great power of all gods
truly they cannot turn their backs on you
in their name "Ennead".[155]

The principal interest of this text is that, unlike the Amun-Re eulogies of the tombs, it represents a pure Amun hymn that comes from the temple liturgy of Karnak. *p3wtj t3wtj ḏsr-ʿ*, as a fixed phrase, indicates Amun as an ithyphallic primeval god revered in Karnak, "most virile (=begetter) of the gods".[156] Likewise, the epithets of the cult appearance *nb šwtj wrrt tpt=k*[157] and the formula *mn jḫt nbt*[158] also refer specifically to cult forms of Amun. Compared with this text of pure Amun theology, which is very probably older than the tomb eulogies, the latter develop a more complex theology that links Amun and Re, and this theology presented at the time what was new and forward-looking.

A third example may also be mentioned in passing: *STG* no.240 (*ÄHG* no. 25) from the tomb of Senenmut. This text also uses the outer form of the eulogy, but comes from a different tradition, viz. the "mysteries" of the sun cult.

## 4. Summary

The Amun-Re eulogies appear in the early period of the Theban solar hymns in such profusion that one can describe the worship of Amun-Re as not simply in its infancy, but in the prime of life. The great interrelationship of texts, their use of the same phraseology and text structure, enables one to conclude that they reflect a theological discourse that was fully developed at the time and was being disseminated by means of hymns. The Cairo text is an example of one such collection. The emergence of such a discourse and the extent to which it spread to the funerary cult (cf. examples from This and El Kab) are quite in keeping with the policy of religious restoration associated with the name of Hatshepsut.[159] She too manifested a religious commitment that in many ways foreshadowed that of Ramesses III. Her example was followed by Tuthmosis III. The emphatic acknowledgement of Amun-Re undoubtedly tells us something about the spirit of

154 On the epithet *ḏsr-ʿ* cf. J.P. Hoffmeier, *The terminology of the "Sacred" in Egyptian* (OBO 59) (Fribourg, 1987), 203f.
155 A pun on *psḏ* "back" and "nine".
156 R. Parker *et al.*, *The Edifice of Taharqa*, 59 n.53.
157 *LL*, 173 n.20.
158 *STG* no.134 (b).
159 S. Ratie, *La Reine Hatshepsout. Sources et problèmes* (Orientalia Monspeliana I, 1979), esp., 318-327. The problem requires a much more detailed and analytical assessment.

In my opinion we have here a literary phenomenon that in some ways can be compared with the "propagandist" elements of Middle Kingdom[160] and Amarna literature.[161] When I use the term "propaganda", I am thinking not so much of the emphasis on rule and the primacy of god together with his unique position in the divine world, for this henotheistic perspective belongs to some extent to the genre style of the eulogy. What strikes me rather is the emphasis on the goodness of god as "benefactor", "shepherd" and "ethical authority", which is based on the royal image of the Middle Kingdom.[162] As the literature of the Middle Kingdom serves to propagate this image of the king, the hymns of the Cairo text also wish to propagate this image of the god among the people. This "publicity" for the god of Thebes, raised to the status of "national god",[163] and the ruling dynasty undoubtedly has a political aspect. But the tomb texts show that the literary phenomenon was backed up by a "movement" of more than simply official character. The content of these texts makes it certain that we have here a first wave of personal piety. This concept could not be more clearly formulated for the Egyptian than in the expression of *STG* no.165: "father and mother for the one who puts them in his heart". The discovery made by Posener that a group of texts with prayers of personal piety come from this early period[164] makes this interpretation certain.

The aim of propagandist statements about the greatness and goodness of god is expressed explicitly in a formula that occurs in a final statement from several hymns of this period: *swꜣš=j mrwt=k ḫt tꜣ* "I will disseminate love of you throughout the land".[165] A stelophore inscription from Heracleopolis is even more explicit:[166] "I will worship you and tell the gods and human beings about your beauty every day." These statements throw some light on the self-understanding of this genre of hymns (inscribed on stelophores and at tomb entrances) as established ways of proclaiming the praise of god or "divine propaganda". We come across them later within the framework of another institution, the temple statue, which can be understood quite explicitly as an intermediary between gods and humans:[167] "I shall build up your greatness in the faces, lord of the gods, and tell people about how beneficent and effective you are." The corresponding formulae that come from personal piety texts are well known.[168] One example from the early prayer ostraca, which are contemporary with our texts, will suffice:

> I want to tell all faces of your power
> for I have seen your power (?)

160 G. Posener, *Littérature et politique dans l'Égypte de la XIIe Dynastie* (1956).

161 *SAK* 8 (1980), 1-32, esp. 11-19.

162 E. Blumenthal, *Untersuchungen*; Posener, *Littérature*; D. Müller "Der gute Hirte", in *ZÄS* 86 (1961), 126ff. and later Chapter 7.

163 On the concept of "state god" as an institution see "Primat und Transzendenz", 17-27.

164 *RdÉ* 27 (1975), 195-210; cf. also *Ägypten:Theologie und Frömmigkeit*, 221-232.

165 *STG* no.67; 220 (stelophore); Theban Necropolis pl. xvii (Stelophore) cf. P.Cairo 58038, v, 6: *mrwt=k zš.tj ḫt tꜣwj* "the love of you is dispersed through the Two Lands"; TT 11 *Urk* IV 444f.: *šms=j kꜣ=k swꜣš=j mrwt=k* "I will follow your ka and disseminate the love of you".

166 W.F. Petrie, *Sedment* II, 49.

167 Cairo CG 42 208.

168 H. Brunner, in *Festschrift E. Otto* (1977), 119-124.; *SAK* 8 (1980) pp.6-8.

I want to raise you on high. to give you praise...[169]

The *topos* of announcing the praise of god is also richly attested in the inscriptions of Hatshepsut.[170]

The eulogistic form, attested in Middle Kingdom hymns and certain passages of the PT, is undoubtedly the most universal and original form of praising god among the Egyptians and the sun hymn in the verbal style represents an exception in comparison with it. It continues to play an important role after this first period, which stretches from Hatshepsut to Amenophis II, in Theban sun hymns. It occurs in:

1. extended offering formulae and similar "divine titularies";
2. hymns of eulogistic form;[171]
3. eulogistic passages of formally complex hymns.[172]

In conclusion, several examples of (1) will be considered.

Offering formulae that extend the divine name with eulogistic descriptions are much more common than my collection of sun hymns (*STG*) might lead one to suppose. I have taken only a few examples that have been developed into texts resembling hymns. Divine titularies of this sort do not occur simply in connection with Amun-Re and the sun god.[173] Examples such as *STG* no.184 (Amenophis III), *STG* text nos. 23 and 258 (19th dynasty) and 94-95 (20th dynasty) (and there are many more) attest to the continuation of this tradition. They show that fixed divine titularies always using the same formula were extended by means of divine names. One example from the accompanying caption to a festival scene in TT 65, which is not included in *STG* may serve to illustrate the point:

| | |
|---|---|
| *ḏd mdw jn Jmn-Rˁw* | To be spoken by Amun-Re |
| *nb nst t3wj ḫntj Jpt-swt* | lord of the Throne of the Two Lands, prince of Karnak |
| *k3-mwt=f ḥrj.tp psḏt* | Bull of his Mother, Chief of the Ennead |
| *q3 šwtj ˁb.tw m nfrw=f* | with the tall Double Feather, whose beauty is boasted of[174] |
| *Jtmw ḫntj jpt=f* | Atum, who stands before his chapel[175] |
| *ˁ3 ḫˁw m ḥwt-sr* | great of appearance in the house of the prince[176] |
| *nṯr špsj ˁnḫ m m3ˁt* | Venerable god, who lives from Maat, |
| *p3wtj ḫpr m ḥ3t* | primeval god, who emerged at the beginning[177] |
| *sḥḏw t3wj m stwt=f* | who brightens the Two Lands with his rays |

169 *RdÉ* 27, 209: O.Cairo 12189.

170 *Urk* IV p.349, 7 p.350, 17; p.351, 7; p.480; p.390 From the time of Tuthmosis I see *Urk* IV p.271.

171 E.g. *STG* no.181, whose "crossword" structure is made easier (perhaps even possible) by the loose apposition of rows of nominal syntagms.

172 E.g. the second part of the Suty-Hor Hymn (*ÄHG* no.89, 31-60).

173 See corresponding eulogies of this period to Osiris, e.g *Urk* IV pp.543ff.

174 *Wb* II, 260.17; id., *STG* no.241, 7. Cf. Zandee, *Amunshymnus*, 333, 337-340.

175 Cf. *STG* no.181, a, 3; P.Cairo 58038, ix, 2; Barguet, *Le temple d'Amon Re à Karnak*, 150; 202; 215.

176 Cf. *STG nos.* 22; 60 (*ḥwt B3* "house of the Ba" instead of *ḥwt sr*).

177 Cf. TT 68 ed. K.J.Seyfried, *THEBEN* VI, 1991, 30f.

| | |
|---|---|
| *sḫm špss ˁnḫ m m3ˁt* | Venerable power who lives on Maat |
| *p3wtj ḫprw m ḥ3t* | Primeval one who emerged in the beginning |

| *b3 špsj prjw m Nnw* | Venerable Ba, who comes from the primeval waters[178] |
|---|---|
| *ṯr ʿ3 njswt nṯrw* | great god, king of the gods. |

The eulogistically extended formulae from the tomb of Nebwenenef (TT 157) are a particularly interesting phenomenon,[179] which cannot be dissociated from the fact that he was High Priest of Amun. What he expresses in his offering formulae is theological knowledge.[180] His eulogy is the linguistic expression of theological work. The object of this work and the subject of the eulogy are to determine the nature of god. There is not just one attempt to do this, but several. The last section of this long series of elaborate attempts to define the nature of Amun-Re is the divine titulary in the 21st dynasty "decrees".[181] In the history of this form, the post-Amarna period, i.e. the religious restoration undertaken by men like Nebwenenef,[182] seems to play an important role. Amun-Re religion, shocked by the catastrophe of Amarna, attempted to define more closely the nature of god. The divine titulary has the character of a "credo" or "confession" only insofar as it establishes the identity of the god exactly. The name alone is not enough, because it does not express the total nature of the god. The name stands next to other names, but the theological statement about his nature aims at an all-embracing and inclusive totality.

This "confessional" character is revealed in the type of divine titulary common in the post-Amarna tombs of Deir el Medina:[183]

| *ḥtp dj njswt Rʿw Ḥrw-3ḫtj* | An offering to Re-Harakhty |
|---|---|
| *Jmn nb nst t3wj* | Amun, lord of the thrones of the Two Lands, |
| *Rʿw pw nb Jpt-swt* | he is Re, the lord of Thebes, |
| *Jmn wbnw m ḥrt* | Amun who rises in the heaven. |
| | |
| *(b) sḫm špss n psḏt* | Venerable power of the Ennead, |
| *nfr-ḥr jrjw nṯrw* | with beautiful face, creator of the gods |
| *q3 šwtj ʿb m nfrw=f* | with high feathers, who boasts with his beauty. |

The theological concern of these divine titularies, the problem of the complex identity of Amun and Re, is revealed most clearly in the chiastic arrangement of vv.3-4:[184]

---

178 Cf. *STG* no.95 (TT 68):

| *nṯr nṯrj ḫpr ḏs=f* | divine god, self-created |
|---|---|
| *sḥḏw t3wj m stwt=f* | who brightens the Two Lands with his rays |
| *b3 špss prjw m nnw* | Venerable ba who came forth from Nun |
| *p3wtj ḫprw m ḥ3t* | Primeval one who emerged in the beginning |

179 *STG*, 148-150, 152-153; cf. Zandee, "Hymnical Sayings".

180 Cf. *Nbwnn=f* on himself: WbZ <1154> *jw rḫ trw nṯr/ḥ3wtj m sʿ3 srḫw=f* "A knowledgeable one, who worships god, a leader in enlarging his commands" (the word *srḫw*, a causative of *rḫ* "to know", occurs only in this formula). On the widespread nature of this topos among high priests cf. "Weisheit, Loyalismus und Fömmigkeit", 18-19.

181 *ÄHG* no.131 and n.154.

182 His installation as High Priest was one of the first official acts of Ramesses II; cf. Kitchen, *RI* III, 282ff.

183 *LL*, 330ff. and n.73; *STG* Text Nos. 241-242.

184 *Jmn nb Jpt-swt* and *Rʿw wbnw m ḥrt* really belong together; cf. *LL*, 330ff.

*R$^{c}$w* *nb jpt swt*

*Jmn* *wbnw m ḥrt*

Theological scholarship is not, however, a regular feature of the universal ideal of knowledge of god, which plays such an important role in New Kingdom inscriptions in the quite untheological form of "taking god into one's heart".[185] In general, it can be said that the eulogy as an attempt to define the nature of god is the most appropriate form in which to present knowledge of god, the form of the "one who has taken god into his heart" and "announces his power" in the eulogistic praise.

185 "Weisheit, Loyalismus und Frömmigkeit" passim.

# CHAPTER FIVE

# BA: HIDDENNESS AND ONENESS. THEBAN AMUN-RE THEOLOGY IN THE RAMESSIDE PERIOD I

## 1. Preliminary observations

The theology to be discussed in this chapter represents a religious model which, for novelty and self-containedness, rivals Amarna religion. Compared with Amarna religion, however, only individual aspects of this theology have been identified by scholars, and the most striking of these is the phenomenon usually summarised under the heading "personal piety".[1] The reason for this is that the new theology, unlike Amarna religion, was not introduced by force, in the form of "revolution from above", or by actively excluding other religious forms, so that the new could be sharply distinguished from the old and as such made easily recognisable. This theology, rather, presents a new context, which was able to accommodate the old; it took many decades to develop, but did so with increasing clarity. We are thus dealing with a structural change of the old religion, which was achieved not only gradually, but also with the traditional forms of expression intact, so that the new often cannot be recognised by the individual new expression, but only by the novel configuration of traditional motifs. Anyone looking at individual aspects will find the following interpretation somewhat arbitrary. The nature of the changes postulated here was significant and fundamental, but the superficial differences between the old and new appear relatively hard to detect. It therefore seems to me indispensable to make a preliminary summary of the motifs and characteristics by which, in my opinion, the new theology can be recognised most clearly:

1. the emphasis on the oneness and hiddenness of the god;
2. the predication of the god as .i."ba" in connection with the concept of hiddenness;
3. the formula of the "one who makes himself into millions", with all its variants;
4. the concept of the god dwelling in the world as "ba", image and body, who has created the world as earth, heaven and underworld for these three constituent elements of his self;
5. the theory of the "life-giving elements", i.e. the concept that god sustains and gives life to the world not only by, but also as light,.i. air, and water;
6. the idea of all-pervasiveness in the form of air, as is expressed in the formula *(Jmn) mnw m jẖt nbt*;
7. the role of this god as god of time and fate in connection with
8. his personal aspect as "ethical authority".

---

1 J. H. Breasted called the Ramesside period "the age of personal piety" in his book *Development of Religion and Thought* (New York, 1912), 344ff.

Every one of these eight motifs has an earlier history, which in some cases is very old. The idea of the "uniqueness" and "oneness" of god is found in the new solar theology and earlier Amun-Re religion (chapter 3 §2.1 and chapter 4). "Ba" predication occurs in the older Re-Harakhty eulogies (chapter 4 §1.2), which call the god *bꜣ ꜥnḫ* "living ba". The "one-millions" formula has its predecessors in Amarna religion and even in *CT* (*STG* text 149c[2]). The concept of god as ba, image and body is paralleled in the idea of the journey of the sun as a nocturnal union of ba and corpse of the god (chapter 2). The theory of the life-giving elements has roots in the older concept of a life god and in the Middle Kingdom ideology of kingship (Sinuhe[3]). The formula *Jmn mnw m jḫt nbt* recalls the earlier *Jmn mn jḫt nbt* (i.e. without the preposition "*m*") cf. *STG* text 134. For the function of the time god compare the relationship of the sun god (chapter 3) with time "produced" by him. The aspect of god as "ethical authority" may be compared with our analysis of section C of P. Cairo 58038 (*ÄHG* 87). Each of these motifs changes its meaning in the new context, in which Amun-Re, throughout the course of the 13th century BC, gradually becomes a personal world-god. This context will be examined in its most characteristic aspects in the following sections.

## 2. Oneness and Hiddenness

*wꜥw Jmn jmnw jr=sn* "Amun is one, in that he is hidden from them". This statement from hymn 200 of the Leiden Amun Hymn, which will be examined in full later on, combines the traditional themes of oneness and hiddenness in a new way.

### *2.1 Oneness*

Time and again the Egyptian sources predicate the oneness/singleness/uniqueness of a god. We have encountered this predicate in two different contexts within the framework of our study:

1. in the new solar theology, where the theory of the oneness of god represents the theological interpretation of the natural phenomenon of the "aloneness" in which the sun makes its remote and hidden journey through the sky;

2. in the theology of the life god, as it is expounded in P. Cairo 58038 (especially section E), where Amun-Re is praised as the source of life for gods, humans and animals.

The Cairo text likewise deals with the sun. The life god Amun-Re is regarded as a solar deity, who develops his life-giving efficacy in the form of the sun. The new solar theology interprets the solar journey theologically as the life-giving and sustaining action of the sun god in the world. Thus, there are many points of agreement between the two concepts. Nevertheless, one has to be careful here to make a distinction. In the context of Amun-Re religion the unifying, centralising view focuses on the problems of life and answers the question where all life comes from and which forces are effective in the emergence, preservation and continuation of life. The focus of attention in the new solar theology, however, is on

---

2 The connection between the two traditions was first demonstrated by E. Otto, *Forschungen und Fortschritte* 35 (1961), 278ff.

3 Cf. *SAK* 8 (1980), 18 n.86.

the cosmic events of the solar journey. It postulates its knowledge of the aloneness and oneness of the sun in radical antithesis to the usual view, according to which the solar journey takes place in the changing constellations of a" personal sphere", grouped around the sun god.

In both theologies, as we have seen, the postulate of the oneness of god does not exclude the existence of other gods. Apart from Amarna the texts constantly mention the gods. They do not appear, however, as individuals with their own names, but collectively. As a result, they do not enter a constellation with the "one god", but are his counterpart, alongside the other living creatures, viz. humans, animals and even plants. In all contexts that mention the oneness of god the question is one of the transcendence of ONE god from the constellations and spheres of the divine world. This phenomenon has, of course, been responsible for the classical idea that the polytheistic structure of Egyptian religion is a sort of façade concealing a basic monotheism. Erik Hornung has examined all expressions of this idea and refuted them, so that it is not necessary to go into detail about them here.[4] He reduces the idea of oneness to uniqueness, which he maintains is applicable to every god as such and is inherent in the concept of god. But this concept of uniqueness, in my opinion, goes too far in the cases that I have dealt with and does not do justice to the related phenomena summarised by E. Otto in his pioneering essay of 1955 (which took the debate on monotheism, then at something of a dead end, to a new level) under the somewhat misleading of "monotheistic tendencies".[5] It was not Otto's intention to reduce Egyptian polytheism to a mere facade. While fully acknowledging that Egyptians regarded reality (and he understood the Egyptian divine world as the spiritual expression of reality) as a multiplicity,[6] Otto was concerned to enquire after the contexts in which experiences and concepts of unity were nevertheless prominent and where the Egyptians tended to reduce the multiplicity of phenomena to ONE form. He names four such contexts, arranged in pairs:[7]

The ruler god and creator god
The god in man and the god of ethics.

These aspects indicate four levels on which the divine might be experienced in the form of "oneness" and not merely uniqueness. Every characterisation of Egyptian creation theology reckons with one, and only one creator. The wisdom that treats the divine on the same level as the human condition speaks only of "god".[8] The theory of "god in man", in my opinion, overlaps with the god of ethics and belongs to quite a different context, and I would therefore like to exclude them here. Unlike Otto, I should like to relate the ruler god, not to the king himself, but to the institution of "national god" as manifested in the king,[9] represented by the king and given to him as father. This "ruler god" belongs to the original forms of

4 *Conceptions of God in Ancient Egypt* (tr. J. Baines) (Ithaca, 1982).

5 "Monotheistische Tendenzen in der ägyptischen Religion", in *Welt des Orients* 2 (1955), 99-110.

6 He describes the "abundance of forms" of the Egyptian divine world as "the building blocks of its theology and its attempt, rooted in religious forms, to understand the world", the "raw material of divine systems that represent speculatively a comprehensive cosmology" (p.99).

7 Ibid. p.100

8 Hornung, *Der Eine*, 32-49; W. Barta, *ZÄS* 103(1976), 79-88; *LÄ* II, 771-774.

9 "Primat und Transzendenz", 17-27.

expression of that experience of unity that refers in this case to the political sphere. Just as cosmic unity may be expressed by the "oneness" of the creator god together with the idea that the world in its multiplicity and variety came from one origin and was designed according to one plan, so the unity of human society may be expressed by the "oneness" of the state or ruler god.

If the results of Otto are added to the results of our analysis, the following six aspects, in which the divine is represented in a special way as a unity, emerge:

Primeval god/creator god/life god
Sun god/ ruler god/ ethical authority.

These aspects never appear individually in the context of a concrete theology: there is no god that is solely a creator god, primeval god etc. They appear always in various configurations and profiles. The god of Amarna religion, for example, is neither "primeval god" nor "ethical authority". The Theban Amun-Re theology of the Ramesside period differs from its predecessors in that it takes not only all six manifestations of the oneness of god for its concept of god, but adds a seventh: the oneness of the hidden god. The oneness of Amun, which by no means denies the existence of the other gods, is based on the fact that he is:

1. the primeval god, who existed before the entire world
2. the creator, who transformed the world from the primeval condition into the cosmos;
3. the life god, who gives life and spirit to the world in the form of the three life-giving elements;
4. the sun god, who completes his journey alone and illuminates and guards the world with his eyes;
5. the ruler god, who exercises rule over his creation and is represented by the king on earth;[10]
6. the ethical authority, who watches over right and wrong, the "vizier of the poor",[11] the judge and saviour, the lord of time, "favour"[12] and fate;
7. the hidden god, whose symbols, images and names are the many gods.

### *2.2 Hiddenness*

The qualities of the secret, the secluded, the inaccessible, the inexplicable form part of a concept of the holy, which may be regarded as an anthropological universal. Egypt is no exception. Indeed, it has been rightly said to have a "sense of its own for what is secret in religion".[13] Thus, the words used in Egyptian to express the concept of the hidden, in a particularly elaborate and varied way, refer primarily and originally to the concept of holiness: *štꜣ* "secret, inaccessible, difficult"; *ḏsr*

10 The role of Amun as king and its development during the New Kingdom, from the oracular interventions into the Thutmoside succession until the Theban theocracy of dynasty 21, exceed the scope of this study and should form the subject of a separate book; meanwhile see J. Zandee, *Numen* 3 (1956), 230-234 and supplement to *Numen* 31 (1975), 167-178, also *Amunshymnus*, 581-952. See also *LÄ* II, 774; "State and Religion in the New Kingdom".

11 G. Posener, "Amon, juge du pauvre", in *Festschrift H. Ricke* (1971), 59-63.

12 *Zeit und Ewigkeit*, 60-64; "Weisheit, Loyalismus und Frömmigkeit", 31.

13 J. Leipoldt and S. Morenz, *Die Heiligen Schriften* (1956), 88.

"secluded";[14] *jmn* "hidden"; *špss* "august, noble": *ḥ3p* "concealed" etc..[15] The hiddenness peculiar to holiness is expressed by keeping the cult image secret and screened off in the sanctuary:

> secret (*sšt3w*) and made holy (*sḏsrw*) are their bodies (*ḏt*)(...)
> more secluded than the events in heaven
> more concealed (*ḥ3p*) than the condition (*sḫrw*) of the underworld
> holier (*w3š*) than what is in the primeval one.[16]

It is expressed through the secrecy surrounding the ritual,[17] through the regulations for the initiation and purification of priests[18] and in temple architecture, the development of which down to the Late Period makes it clear how much importance was attributed to this aspect of the holy throughout Egyptian religious history. In the Late Period the temple sanctuary was surrounded by several "mantles", which screened it from the profane world outside.[19] To reveal the cult secrets would, in the eyes of the worshippers, unleash a cosmic catastrophe.[20]

The concepts used to describe the hiddenness of the holy are also used to express the obscurity of certain cosmic regions related to the terrestrial Here and Now in the same way as the holy is related to the profane: heaven and underworld. Unlike the hiddenness that is generally contained in the concept of the holy, the specific hiddenness of heaven and underworld is associated in a particular way with the gods who control these regions: Osiris and the sun god. The most profound secret is the midnight union of the two gods, presented as both a union of "ba"; and corpse (the texts refer to this "corpse" using the word *sšt3w* as if it were the essence of a holy mystery) and as a union of the two gods in a single united ba (*b3 dmḏw*).[21]

A third concept of hiddenness is associated with the "self-generated" primeval god, who has no parents. witnesses of his birth or colleagues that know his name. The "anonymity" of this god is certainly the oldest and most prominent characteristic of his hiddenness:[22] he appears in the PT as:

"the great god, whose name is not known."[23]

---

14 S. Morenz, *Ägyptische Religion* (1960), 105ff.; J.P. Hoffmeier, *Sacred in the Vocabulary of Ancient Egypt. The term ḏsr, with special Reference to Dynasties i-xx* (OBO 59) (Fribourg, 1985).

15 These constituent elements of the Egyptian concept of holiness have often been misunderstood and words like *ḏsr* and *špss* translated by terms such as "splendid", which in fact have the opposite meaning. That *špss* is associated with the idea of hiddenness is clear from passages such as *STG*, text 87, 10 about *Jmn-rn=f: sšpss sw r rmṯw nṯrw 3ḫw mwtw* "who has made himself *špss* with respect to humans, gods, the transfigured and dead".

16 *Urk* IV 99 cf. Mariette, *Abydos II*, 31; Hoffmeier, *Sacred*, 150.

17 P. Barguet, *Le Papyrus Louvre 3176*, 24 and n.9; *LL*, 19ff. and n.3, and passim.

18 References in Morenz, *Ägyptische Religion*, 106ff.

19 F. Daumas, in *Propyläen Kunstgeschichte* 15 (1975), 197.

20 *Urk*. VI, pp.122ff.; similarly Iamblichus, *De Mysteriis* VI.5 ed. des Places, 186. Cf. also P.Leiden I 347, V, 11-12: "who makes secret the cult images of the gods who are at their places" (unpublished, quoted by Zandee, *Amunshymnus*, 78.

21 Hornung, *Conceptions*, 93-96.

22 See the collection of pertinent passages in Zandee, *Amunshymnus*, 126-133. On *Jmn rn=f* see *STG* Texts 87(k) and 253(m), Zandee, 131-133.

23 PT 276c = *CT* VI 162 n-p; cf. also *CT* II 154d and 221e; IV 70b; II 157a (plural). For *št3 rn* cf. *CT* VI 389 i-k.

This concept of god appears perhaps in the earliest stages of Egyptian religion, certainly in the period of the New Kingdom that interests us here, in connection with the theology of the sun god. When the funerary texts, for example, speak of offerings on the altar of *Jmn rn* (hidden of name), the offerings of the sun god in Heliopolis are meant.[24] The well-known myth of the Cunning of Isis, which has survived in the form of a magical spell, lends this idea of the sun god as an "anonymous" primeval god the inconsistent and somewhat burlesque form typical of Egyptian stories.[25] This concept of an anonymous god, rooted in a beginning not witnessed by anyone, was taken over from solar theology by Amun-Re theology in the Ramesside period. One reason is undoubtedly the word-play possible in the name *Jmn/Jmn rn=f*. But the main reason was that this concept of hiddenness, unlike all the others, is by definition associated with the concept of oneness:

*šꜣꜥ ḫpr m zp tpj*
*Jmn ḫprw m ḥꜣt nn rḫ bs=f*
*nn ḫpr nṯr nb ḫr-ḥꜣt=f*
*nn kjj nṯr ḥnꜥ=f ḏd=f qj=f*
*nn wn mwt=f j-jrjj.n=s rn=f*
*nn jtj=f stj sw ḏdw jnk pw*
*nbjw swḥt=f ḏs=f*
*sḫm štꜣ mswt qmꜣ nfrw=f*
*nṯr nṯrj ḫpr ḏs=f*
*ḫpr.n nṯr nb ḏr šꜣꜥ=f sw*
*nn jtj=k j-jrj-tw*
*nn hꜣb.n=k m ḫt n ḥmt*
*nn Ḫnmw r qd...*
*bw rḫ.tw qj=k jnw (=k)*
*ḥꜣtjw ṯmḥjj r rḫ=k*
*wtn.tw pḏ.tw nnj.tw*
*ꜥꜣ-tw tnj-tw*
*ḏrj-tw wdn-tw m ḏrw=k*
*nḫt-tw pḥtj-tw*

The one who initiated the emergence at the beginning
Amun, who emerged at the beginning, whose origin is not known
who was not preceded by any god
There was no other god with him, who could say what he looked like
He had no mother who created his name[26]
He had no father to beget him or to say "He is my flesh and blood"[27]
Who formed his own egg
Power of secret birth, who created his beauty
most divine god, who came into being alone

---

VI 389 i-k.

24 P.Berlin 3050 VI 2-3: "Let Pharaoh receive the offerings in the Benben House on the altar of *Jmn-rn=f*".

25 Translation and references in Brunner-Traut, *Altägyptische Märchen* (Munich, 1976), 115-120.

26 Creation of the name through the mother: cf. Posener, *RdÉ* 22 (1970), 204f.

27 In these words the father recognizes himself in his child and knows the child as his child; cf. *LL*, 99 with n.41.

every god came into being after he had begun himself[28]
You have no father who created you[29]
You do not enter into the body of a woman
No Khnum formed...
Neither your form nor nature is known
hearts long[30] to know you
people pierce, stretch themselves and grow weary
you are (too) great and exalted
firm and wide-ranging
strong and powerful.[31]

The concept of a god "whose birth is secret",[32] "whose place of origin is not known",[33] of a god whose birth is not witnessed, but (and this is crucial) who keeps the secret of his nature concealed from all who are born after him: "who formed himself and kept himself hidden from gods and humans",[34] this concept of god became a central theme of Ramesside theology. Oneness and hiddenness of god do not, however, refer to the world before creation. There was no one in that pre-world from whom the god could have kept himself hidden. The concept of hiddenness means rather a relationship of god to the world, which came into being after and from him. He is alone as the hidden one who cannot be fathomed by gods or humans. He is hidden as the One Alone, whose birth was not witnessed. In the context of Amun-Re theology the idea of the hiddenness and oneness of the primeval god, which referred to the world before creation in the framework of solar theology, underwent a change of meaning. The temporal relationship of unity and multiplicity was transformed into an ontological one.[35] The one and the hidden one inhabits an ontological, but not a temporal Beyond. This concept of divine transcendence is most clearly expressed in Hymn 200 of the Leiden Amun Hymn.

28 P.Leiden J 350, IV, 9-11; Zandee, *Hymnen*, 71-75; *ÄHG* no.137.
29 Cf. P.Leiden I 344 vso. I.4: "who created his father, begot his mother", Zandee, *Amunshymnus*, 24-27.
30 See Ani IX, 3.
31 Černý-Gardiner, *Hieratic Ostraca*, pl.106.
32 *št3 mswt*: cf. P.Leiden J 350 IV 11; Zandee, *Hymnen*, 74; P.Berlin 3049 VI 7-8; *ÄHG* no.131, 10; *STG*, text 42a(i). On *ḏsr mswt* cf. P.Leiden J 344 I 1. ed. Zandee, 17-18; cf. also stela of Haremhab BM 551 = *ÄHG* no.58, 18-20.
33 *STG* Text 114, 11(c).
34 P.Strasbourg 7 v.2. On the self-creation of the primeval god see J. Zandee, *Hymnen*, 38-39
35 This does not exclude the possibility that the temporal relationship between unity and multiplicity is simply a metaphorical expression of the ontological one, in the sense of "temporizing of essence" (K. Burke); cf. "'Häresie'", *Saeculum* 23 (1972), 115ff., esp. notes 28 and 31. But I believe I can now see the historical development more clearly than was possible in earlier works. The term "hidden unity" IN (as distinct from BEFORE) the multiplicity belongs specifically to Ramesside Amun-Re theology.

## 3. Transcendence and Hidden Unity

### *3.1 Transcendence and Personification (according to P. Leiden J 350 IV,12-21)*

*štꜣ ẖprw ṯḥn jrw*
*nṯr bjꜣjjtj ꜥšꜣ ẖprw*
*nṯr nb ꜥb=sn jm=f*
*r sꜥꜣ-sn m nfrw=f mj nṯrj=f.*

*Rꜥw ḏs=f zmꜣw m ḏt=f*
*ntf pꜣ wr jmj Jwnw*
*jw ḏd.tw tꜣ-tn jr=f*
*Jmn prjw m Nnw sšm=f ḥrw.*

*kjj ẖprw=f m ẖmnw*
*pꜣwtj pꜣwtjw msjw Rꜥw*
*tm=f sw m Jtmw ḥꜥw wꜥ ḥnꜥ=f*
*ntf Nb-r-ḏr šꜣꜥ wnnt.*

*bꜣ=f pw ẖr.tw pꜣ ntj m ḥrt*
*ntf pꜣ ntj m dꜣt ẖntj jꜣbtt*
*bꜣ=f m pt ḏt=f m jmntt*
*ẖntj=f m Jwnw šmꜥw ḥr wṯz ḥꜥw=f.*

*wꜥ Jmn jmnw-sw jr=sn*
*sḥꜣpw-sw r nṯrw bw rẖ.tw jwn=f*
*wꜣjw-sw r ḥrt*
*mḏw-sw r dꜣt*

*bw rẖ nṯrw nbw qj=f mꜣꜥ*
*nn sšm=f prẖw ḥr zšw*
*nn mtr.tw jr=f ḏrjjwt*

*sw štꜣ r kfꜣ šfjjt=f*
*sw ꜥꜣ r nḏnḏ=f*
*wsr r rẖ=f*

*ẖr ḥr-ꜥ m mwt n ḥr-n-ḥr*
*n wḏ rn=f štꜣ ẖmw rẖw*
*nn nṯr rẖ njs sw jm=f*
*bꜣjj Jmn-rn=f mj štꜣ=f*

Secret of transformations and sparkling of appearances
marvellous god, rich in forms
All gods boast of him
to make themselves greater with his beauty to the extent of his divinity

Re himself is united with his body
He is the Great One in Heliopolis
He is called Tatenen

Amun, who comes out of the primeval waters to lead the "faces".

Another of his forms is the Ogdoad
primeval one of the primeval ones, begetter of Re
He completed himself as Atum, being of one body with him
He is Universal Lord, who initiated that which exists.

His ba, it is said, is the one who is in heaven
it is he, the one who is in the underworld, who rules the east
His ba is in heaven, his body in the west
his image is in the southern Heliopolis and wears his diadem.

One is Amun, who keeps himself concealed from them
who hides himself from the gods, no one knowing his nature
He is more remote than heaven
he is deeper than the underworld.

None of the gods knows his true form
his image is not unfolded in books
nothing certain is testified about him.

He is too secretive for his majesty to be revealed
he is too great to be enquired after
too powerful to be known.

People fall down immediately for fear
that his name will be uttered knowingly or unknowingly
There is no god able to call him by it
He is ba-like, hidden of name like his secrecy.[36]

The form of this magnificent hymn is comparable with that of a sonnet: its bipartite division into two unequal halves (8/8 and 7/7) is based on antithesis of thought, a change of aspect. The first part is a piece of "positive theology" and decribes how the god is personified on earth in the other gods: this personification is represented by

(a) the eight primeval gods (vv.9-10);

(b) the three gods of the "imperial triad",[37] viz. Re-Atum (4-5, 11-12), (Ptah)-Tatenen (7) and Amun (8, 16).

Their relationship to him is explained in relatively elaborate terminology: Re is *zm3w m ḏt=f* ("united with his *ḏt*-body"[38]), Atum is *ḥᶜw wᶜ ḥnᶜ=f* ("sharing one body with him"[39]), Tatenen and Amun "it is said to him", "he is (*ntf*) the Great One in Heliopolis" and "Lord of All" (both descriptions of Atum), the eight primeval gods of Hermopolis are his "other forms" (*kjj ḫprw*).[40] Finally, the theory of the three

36 Zandee, *Hymnen*, 75-86; *ÄHG* no.138.

37 On this concept cf. Hornung, *Conceptions of God*, 219-221.

38 Another interpretation is also possible: "(He is) Re himself, in that he is united with his (Re's) body", an allusion to the ancient Heliopolitan idea of the nocturnal union of the sun god with his underworld body (*STG*, text 158(n)), which also features in the Leiden Papyrus I 350 I.1, IV 15-16 and VI 12-13 (cf. J. Zandee, *Hymnen*, 3-4, 81 and 110).

39 On this formula cf. H. Brunner, *Die Geburt des Gottkönigs*, 65ff. and *LL*, 100 and n.47.

40 This concept derives from the cosmogonic "transformation theory"; cf. *Zeit und Ewigkeit*, 21-23 and

constituent elements of the divine person (ba, image and body) is put into the context of the earthly personified presence of the god.

The second part is a piece of "negative theology"[41] and reads like a revocation of all the theological scholarship displayed and developed in the first part. The subject of this first part was not the one, but the many gods who reflect his nature in the world. Amun of Thebes also belongs there. The "one Amun" is not only hidden "from them". He is hidden absolutely. No statement about him is possible. He is still beyond heaven and the underworld, the holy and otherworldly regions of the world. He is even hidden from the gods, who reflect his unfathomable nature in this remote sphere. He is even more hidden from humans. The scriptures give no information about him. He cannot be explained by any theory. The final stanza clearly expresses the concept of the Ineffable God and associates it with the two significant epithets "having the quality of ba" and "he who keeps his name hidden". This shows that they belong together. The god is called "ba", because there is no name for him. His hidden all-embracing abundance of essence cannot be apprehended. "Amun" is merely a pseudonym, used to refer to the god in that worldly, albeit other-worldly, sphere of personification. Basically, every divine name is a name of the hidden one, but the term "ba" is used when the hidden one behind the many personifications is meant.

In this theologically most mature statement the relationship between the one and the many is "de-temporalised". The one is not regarded as the primeval god before the many, whose unity becomes plurality in creation, but as the one in the many, a hidden power (*b3*), which assumes form (*ḫpr*) in the many gods and makes them into gods. Far from being a sort of "mana" or abstract principle, it is a personal nature that transcends questions and research or knowledge and speculation.

### *3.2 "Ba"*

#### *3.2.1 Instances where "ba" and "transformation" appear together*

| | |
|---|---|
| (1) *jnḏ ḥr b3 ḏsr ḫprw* | Hail to the ba, sacred of forms[42] |
| (2) *jnḏ ḥr=k b3 sṯn ḫprw* | Hail, ba, sublime of forms, |
| *jtn sšp ḥḏḏwt* | sun radiant with light[43] |
| (3) *b3 sṯn ḫprw jrjw wnnt* | Ba, sublime of forms, who made that which exists[44] |
| (4) *zr ꜥ3 ḫprw* | Ram, great of forms[45] |

notes 57, 58, and 60; *ÄHG* pp.67ff.; "Primat und Transzendenz", 30ff.

41 This classification is also used by E. Topitsch, *Gottwerdung und Revolution* (1973), 17ff., though the antithetical structure of the entire hymn is not taken into account; cf. *LÄ* II, 775 and n.185.

42 *ZÄS* 72, 101ff. no.24.

43 P.Berlin 3049, II = *ÄHG* no.127A, 1-2.

44 Sobek-Re P.Strasbourg IV 15 = *ÄHG* no.144C, 62.

45 Litany of sun no.26 ed.Hornung, *Das Buch der Anbetung des Re im Westen* (ÄH 2) (Geneva, 1975) I, 31.

These passages illustrate the original meaning of the lexeme *bꜣ*, explained by E. Wolf-Brinkmann as "capacity to assume forms"[46]. They designate an aspect of the complex ba-concept, which distinguishes the ba as the one (potential) power from the many (actual) transformations or forms. Ba is the power that "happens", materialises (*ḫpr*) in forms.

### *3.2.2 Instances where "ba", "hiddenness", "holiness", and "greatness" appear together*

| | |
|---|---|
| (5) *bꜣ štꜣ m-m nṯrw* | secret ba among the gods.[47] |
| (6) *bꜣ štꜣ jr.n=f šfjt* | secret ba, to whom respect is shown.[48] |
| (7) *bꜣ štꜣ wbnw m nnw* | secret ba, who rises from the primeval waters.[49] |
| (8) *bꜣ štꜣ šfj ḥꜣt* | secret ba with ram-headed face.[50] |
| (9) *bꜣ štꜣ ḥrw wr šfjt* | ba of secret faces, great of majesty.[51] |
| (10) *bꜣ špss wbnw m nnw* | illustrious ba who rises from the primeval waters.[52] |
| (11) *bꜣ špss ḫprw m ḥꜣt* | illustrious ba, who came into being at the beginning.[53] |
| (12) *bꜣ špss prjw m nnw/ pꜣwtj ḫprw m ḥꜣt* | illustrious ba, who comes from the primeval waters primeval one who came into being at the beginning.[54] |
| (13) *bꜣ špss jmj jtn=f* | illustrious ba who is in his disk.[55] |
| (14) *bꜣ špss jmj ꜣḫt=f* | illustrious ba who is in his horizon.[56] |
| (15) *bꜣ špss wbnw m ḥrt* | illustrious ba, who rises in heaven.[57] |
| (16) *bꜣ ꜥꜣ nṯrj wbnw m pt* | great divine ba, who rises in heaven.[58] |
| (17) *bꜣ wr sšp.n=f tꜣwj* | great ba, he has illuminated the Two Lands.[59] |
| (18) *bꜣ ḏsr mdt wtt nṯrw ꜥpr sw m jrw=f n rḫ.n.tw=f* | ba, of sacred words, who begat the gods who equipped himself with his forms. He cannot be known.[60] |
| (19) *bꜣ špss wbnw m hrt* | illustrious ba, who rises in heaven, |

46 E. Wolf-Brinkmann, *Versuch einer Deutung des Begriffes "bꜣ" anhand der Überlieferung der Frühzeit und des Alten Reiches* (Ph.D. thesis Basel, 1968). Cf. also W.A. Ward, *The Four Egyptian Homographic Roots Bꜣ*, (Studia Pohl 6) (1978), 67-88, who is more interested in the lexicographical than religious-historical understanding of the term. Rather curiously L.V. Zabkar in his *Study of the Ba Concept in Ancient Egyptian Texts* (1968) appears quite oblivious of the meaning which "*bꜣ*" acquired in Ramesside Amun-Re theology: he does not deal with the relevant passages at all.

47 Hibis 32, 32 = *ÄHG* no.129, 168.

48 Hibis 32, 2; P.Mag.Harris (s.bel.) = *ÄHG* no.129, 6.

49 P.Luynes; P.Chester Beatty VIII, 12.

50 Hibis 32, 31 = *ÄHG* no.129, 158.

51 OIP XXV pl.23 = *ÄHG* no.196, 13.

52 E. Naville, *The Temple of Deir el Bahari V*, 149.

53 Neschons 2 = *ÄHG* no.131, 3.

54 *STG*, text 95 cf. ch.4.

55 *STG*, text 242, 8(q).

56 G. Lefebvre, *Le tombeau de Petosiris* II, 33.3.

57 Turin 3070.

58 Sobek Re (P.Strasbourg 2+7, *ÄHG* No. 144A), III 2.

59 BM 1224.

60 BD 15 I; *ÄHG* no.24, 15-17.

| | |
|---|---|
| *[št3 ms]w ꜥš3 ḫprw* | [with secret birth] and many manifestations.[61] |
| (20) *b3 jmn št3 sw r jrt.n=f* | hidden ba, who conceals himself from his creation.[62] |

Compare these with the passages assembled by Sethe in *Amun* (§232). On the surface most passages seem to deal with the sun as a "visible manifestation", which is frequently cited in the eulogies as *b3 ꜥnḫ*.[63] It is noticeable, however, that the epithet *ꜥnḫ* is here missing. As Goedicke notes, ba is a bifocal term, which can designate both the hidden power and the visible manifestation.[64] Which of these aspects is meant has to be made clear through explanatory epithets. The epithet *ꜥnḫ* tends to explain the ba-concept as a visible manifestation, while epithets such as *št3, ḏsr, špss* tend to explain it as the hidden power. Likewise, ba in association with *ḫprw*, which alone refers to the visible manifestation of a power "become event", refers to the hidden side of the power concept. This concept becomes clearest in larger contexts.

### *3.2.3 "Ba" and the life god personified in the elements*

The hymn of Ramesses III to Amun-Re does not address the god by name, but begins as follows:

| | |
|---|---|
| *šꜣꜥ=j ḏd wr=k m nb nṯrw* | I will begin to say your greatness as lord of the gods |
| *m b3 št3 ḥrw wr šfjt* | as "ba" with secret faces, great of majesty |
| *jmn rn=f s[ḥ3p] sšm=f* | who hides his name and conceals his image |
| *n rḫ.tw qj=f m zp tpj* | whose form was not known at the beginning.[65] |

In the verses that follow, to be considered later in detail, the hymn develops the theory of the life-giving elements, in which the god materialises in the world. This text praises Amun as a cosmic god, whose body is the world. By praising this god as "ba" and not with his usual name, the hymn refers to god as the "ba" of the world, the "vital principle" of the cosmos, which gives life to the cosmos in the same way that the human ba gives life to the individual human being.

With the possibility of the aspect change inherent in the concept of ba, the expression also refers to the plurality of the cosmic manifestations and not only to the one life-giving principle in and behind them. Thus, his "ba's" are the life-giving elements and they can be experienced in the cosmos as the ways in which god works. By making use of this concept Ramesside Amun-Re theology refers not to a specific power, but to the concept of absolute power, responsible for absolutely all effects, whose visible manifestation is the entire cosmos.[66]

---

61 P. Vernus, *BIFAO* 75(1975), 29.

62 *Urk* VIII 18h.

63 Chapter 4 §1.2

64 H. Goedicke, *The Report about the Dispute of a Man with his Ba* (1970), 25; "Primat und Transzendenz", 35.

65 OIP XXV, pl.23 = *ÄHG* no.196, 12-15.

66 Cf. also the form of the "Bes pantheos", whose seven heads represent the "7 ba's of Amun-Re", in which the hidden world god is not only incarnate within the world but also as the world; cf. "Primat

The origins of this theology point back to the Middle Kingdom. In the "Book of Shu", Coffin Text spells 75-82, wind is thought to be the ba of the air god Shu, into which the deceased wishes to be transformed. In the Book of the Celestial Cow, that is to say in the time of Tutankhamun at the latest, there is an article of developed Ba theology:

| | |
|---|---|
| *B3 pw n Šw: ṯ3w* | The ba of Shu is air |
| *b3 pw n Nḥḥ: ḥwjt* | The ba of Neheh is rain |
| *b3 pw n Kkw: grḥ* | The ba of darkness is night |
| *b3 pw n Nnw: Rᶜw* | The ba of the primeval ocean is Re |
| *b3 pw n Wsjr: B3-nb-ḏdt* | The ba of Osiris is the Ram of Mendes |
| *b3 pw n Sbk: msḥw* | The ba of Sobek is crocodiles |
| *jw b3 n nṯr nb m ḥf3w* | The ba of every god is snakes |
| *jw b3 n ᶜpp m b3ḫw* | The ba of Apophis is (in) the eastern mountains |
| *jw b3 n Rᶜw ḫt t3 r ḏr=f* | The ba of Re is throughout the entire land.[67] |

The last equation refers to the omnipresence of light and is therefore a piece of the new solar theology (chapter 3 §4.4). The *Teaching of Ani* is similar: "he gives his power in millions of forms" (*sw dd b3w m ḥḥw nw ḫprw*)[16]. Ramesside Amun-Re theology built on these concepts from solar theology. But it went further, by regarding not only the light but also the totality of the energies that perform a life-giving function in the world as proofs of power, manifestations, ba's of Amun. This is clearly opposed to Amarna religion, where the concept "ba" does not occur and the corresponding category is *ḫprw*: the visible world is *ḫprw* of god, i.e. it proceeds from him, but is not itself divine.[69] Ramesside ba theology reaches its high point in the theory of the 10 ba's of Amun, developed in a tremendous hymn. Unfortunately, of the ten cantos, each one devoted to a ba, only the first three have been preserved. But an introductory hymn, in the form of a Morning Canto, names all ten of them, so that the system as such is recognisable.[70]

In the first five ba's we find once again those life-giving elements. The first pair of ba's are the sun and moon, which can also be explained as the right and left eye of the cosmic god. Then come the ba's of Shu and Osiris for air and water. The fifth ba is not that of Geb for earth, as one might expect, but that of Tefnut. The theological interpretation is given in the hymn. Sun and moon represent not light, but time, which appears here also as a cosmic life-giving energy. Light is attributed to the ba of Tefnut, the goddess of the flaming uraeus snake. The life-giving elements here are thus time, air, water and light. When they are represented, all five ba's wear the insignia of their cosmic manifestation on their head: sun, moon, sail, 3 water bowls (*nw*) and torch. Up to that point we find ourselves on known ground,

---

und Transzendenz", 12ff.

67 E. Hornung, *Der ägyptische Mythos von der Himmelskuh* (OBO 46) (Fribourg, 1982), 26f., 47.

68 P. Boulaq 4, VII, 15; A. Volten, *Studien zum Weisheitsbuch des Ani*, 111-112, 115; cf. *Saeculum* 23, 125 n.63.

69 Cf. *Saeculum* 23 (1972), 109-126 and "Akhanyati's Theology of Life ant Time".

70 J.C. Goyon, in R.A. Parker, J. Leclant, J.C. Goyon, *The Edifice of Taharqa* (Providence, 1979), 69-79; 40-41; pl.27. Cf. *ÄHG* no. 128; Barucq-Daumas, No.88; *TUAT* No.13, p.865-868. A parallel demotic text has been published by M. Smith, *Enchoria* 7 (1977), 115-149.

even if this Pentad is otherwise not attested.[71]

The second group of 5 ba's takes us into theologically new territory: they represent five classes of living creatures. This theology therefore distinguishes between cosmic and animal life.The five life-giving cosmic elements are paired with five classes of life-endowed animate creatures:human beings, quadrupeds, birds, creatures of the water and creatures of the earth, such as snakes, scarabs and the dead. The ba of human beings has human form and is called "royal ka"; the ba of quadrupeds is lion-headed and is called "ram of the rams"; the ba for birds has human form and is called Harakhty; the ba of aquatic creatures has a crocodile head and is called "ba of those in the water"; the ba of terrestrial creatures has the head of a snake and is called Nehebka. The system is illustrated in the following table:

First Pentad:

| Ba | "in his name" | function |
|---|---|---|
| Ba in the right eye | Re of every day | time |
| Ba in the left eye | full moon | time |
| Ba of Shu | remaining in all things | air, wind |
| Ba of Osiris | Eldest Nun | water |
| Ba of Tefnut | The one who awakes whole | light |

Second Pentad:

| symbol | class | "in his name" |
|---|---|---|
| human | human beings | royal-ka |
| lion | quadruped | falcon |
| falcon | bird | Harakhty |
| crocodile | aquatic animal | Ba of aquatic creatures |
| snake | terrestrial " | Nehebkau |

Perhaps the most puzzling feature of this theology is the place assigned to the king. The king belongs to the ten ba's; he is one of the ten worldly manifestations in

71 An illustration of the otherwise largely unpublished representation of the 10 ba's of Amun in the crypt of the Ptolemaic Opet Temple at Karnak may be found in: C. Traunecker, *Les dieux de l'Égypte*, (Que sais-je? 1191) (Paris, 1992), 97 fig. 8.

which the god gives life to, animates and organises the world; he is indeed the divine energy responsible for human beings. Not the king himself, of course, but the royal ka, i.e. the divine institutional principle of kingship, embodied in each king and identical with Horus.[72] Kingship is a cosmic energy, like light and air: in it is manifested the power of god that animates, takes care of and orders the human world.

This theology is not only given linguistic expression in a hymn, but is also translated into cult action in the form of a ritual. This ritual is known to us from the Taharqa building next to the Sacred Lake in Karnak, in which the wall reliefs are unfortunately very badly damaged, and from the Opet Temple in Karnak, in whose crypts a well-preserved variant has been discovered by C.Traunecker.[73] The fact that the cult was performed in a crypt indicates that it was a secret cult. The hymn too is surrounded by indications of secrecy. In the Hibis temple version it bears the title: "Book of the Secrets of Amun Written Down on Boards of *Nbs*-Wood".[74] We find ourselves here on the threshold of Hermetism and the Greco-Egyptian magical papyri, which to some extent develop a similarly complex theo-cosmology.[75]

### *3.2.4 Ba and the All-One*

Section G of the Harris Magical Papyrus contains a short version of one of the most important Amun-Re hymns. Thus, the hymn can be dated to the 19th dynasty, though the earliest surviving complete version occurs in the Hibis temple from the Persian Period. The short version is as follows:

*jnḏ ḥr=k wꜥ jrjw-sw m ḥḥw*
*ꜣwj=f wsḫ=f nn drw=f*
*sḫm spd msjw sw ḏs=f*
*jꜥrrt ꜥꜣt nbj*
*wrt ḥkꜣw štꜣ jrw*
*bꜣ štꜣ jrjj.n=f šfjjt*

*njswt-bjt (Jmn-Rꜥw) -ꜥ.w.s- ḫprw ḏs=f*
*ꜣḫtj Ḥrw jꜣbtj*
*wbnjj sḥḏw sšp*
*jꜣḫw ꜣḫ r nṯrw*

*jmn.n=k tw m Jmn wr*
*jtn=k m ḫprw=k n jtn*

---

72 A similar concept of kingship as an intramundane manifestation of god's creative and preserving power is expounded in P.Leiden I 344 vso. IX.9, Zandee, *Amunshymnus*, pp.873-76; XI.1-2, Zandee, ibd., pp. 995f. where the king is called the "Ka" of God.

73 Mentioned by J.C. Goyon, *Edifice*, 69ff.

74 N. de Garis Davies, *The Temple of Hibis in el-Khargah Oasis III: The Decoration*, (MMA Eg.Exp. 17) (New York, 1953), pl. 31 (the transl.in *ÄHG* no.128, 1-2 must be corrected accordingly).

75 Cf. esp. R. Merkelbach, M. Totti (eds.), *Abrasax. Ausgewählte Papyri religiösen und magischen Inhalts*, (Abh.d.Rheinisch-Westf. Ak.d.Wiss., Sonderreihe Papyrologia Coloniensia. XVII-) (Opladen, 1990-) see under "Gebete".

*ṯ3-tnn sṯnj sw r nṯrw*
*j3w rnpj zbbw nḥḥ*
*Jmn mn jẖt nbt*
*nṯr pn š3ᶜ t3 m sẖrw=f*

Hail, one who makes himself into millions
  whose length and breadth are limitless[76]
power in readiness, who gave birth to himself
  uraeus with great flame
great of magic with secret form
  secret ba, to whom respect is shown

King Amun-Re (l.p.h.), who came into being himself
  Akhty, Horus of the east
the rising one whose radiance illuminates
  the light that is more luminous than the gods

You have hidden yourself as Amun the great
you have withdrawn in your transformation as the sun disk[77]
Tatenen, who raises himself above the gods

The Old Man forever young, travelling through *nḥḥ*
Amun, who remains in possession of all things
this god who established the earth by his providence.

The tripartite text (6/4/6) deals in the last stanza with the well known tripartite form of the god as "imperial triad", not in the form of his worldly manifestation, but in a threefold form of his hiddenness, which is revealed by the word play in the three divine names Amun, Aten and Tatenen. As Amun he has "hidden himself" (*jmn*); as the sun disk he has removed himself (*jtn*);[78] as Tatenen he has elevated himself above the gods (*ṯnj*). As the sun he is the god of time, periodically alternating within endless time as an old man and a youth; as Amun he is the breath of life "ever present in all things"; as Tatenen he is the creator, who has arranged the world according to his "design".

The middle stanza of four lines combines the aspects of "ruler god" and "sun". The divine name Amun-Re receives not only the royal title *njswt-bjt*, but is even written in a cartouche. These cartouches, attested in the New Kingdom and very common in the Late Period,[79] occur not only for Amun-Re,[80] but also for Osiris,[81]

76 On the concept of the "limitlessness" of god cf. *sdg3 sw jwtj jn ḏrw=f* "who concealed himself, whose limits cannot be attained" vso ii, 8-9, Zandee, *Amunshymnus*, 120-126 (on *nn ḏrw=f*: p.125). Cf. P.Berlin 3049, 16, 6 and *Urk* VIII, 116: *nn ḏrw ḥpt=f* "whose circuit has no limits".

77 This is one of the very few instances where the sun in other than Amarna texts is called *ḫprw* of the god (cf. ch. 3 n.7) and doubtless refers to the concept of the divine "transformations" in which the sun forms the last stage of the cosmogonical and transformational process of the primeval god.

78 Cf. Neschons = *ÄHG* no.131, 86; the verb jtn is also attested elsewhere in Ramesside hymns, apart from word-play with *jtn* "sun"; cf. P.Berlin 3049 IV 1 = *ÄHG* no.127A, 63-64: *Imn Rᶜw jrjj pt n b3=f sḥḏw t3wj/ jtn=f sw m hrt n ḏt*; cf. also Sobek Re (P.Strasbourg 2+7, *ÄHG* No. 144A), III, 22-23.

79 Cf. Zandee, *Amunshymnus*, 594-602.

80 Neschons 39.

81 Earliest example dates from the 13th Dynasty (Sethe, *Lesestücke*, 63, 22); J. Leclant, *Recherches*

Ptah[82] and Re,[83] as well as, of course, for the god of Amarna.[84] In Amarna the royal title of the god refers not to the idea of mythical primeval kingship,[85] but to a current theocratic concept of rule,[86] just as *mutatis mutandis* in the Theban theocracy of the 21st dynasty.[87] But one should not categorise the other passages too quickly as "mythological". Here too the theocratic idea of rule embodied in a "national god" and exercised by the earthly king acting only as a representative is meant. In Ramesside theology rule by the king belongs to the aspects of the divine nature and must not be reduced either to a mythical primeval kingship or to a purely divine kingship. The earthly king is a manifestation of the divine nature in the world.[88] His counterpart in heaven is the sun.

The first stanza deals with the aspect of the god that is of particular interest to us: the aspect of the hidden nameless power, for neither the divine name Amun (-Re) nor the description *nṯr* (usually translated as "god") appear sufficient. This accounts for the use of paraphrases such as "power-bearer" (*sẖm*), "uraeus" (*jꜥrt*), "great of magical power" (*wr ḥkꜣw*) and, finally, what has to be regarded as the *nomen ipsum* of this concept of god *bꜣ štꜣ* "hidden ba". This stanza is quite different from the second one, which not only names the hidden god, but also emphasises this name with cartouche and titles. There can scarcely be a clearer expression of the fact that the name too is only an aspect of the god, which he uses when he exercises rule over the world. As a nameless and secret ba the god is unlimited and omnipresent. The forms in which his power manifests itself are the million-fold Totality.

---

*sur les monuments thébains de l'Époque dite Éthiopienne* (1965), 199 n.1; J. Bergman, *Ich bin Isis* (1968), 76 n.1.

82 Bergman, *Isis*, 71ff.

83 P.Cairo 58038 II 2; C. Maystre, "Vache du Ciel", *BIFAO* 40 (1940), 70 and 72; E. Hornung, *Himmelskuh*, 7-8; G. Fecht, *ZÄS* 85 (1960), 102; Bergman, *Isis*, 76; For a summary of mythical primeval kingship of the gods cf. U. Luft in *Studia Aegyptiaca* IV, 78-154.

84 *LÄ* I, 526ff.

85 G. Fecht, *ZÄS* 85 (1960), 101ff.

86 *JNES* 31 (1962), 151ff.

87 The standard text for the contemporary version of divine kingship is the Decree for Neskhons (*ÄHG* no.131), esp. 95-100. For a summary see Hornung, *Conceptions*, 140ff.

88 Cf. P.Leiden I 344 vso ix, 9-x, 1 where the idea of god's presence in the king is developed in the most explicit form:

| | |
|---|---|
| *zmꜣ=k nst=k nt ꜥnẖw* | you unite yourself with your throne of the living |
| *sḥtp kꜣ=k jmj dbꜣt* | your ka, which is in the palace, is pacified |
| *ꜣw n=k nfrw=k* | your beauty is extended for you(?) |
| *tmw m šmsw=k* | all are in your following |
| *hnw=sn r-gs ṯbwtj=kj* | they rejoice beside your sandals |
| *ḏt=k pw jmj jb n njswt* | your body is what is in the heart of the king |
| *dd=f bꜣw=f r ẖftjw=k* | he proves his power against his enemies. |
| *ḥms=k ḥr-tp rꜣ n bjtj* | You sit on top of the mouth of the King of Lower Egypt |
| *mdw=f ẖft wḏ.n=k* | he speaks according to what you have ordered. |
| *ẖm=k sptj nb ꜥnẖ wḏꜣ snb* | your chapel are the lips of the lord (l.p.h.) |
| *ḥm=k ꜥnẖ wḏꜣ snb m-ẖnw=f* | your Majesty (l.p.h) is inside him. |

## *3.3 One and All*

### *3.3.1 Ramesside texts*

| | |
|---|---|
| (1) *Wnn-nfr pꜣ nb r nḥḥ nb ḏt* | Wannafre, you lord of eternity and everlastingness |
| *pꜣ nṯr wꜥ jrjw sw m ḥḥw* | you One god who made himself into millions.[89] |
| (2) *ḫprw wꜥw msjw sw m ḥḥw* | Who came into being alone and gave birth to himself as millions.[90] |
| (3-5) *nṯr wꜥ jrjw sw m ḥḥw* | One god who made himself into millions.[91] |
| (6) *ḫprr ḫpr m ḥḥw* | Khepre who emerged as millions.[92] |
| (7) *jnḏ-ḥr=k bsw sw m wꜥ* | Hail to you, who brought himself forth as one |
| *qmꜣ.n=f ḥḥw mj ꜥšꜣ=sn* | and who created millions in their abundance.[93] |
| (8) *wꜥ wꜥw ḏt=f ḥḥw* | The One Alone, whose body are millions.[94] |
| (9) *jjw m nṯr wꜥ [jrjw sw m] ḥḥw* | Who came as One god[95] and [made himself into][96] millions.[97] |
| (10) *jnḏ-ḥr=k nṯr wꜥ jrjw sw m ḥḥw* | Hail to you, One god who made himself into millions |
| *ꜣwj=f wsḫ=f nn ḏrw=f* | whose length and breadth are without limits.[98] |
| (11) *wꜥ jr.n=f sw m ḥḥw* | The One who made himself into millions.[99] |
| (12) *jw=f wꜥ jrj=f sw m ḥḥw* | Who being one makes himself into million.[100] |

### *3.3.2 Late Period texts (selection).*

| | |
|---|---|
| (13) *jjw m wꜥ ṯnj=f sw m ḥḥw* | Who came as One and distinguished himself as millions.[101] |
| (14) *wꜥ jrjw ḥḥw* | The One who made millions.[102] |
| (15) *ntk šꜣꜥ ḫpr m wꜥ jrjw ḥḥw* | You started becoming as the One who made millions[103] |
| *pr ḥfn m nṯrtj=fj* | hundreds of thousands came forth from his two divine eyes. |
| (16) *wꜥ pfj jr.n=f sw m ḥḥw* | that One who made himself into millions.[104] |
| (17) *sw m nṯr wꜥ qmꜣ ḥḥw ḥfnw* | he is the One god who created millions and |

89 TT 51 ed. Davies, pl.IX.

90 *STG* Text No. 149.

91 *STG* Text No. 148; STG, text no. 43 (TT 34, Saite period but using a Ramesside model); Neschons, var. = *ÄHG* no.131, 7.

92 *STG* Text No.42a (TT 34).

93 P.Louvre 3292 = *ÄHG* no. 47, 1-2.

94 P.Leiden I 344 vso iii, 3, Zandee, *Amunshymnus*, 168-176.

95 Cf. no. 20.

96 The completion follows Zandee, *Hymnen*, 76 with n.1.

97 P.Berlin 3049, ii, 3 = *ÄHG* Nr.127A, 5-6.

98 P.Mag.Harris iv, 1-2 = *Hibis* 32, 1.

99 *Hibis* 31 B 2-3 = *ÄHG* Nr.128; *Taharqa* pl. 28 ed. Goyon, in R. Parker *et alii*, *The edifice of Taharqa*, 74 with n.12.

100 Černý, *Grafitti*, 17 no. 1285a, 1.2.

101 *Urk* VIII, 1 § 3b.

102 *Urk* VIII, § 68b, cf. 138b: *wꜥ ḥḥ ḥḥw rn=f* "The One, million of millions are his name".

103 Medamud Nr. 249, 7; cf.E. Drioton, *Medamoud* (1925), 109.

104 *Edfou* III, 34

| | |
|---|---|
| | hundreds of thousands.[105] |
| (18) *nḫb wr jtj jtjw msjw sw ḏs=f* | Big Lotus, father of fathers who created himself |
| *wbnw m wʿw sḫpr.n=f ḥḥw* | who rose as one and brought forth millions.[106] |
| (19) *nṯr wʿ jrjw ḥḥw* | One god who made millions |
| *ꜣw=f wsḫ=f nn ḏrw=f* | whose length and breadth are without limits |
| *šꜣʿ ḫpr nn wp ḥr=f* | who initiated becoming, there being none besides him |
| *ḫpr nṯr nb ḥr sꜣ=f* | every god came into being after him.[107] |
| (20) *njswt-bjt jrji sw m ḥḥw* | king who made himself into millions |
| *jtj jtjw mwt mwwt* | father of fathers, mother of mothers.[108] |
| (21) *jjw m wʿw jrj sw m ḥḥw* | Who came as one and made himself into millions.[109] |
| (22) *jrjw sw m ḥḥw nṯrw* | Who made himself into millions of gods |
| *qmꜣw m ḥʿw=f* | created as/from his body.[110] |
| (23) *nṯr wʿ jrj sw m ḥḥw nb* | One god who made himself into all millions |
| *jrj wnnt m rꜣ-ʿwj=fj* | who created what exists with the work of his hands |
| *pꜣwtj šꜣʿ ḫpr* | the primeval one who initiated becoming |
| *ṯz spꜣwt m sḫrw=f* | who organized the nomes with his plans.[111] |
| (24) *wꜣw m ḥrw tkn m msḏr* | distant of face but close of ear (= in listening).[112] |
| *m wʿ ḥḥw nn rḫ jnm=f* | as One-and-Millions, whose nature nobody knows.[113] |
| (25) *wbn m wʿ sḫpr.n=f ḥḥw* | who rises as one, he brought forth millions.[114] |
| (26) *wbn=f m wʿ qmꜣ.n=f ḥḥw* | he rises as one and has brought forth millions.[115] |
| (25) *una quae es omnia* | one who are all things.[116] |

### *3.3.3 The meaning of the formula*

All New Kingdom passages of this much discussed[117] formula come from Thebes and refer, with the exception of no.1, to Amun-Re.[118] This too shows that we are

105 *Edfou* V, 80.

106 *Edfou* III, 60; sim. VI, 348, 7ff. Cf. also *Edfou* V, 156.1; VI, 101.3; VI, 348, 9.

107 *Philae* II, 49, 27-30.

108 *Philae* II, 29.8.

109 *Philae* 2924 (Osiris), cf. (8), (12).

110 *Philae* 885 WbZ 1208.

111 Esna no. 387, 3-4; cf.S. Sauneron, *Esna* III, 386; V, 220.

112 cf. infra, p.

113 Esna Nr. 387, 5-6 ed. Sauneron, *Esna* III, 368; *Esna* V, 221.

114 *Edfou* V, 156.1, quoted after Zandee, *Amunshymnus,* 171.

115 *Edfou* VI, 348.8-9, after Zandee, *Amunshymnus*, 171.

116 According to Junge, in W. Westendorf (ed.), *Aspekte der spätägyptischen Religion*, 102. References of corresponding formulas in the *Corpus Hermeticum* in *Zeit und Ewigkeit*, 31 notes 93-94 and "Primat und Transzendenz", 38.

117 Sethe, *Amun* § 200; Otto, in *Forschungen und Fortschritte* 35 (1961), 278 and *Gott und Mensch*, 106; Hornung, *Conceptions*, 164; J. Zandee, *JEOL* 18 (1964), 255; *Saeculum* 23 (1970), 125; "Primat und Transzendenz", 30; Zandee, *Amunshymnus*, 168-176; M. Bilolo, *L'Un, devient-il multiple? Approche pragmatique des formules relatives à "l'Un «comme multiple»" ou à l'"auto-différenciation" de l'Un dans les hymnes thébains du Nouvel Empire*, (Habil.Schr) (Zürich 1992).

118 In the case of Osiris only the "millions" of dead must be meant, who have become "Osiris" = have "emerged" from him (*ḫpr m*). The god of the dead refers to the millions of dead in the same way that the life god refers to the millions of living creatures.

dealing here with a piece of Ramesside Amun-Re theology and have to interpret it in the context of this theology. The formula has a "canonical form", as in nos. 1,3,4,5,11 and 22:

| | |
|---|---|
| *nṯr wᶜ jrjw sw m ḥḥw* | the One God who made himself into millions |

The other passages are variants of this basic form. The problems presented by the interpretation of this formula can be summarised as follows:

(a) *nṯr wᶜ*: does the predication of "oneness" refer to the "aloneness" of the primeval god before creation or to the all-oneness of god in creation?

(b) *jrjw sw*: does it refer to the creation at the beginning or to the continuous stream of the all from the one?

(c) *ḥḥw*: does this refer to the millions of gods or the totality of living creation or a concept of everything (Greek πᾶν / Latin *omnia*)?[119]

Hornung has interpreted it in a temporal sense. He regards "oneness" as the condition of the god before creation. He regards the verbs describing the creation (1,3,4,8,9-12,14-16,19-42 cf. 2,7,17-18) or emergence (6) of the many from the one as a description of primeval creation. He regards the "millions" as the polytheistic divine world that represents existing reality.[120] By and large, these views are supported by the texts, almost all of which refer to creation. Occasionally, the temporal relationship between oneness and allness is also expressly emphasised by the additional statement that all gods emerged after the one. It is not therefore a matter of disputing Hornung's interpretation, but of asking whether the formula, apart from its undeniable reference to creation (which, as such, introduces nothing new in Egyptian religious history), aims at a concept of god like that expressed by the Latin formula *una quae es omnia*. Passages such as nos.8 and 24 clearly point to this. But even passage no.11, the starting point of this analysis, cannot be reduced to pure creation theology. In §3.2.4 I tried to prove that the corresponding stanza of this hymn dealt with the concept of a god as a "hidden power" (*bꜣ štꜣ*) and the source of the million-fold plurality in which he unfolds and extends into the "boundless".[121] This boundlessness is not predicated of the world, but of the god to whom the hymn

119 *ḥḥw* clearly means "millions" and not, as Sethe suggested, the "all-pervasive air" personifed in the god Hah (§201). The god Hah does not occur in this connection until the Ptolemaic period (cf. É. Drioton, *ASAE* 44 (1944), 127(c)).

120 *Conceptions*, 170: " 'Millions', enormous and unfathomable but not infinite multiplicity, are the reality of the world of creation, of all that exists." Is it really legitmate to speak of *ḥḥw* as if it were something finite ? It obviously does not mean a finite number (i.e. a million as distinct from a million and one), but rather incalculable abundance. It should also be borne in mind that the idea of infinity, expressed in *ḥḥw*, is a category of chaos, just like the concept of "undifferentiated unity". When the cosmogonic concept of differentiation is meant, the phrase "one who becomes three" is used, not "one who becomes millions" (*CT* II 39; cf. Otto, *Saeculum* 14, 267 and 274.) Cf. also the text on the coffin Cairo CG 6234: "I am the one, who became two/I am the two who became four/I am the four who became eight"; cf. Maspero, in *Receuil de Travaux* 23 (1901), 196-197.

121 Cf. Leiden Stela V 70 = *ÄHG* no.90, where the sun god is addressed as *ḥḥw pwjj nn rḫ.tw ḏrw=f/ḫprr nn rḫ.tw ḏt=f* "that *ḥḥw* whose limits are not known, scarab whose body is not known". The text derives from the period very close to that of Amarna and thus belongs to the "new solar theology". It probably means the "boundless" omnipresence of the light, in the sense meant in Chapter 3 §2.4.

is addressed. Accordingly, god is the million into which he has created and transformed himself: *unus qui est omnia*. "Million" is his *ḏt*-body,[122] his *ḥᶜw*-body[123], his *ḫprw*-transformation-manifestation[124] and even his name: *ḥḥ n ḥḥw pw rn=f* "'million of millions' is his name".[125] By transforming himself into the million-fold reality, god has not ceased to be one. He is the many in that mysterious way, hidden and present at the same time, which this theology is trying to grasp by means of the ba-concept. A common text even goes so far as to describe god as the ba of gods and humans, i.e. "the millions":[126]

| | |
|---|---|
| *wᶜ wᶜw qmꜣw wnnt* | The One Alone who created what is |
| *bꜣ špss nw nṯrw rmṯw.*[127] | the illustrious Ba of gods and humans |

By linking the ba concept and the theology of the hidden, it becomes clear in what respect this formula goes beyond the traditional creation theology of the opposition between unity and plurality. There are already antitheses in the earlier Theban texts that seem to prefigure the Ramesside one/all-formula "*wᶜ ḥḥw*". For example, P. Cairo 58038 in two places contrasts the one "solitary" creator and life god (*wᶜ wᶜw*) of everything with the world created and sustained by him:

| | | |
|---|---|---|
| VI,2-3 | *twt wᶜ /jrjw ntj nb* | You are the One who created what exists |
| | *wᶜ wᶜw /jrjw wnnt* | the One Alone who created what is.[128] |
| VI,7 | *jnḏ ḥr=k /jrjw nn r-ꜣw* | Hail to you, who created all this |
| | *wᶜ wᶜw / ᶜšꜣ ᶜwj=fj*[129] | the One Alone with many arms |

In the context of this hymn, the concept of "all that is" *ntj nb/wnnt nbt* is then explained as the totality of living creation, from gods and humans to worms, fleas and mice. A passage attested in several early Theban texts is even closer to our formula:[130]

| | |
|---|---|
| *nb ḥḥw jwtj snnw=f* | lord of millions without his equal |

122 P.Leiden I 344 vso. III, 2-3.

123 *Edfou* III, 34.9-10.

124 *ḫprw=f m ḥḥw*: stela of Ramesses III, Kitchen, *RI* VI, 452.8.

125 *Urk* VIII §138b. Of Yahweh, on the contrary, it is said: "'One' is his name" (Zach. 14, 9), cf. C.H. Gordon, "His Name is 'One'", in: *JNES* 29 (1970), 198-99.

126 On this meaning of *ḥḥw* cf. *STG* Text 149(c).

127 Hymn to the primeval god in the "Livre que mon fleurisse" in P.Berlin 3030 VIII-IX; P.Louvre 3336 I 1-16; P.Brussels published by Speelers, *Recueil des Travaux* 39 (1917), 28ff.

128 Id.: Neschons 2-4, *ÄHG* 131, 5-10; on *wᶜ wᶜw* as predicate of the creator god cf. Zandee, *Amunshymnus*, 173-176.

129 This opposition of unity and diversity, in form of the one god with many arms, has been recognised as a verbal anticipation of the iconic type of the "radiant Aten", cf. Hornung, *ZÄS* 97(1971). The common background is provided by the concept of life-god. Also in the P. Cairo 58038 we are therefore dealing with the opposition of singleness (as sun) and multiplicity of immanent life-giving manifestations.

130 *STG* Text 130 = *STG*, text 176. The chiastic structure of this couplet reveals the following scheme (a = multiplicity/b = unity):

| | |
|---|---|
| a | b |
| a' | b' |

| | |
|---|---|
| *wᶜw jrjw ntt qmꜣ wnnt* | One, who created what is and made what exists |

Not only is the conceptual pairing *wᶜ/ḥḥw* used, but the description of god as "lord of millions" goes beyond pure creation theology.

The antithesis betwen *wᶜ* and *ḥḥw* also occurs in the two most important hymns of Amarna religion. The Great Hymn contrasts the one with the million-fold forms of the phenomenal world of nature that has been produced by his light:[131]

*jrjj=k ḥḥw n ḫprw jm=k wᶜw*
*njwwt dmjw*
*ꜣḥwt mtn jtrw*

You create millions of forms from yourself, the one,
cities and towns
fields, paths and river.

This concept of a world made habitable by light and arranged into a cosmos is never described, outside Amarna, by the expression "millions". But the passage in the Small Hymn is much closer to the usual understanding of this expression:[132]

*jrjj=k pt wꜣ.tj r wbn jm=s*
*r mꜣꜣ jrt.n=k jw=k wᶜ.tj*
*jw ḥḥw n ᶜnḫ jm=k r sᶜnḫ sn*

You made heaven remote to rise in it
to see all that you created, you being alone
but there being millions of lives in you (for you) to make them live.

Both passages deal not with the passages at the beginning and self-development of a pre-existent one into the million-fold reality of the present state, but with the present relationship of the god to the world, which proceeds from the one as million-fold reality in a continuous process.

Neither in Amarna religion nor in the passages of the earlier Theban Amun-Re eulogies cited is the antithesis between unity and multiplicity (or better, all-oneness) linked with the concepts of the hidden, the mysterious or the unfathomable or even with the concept of the ba. Theban Amun-Re theology of the pre-Amarna period seems to have succeeded in uniting this antithesis (which was not expressed as pure creation theology, but as the relationship of the life god to the created world to which he has given life) with polytheism in the hierarchical sense, where the one has precedence over the many. Amarna religion perceives the relationship between god and the world as the visible contrast between the sun and the earth: the earth, being the world of creation to which life has been given, comes forth new every day from the one source of life.

The unity of god becomes a problem only when it has to be made to harmonise with the idea (realised in polytheism) of the divinity of the world, without being reduced to the before/after solution of creation theology. That is the situation of

131 Sandman, *Texts from the Time of Akhenaten*, 95, 12-13. On this passage cf. G. Fecht, *ZÄS* 94 (1967), 33; *STG* Text 54 (x).

132 Sandman, *Texts*, 15, 1-9; cf. *STG* Text 253(s).

the Ramesside period. The unity of god is realised as neither pre-existence nor monotheism, but as transcendence, as a "hidden unity", in which all living plurality on earth has its origin and whose inscrutable nature can be experienced and stated only in "colourful reflection" of the polytheistic divine world.

The predication "the One who made himself into a million" means that the god, by creating the world, transformed himself into the totality of divine forces which are operative in the creation and maintenance of the world and that all the gods are comprised in the One. It is more than probable that the corresponding predication of Isis as "the one who is all" translates and continues this form of predication. She is called *una quae es omnia*[133] or μούνη εἶ σὺ ἅπασαι[134] meaning that in her divine being all the other goddesses are absorbed or united. She is also called *myrionyma* "with innumerable names", which means that all divine names are hers and that all other deities are merely aspects of her all-encompassing nature. This idea occurs also in the *Corpus Hermeticum*: all names are those of one god.[135] The famous proclamation "One-and-All" ( ἓν καὶ πᾶν, ἓν τὸ πᾶν and so on), the *Credo* of Hermetism, has the same origin as the Isis formula *una quae es omnia*.[136] Alchemistic and Hermetic manuscripts transmit this motto through the Middle Ages into the pantheist revival in the 18th century.[137]

133 Ex voto inscription from Capua, 1st or 2nd cent. AD, *Corpus Inscriptionum Latinarum* X 3800 : *Te tibi una quae es omnia dea Isis*. F. Dunand, "Le syncretisme isiaque", in F. Dunand and P. Levêque (ed.), *Les syncrétismes dans les religions grecque et romaine*, (Colloque de Strasbourg, Bibliothèque des Centres d'Études supérieures spécialisés), (Paris 1973), 82 n.1. L. Vidman, *Sylloge inscriptionum religionis Isiacae et Sarapidae* (Berlin, 1969), No. 502. V. Tran Tam Tinh, *Le culte des divinités orientaux en Campanie* (Leiden, 1972), 41ff.; 77; 199-234.

134 Hymn of Isidorus from Medinet Madi cf. Vera F. Vanderlip, *The Four Greek Hymns of Isidorus and the Cult of Isis*, (American Studies in Papyrology XII) (Toronto, 1972), 18f.; E. Bernand, *Inscriptions métriques de l'Égypte gréco-romaine*, Paris 1969, Nr. 175, 632ff.; M.Totti, *Ausgewählte Texte der Isis-Serapis Religion*, (Subsidia Epigrapha XII) (Opladen, 1985), 76-82; F. Dunand, "Le syncrétisme isiaque", 79-93. On Isidorus cf. Drijvers, *Vox Theologica* 32, 1962, 139-50.

135 C.H. IV.10, Nock-Festugière I, 64; Asclepius §20 = II, 321.

136 ἓν καὶ τὸ πᾶν as a Hermetic device: Festugière, *C.H.* II, 234ff. n.8. As an alchemistic device cf. Festugière, *Alchimistes grecs* I 84, 13. Cf. J. Assmann, *Zeit und Ewigkeit im Alten Ägypten* (Heidelberg, 1975), 31 n.94; id., "Primat und Transzendenz. Struktur und Genese der ägyptischen Vorstellung eines 'Höchsten Wesens'", in W. Westendorf (ed.), *Aspekte der spätägyptischen Religion* (Wiesbaden, 1979), 38; *Monotheismus und Kosmotheismus*, 18f.

137 T. McFarland, *Coleridge and the Pantheist Tradition* (Oxford, 1969).

# CHAPTER SIX

# COSMIC GOD AND SAVIOUR. THEBAN AMUN-RE THEOLOGY OF THE RAMESSIDE PERIOD II

## 1. Creation

### *1.1 Creation theology as "natural philosophy"*

Creation theology is primarily "natural philosophy", i.e. it formulates not so much theological knowledge as cosmological, biological and anthropological knowledge.[1] The great and, as it were, genuine creation theologies of Egyptian religious history express a cosmology rather than a concept of god. The spiritual situation of the Ramesside period is characterised by the juxtaposition of different cosmologies (=creation theologies) that do not so much compete with each other as tell pretty much the same truth. Their relationship to one another is best described by the modern concept of complementarity.[2] This is not the place to review these creation accounts in detail.[3] On the other hand, in order to understand the eclecticism of the Theban texts, we have to take a brief look at the spiritual home of the ideas brought together in those texts.

#### *1.1.1 Heliopolis*

The earliest creation mythology, which influenced all later ones, is that of Heliopolis. Its distinctive characteristic is the strict "biomorphic" view of the cosmogonic processes.[4] The central concepts of this mythology are *ḫpr* and *ḫprw*, which means "arise from/become" and "embodiment/emanation" respectively. It

1 R. Hönigswald, *Vom erkenntnistheoretischen Gehalt alter Schöpfungserzählungen* (1957); G. von Rad, "Hiob 38 und die altorientalische Weisheit", Supplement to *Vetus Testamentum* 3 (1955), 293-301; on the concept of natural philosophy ("Naturlehre") cf. S.Morenz, *WKZM* 54 (1957), 119ff.

2 Hornung, *Conceptions*, 237-24. Unlike Hornung I do not understand the relationship between divine unity and multiplicity as juxtaposing polytheism and "henotheism" in the sense of complementarity. I think that the Egyptians attempted to integrate these poles into a dialectical relationship rather than simply leave them to exist "side by side". On the concept of complementarity cf. U. Berner, *GM* 20 (1976), 59-71.

3 S. Sauneron and J. Yoyotte, "La naissance du monde selon l'Egypte ancienne" in *Sources Orientales* I (1959), 17-91; S. Morenz, *Ägyptische Religion*, 167-191; S.G.F. Brandon, *Creation Legends of the Ancient Near East* (1963) Chapter 2.; J.P. Allen, *Genesis in Egypt. The Philosophy of Ancient Egyptian Creation Accounts*, (YES 2) (1988); *LÄ* V s.v. Schöpfung.

4 On the terminology and criteria used to distinguish "bio-" and "technomorphic" models of world creation cf. E. Topitsch, *Gottwerdung und Revolution*, 39ff.

thinks of the world as a sort of emanation of god.[5] Typical of this thought are the metaphors of "secretion": the first gods were spat and coughed out, while men arose from the tears of god.[6] Even when the "issuing from the mouth" is no longer understood as secretion, but as a speech act, the names of the gods arise, as it were, incidentally and certainly unintentionally from the conversations of the god with himself or the primeval waters from which he emerged.[7]

The first stage of creation came about unintentionally. Planning began only with the meaningful establishment of the world for the creation that proceeded from the primeval god. Creation took place in two stages, associated with the names of Atum (the origin of the emanation) and Re (the creator of the cosmos). The main parts of the Heliopolitan mythology refer probably to the efficacy of Re, as the scenes in the sun chapel of Niuserre suggest (and the *Teaching for Merikare*).[8] The Shu theology of the *CT* distributes the two aspects between Atum and Shu as father and son respectively: Atum as the origin of the *ḫprw*, Shu as the life god who arranges and guarantees their physical well-being.[9]

### *1.1.2 Memphis*

The polar and deliberate opposite of the Heliopolitan system is presented by the theology of Memphis, which postulates a world created according to the plan of a demiurge. Ptah is the god of artists, sculptors and craftsmen. Creation in this system is an act of separation: water from land, light from darkness, heaven from earth. The crucial idea in this system is that separation is essentially a conceptual act. The most important organ of creation is not the hand that carries out, but the heart that plans and the tongue that formulates. However old the "Memphite theology" might be,[10] the basic core of the system is of great antiquity. In the Ramesside period the Memphite theology was associated with the idea of the primeval hill (i.e. the creation of space through the division of land and water) and the idea of the ingeniously devised creation plan brought to fulfilment by the

5 The *locus classicus* of this theory is P.Bremner Rhind XXVI,21-XXVII,5 and XXVIII,20-XXIX,6; cf. Sauneron and Yoyotte, "Naissance",48-51 and 27ff.; D. Lorton, in *SSEA* 7 (1977), 17-23; Allen, *Genesis*, 28-31 (text 9); Zandee, *Amunshymnus*, 168ff. objects to an incautious use of the notion "emanation", which belongs within the context of Neo-Platonism and Gnosis and must not be applied anachronistically to ancient Egyptian religion. This is right, but it is precisely this reflection about the origin of the universe where Neo-Platonism comes closest to ancient Egyptian conceptions. What is important is the difference between entities, which emerge or "emanate" (*ḫpr*) out of god's own substance and those which he creates out of external material.

6 *CT* VII 464-465; cf. also infra §1.4.

7 Cf. the emergence of the "Eight Heh Gods" on the occasion of a conversation between Atum and Nun *CT* II 5-8; cf. Sauneron and Yoyotte, "Naissance", 47.

8 On the nature philosophy of the sun temples cf. E. Edel, *Zu den Inschriften auf den Jahreszeitreliefs der Weltkammer* (1961), 243.

9 S. Morenz, *WKZM* 54 (1957), 119ff.; A. de Buck, *Plaats en betekenis van Sjoe*, 21-35. Allen, *Genesis in Egypt*, 14-27.

10 Sethe, *Dramatische Texte*; H. Junker, *Die Götterlehre von Memphis;* S. Sauneron/J.Yoyotte, loc.cit, 62-64; J.P. Allen, *Genesis* 42-47, 91-93 (text 15). F. Junge, *MDIK* 29 (1973), 195-204; H.A. Schlögl, *Der Gott Tatenen* (OBO 29) (1980), 110ff.

Word.[11]

### *1.1.3 Amarna*

Questions about primeval origins are of no importance in Amarna religion.[12] The specific contribution of Amarna to the history of Egyptian ideas about creation is the consistency with which creation was thought of as *creatio continua* and related to the present god-world relationship. The Great Hymn gives authoritative expression to this creation theology in vv.59-104; this section falls into two parts: the first is a sort of embryological treatise, while the second in general deals with the subject of the well-orderedness of the world. The embryological text represents a transformation of the traditional Heliopolitan theme of the emergence of life, by transferring it from the phylogenetic level to the ontogenetic level: from the creation of humankind to the creation of the child in the womb. It is perhaps best described as a *Naturlehre* (natural philosophy).

The second part gives predominantly cosmological knowledge, when it praises the well-orderedness of the world in the plurality of skin colours and languages in the human race and their various living conditions based on the division between rain and flood water.[13]

### *1.1.4 Khnum*

Among the late hymns of Esna are anthropological texts that describe the condition and function of the individual bodily organs in minute detail and in accordance with the most advanced stage of scientific knowledge available at the time.[14] Khnum is the creator of humans par excellence. The Esna theology is thus the only one that distinguishes between world and human creation and makes the androgynous primeval deity Neith the creator of the world.[15] The creation activity of Khnum, devoted exclusively to humans, is associated with the specifically anthropological phenomena of the ka and individuality. In the Final Judgement the heart is called "my Khnum". The name of the god often appears in connection with personifications of personal fate, such as Shai, Meskhenet and Renenet.[16]

---

11 In a list of passages on "Creation by the Heart" (infra, pp. ...) Ptah is notably prominent (texts 5-9), Cf. also Morenz, *Ägyptische Religion*, 172-174.

12 *Saeculum* 23 (1972) pp.119ff. The only exception which I know of is an early inscription where Aten is referred to as "the noble god of the first time", see H. Brunner, in *ZÄS* 97 (1971), 12-18. "Theology of Light and Time", ...

13 Cf. Allen, "The Natural Philosophy of Akhenaten", *YES* 3. For the motif of the heavenly Nile cf. *ÄHG* nos.127B, 45f.; no.195, 166; 143, 46, 100ff., 164f. (cf. p.590 ad loc.); 144C, 39; 214, 29-32 (=Book of the Dead, ch. 183); 242, 7-8 (D. v.d.Plaas, *De hymne aan de overstroming van de Nijl* (Diss. Utrecht) (1980), 16f. and 60-63); cf. A.P. Zivie (1983), "Regen", in *LÄ* V, 201-206, esp. 202 and 204.

14 Especially Sauneron, *Esna* V, 95ff.; *Esna* III no.250; Assmann, "Lieder und Gebete II", in O.Kaiser et al., *Texte aus der Umwelt des Alten Testaments* II.6 (1991), 909-11.

15 Sauneron and Yoyotte, "Naissance", 72.

16 *MDIK* 28 (1972), 61; Fecht, *ZÄS* 105 (1978), 24. On Khnum as creator of the individual see also Brunner, *LÄ* I, 303ff

Missing from this survey is the name "Hermopolis". The theology of the.i. eight primeval gods, usually associated with this city because of its Egyptian name (which means "the eight"), plays a very important role in the theology of Amun and it can scarcely have been regarded in the Ramesside period as an "import" from Middle Egypt. It is more likely to have been developed as a specifically Theban contribution and, incorporating the doctrines of Memphis and Heliopolis, to have become a comprehensive creation theology.

### *1.2 The transformation of the primeval god: the "imperial triad" as stages in cosmogony*

*ẖmnw ẖprw=k tpj*
*r km=k nn jw=k wᶜ.tj*
*sšt3 ḏt=k m-m wrw*
*jmn.n(=k) tw m Jmn m-ḥ3t nṯrw*

*jrjj=k ẖprw=k m t3-ṯnn*
*r šms p3wtjw m p3wt=k tpt*

*wṯz nfrw=k m k3-mwt=f*
*ḥrj=k tw m jmj-pt mn.tj m Rᶜw*

*jj.tj m jtjw jrjw z3=sn*
*(r) jrt jwᶜ mnḫ n msw=k (...)*

The Eight were your first form
so that you might complete this, you being one[17]
Your body was secret among the old ones
because you kept yourself hidden as Amun at the head of the gods

You took your (next) form as Tatenen
to lead the primeval ones in your first primeval period

Your beauty arose as Bull of his Mother
You withdrew as the one in heaven, remaining as Re

You returned in the fathers as creator of their sons
to make an excellent heritage for your children (...)[18]

P. Leiden J 350, which contains the most elaborate statement of Ramesside Amun theology, develops a creation theology that clearly attempts to integrate Heliopolitan and Memphite traditions in a new comprehensive cosmology. In this theology, the main ideas of the three religious centres of the country (Thebes, Memphis and Heliopolis) are distributed in the three stages of the cosmogonic process.

---

17 Cf. Junge, in: "Wirklichkeit und Abbild", 105 with n.59. In Amun the eight become one. Cf. P.Berlin 13603 (Sauneron,Yoyotte, op.cit., 58 doc.15).

18 P.Leiden J 350 III 22-27; Zandee, *Hymnen*, 63-66; *ÄHG* no.135.

The first stage, i.e. the "first transformation/impersonation (*ḫprw*)" of the all-embracing god, is represented by the "eight primeval gods" that embody pre-existent chaos. Amun is present in them in a hidden way: as a hypostasis of their unity.[19] The second stage, the second transformation/impersonation, is the primeval hill that appears from the waters of chaos, on which the god (up to that point without a place) can set foot and begin the work of creation. This stage is associated in the text with the emergence of the "primeval gods", *pꜣwtjw*, by which term perhaps Shu, Tefnut, Hike and others are meant. The third stage, removal to heaven, follows hidden pre-existence and the first self-coagulation or solidification[20] in form of the primeval mound. When heaven is created and the god removes himself to it, he creates a sphere, in which he is alone and separate from those who have come forth from it.

The names of the gods associated with this cosmogony (Amun, Tatenen and Re) form the "imperial triad", which here, like the Heliopolitan Ennead, represents a cosmogonic scheme of succession, without doubt the principal concern of the text. In this way the theologies of Memphis and Heliopolis are integrated as stages in a complex cosmogonic process within the Theban cosmogony. Although there were different creation theologies, there was unanimous agreement that the world was created by only one god. These various theologies must have created a problem for Egyptian theologians whenever they had to expand a local temple theology or design a universally acceptable cosmology. The first plan of such a universally binding cosmology is provided by Amarna religion, which solved the problem of other gods in a simple and brutal fashion. Even Theban theology seems to have come up with the claim to formulate a universally valid cosmology. This much is evident from its use, among other things, of the medium of literature, as can be seen in P.Leiden I 350 (the most important text), P. Chester Beatty IV (recto) and P. Leiden I 344 (verso).[21] P. Leiden I 350 was intended to be universally acceptable in Egypt, hence its emphasis on the role of the "imperial triad".[22]

The real concern of this creation theology is not cosmological, but theological and political. It does not so much put forth a model of natural philosophy,[23] but rather a solution to a theological problem that seeks to integrate the various cosmologies, which overlap with each other and represent indispensable knowledge, into a single creation theology and to understand the various gods as

19 Sauneron and Yoyotte, 34 and 53. Many passages concerning the "eight", mostly from ptolemaic sources, in Zandee, Amunshymnus, 32f.

20 *CT* I 316a, 318a, 336a. The cosmogony of P.Bremner-Rhind also speaks of an act of "coagulation" (*ṯz* cf. *Wb*. V p.398, 12-15) of the primeval god: *ṯz.nj jm m nnw m nnjwt* "I became solid there in Nun in Inertia". *m nnw m nnjwt* also occurs in Tura Hymn 11-26 cf. §4.3.1. On the concept of inertia as a quality of Chaos cf. Morenz, *Ägyptische Religion*, 175. On the text cf. D. Lorton, Newsletter *SSEA* 7.4 (August 1977), 17-23.

21 Ed. Zandee, *Amunshymnus*. The recto contains the famous *Admonitions*.

22 P. Cairo 53038, the so-called Cairo Amun Hymn, is also a literary manuscript. Already the older Theban Amun-Re theology shows clear signs of spreading throughout the whole of Egypt

23 Only the last two verses of the extract quoted from P.Leiden J 350 III 22-27 reveal a concern with "natural theology": the creator, who has "withdrawn" to heaven as the sun at the same "returns", in order to function as sexual potency in men. In the same way, Ptah, according to the Memphite Theology, functions as knowledge and speech in all hearts and tongues. The "theory of propagation" is characteristic of Ramesside and late creation theology. Cf. n.44.

"transformations/impersonations" of a single all-embracing god. Although this theology survived into the Greco-Roman period, there is no trace of it in the tomb hymns. Even the great theological hymns of the Ramesside period (*ÄHG* 127-131) contain no traces of these ideas, except for the Berlin Ptah Hymn.[24] However, before we examine the treatment of the creation theme in the tomb hymns, let us look at the only two hymns that deal with this theme, not in the eulogistic form (i.e. the nominal style of predication, where the subject is the creator), but rather as an account in the narrative style.

### *1.3 Narrative creation hymns from Thebes*

#### *1.3.1 The Tura Hymn*

Despite the fact that this hymn was recorded in a cave among the Tura quarries near Heliopolis, in a niche originally provided with folding wooden doors,[25] it actually originated in Thebes. This is clear not only from the first few verses,[26] but has been confirmed by parallel texts discovered in the tomb of Neferhotep (TT 50: time Horemheb = *STG* text 62d). The hymn obviously dates from the Amarna period. Since Theban Amun-Re hymns naturally were forbidden in Amarna, this hymn was recorded in a remote place, where there was probably a secret Amun cult operating.

The Tura Hymn supplements the Cairo Hymn in precisely the aspect that was so strikingly absent from the latter: the creation. The interesting feature of this treatment is the narrative form. The individual cosmogonic events are narrated in verbal sentences and follow each other chronologically.

1. Coagulation in the primeval waters. The plurality of gods as the limbs of the divine body taking shape[27]

| | |
|---|---|
| *bs.n=f m ḫpr ḏs=f* | He came forth as self-created |
| *ᶜwt nbt ḥr mdt ḥnᶜ=f* | all his limbs speaking to him |
| *qd.n=f sw n ḫprt pt tꜣ* | He formed himself before heaven and earth came into being |
| *jw tꜣ m nnw r-jmjtw nnjw* | the earth being in the primeval waters in the midst of the "weary flood"[28] |

2. Creation of the earth (primeval hill) as a place for the gods who have emerged from the monologues of the god

24 *ÄHG* no.143 70-79 and p.590. On the Late Period forms cf. *ÄHG* p. 587 (no.135) and no. 144, 14-18 (p.593). Cf. also *Zeit und Ewigkeit*, 21-23; "Primat und Transzendenz", pp.30-31.

25 M. Bakir, *ASAE* 42 (1943), pp.83ff.

26 *ÄHG* no.88, 1-6. For a parallel to the beginning cf. *STG*, Text 236 (TT 323) and *STG*, Text 72 (TT 55).

27 On this idea cf. *LÄ* II, 775, esp. n.190-193.

28 Or, with Zandee, *Amunshymnus*, 36f.: "between these" (*nn* = demonstrative, referring to "heaven and earth"). the words ... *jmjtw nn* occur in a similar context in P.Leiden I 344 vso, i, 7.

| | |
|---|---|
| *šꜣꜥ.n=k js jrt tꜣ pn* | you have started to create this land |
| *r smn prt m rꜣ=k* | to establish what has come from your mouth (=the gods) |

### 3. Division of heaven and earth. The earth as bearer of "images"[29]

| | |
|---|---|
| *ꜥḫ.n=k pt dꜣr.n=k sꜣṯw* | You have raised heaven and kept earth down |
| *r swsḫ tꜣ pn n tjt=k* | to make this land wide enough for your image |

### 4. "First transformation" as the sun. Creation of the light

| | |
|---|---|
| *jrj=k ḫprw tpj m Rꜥw* | You have taken on your first form as Re |
| *r sḥḏ tꜣwj n jrj=k* | to illuminate the Two Lands for that which you have created. |

### 5. Creation plan

| | |
|---|---|
| *m [kꜣ]*[30]*.n jb=k wꜥ.tj* | as your heart [planned], you being alone |
| *jrj=k st nṯrw n šmsw=k* | You created them, the gods being in your retinue |
| *ḏr prj=k wꜥ.tj m nnw* | after you came forth alone from the primeval waters |

### 6. Creation of life on earth

| | |
|---|---|
| *jr=k rmṯw ꜥwt mnmnt* | You created humans together with creatures great and small |
| *ḫprwt wnnt nbt* | and all that has come into existence and all that exists. |

### 7. Hymn of thanksgiving and praise of creation.

The following seven verses describe the praise and joy of creation. After that comes the last song of the hymn once again in the vocative form. It deals with the preservation and "well-orderedness" of the world, in which everything that lives has its place and is able to survive. Unfortunately, it is so damaged that only the outline can be reconstructed:

| | |
|---|---|
| *jnḏ ḥr=k jrjw nn [r-ꜣw]* | Hail, the one who has made all this[31] |
| *dwꜣ tw pꜥt rḫjjt* | 'patricians' and commoners worship you |
| *ftft n=k [ꜥwt nt ḫꜣswt]* | [animals of the desert] leap before you |
| *sjꜣ=[sn tw mj] wrḏ=k ḥr=w* | [they] know [you how] you took pains with them[32] |
| *smn=k tꜣwj n psḏt* | You have established the Two Lands for |

29 On the image of god on earth cf. below, 174ff. There the cult-image in Thebes is mentioned.

30 Only the determinative is preserved, one square is missing. The verb *kꜣj* is normal in this context, see p.164 with note 40.

31 Id. P.Cairo 58038, VI,7; cf. P.Leiden I 344 vso i,11: *ntf jrjw nn r-ꜣw* "he is the one who made all this", Zandee, *Amunshymnus*, 61ff.

32 See ch.3 § 2.6.

| | |
|---|---|
| | the Ennead[33] |
| *[rdj.n=k z nb] ḥr st=f* | and [put everyone] in their place[34] |
| *jrj.n=k n=sn ꜥwt [mnmnt]* | You have made for them creatures great and small |
| *pꜣjj [nb ẖnnt nbt]* | everything that flies up and alights |
| *smw snw* | grasses and trees |
| *ẖꜣw rnpjjw* | bushes and plants |
| *s[sn=sn ṯꜣw n dd=k]* | [they breathe the air that you give] |
| *[jj ?] ḥꜥpj ḥr [bꜥḥ? snmt? tꜣ] r ḏr=f* | The inundation [comes to flood/nourish] the entire [land.] |
| *[wbn=k m ꜣḫt]* | [You arise in the horizon] |
| *[r sḥḏ] n=sn rꜥw nb* | [to shine] for them every day. |

This treatment of cosmogony differs from that of the traditional Heliopolitan theology in several respects. Shu and Tefnut are not mentioned. The creator does not enter a constellation with the divine world that proceeds from him. He does not "become three", but remains one. But the gods are the first beings to emerge after the god has come to and implanted himself in a body. They come into existence both as limbs of this body and from the words that the god exchanges with his limbs.

Humans do not come into existence in the primeval age, as "tears of the god",[35] but are created after the world is made in its present state, where heaven has been separated from earth and light from darkness. This "wise"[36] arrangement of the world is conceived by the heart of the creator and corresponds with the Memphite theology. Humans are created together with animals and "everything that exists". It is clear in the third hymn, however, that the foundation of the earth happens for the sake of the gods, while the creation of animals and plants is clearly intended for humans, who will be sustained by [air?], inundation and [sun].[37] This anthropocentric interpretation of the theology follows that of *Merikare*. We must not forget that, although *Merikare* is much earlier, the extant mss. are exactly contemporary with the Tura Hymn

### *1.3.2 The Hibis Hymn pl.32 (=ÄHG 129)*

As extracts from the Harris Magical Papyrus show, the Hibis Hymn, written down in the Persian Period, originates in the Ramesside era. The first stanza deals with individual acts of creation, such as the separation of heaven and earth and the foundation of the starry sky (vv.23-25 and the emergence of humans and gods from the eye and the mouth (vv.35-36) and aspects of the nature of the creator, such as the lord of millions, primeval god, origin of the gods (vv.28-31). The account proper

---

33 This refers to the foundation of the temple and the cult, an uncommonly frequent subject in New Kingdom hymns. The following references are from *ÄHG*: no.26,39f.; 38,7-9; 101,5-7; 104,19f.; 127A,115; 127B,139; 130,109f.; 144,5-15.24f.; 144C,64; 192,24; 222,10f.,41f. see p.613 to no.192,24. Cf. also P.Leiden I 344 vso II,2-3 and Zandee, *Amunshymnus*, 75-88.

34 Cf. Amarna Great Hymn *ÄHG* no.92,85.

35 Cf. below, 167f.

36 P.Louvre 3292 and later n.192. The motif of wisdom is also echoed in the exclamation *smnḫ-wj sj sḫrw=k pꜣ nb nḥḥ* "how effective your plans are, lord of *nḥḥ*" (Great Hymn *ÄHG* no.92.100). Cf. also Chapter 3 §2.5 notes 129-130.

37 This restoration assumes that the stanza has been constructed according to the triad of life-giving elements: air-water-light. Cf. also §2.2

begins in v.37. It occupies a stanza of 15vv. (37-51), which describe in great detail the primeval stage, viz. the self-creation of the god in the midst of chaos as "child of the Eight",[38] without father and mother, but himself "father of fathers and mother of mothers".[39] The second stage is the creation plan, the conceptualisation of the cosmos. This unusually detailed description too requires a stanza of 18 lines, though it is regrettably badly damaged (52-69). The text mentions repeatedly that the god "counsels with his heart" (*nḏnḏ jb=f*), "plans" (*k3j*)[40] "devises "(*w3w3*) and "orders" (*wḏ*).

The third and longest passage of this creation narrative describes in 26vv. the implementation of this creation plan (70-95):

1. vv.70-71: raising and solidifying heaven, with the sun in it;[41]
2. v. 72 : extending the earth and surrounding it by the ocean;
3. vv.73-74: forming (*qd*[42]) living creatures, viz. humans,[43] large and small animals, birds, fish, and worms;[44]
4. vv.75-78: creating the possibility of propagation;[45]
5. vv.79-83: dividing countries and their living conditions;
6. vv.84-86: differentiating humans according to colour and language;[46]
7. vv.87-90: organising the human body and its limbs;
8. vv.91-94: living conditions of fish and birds.[47]

The subject of this stanza is the well-orderedness of the world, which has resulted from the well-devised conception of the creation plan and is praised in the Great Hymn of Amarna: *smnḫ.wj sj sḫrw=k* "how effective are your plans".[48] In this stanza the cosmological tradition of creation theology is continued as natural philosophy

38 Sauneron-Yoyotte, "Naissance", 54-58; P.Berlin 3055, 20, 6-7 ; *ÄHG* no.125, 11-12; *ÄHG* no.126, 11; *ÄHG* no.192, 15-16.

39 *STG* Text 108b; Kitchen, *RI* vol. III, 18-19; P.Leiden J 350 V 3-4; P.Leiden I 344 vso II,1, Zandee, *Amunshymnus*, 67-70; Sauneron, *Mélanges Mariette* (1962),240-242.

40 The Memphite Theology also uses the terms *k3j* and *wḏ*; cf. H. Junker, *Die Götterlehre von Memphis*, lines 56 and 57 (twice). Hatshepsut, in her coronation text (chapelle rouge) calls Amun *k3j ntt nbt* "who planned everything existing" (ed.Lacau-Chevrier, 99); sim. P.Leiden I 344 vso vi.3, Zandee, *Amunshymnus*, 505, 515f.

41 *STG* Text 59a; Text 204,5; BD (Nakht) col.21: *qm3w pt smnw sw m ḫnw=s*; text 209; O.Michailides 15 vso 15; *Aeg. Inschriften II*, 66-67 (Berlin 6910) = Ptah as creator of heaven; P.Greenfield pl. XXXI (for this and parallel passages cf. *Zeit und Ewigkeit*, 38); pGreenfield XXX,3 : *jrjw pt smnw sw m ᶜwj=fj/ jr n=f ᶜ n wbn jm=s* "The one who made heaven and made it fast with his arms/ who made for himself a place for rising in it".

42 On *qd* as the specific activity of the creator of mankind Khnum cf. *SAK* 8 (1980), 5ff and 19. Zandee, *Amunshymnus*, 71-74.

43 According to verse 35 humans emerged already before the creation of the world from the "tears" of god. It is the old Heliopolitan theology, still adhered to, about the origin of the human race (see later §1.4). In this version it may well be that there is no allusion to the physical corporeality of humans, which is created only now with the animals.

44 For similar catalogues of animals cf. *STG* Text 156 (n).

45 S. Sauneron, *BIFAO* 60 pp. 19ff.; J. Yoyotte, *BIFAO* 61, 139-146: D. Müller, *Aegypten und die griechischen Isisaretalogien* (1961), 45. Cf. Zandee, *Amunshymnus*, 88-90 (bulls and cows).

46 Sauneron, *BIFAO* 60, 31ff.

47 On the possibilities of life for fish, which also breathe in water cf. *STG* Text 54, 20-21 (q).

48 Cf. Chapter 3 §2.5, esp. notes 129-130.

The next stanza (96-107) reports in twelve verses what has to be understood as the fourth and final stage of creation: the removal of god to heaven to consider his work. His eyes are the light that endows creatures with the ability to see:

| | |
|---|---|
| *sw=f sw m ḥrt sdg3.n=f jrw* | He (removed himself?) to heaven to observe the creatures;[49] |
| *sdg3.tw=f m-ḫnw dg3=f* | One sees by means of his seeing. |

This theme, foreshadowed in the Teaching of *Merikare*,[50] plays an important role in the new solar theology and has already been dealt with (Chapter 3).[51] There it does not feature in the context of a creation theology, but describes the present-extratemporal constitution of the world as a theological interpretation of cosmic phenomena. As a final stage of creation this withdrawal, by which the creator distances himself from creation at the end of his work to contemplate the whole, acquires another meaning. In the myth known as the Celestial Cow the idea is obvious that the sun god ruling over his creation ruled over "humans and gods together" (*m jḫt wꜥt*) at the beginning. Only after the rebellion of humans against their creator and an unsuccessful attempt to destroy them does the sun god become tired of human beings. Thus, heaven is raised up on high and the gods are separated from humans.[52] The idea of distance is temporalised in this myth, in the typical fashion of mythical thought. The world as it is today (divided into the Now and the Hereafter, into a divine world that is remote and can be visualised only by images and symbols and into an earthly world administered on behalf of the creator by a deputising king) is a relatively recent establishment. It was not preceded by pure "chaos", but by a state where all living creatures lived together, which possibly had characteristics of a golden age.[53] Thus, the theme of the creation of heaven and the

49 Zandee, *Amunshymnus*, 52 n.298 prefers to read *jrtj* "he placed himself in the sky and made the eyes see; one is enabled to see by his glance".

50 *STG* Text 253 (u). Other passages include BM 170 (in I.E.S. Edwards, *Hieroglyphic Texts* vol. VIII pl. 34): *wbnw m [pt] rꜥw nb/ r m33 t3w jr.n=f* "Who rises in [heaven] every day/ to see the lands which he has created"; Edfu III 340: *dg3=k jr.n=k pr nb jm=k/k3 ḥꜥꜥ jb=k m jr.n=k* "You look at what you have done, all that goes forth from you/ then your heart rejoices at what you have done". The passages in *ÄHG* are assembled in p. 513 n.39.

51 Cf. P.Leiden I 344 vso v,9-10: *nn m33=sn m ḥrw=sn, dgg=sn m nṯrwtj=kj* "they do not look with their faces, they see by virtue of your divine eyes"; cf. Zandee, *Amunshymnus*, 455ff.

52 L. Kákosy, "A nap kiralysaga. Az egyiptomi aranykormitoszok". *Vilagossag* 17 (1976), 229-233. Cf. also *GM* 25 (1977), 34. On the interpretation as "original sin myth" cf. *GM* 25, 40. In general cf. W. Staudacher, *Die Trennung vom Himmel und Erde. Ein vorgriechischer Schöpfungsmythos bei Hesiod und den Orphikern* (1942). Cf. also H. te Velde, "The Theme of the Separation of Heaven and Earth in Egyptian Mythology", *Studia Aegyptiaca* 3 (1977), 161-170. On the interpretation of the Cow Book as an "aetiology of the incomplete" cf. E. Hornung, *Der ägyptische Mythos von der Himmelskuh* (OBO 46) (1982). For further references on theme of the separation of heaven and earth cf. *Ma'at*, 174-177.

53 The text does not say that the condition of the world was better before the raising of heaven and the withdrawal of the sun god. I agree with Otto (in *Religion en Égypte hellénistique et romaine* (1967), 93-108) that distinct ideas of a golden age do not occur in Egypt until late but should not necessarily be understood as the product of Greek influence. They arise rather from a specific understanding of time and history, which is also expressed in the formation of an eschatological soteriology and is similarly a product of basic Egyptian ideas (cf. "Königsdogma und

withdrawal of the creator to it is associated with ideas of remarkable range and importance, and this may explain the frequency of the subject in Ramesside hymns.

The following stanzas of the Hibis Hymn look like a continuation of this theme. In fact, however, the transition into the style of the eulogy marks also a thematic break. What follows mentions the giving life to and preservation of creation, the theory of "life-giving elements", which are examined in §2. It is characteristic of Egyptian creation ideas that they allow the work of creation to make a smooth transition to the work of preservation. The creation is only the "First Time" in a continually recurring *creatio continua*.[54]

### *1.4 The theme of creation in Ramesside tomb hymns*

Although the theme of creation plays an important role in Ramesside tomb hymns, a characteristic that distinguishes them from the earlier traditions, there is no text that provides a narrative account of cosmogonic events, not even a text where the theme of creation is a central one.[55] The praise of the creator always goes together with other aspects of divine nature and activity. If one ignores mere epithets, such as *pꜣwtj* etc., and considers details connected with the creation theme, it can be established that the cosmogonic process is important only in its final stages. The texts refer, only en passant and in short formulae, to the primeval condition in the waters of chaos. The "Eight" are hardly mentioned at all.[56] Shu and Tefnut are mentioned here as rarely as in other texts of Theban theology.[57] Here too it is clear that the real concern of the reflections about the origin of the world is theological: it is here that the concept of the oneness of god is most clearly expressed. This, and the creation as such, was the great issue of the time: there was no creation before god[58] and none after him[59] and none at the same time.[60] Everything was created by One Alone, and this One created everything.[61]

The other idea that plays a central role in creation theology passages of the tomb hymns refers to the fact that humans and gods originate in god and to the anthropocentric meaning of creation, which was set in motion primarily for the sake of these creatures that had come forth from the primeval god. This is the meaning

---

Heilserwartung" in D. Hellholm (ed.), *Apocalypticism*, repr. in *Stein und Zeit*, 259-87). Cf. also L. Kákosy, "Ideas about the Fallen State of the World in Egyptian Religion", *Acta Orientalia Hungarica* XVII (1964), 205ff. The hymns that praise the raising of heaven as a cosmogonic act obviously do not speak of a "fall". The question here is quite simply whether this act involves the idea of a periodisation of creation in contrast to the stages of the cosmogonic process. On this problem cf. Sauneron-Yoyotte, 42ff.

54 Morenz, *Ägyptische Religion*, 174ff.; Sauneron-Yoyotte, 77. The expression is attested only from the Heracleopolitan period (cf. E. Otto, *Gott und Mensch*, 95).

55 A possible exception is *STG* Text 149.

56 Once in corrupt context: *STG* Text 43.

57 *STG* Text 42a mentions the "twins"; cf. also P.Berlin 3049 = *ÄHG* no.127B,2 08. P. Leiden J 350 V 16 = *ÄHG* no.141 does not refer to the cosmogony.

58 *STG* Text 54: 14ff.; also P.Berlin 3049 = *ÄHG* no.127B, 120.

59 *STG* Text 253,25[p].

60 *STG* Text 113,55 and Text 62d [i]; Cf. *STG* note (i) *ad* Text 62d.

61 *STG* Text 151[o]; 155[a]; 130[d]; Cf. also Text 41 (1) and 62b (a) on the formula *jrjw wꜥ* "One creator" and J. Zandee, *Hymnen*, 70 on P.Leiden J 350 IV,6.

of the extraordinarily common formula that humans issued from the eye and gods from the mouth of the primeval god:

| | |
|---|---|
| (1) *prr.n rmṯw m jrtj=fj*<br>*ẖprw nṯrw tp rꜣ=f* | humans issued from his eyes<br>the gods emerged on his lips.[62] |
| (2) *pr.n rmṯw m jrtj=fj*<br>*nṯrw jmj sptj=fj* | humans issued from his eyes,<br>the gods from his lips.[63] |
| (3) *nb nṯrw jrjw rmṯw*<br>*pr.n=n r-ꜣw m jrt=f* | lord of gods, creator of humans,<br>we all came forth from his eye.[64] |
| (4) *nn wn ꜥnḫ m ẖmt=f*<br>*pr.n m jrt=f r-ꜣw* | there is no life without him<br>for we came all forth from his eye.[65] |
| (5) *bjf(?)=f bw nb m jrtj=fj*<br>*ẖpr nṯr m rꜣ=f* | he ... all people from his eyes,<br>but the gods issued from his mouth.[66] |
| (6) *r smnḫ ꜥwt qmꜣ.n=f*<br>*rḫjjt prt m jrt=f* | ...in order to provide for the cattle which he created,<br>commoners that came forth from his eye.[67] |
| (7) *ẖpr rmṯw m jrt=f*<br>*ꜥwt nbt qmꜣ.n jb=f*<br>*ẖt-n-ꜥnḫ m rwḏw ꜥwt=f* | humans emerged from his eye<br>all the cattle that his heart has created,<br>and the fruit-trees from the secretions of his limbs.[68] |
| (8) *smḏw=k nṯrw (...) jj=k*<br>*rmṯ m rmjwt jrt=k* | you provided the gods ... ?<br>and humans from the tears of your eye.[69] |
| (9) *prj nṯrw m rꜣ=k*<br>*rmṯw m jrt=k* | gods issued from his mouth<br>and humans from his eye.[70] |
| (10) *prj rmt m nṯrwtj=fj*<br>*nṯrw m tp-rꜣ=f* | humans issued from his divine eyes<br>and the gods from the utterance of his mouth.[71] |
| (11) *prj nṯrw m rꜣ=f*<br>*rmṯw m jrt=f* | the gods issued from his mouth<br>and humans from his eye.[72] |
| (12) *qd=f rmṯw m rmjwt jrt=f*<br>*smḏw=f ẖrt nṯrw* | he built humans with the tears of his eye<br>and provided for the needs of the gods.[73] |

62 P.Cairo 58038,vi,3. *prr.n* must be a mistake; read *prrw* or *pr.n*.
63 *STG* Text no. 188 (e).
64 *STG* Text 232 (r).
65 O.Cairo 25208 = *ÄHG* no. 193.21-22.
66 *RT* 13, 163.16.
67 Stele Cairo JE 28569 cf. chapter 3 note 147.
68 *STG* Text No. 159 (a).
69 O.Cairo 25210.
70 Hymn of Ramesses III, *OIP* XXV pl. xxv = *ÄHG* no. 196.
71 Neschons, 19-21 = *ÄHG* no. 131, 50-51.
72 P.Berlin 3049,ii,6 = *ÄHG* no. 127A, 17-18.
73 O.Cairo 25207 = *ÄHG* no. 192, 17-18.

| | |
|---|---|
| (13) *jr.n=f rmṯw m nṯrt=f* <br> *qꜣꜥ.n=f nṯrw m rꜣ=f* | he made humans from his divine eye <br> and spat the gods from his mouth.[74] |

cf. also

| | |
|---|---|
| (14) *sḫpr.n=j nṯrw m fdt=j* <br> *jw rmṯw m rmjjwt nt jrt=j* | I caused the gods to emerge from my sweat <br> but humans are the tears of my eye.[75] |
| (15) *nṯn rmjt ꜣḫt m rn=tn n rmṯw* | you are the tears of my shining eye in your name "humans".[76] |

The theme still plays an important role in Greco-Roman texts[77] and is related in a way, that has yet to be explained, to the particularly Orphic[78] and generally Greek idea[79] that the gods issued from the laughter, humans from the tears of the primeval creator god.[80]

The relationship between tears and human beings in Egyptian texts is clearly based on the homophony of the words *rmṯ* (human beings) and *rmjt* (tears) (cf. example 15). In the *CT*[81] and the *Apophis Book*[82] there are traces of a myth that places this weeping of the primeval god (which led to the creation of human beings) in the cosmogonic process. The first creatures to issue from the primeval creator, Shu and Tefnut, take flight into the still spaceless and boundless ante-world. The primeval god then sends his "one eye" to look for them:

> Then Atum sent his One-Eye forth to look for me and my sister Tefnut (*CT* II 5b)
> It was my Eye that brought them (Shu and Tefnut) back to me after they had withdrawn from me.
> As I wept over them (Shu and Tefnut), human beings emerged as tears that fell from my eyes.[83]

It is these "humans", the issue of the primeval god, who are mentioned several times in the *CT* as *wnḏwt*.[84] The expression *wnḏwt* ascribes human beings to the

---

74 *Hibis* 32.7 = *ÄHG* no. 129, 35-36.

75 *CT* VII 464-65; Hornung, *Der Eine*, 141; Zandee, *Amunshymnus*, 74.

76 Book of Gates, 5th hour, sc.30 (Hornung, *Pfb.I*, 178).

77 E. Otto, *Gott und Mensch*, 58ff.; S. Schott and W. Erichsen, *Fragmente memphitischer Theologie in demotischer Schrift* no.2,12; Sauneron, *Esna* V 261 (a).

78 Orph. fr.28 Abel.

79 A. Dieterich, *Abrasax*, 28; Proclus on Plato, *Republic* 385. Cf. infra, n. 85.

80 Esna no.272,2-3; cf. also Sauneron, *Esna* V, 142.

81 *CT* II 5b and 33d; IV 174-175.

82 P.Bremner-Rhind 29, 3-4; the short version (27,1ff.) is more explicit; cf. Sauneron-Yoyotte, "Naissance", 51.

83 *rm.n=j ḥr=sn ḫpr rmṯw pw*
*m rmw prjw m jrt=j* (p.Bremner Rhind 27.2-3).
The weeping of the primeval creator is mentioned also in *CT* IV 175f., but without reference to the emergence of human beings. Cf. also *CT* VI 344 f-g and Hornung, *Conceptions*, 142.

84 *CT* I 376/77c. The word probably derives from *nḏ* "to act on behalf of someone" and means "clients"; cf. *CT* I 128b, 129e, 130e, 131e, 144c, 153e, 163e, 176o and Wb.I, 326, 5-6. Also A. Piankoff, *Les Chapelles de Tout-Ankh-Amoun*, pl.19 and J. Barns, *JEA* 54 (1968), 74.

creator god in the same sense that they are called "his animals and his herd" (*ꜥwt*).[85] In the light of these associations, we can understand the meaning of the motif, which explains the tenacious retention of it even in quite unmythological texts.[86] Humans do not belong, like animals and plants, to the created and well-appointed world, but, like gods, they themselves are the creatures that issued from the primeval god at the beginning for whose sake the world was created. Moreover, it is worth noting that of the passages quoted only nos. 3,8 and 14 mention the word play of "tears" and "human beings", so that the "weeping" of the creator and its reasons remain obscure. There seems to be no idea that human beings are especially associated with suffering (as in the Greek texts, where the origin of humans from weeping is contrasted with the origin of gods from laughter).[87] More important for the Egyptians is the relationship of humans to the eye. Their character as "ocular creatures", expressed in the terms *jrt nbt* and *ḥr nb*, plays a fundamental role in the new solar theology. It is one of the basic concepts of a religious anthropology to which the Egyptians unwaveringly adhered.[88] "Everything that has eyes" (by which humans were always meant) springs forth from the "eyes" of the primeval god.

Equally crucial to the Egyptians was the idea of the creation of the gods through the word. Passages such as no.14 reveal that it was still alien in the Middle Kingdom.[89] Even if the gods here occasionally emerge from words, it is not associated with the idea of an intentional act of creation. Words are rather a sort of secretion, such as tears, sweat, coughing, spitting etc..[90] The idea of creation by the word, therefore, is probably not much older than the 18th dynasty.[91] It makes the world proceed not from more or less accidental utterances, but from an order conceived "in the heart", which is fulfilled in the form of a statement. Creation through the word is first and foremost creation through the "heart", the planning wisdom of god:

| | |
|---|---|
| (1) *Rꜥw k[ꜣjw] ntt*<br>*nb tꜣ-tmmw jrjw wnnt* | Re who planned everything that exists,<br>lord of humankind, creator of what exists.[92] |
| (2) ... *m [kꜣ].n jb=k* | ... as your heart [planned].[93] |
| (3) *qmꜣ.n=k tꜣ n*<br>*jb=k jw=k wꜥ.tj* | You created the earth according to<br>your will, you being alone.[94] |

85 Cf. Chapter 3 §2.5 (end).

86 E.g. *Hibis* 32, where it is mentioned beneath the "forming" (qd) of people; an other interpretation (based on *CT* VI 344f-g) gives Hornung (s.n.81).

87 On the motif of the creation of the gods by laughter cf. the Leiden *Cosmopoiia* (*Papyri Graecae Magicae* XIII, 161, 167) and the Hermetic treatise *Kore kosmou*, *Corpus Hermeticum* ed. Nock-Festugière IV, p.4. Cf. also Orph. fr. 28 Abel; A. Dieterich, *Abraxas*, 28; Proclus, ad Plato, *Republic*, 385.

88 Otto, *Gott und Mensch*, 41 and 47-50; Brunner, *LÄ* I, 303ff.

89 But cf. Louvre C 3,16 in A. Moret, *Mystères Égyptiens*, 64 and A. Gayet, *Stèles de la XIIe Dynastie* (1889), pl. IV.

90 Sauneron-Yoyotte, 39ff.

91 *pace* Zandee, *Amunshymnus*, 74.

92 BM 29944 ed. Stewart, *JEA* 53,37.

93 Tura-Hymn, 14.

94 Amarna *ÄHG* no.92,79.

| | |
|---|---|
| (4) *jrjw tȝ m ḥḥ n jb* | The one who created the earth as an investigation of his heart.[95] |
| (5) (Of Ptah) *qmȝ jȝwt*<br>*msjw nṯrw m jr.n jb=f* | The one who created technology<br>and gave birth to the gods as a creation his heart.[96] |
| (6) (Of Ptah) *jrjw ḥmw*<br>*m gm.n jb=f* | The one who created the arts<br>as a discovery of his heart.[97] |
| (7) (Of Ptah) *jrjw pt*<br>*m qmȝ.n jb=f* | Who made heaven<br>as the creation of his heart.[98] |
| (8) (Of Ptah) *ḏdt m jb=f*<br>*mȝȝw ḫpr=sn* | The things that are said in his heart<br>one sees that they come into being.[99] |
| (9) (Of Ptah) *ḥmw tȝ*<br>*m sḫrw n jb=f* | The one who formed the earth<br>by the providence of his heart.[100] |
| (10) *ḫpr rmṯw m jrtj=fj*<br>*ꜥwt nbt qmȝ.n jb=f* | human beings arose from his eyes<br>and all animals which his heart created.[101] |
| (11) *šȝꜥ [ntt] nbt*<br>*m qmȝ.n jb=f* | The one who initiated everything<br>that exists as a creation of his heart.[102] |
| (12) *jrjw pt tȝ m jb=f* | The one who created heaven and earth with his heart.[103] |
| (13) *sqn.n=f tȝ sḫpr tnw*<br>*ḥr tp <rȝ=f>*.[104]<br>*m sḫrw n jb=f* | He settled the earth and caused the primeval hill to emerge<br>through his first utterance<br>by the providence of his heart.[105] |
| (14) *mȝȝ jr=k r ḥm.n jb=k*<br>*sȝr nbjw ntt šȝꜥ wnnt* | Look at what your heart has formed<br>wise one, who has formed all that is and initiated what exists.[106] |
| (15) *nṯr pn šȝꜥw tȝ m sḫrw=f* | This god who first established the earth by his providence.[107] |

95 Leiden K1.
96 Berlin 6910 *Äg.Inschr.*II,66-67.
97 TT 44(5) (unpubl.).
98 P.Harris, I,44,5 = *ÄHG* no.199,7.
99 Copenhagen A 719 = *ÄHG* no.223,7.
100 P.Berlin 3048,III,1 = *ÄHG* no.143,22.
101 *STG*, Text 159.
102 P.Berlin 3049,XI,3-4 = *ÄHG* no.127B,80.
103 Neschons, 9-10 = *ÄHG* no.131,26.
104 Det. "man with hand on mouth" behind *ḥr tp* suggests that here a word for "utterance" is meant.
105 *Sobek Re* (P.Strasbourg 2+7) IV 9-10 = *ÄHG* no.144C, 38.
106 P.Louvre 3292 = *ÄHG* no.45,11-12.
107 *Hibis* 33,4-5 = *ÄHG* no.130,22.

| | |
|---|---|
| (16) *mꜣṯ.n jb=f ḫpr ḥr-ᶜ* | That which his heart planned materialises immediately.[108] |

The theme also features in Late Period texts[109] and, of course, in the Memphite Theology, which need not concern us here.[110]

In the transition from the 18th to 19th dynasty, the idea of creation through the word was extended from the creation of the divine world, to which it had up to that point been limited, to the creation of the whole cosmos, "everything that exists".[111] The idea of verbal creation, according to a plan conceived in the heart, emphasised the organisational aspect of the created world, its rational character. What was conceived in the heart of god and came forth from his mouth were not the things themselves, but the "names of all things",[112] which the Egyptians imagined to be arranged hierarchically in the form of an onomasticon. An onomasticon does not enumerate individual objects, but classes of objects.[113] It can therefore be understood as an exhaustive inventory of the cosmos and a replica of its structure. The doctrine of verbal creation envisaged the well-appointed nature of the world, its fullness and order, and attributed them to the wisdom of the creator, the spiritual conception in the heart. This was an aspect of the world especially emphasised in Amarna religion, which also influenced Psalms 104 and Wisdom in Hebrew literature.[114]

### *1.5 Excursus: The Role of Thinking, Speaking and Writing in the Memphite Theology*[115]

The Memphite Theology has always been interpreted as the closest Egyptian parallel to the Biblical idea of creation through the word.[116] But there are two

108 *Urk* VIII 138k; Esna No. 206.2.

109 Sauneron, *Esna* V p.361 no. 260,10; p.220 no.387,3; Otto, *Gott und Mensch*, 58; Zandee, Amunshymnus, 31.

110 H. Junker, *Die Götterlehre von Memphis*, 56; Morenz, *Ägyptische Religion*, pp.172-174. Allen, *Genesis*, 42-47 text 15. See infra, § 1.5.2.

111 In detail *STG*, Text 149 (L).

> Who created heaven and earth and gave birth to human beings,
> who brought forth all that is through the utterance of his mouth.
> Who spoke and it happened, who gave birth to what exists,
> Great One, creator of the gods and human beings.
> Who came into being alone and gave birth to himself as millions.
> It was his limbs that answered,
> it was his tongue that formed everything he created.

112 *Memphite Theology* 55 = *mꜣṯ rn n jḫt nbt*; similarly P.Berlin 3055, XVI, 3ff. = *ÄHG* no. 122,7.

113 This is true of entities such as "heaven", "sun", "moon" "king", which have to be understood as one-element classes.

114 Cf. note 1.

115 H. Junker, *Die Götterlehre von Memphis* p.56; Morenz, *Ägyptische Religion* pp.172-174. Allen, *Genesis*, 42-47 text 15.

116 Cf. Klaus Koch, "Wort und Einheit des Schöpfergottes in Memphis und Jerusalem. Zur Einzigartigkeit Israels", *Studien zur alttestamentlichen und altorientalischen Religionsgeschichte*

points of difference between the Egyptian and the Biblical text which I think are decisive. Firstly, stress is laid (and this, as we have seen, is generally true of Egypt, but especially true of the Memphite Theology) not so much on the act of speaking, but on the preceding act of conceiving the world. Creation is achieved, in the first place, by the thinking 'heart', and only in the second place by the speaking 'tongue'. Secondly, the Memphite idea of a linguistic conception of the universe seems to me, in spite of the 'tongue', to refer to writing as much as to speaking. Since there are good arguments in favour of dating the Memphite Theology in the Ramesside period or later, it seems to me essential to include at least a brief and cursory treatment of the passages relevant in the present context. The translation follows closely Allen's rendering:

> Through the heart and through the tongue something developed (*ḫpr*)
> into Atum's image (*tjt*)
> Great and important is Ptah,
> who gave life to all the gods and their kas as well
> through his heart and his tongue
> through which Horus and Thoth both became (*ḫpr*) Ptah.
> It has come about (*ḫpr.n*) that the heart and tongue have control of all limbs,
> showing that he is preeminent in every body and in every mouth
> of all the gods, and all people, all animals, and all crawling things that live,
> planning and governing everything he wishes.
> His Ennead is before him in teeth and lips,
> that seed and those hands of Atum:
> for it is through his seed and his fingers that Atum's Ennead came into existence (*ḫpr*),
> but the Ennead is teeth and lips in this mouth
> that conceived (*mꜣṯ*; not: 'pronounced') the name of everything,
> and from which Shu and Tefnut emerged
> and gave birth to the Ennead.
> The eye's seeing, the ear's hearing, the nose's breathing of air send up to the heart,
> and *it* is what causes every conclusion to emerge;
> it is the tongue that repeats what the heart plans.
> So were all the gods born,
> Atum and his Ennead as well,
> for it is through what the heart plans and the tongue commands that all *divine speech*
> (*mdw nṯr*) has come into existence (*ḫpr*).
> So were the male life-principles made
> and the female life-principles set in place
> they who make all sustenance and every offering
> through that word that makes what is loved and what is hated.
> So has life been given to him who is calm
> and death to him who does wrong.
> So has been made all construction and all craft,
> the hand's doing, the feet's going, and every limb's movement,
> according as he governs that which the heart thinks,
> and which emerges through the tongue,
> and which facilitates everything.
> It has come about that Ptah is called "He who made all and caused the gods to come into
> existence",
> since he is Tatenen, who gave birth to the gods,

(Göttingen, 1988), 61-105.

from whom everything has emerged,
food offerings and sustenance, god's offerings and every perfect thing.
So it is found and recognised that his strength is greater than that of the gods.
So has Ptah come to rest after his making everything
and all divine speech (*mdw-nṯr*) as well,
having given birth to the gods,
having made their villages,
having founded their nomes,
having set the gods in their cult-places,
having established their bread-offerings,
having founded their shrines,
having made their bodies resemble what contents them.
So have the god entered their bodies
of every kind of wood, every kind of mineral, every kind of fruit,
everything that grows all over him, in which they have come into existence
So have been gathered to him all the gods and their ka's as well,
content and combined in the lord of the two lands.

At first sight the text says nothing about writing, but only about the planning heart and the speaking tongue, the heart being given an obvious precedence over the speaking tongue. In the Bible there is no mention of God's planning the world. But what the heart conceives is not the sound, which will pass through the mouth, but the meaning, and, what is more, the shape or form, the design of everything which will be named by the speaking mouth. For Ptah is the god of art. Now hieroglyphs were considered by the Egyptians to be a genre of art.[117] Thoth was the god of writing, but Ptah was the god of hieroglyphs, because he invented the forms that were to make the sounds visual. Once one becomes aware of this connection, one realises that the term "hieroglyphs" actually occurs twice in the text. This has not been recognised up to now, but it is nevertheless quite obvious: the term *mdw-nṯr*, which has been rendered as "divine speech", means "hieroglyphs".

The Egyptian word for "hieroglyphs", which the Greeks translated as *ta hiera grammata* is *zš n mdw nṯr* "the writing of divine speech".[118] Thoth, the god of writing, is called "the lord of divine speech".[119] The sacred texts which were written in hieroglyphs are called "scrolls of divine speech".[120] Thus it is quite evident, that "divine speech" refers to the *signs* (and not to the *sounds*), which Thoth commands, which the sacred books contain and which constitute the sacred script.

What does the text teach us about hieroglyphs? The notion occurs in two sentences: "it is through what the heart plans and the tongue commands that all ***divine speech*** (*mdw nṯr*) has come into existence (*ḫpr*)." This is very clear. The heart conceives the forms and the meanings, and the tongue pronounces the sound, i.e. the phonetic value. The result is the hieroglyph. The second sentence reads: "So has Ptah come to rest after his making everything and all *divine speech* (*mdw-nṯr*) as well". It is the epitome of the creation process as narrated in the preceding sections. Total reality is summed up by the duality of "things" and "hieroglyphs". This dichotomy corresponds exactly to what we would distinguish as "types" and "tokens".

117 H.G.Fischer, *L'art et l'écriture dans l'Égypte ancienne* (Paris, 1986).
118 *Wb*. II, 181.2
119 *Wb*. II, 181.6
120 *Wb*. II, 181.1

Ptah, the creator and chief-artist, invents the types or models in his planning heart, and fills the visible world with tokens. He did not write, but he invented the hieroglyphs by inventing the shapes and names of everything. Thoth, the god of writing, did not *invent*, but merely *found* the script: thus in the Onomasticon of Anememope the notion of "every word" is expressed as "everything that Ptah has created and that Thoth has written down".[121] Writing only carries out what is already implicit in the structure of reality.

This structure is "hieroglyphic". It is a kind of Platonism. Plato interprets the visible world as the infinite material impression of a finite set of immaterial ideas. The Egyptians interpreted the visible world as a kind of infinitely ongoing series production which very faithfully follows an original finite set of types or models. And this same set is also represented by the hieroglyphic system.

### *1.6 The three-tier world and the triune god*

Peculiar to the Ramesside period and, to some extent, antithetical to the cosmology of Amarna religion is a creation theology where the creator appointed a three-tier world for the tripartite forms of his earthly personification.[122] Heaven, in its unreachable height and remoteness, for his ba; earth, in its endlessness and boundlessness, for his image (*ẖnntj*); the underworld, in its unfathomableness and hiddenness, for his body/ corpse (*ḏt/ḫ3t*).

In Amarna cosmology the underworld was unimportant.[123] Amarna divided the world very clearly and rationally into heaven and earth, above and below, as the spheres of god and creation. God created heaven for himself as the place from which he was able to contemplate creation and, by means of the life-giving rays of his eyes, summon it into life every morning. The cosmology of traditional sun religion was much more complex. By including the underworld in the sphere of the sun god and adopting the concept of his nocturnal journey, which would bring him into contact with the dead, the subterranean gods and ultimately his own dead body, the world was divided into a terrestrial Here and Now and a celestial/subterranean Beyond.

The cosmology of Ramesside Amun theology derived from the novel concept of an omnipresent god, who filled the world, not with his light from outside (like the sun god of Amarna and the new solar theology), but from inside with his "power". This concept of god gave rise to that cosmogonic concept that appropriates the

---

121 A.H.Gardiner, *Ancient Egyptian Onomastica* (Oxford 1947), I, *1.

122 Cf. the references collected by Zandee, *Amunshymnus*, 190f.

123 Though not specifically emphasised, this much is clear from the well-documented overview given by L. Zabkar, *Ba Concept*, 156-159 of the Amarna ideas about life after death that affect the ba. This reduction of cosmology to heaven and earth is quite clear from the fact that the underworld journey is replaced by the description of night in solar journey hymns; cf. Chapter 3 §3.3. If the "progressiveness" of a system in the process of social evolution is determined by the degree of its complexity, Amarna cosmology has taken a step backwards: it is much less complex than traditional Egyptian cosmology. Indeed, it was a revolution, not an evolution, that ensured its acceptance. In terms of systems theory one might say that the low level of its complexity was not appropriate for the time; it was not able to make sense of the world for the Egyptians of that period.

terminology of traditional solar theology, the idea of "ba" and corpse, to express something quite new by adding a third component: the image. The creator god made the heavens high enough for his ba,[124] the earth wide enough for his image and the underworld deep enough for his corpse,[125] all of which expressed the idea of divine co-extension with the world. God created the world in the process of creating and extending himself. This was not simply a "withdrawal", as in the new solar theology tradition, but an extension simultaneously in all directions. God filled the world from inside to its boundaries and, according to Hymn 200 of the Leiden Amun Hymn, beyond (chapter 5, §3.1).

As always when a new concept makes use of traditional terminology, it is a delicate undertaking to detect it among the various formulations used by the texts. But *STG* text 17 makes clear use of it:

| | |
|---|---|
| *pt ẖr bꜣ=k ḥr sṯz ꜣḫw=k* | Heaven has your ba and raises up your radiance |
| *dꜣt ẖr ḥꜣt=k ḥr sḥꜣp ḏt=k* | The underworld has your corpse and conceals your body |
| *tꜣ pn ẖr ẖnntj=k* | This land has your image |

Taking this as a starting point, one would also like to apply the new concept to all those cases where the image on earth is mentioned next to heaven/ba and underworld/corpse, e.g.

(1) P. Leiden J 350 IV 15-16 (ch. 5, §3.1)

(2) P. Leiden J 350 VI 12-13[126]

| | |
|---|---|
| *dꜣt štꜣt ḥr sḥꜣp nb=s* | The secret underworld conceals its lord; |
| *ḏbꜣtj jmj ḥꜣw=s* | the one in the coffin is resident there. |
| *bꜣ=f jmj pt* | His ba is heaven, |
| *ḥwt=f Wꜣst n ẖnntj=f* | his mansion is Thebes for his image; |
| ... *n sꜥḥ=f ntj m dꜣt* | ... for his mummy which is in the underworld. |

124 Cf. *STG* Text 141, 23q: "You created heaven for your ba, when you were alone"; *STG* Text 255,8g: "Who created heaven to raise his ba". Further examples in *ÄHG* no.100,23.

125 The motif is also found in the context of solar theology in the binary form that contrasts only heaven and underworld (also heaven and earth): (1) Pleyte and Rossi pl.146,8 *jrjw tꜣ r sḥꜣp ḏt=f/ꜥẖ pt n bꜣ=f* "who made the earth to hide is body/who raised high the heaven for his Ba"; (2) text 256 and TT 178,8 *jrjw n=f pt r sqꜣ bꜣ=f/dꜣt r sḥꜣp ḏt=f* "The sky was made for him to elevate his Ba/the netherworld (was made) to hide his body" (TT 178,8 reads *smḏw dꜣt n ẖꜣt=f* "the netherworld was made deep for his corpse"); (3) text 113,56ff. *[sštꜣ.n=k dꜣt] r sḥꜣp sšm=k/ꜥẖ=k pt r sꜣẖ [bꜣ=k]* "you made secret the netherworld to hide your image/you raised high the sky to glorify your Ba"; (4) *Edfou* III 186 *ꜥẖ pt n bꜣ=f wbn=f jm=s/dꜣt štꜣ.tj <r> ḥꜣp ḏt=f* "who raised high the sky to rise in it/the netherworld is made secret <to> hide his body"; (5) Quibbell, *Saqqara* IV, pl.73.3 *oẖ pt m sṯzw [šw n] ꜣḫt=f/ḏt=f mnẖ[tj m dꜣt]* "who raised high the sky in the air for his light-eye/whereas his body is perfect in the netherworld"; (6) BD 15B II (Berlin 7317) = *ÄHG* no. 44 and 62 (here in the sense of the new solar theology as heaven and earth) *ꜥẖw pt r ḥpt jrtj=fj/jrjw tꜣ r swsẖ jꜣḫw=f* "who raised high the sky for the circuit of his two eyes/who made the earth to enlarge his radiance". Cf. Zandee, *Hymnen*, 3-4.

126 Zandee, *Hymnen*, 110-111.

(3) P. Berlin 3050 VIII 1-3[127]

You have raised heaven to raise your ba,
you have kept the underworld concealed for your falcon image.
You have raised heaven as far as your arms reach,
you have extended the earth as far your footsteps reach.
Heaven acclaims you because your ba is so powerful,
the earth trembles before you because your image is so holy.

(4) P. Berlin 3049 = *ÄHG* 127A

63-64: The one who created heaven for his ba
to illuminate the Two Lands;
66-67: the one who conceals the underworld to hide his "secret";[128]
84-85: the one who wears the crown in Thebes
in that cult image of his, which is bigger than the gods.

(5) *Edfou* III 196

His ba is in the horizon,
his body is in the underworld,
his august image (*ᶜẖm*) is on the great throne[129]

(6) *Urk*. VIII §12b[130]

The one who raised the curtain of heaven, settled on his ground,
to make his horizon secret for his ba.
The one who made this land and created what is in it
for his exalted image;
who made the underworld dark and unending (*kk.tj ḥḥ.tj*),[131]
to hide his *ḏt*-body in it;
who made a gate from one to the other because he wanted,
to walk about and see what he had created.

(7) Graffito of Osorkon in Daressy, *Rec.Trav*. 18 (1896)

The one who raised up heaven, appearing in it;
it (heaven) endures under his sun,
as the underworld under his body,
to conceal his secret.
The great one, who came into being at the beginning,
the Two Lands bear his image (read: *ẖnntj=f*)

Some of the passages do not refer to creation, but describe a constitution of the world that is both present and atemporal (nos. 1,2,5). This seems to be the meaning

127 *ÄHG* no.22D,2-11; cf. *LL*,305.
128 On designation of the corpse of the sun-god as "his secret" s. *LL*,84-86.
129 Cf. *Edfou* I 495.17: "the heaven is elevated for his Ba, the underworld is founded for his corpse, the earth is hacked up (?) read "established"? for his images (*ᶜẖm*).
130 Cf. Sethe, *Amun*, § 150; "Primat und Transzendenz", 12.
131 Cf. *STG*, text 156(d).

of this *topos*, even where it is formulated as a cosmogonic image. Like the topos of the life-giving elements to be discussed in the next section, this one merges in with the concept of a world god. By inhabiting and filling the world as ba, image and body (viz. the three aspects of his person), he personifies the cosmos:

> His body is the wind,
> heaven rests on his head,
> the primeval waters bear his "image",
> his priest is the "falcon on the palace facade"( = the king).[132]
>
> Your feet are on the earth,
> your head is in the sky.[133]
> You stand up with the strength of your arms,
> but your weight rests upon the secret.
> The sky is over you, the underworld beneath you,
> Geb is able to conceal you;
> they do not know what arises from your body.
> Your strength raises water to heaven,
> the clouds are the breath of your mouth,
> the wind is the air in your nostrils.[134]
>
> You are the sky, the earth and the underworld,
> you are the water, you are the air between them.[135]
>
> Your eyes are the sun and the moon,
> your head is the sky,
> your feet are the underworld.[136]

We are dealing here with the origin of a conception of the divine which was to become supremely important in Late Antiquity: the "cosmic god", the supreme deity in Stoicism, Hermetism and related movements,[137]

> whose head is the sky,
> whose body is the air,
> whose feet are the earth.
> You are the ocean.[138]
>
> The celestial universe is my head,
> my body is the ocean,
> the earth is my feet,
> my ears are in the ether,

132 *Hibis* 33 = *ÄHG* no.130,25-28.
133 Cf. P.Leiden I 344 vso IV.11: "who strides on earth, his head in the sky"..
134 P.Berlin 3048 = *ÄHG* no.143,90-102.
135 *Hibis* 33 = *ÄHG* no.130,205f.
136 *STG*, Text 88,12-15.
137 A.J. Festugière, *La révélation d'Hermès Trismégiste* II: *Le dieu cosmique* (Paris, 1949).
138 R. Merkelbach, M. Totti, *Abrasax. Ausgewählte Papyri religiösen und magischen Inhalts* I (Opladen, 1990), 136f., cf. ibd., 127-134 for similar Greek texts and for their striking parallels with Ramesside theology.

my far shining eye is the light of Helios.[139]

## 2. Life

### *2.1 The concept of the life god*

Just as Egyptian religion permits us to speak of the concept of the "creator god" in connection with various gods (but the "creator" being always in the singular), the question of giving life to and preserving creation is always associated with the life god. The life god is usually the creator, who takes responsibility for his creation. As far as I know, the only exception to this is the Shu theology of the Middle Kingdom, which will be discussed presently. The texts, however, can be divided very precisely between (a) the origin of coming into existence, (b) the establishment of the cosmos and (c) its continuing provision with life, soul and movement. These three categories correspond to the concepts of primeval god, creator god and life god, which have to be kept apart, even if the next stage of theological reflection is anxious to equate them.

The concept of the life god probably dates back to the Old Kingdom in the divine name *ʿnḫw* "the living".[140] We can, however, be more certain in the case of the theology of Shu the air god, which is presented in spells 75-80 of the *CT* in a form that has been slightly adapted for the purposes of "funerary literature" and dates from the beginning of the Middle Kingdom.[141] Shu appears here as a god of the air between heaven and earth and god of the breath of life "in the nostrils" of the individual creatures.[142] It is his duty to give life to creatures and provide them with the conditions necessary for life and keep them alive, and he does this on behalf of his father Atum the creator god.[143] Thus, there is a distinction between creator and life god, even though the association between father and son approaches a unity of natures in terms that bring to mind the Christological formulae of the Early Church.[144] As life god Shu is called *ʿnḫ*[145] and *nḥḥ*.[146] Just as the individual life unfolds in the "lifetime" (*ʿḥʿw*) allotted to it from the inexhaustible supply of time (*nḥḥ*),[147] the absolute life of the life god, from which all life proceeds, unfolds in the absolute *nḥḥ*-endless time, which gives rise to individual years and "life-times".[148]

I am life, the lord of years
the living one of *nḥḥ*-endless time

---

139 Macrobius, *Saturnalia* I 20, 16-17; R. van den Broek, in *Hommages à Marten J.Vermaseren,* (EPRO 68.1) (Leiden, 1978), 123-141; Merkelbach, loc.cit., 129f.

140 H. Junker, *Der Lebendige als Gottesbeiname im Alten Reich*, Anz.AW Wien (1954), No.12.

141 A. de Buck, *Plaats en betekenis*, 16ff, (esp. 21-25); Zandee, *Hymnen*, 131ff.

142 *CT* II 42-43; de Buck, *Plaats*, 21.

143 *CT* II 43; de Buck, *Plaats*, 22; "Primat und Transzendenz", 25.

144 de Buck, *Plaats*, 32ff.; *Ma'at*, 172-74.

145 Numerous references in de Buck, 22-23.

146 de Buck, 23.

147 On *ʿḥʿw* and *nḥḥ* cf. *Zeit und Ewigkeit*, 11-18 and 54-57

148 *LL*,87-88; *Zeit und Ewigkeit*, 36-41.

the lord of *ḏt*-endless duration.[149]
But N is life
the heir of *nḥḥ*-endless time
who spends *ḏt*-endless duration.[150]

In the New Kingdom we come across the concept of the life god in various contexts, which we have already discussed: in the early theology of Amun-Re, as it is presented in P. Cairo 58038 (cf. chapter 4 §3) and especially in the new solar theology,[151] above all in Amarna religion, where the concepts *ʿnḫ* and *nḥḥ* are of central importance in determining the concept of god (chapter 3 §2.5). Amun theology of the Ramesside was based on these traditions. It attained to the concept of a life god. Unlike the Aten and the still purely solar life god aspect of early Amun-Re theology which brought life to the world "from outside" by means of "radiating hands",[152] he gives life to the world macrocosmically from inside and operates microcosmically as a life force in every single living creature. This concept is expressed in the old formula, modified by the introduction of the preposition "*m*" in "*Jmn mn m jḫt nbt*".[153] It was the "pneumatic" aspect of the air as the breath of life that was now conceptually distinguished quite clearly from the cosmic aspect,[154] even if Amun personified both, as Shu does in the *CT*. Amun was "the breath of life in the heart of all things",[155] an "omnipresent hidden power of life".[156] He too, as personification of cosmic life like Shu before him, personified cosmic "endless time", within which this life is completed and which came to be interpreted as the life-span of the world god himself, whose life movement brought forth time. Time as cosmogonic energy, which brings forth everything that exists in it,[157] is a *modus operandi* of the life god, since the concepts of "time" and "life" are inseparable in Egyptian.[158] Like Shu in the Middle Kingdom, Amun was called quite simply "life".[159] In view of their many writings with *-jj*[160] and *-w*,[161] a translation like "the

149 *CT* II 39.
150 *CT* VI 389g.
151 The text published in Quibell, *Exacavations at Saqqara* IV, pl. 73.3, which can be restored with the help of P.Berlin 3048 (=*ÄHG* no.143,10) is an important one: "Radiant One, life of the gods (cf. P.Leiden J 350 II 10)/illustrious one, who rises in the east.../living one, when he opens up the darkness". Cf. also P.Berlin 3049 IX,3: *pꜣ ʿnḫjj nṯr jwtj sk m-m skjjw/rnpjj n rʿw nb nn jnw ḏrw=f* "You living one, god, who does not perish among the perishable ones, who is renewed every day without reaching his limits". On the solar conception of the life god and its relationship to "endless time" cf. *LL*, 87-88.
152 Cf. chapter 5, note 121 (93); *Saeculum* 23, 117-118.
153 Cf. *STG*, text 134(b) and Sethe, *Amun* §§219-230.
154 On the possible connections between Amun, the Hebrew concept of *ruaḥ* YHWH and the Greek concept of pneuma cf. Merkelbach/Totti, *Abrasax*, II, 34-42.
155 Cf. Sethe, *Amun* § 193; Esna No.249.4, Sauneron, *Esna* V,89.
156 Zandee, Hymnen, 132 with regard to the Shu-theology of the Coffin-texts.
157 *Zeit und Ewigkeit*, 36-41.
158 Cf. *LL*, 87-88; many references in *Zeit und Ewigkeit*, 30-41, 49-63.
159 *ʿnḫ* with god-det.: Berlin 818; *FIFAO* 20,119f.; Deir el Medine No.280; O.Cairo 12225 ed.Posener, *RdE* 27,206; *Urk* VIII § 65c; *Hibis* 31 B 29-30; P.Ch.Beatty IV,6,4-5 = *ÄHG* no.195,71; P.Berlin 3048,X,7 = *ÄHG* no.143,248; cf. Sethe, *Amun* §§ 205-6; Otto, *Gott und Mensch*, 110-111.
160 E.g. P.Berlin 3049,IX,3; *Hibis* pl.32,9; Mariette, *Monuments divers* pl.46; *Urk* VIII § 139d; Barguet, *Le temple d'Amon-Re*, 303.

living" might be more precise, but the meaning is the same.[162] As in the Middle Kingdom, the personification of the *modus operandi* of the life god and the form in which every creature participates in his operation were concentrated in the idea of the "breath of life" (*ṯȝw n ʿnḫ*). Thus, Amun as life god became the god of the breath of life and was invoked as such, for example, in scene VIII of the Late Period Birth Mystery.[163] As in the Middle Kingdom, this breath of life of the individual was associated with the cosmic element of the air in such a way that Amun also appeared as air god. The air was no more than his own breath of life, just as endless time represented the temporal form of his own life span.[164] His nature cannot be reduced, as Sethe suggested, to that of a pure air god. Indeed, whenever the cosmic activity of Amun in the form of air is mentioned, water and light are also mentioned in the same context. It is the three elements together that make up his manifestation as life god.

### *2.2 The* topoi *of the life-giving elements and the emergence of the Ramesside idea of the world god*[165]

#### *2.2.1 Examples*

(1) *STG* Text 206

| | |
|---|---|
| Water | The one who brings up the Nile, so that they have food to eat,<br>who brings good to everyone. |
| Light | When he rises, human beings come to life, their hearts come to life when they see him. |
| Air | The one who gives air to those in the egg,<br>who keeps fish and birds alive,<br>who takes care of the mice in their holes and similarly of worms and fleas.[166] |

(2) *STG* Text 17 = STG *Text* 186

| | |
|---|---|
| Air | You have taken on your form as breath of air,<br>to give it to the nostrils.<br>Life is possible only when you will it.<br>You are the creator who gives birth with your mouth, eyes and arms. |
| Water | The Nile wells up in his caves,<br>it waits to go forth from you. |

161 So the formula in the OK (Junker,op.cit.).

162 The context makes it clear that the idea of 'life', even in the participial form 'the living', is meant transitively, as energy that gives life. Sethe and Otto both translate 'life', while Barguet renders it 'celui qui est la vie'. On Osiris as *ʿnḫ(jj)* cf. Derchain, *Pap.Salt 825*, (72); Junker-Winter, *Philä* II, 203.29.

163 Daumas, *Les Mammisis des temples égyptiens* (1958), 428ff.

164 On air and time see *Zeit und Ewigkeit*, 40 n.137, 63 with n.74.

165 Cf. "Primat und Transzendenz". Neither the late sources nor the religious-historical parallels quoted in this article (pp.7-13) will be repeated here.

166 S. Text 206 (h) for the relation of this text to P.Cairo 58038 and Text 212 and a stela in Stockholm (*ÄHG* no.163).

Light — King of Endless Time as chief of the gods,
they see and live through you.
The heaven carries your ba and raises your radiance,
the underworld contains your corpse and conceals your body.
Your name is a source of jubilation and exultation.
Water is inundated with gold from your influence,
heaven is faience for your sake.

## (3) P. Leiden J 350 V 19ff. (239)

His ba is Shu,
his heart is Tefnut,
Light — he is Harakhte who is in heaven.
His right eye is the day,
his left eye is the night;
it is he who leads the "faces" on all ways.[167]
Water — His body is Nun,
it contains the inundation
which brings forth everything that is and preserves all that exists.
Air — His breath is the breath of life to all nostrils,
he determines the fate and prosperity of everyone.[168]

## (4) O. Vienna 6155 and O. Cairo CG 25214 (242)

Light — You have created yourself as the day-time sun (*šw*)[169]
and night-time moon,
Water — since you are simultaneously the Nile[170] that keeps human beings alive
Air — and the air that allows windpipes to breathe.

## (5) *STG* Text 156

Life — Life belongs to you, there is no other,
to give life to every face (...)
Light — You are the light that drives away the darkness;
no eye lives that does not see you.
Air — You are the air that enables windpipes to breathe.
There is no bird of prey that can live without you.
Water — You are the Nile that keeps human beings alive,
no face lives without your presence.

## (6) The Hymn of Ramesses III[171]

Light — Your skin is the light,

---

167 Similarly the direct identifier *ntf* "he is" alternates with other forms of the relationship of the god to other gods in IV,12-21; cf. above §3.1. On the motif of the "ways" cf. Chapter 3 §2.4

168 The typical connection between "air" and "fate", cf. *LL*,216 with n.137; *Zeit und Ewigkeit*, 63f.

169 *šw* as opposed to *jʿḥ*, i.e. 'sun'(not 'light'). On *šw* as the Late Egyptian equivalent of *jtn* cf. S. Schott, *Die Deutung der Geheimnisse*, 79, where Middle Egyptian *jtn* is rendered by Late Egyptian *pꜣ šw n dwꜣ* "the sun of morning" in the "Ritual for Warding Off Evil" 95, 20/21.

170 *jw=k m ḥʿpj*, not: *ntk*...!

171 *OIP* XXV, pl.23; *ÄHG* no.196.

| | |
|---|---|
| | your breath is the "fire of life" (*ʿnḫt*),[172] |
| | all precious stones are united on your body. |
| Air | Your limbs are the breath of life to every nose, |
| | inhaling you brings life. |
| Water | Your taste is the Nile, |
| | people anoint with the radiance of your light-eye (...). |
| Earth | Coming and going is possible when you appear |
| | as earth god |

## (7) Neskhons = *ÄHG* no.131

| | |
|---|---|
| Light | Radiant torch with great light, |
| | the sight of you enables people to see.[173] |
| | People spend the day looking at him and do not get their fill. |
| | When the day dawns, all people worship him.[174] |
| | Glittering of appearance in the midst of the Ennead, |
| | his form is suitable for every god.[175] |
| Water | The Nile comes, the north wind blows upstream |
| Air | inside this secret (*štȝ*) god.[176] |

## (8) Graffito of Osorkon[177]

| | |
|---|---|
| Time | The one who rises in endless time (*nḥḥ*), |
| | who sets in endless duration (*ḏt*)[178], |
| | who reaches the bounds of eternity (*mz ḥntj*...). |
| Light | The one who is reborn as nocturnal light |
| | in its effective (*mnḫ*) form as the moon. |
| Water | The one who comes as the Nile, to flood the Two Lands, |
| | who keeps every mouth alive with his discharges; |
| Air | he is the air, which wafts down from space, |
| | to allow everyone to breathe. |

## (9) The Stela of the Exiled[179]

| | |
|---|---|
| Air | He is a Khnum, the excellent potter, |
| | the breath of life, |
| | the breath of the north wind; |
| Water | a high Nile, whose ka provides life, |
| | which takes care of gods and men. |
| Light | The day-time sun, the moon of the evening |
| | which crosses the sky without becoming weary. |

---

172 Cf. *Urk* VIII 1g, Sethe, *Amun* § 202.
173 Id. *Hibis* 32, see supra.
174 = *STG,* Text 83,11-12.
175 For such phrases s. "Primat und Transzendenz", 37.
176 Cf. *Hibis* 32 = *ÄHG* no.129,144-45.
177 Ed. Daressy, in *RT* 18 (1896), 182.
178 On the typical correlation of *nḥḥ* with sunrise and *ḏt* with sunset cf. *Zeit und Ewigkeit*, 44 note 155.
179 Ed. v.Beckerath, in *RdE* 20 (1968), 7-36.

## (10) *Hibis*,33,5-5 (*ÄHG* no.130)

| | |
|---|---|
| Air | his body is the wind, |
| | the sky rests on his head, |
| Water | the primeval waters bears his secret. |
| | The falcon on the palace facade (king) is his priest, |
| Light | the sail wind bears him on his voyage to the west |
| | when he travels to the secrets of the underworld. |

## (11) *Esna* no.387,4-5[180]

| | |
|---|---|
| Light | The one who allows everyone to travel the ways and sail upstream and down |
| | by the sight of his eyes (*nṯrwtj=fj*)[181] |
| Water & Air | The Nile (*Nnw*) comes forth, the north wind blows upstream |
| | at the behest of this exalted god. |
| | He comes as the inundation when he chooses, |
| | to fill the Two Lands with his benefits. |
| Life | Life that makes all things live (*jrj ˁnḫ jḫt nbt*). |
| | Water and air are in his bequest, |
| | he gives them to whom he will. |

## (12) P. Berlin 3049 (*ÄHG* no.127A,99-110)

| | |
|---|---|
| Light | Your sun shines, every face can see, |
| | since your right eye appeared at the beginning. |
| | Your left eye, it drives away the darkness; |
| | heaven rejoices when it is reborn. |
| | Its light in the night is like that of the day, |
| | there is no end (*sk*) to your rising. |
| Water | The Nile streams with your dew (*jꜣdt*), |
| | it is rejuvenated in your body |
| | Everything that it produces belongs to you, for you have created it. |
| | All faces live from the nourishment you give them. |
| | Inexhaustible one, who never become weary of keeping alive what you have created. |
| Air | Nostrils breathe the air that you give, |
| | the sky comes with its north wind |
| | as the breath of your mouth. |

## (13) P. Berlin 3048 (*ÄHG* no.143,100-125 in excerpts)

| | |
|---|---|
| Water & Air | Your strength raises the water to heaven, |
| | the clouds are the breath of your mouth, |
| | the [winds] are the breath of your nose, |
| | your spittle is on the mountains |
| | and envelops the leaves of the trees on all desert hill-tops with water. |
| | The one who encircles the two banks of heaven. |
| | Ocean to the end of Nut.(...) |
| | There is none who can live without you, |
| | for it is from your nose that the air comes |

---

180 Sauneron, *Esna* III 368,V 220-21.

181 A fine example of the "way motif" as an expression of the world made "habitable" by light; cf. Chapter 3 §2.4.

| | |
|---|---|
| | and from your mouth that the flood comes. |
| | The "tree of life" grows upon you, |
| | you make the earth green, so that the gods have more than enough, |
| | as well as human beings and animals. |
| Light | It is your light that makes them see. |
| | When you set, the darkness comes. |
| | Your eyes create light (...) Your right eye is the sun, |
| | your left eye is the moon, |
| | your retinue are the unwearying ones (stars). |

## (14) *Hibis*, 31: the Ten Names of Amun.[182]

| | |
|---|---|
| Light: Sun | The one whom those in the nomes see,[183] |
| | the light of the Two Lands, |
| | the bull of the inundation, who lives eternally |
| | in his name: Re, every day. |
| Light: Moon | Living of births, who rules over his left eye, |
| | who is loved by the whole world |
| | in his name: full (*mnẖ*) moon, |
| Air | God of the *jb* and *ḥꜣtj* hearts, |
| | who breathes out air and enables the windpipe to breathe: |
| | Amun, remaining in all things, |
| | ba of Shu for all gods. |
| Water | The body (=incarnation?) of life, which creates the "wood of life", |
| | the corn god who overflows the Two Lands, |
| | without whom nothing lives in Egypt in his name: Great Nile.[184] |

The following hymn, vv.58ff., treats the ba's *in extenso.* In Hibis only the first three cantos, referring to the first three ba's, are recorded:

58-85 : Amun=Atum-Khepre-Re, Primeval God, Creator, Sun God.
86-102 : Amun=Atum, Osiris, Thoth (the Moon)
103-133: Amun=Shu (Wind and Breath of Life).

---

182 Cf. J.C. Goyon in R. Parker *et* al., *The Edifice of Taharqa*, 69-79. There is a parallel for part of this hymn on a demotic ostracon; cf. M. Smith, *Enchoria* VII (1977), 149-155; other parallels exist in Philae, ed. H. Junker and E. Winter, *Das Geburtshaus des Tempels von Philae* (DÖAW Sonderband) (Vienna, 1965), 426F. and Karnak, Temple of Opet (unpublished). See chapter 5, §3.2.3.

183 In accordance with Goyon, op.cit.

184 The following six names are formed after another scheme, which clearly indicates that they belong to another level:

| | |
|---|---|
| (5) *Rs-wḏꜣ* | *nṯr jrjw sšp* |
| "The one who wakes up whole"(=Osiris) | "god, who makes the light" |
| (6) *Kꜣ-njswt ꜥnẖ* | *nṯr ḥnmmt* |
| "Living Royal Ka" (=Horus) | "god of humankind" |
| (7) *bꜣ bꜣw* | *nṯr ꜥwt mnmnt* |
| "Ram of Rams" ( xiLL,78-87) | "god of animals large and small" |
| (8) *ḥrw-ꜣḫtj* | *nṯr sḏrw* |
| Harakhty | "god of reptiles" |
| (9) *bꜣ jmjw mw* | *nṯr msḥw* |
| "ba of those in the water" | "god of crocodiles" |
| (10) *Nḥbkꜣw* | *nṯr jmjw qrst=sn* |
| Nehebkau | "god of the dead". |

The fourth canto would then have treated Amun as Nun, an aspect of the god that was particularly important in the Ethiopian Period.[185]

(15) *Hibis*, 32 (*ÄHG* no.129,107-151)

As an appendix to the four stages of the cosmogonic process represented in four great songs
I 37-51:Self-creation as primeval god.
II 52-69: Conception of creation "in the heart".
III 70-95: Implementation of the creation plan.
IV 96-107: Withdrawal as sun.
The following stanzas are devoted to the subject of preserving creation
V 108-129: Solar journey.
VI 130-151: Life-giving elements:

| | |
|---|---|
| Light | He has created heaven under his control<br>and travels in it to illuminate the earth for his children.<br>He travels north and south and considers what he has created,<br>his eyes irradiate the Two Lands. |
| Time | His left eye is in the night, when he is the moon<br>to distinguish the times of the day, months and years.<br>His sun is in the day, his moon in the night;<br>he never ceases,<br>he endures in millions and billions,<br>his kingship reaches to the end of time. |
| Water | The bringer of the Nile, he has opened its source caves,<br>he has caused the water to pour forth from its caves;<br>it swells and recedes according to his will.<br>He spews forth and swallows as he pleases. |
| Air | The south wind blows north and the north wind blows south,<br>The west and east winds are in his nostrils.<br>Storms have their day and stars their duty according to the command of this illustrious god ... |

### 2.2.2 Origin and development

We first come across the idea of a triad of life-giving elements in the loyalist tradition of the Middle Kingdom,[186] where the role of the king was presented as that of an all-embracing provider, either in the form of someone controlling the elements, as in Sinuhe:[187]

| | |
|---|---|
| Light | The sun rises for your sake. |
| Water | Water in the river is drunk only when it pleases you. |
| Air | Air in the heaven is breathed only when it pleases you |

185 Cf. J. Leclant, *Recherches sur les monuments thébains de la xxv.e dynastie, dite éthiopienne*, *BdE* 36 (1965), 240-41.
186 Cf. *SAK* 8 (1980), 16-19.
187 B 232-234.

or in the form of a metaphorical identification, as in the Loyalist Instruction:[188]

| | |
|---|---|
| Light | He is Re who enables us to see<br>one who illuminates the Two Lands more than the sun. |
| Water | He is one who makes things grow more than a high Nile<br>he has filled Egypt with the "wood of life" |
| Air | When he becomes angry, noses 'freeze'<br>when he is pacified, they can breathe. |

This tradition is taken up by the strongly loyalist texts of Amarna,[189] which praise the king as

| | |
|---|---|
| Light | light of every single land<br>whose sight enables people to live |
| Water | Nile of human beings,<br>whose ka causes people to be satisfied |
| Air | God, who creates great things and forms small ones<br>air for the nose, which makes breathing possible.[190] |

These *topoi* reveal the king as a life god on the social level. His efficacy as the one who provides all, gives life to all and determines fate is represented as a set of cosmic metaphors intended to express the all-embracing nature of this efficacy; but at the same time they are always meant in the social sense. The king is not simply light, air and water, but is "for" humans or, more significantly, those who are loyal.[191] It is precisely this limitation that becomes invalid when these topoi are used in the realms of theology to present the operations of god in the world as those of the all-embracing god. With reference to the god, light, air and water are not metaphors, but are meant literally as cosmic energies in which the life-giving energy is manifested. If Shu as god of air and the breath of life was life god, and Amun-Re and Aten as the sun also fulfilled this function, the Ramesside life god brought this tradition into an all-embracing synthesis, by explaining the totality of the "elements" (light, air and water) as cosmic activities of the life god, who is thus god of light, air and water in one.

This concept developed in the course of the 19th dynasty from the theistic idea of a god controlling the elements to the "pantheistic" idea of a god personified in the elements, i.e. to the idea of a world god, whose eyes are the light, whose breath is the air and whose sweat is the water. Example 1 (*STG* text 206 from TT 215: Seti I) stands at the beginning of this development: it has taken its material almost completely from P. Cairo 58038 and merely re-arranged it according to the new tripartite scheme of the elements, probably inspired by Amarna religion. Example 2, a text recorded in TT 194 and 23, is from the 19th dynasty: it too has used an earlier model that has nothing in common with the "elements" model:

188 G. Posener, *L'Enseignement loyaliste* (1976), 21f., 68f. (§ 3).
189 With more details: *SAK* 8 (1980), 1-32.
190 Inscription in the tomb of Panehsi = *ÄHG* no.234. An almost exact copy of the text, also referring to Khonsu, appears on a Ramesside block statue in the Mut temple (CG 917); cf. *SAK* 8 (1980),1ff.
191 *SAK* 8 (1980), 18 n.83.

*STG* Text 253

> You have taken on your form as breath of life
> to give it to the noses
> life is possible only when you wish it.
> You are the one who creates children of children
> with your mouth, eyes and hands.

In the model further predicates of the creator are attached. The activity of god as the life-giving breath of air is associated with his creation, e.g. in a hymn of the Berlin Amun Ritual:[192]

> You are the one who gives air to every nose
> to make live what you have created with your hands
> you are the god who create with your hands
> you alone, and no other is with you

The Suty-Hor hymn treats this dual aspect of god as breath of life and creator in the brief formula:[193] "Khnum and Amun of humans".

The Great Hymn of Amarna, also referring to the manifestation of god in the breath of life, devotes its embryological excursus to him. Here, and in *STG* text 253, we are dealing with the new solar theology.[194] Example 2 (*STG* Text 17=186), however, continues differently. It mentions the Nile in connection with the air form of the god and, adding a reference to the sun as ba, proceeds to the theology of the threefold impersonation of god as ba, image and body in the three cosmic regions of heaven, earth and underworld:

| | | |
|---|---|---|
| 27-32: | air | (*ẖprw*) |
| 33-34: | Nile | (*pr ẖntj*) |
| 37 : | sun - | *bꜣ* |
| 38 : | | *ẖꜣt* |
| 39 : | | *ẖnntj* |

Air and Nile are related to the god in a way that clearly transcends mere divine control of these elements. He "transforms himself" into air and the Nile "proceeds from him". Light, the sun, is specified as the ba of the god, a concept that for its part is a constituent element of a threefold system, just like the light. As a result of the interlocking[195] the internal connection of both triadically organised conceptions emerges clearly: both refer to the connection between god and world. As life god and creator of living things god gives life to the world in the form of the three life-giving elements; as world creator god fills the world, which he has created as a space for his tripartite personification:

---

192 P.Berlin 3055 = *ÄHG* no.125,21-24.

193 *ÄHG* no.89,40.

194 S. ch.3 § 2.5.

195 The same interlocking also occurs in P.Leiden J 350 III,1-2: "The sun disk of heaven shines before you (*n ḥr=k*)/the Nile streams forth from its source because of your divine primevality/The earth has been established for your image/What Geb causes to grow belongs to you alone".

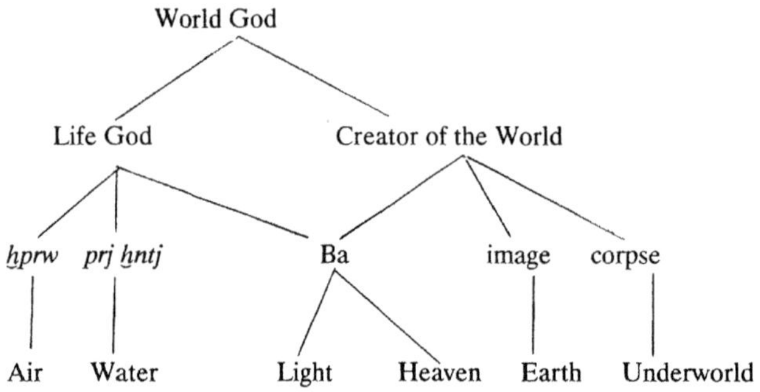


This scheme makes it clear how far we are from the clear-cut concept of a world god in the proper sense. Only from the 20th dynasty onwards (exx. 4-6 come from the 20th dynasty) does this concept receive its canonical formulation.[196]

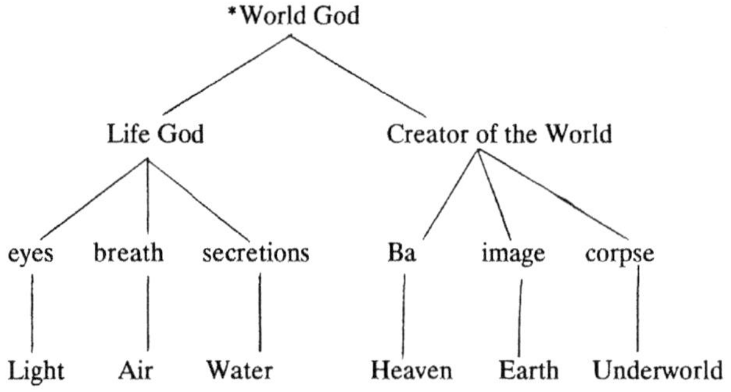


We need not examine the numerous passages of this concept of god in the Greco-Roman temple inscriptions.[197] But I should like to select a typical text, which connects this idea of a life god with the aspects of the creator and primeval god and subordinates them all to the overlapping and all-embracing concept of the "hidden ba". In doing so, it expresses the quintessence of Theban theology:[198]

> The exalted ba as king of the gods continues
> to spend endless time,
> while endless duration is before you.[199]

---

196 This, unlike its predecessor, is an imaginary structure (hence the asterisk) that does not correspond to any concrete Egyptian text, but may illustrate the point I am trying to make.
197 See "Primat und Transzendenz", 5-13.
198 *Urk* VIII § 1g.
199 Cf. on such phrases with *ḏt* (never *nḥḥ*): *Zeit und Ewigkeit*, 68-69.

He is the exalted ba, who arose at the beginning
The creator of heaven, earth and the underworld
Who creates life, namely, wind, light, water (*qbḥt*)
and "fire of life", from which everything lives.

The text once again makes it clear that these topoi deal principally with the idea of life-giving. This explains why there are three elements. But when it is principally a question of the elements that *constitute* (and not only sustain) the world, a fourth element is added: the earth. This question also becomes the subject of the theology concerning Amun-Re as a world god. To clarify it the ba concept is used once again: Amun-Re is represented in the sun chapel of Medinet Habu as a "ba with four heads and a neck",[200] in whom four ba's are united:[201]

| | |
|---|---|
| ba of Osiris : | water |
| ba of Geb : | earth |
| ba of Shu : | air |
| ba of Khepre : | light. |

In this theory of the elements, widespread in the New Kingdom and Late Period, the four elements are represented as four ba's uniting into (or as) one ba[202] and there are four cosmic regions which together form the cosmos (and correspond to the four generations of the Heliopolitan Ennead).[203] In the case of the life-giving elements it is more a matter of energies that give life to the cosmos. In late Ramesside world-god theology both of these aspects merged, with the result that there too the earth was occasionally added.[204]

200 Cf. *STG* Text 156 and p. 207, note (t); J.C. Goyon, *Les dieux gardiens*, 117 n.6; M.C. Betrò, *EVO* 12 (1989), 43 (d).

201 Medinet Habu VI 420 B.2, cf. the parallel text in the Book of the Day, see M.C. Betrò, *EVO* 12 (1989), 37-54. J.C.Goyon, *Les dieux gardiens*, 117 n.6.

202 The first occurence is in the Ani copy of the BD in a vignette accompanying c.17 (=*Urk* V,50). In the Saite Period the ram of Mendes was seen as the union of the 4 ba's = elements; cf. Wild, in *BIFAO* 60 (1960), 57 n.3; *LL*, 80; Sauneron, *Esna* IV, No.405,1-2; 431,2; 437,6; 441,2; Sander-Hansen, *Die religiösen Texte auf dem Sarg der Anchnesneferibre*, 128; *Urk* VI, 75, 18; Goyon, in Parker *et al.*, *The Edifice of Taharqa*, 79 n.80. See also Betrò, op. cit. On Osiris as water cf. the ancient idea of the Nile as a discharge of Osiris cf. Pyr 848a ff.; *CT* IV 130; *Urk* IV 1779; Mariette, *Abydos* II 54/55 = *ÄHG* no.220,23-25; O.Cairo 25209; Caminos, *MDIK* 16, 21.8-9,22 passim; Bonnet, *RÄRG* 571; Frankfort, *Kingship and the Gods*, 190ff.; Junker, *Das Götterdekret über das Abaton*, 37ff.

203 If Atum is inserted for Khepre. Cf. Assmann, *Das Grab des Basa*, AV 6 (1973), 72-73 (on the tetradic nature of the elements).

204 Cf. example text 6 (*ÄHG* no.196).

# CHAPTER SEVEN

# JUDGE AND SAVIOUR: THE GOD OF THE INDIVIDUAL

## 1. The Problem of Personal Piety

The problem of 'personal piety', in Ancient Egypt, is briefly this: are we dealing (a) with a structural feature of Ancient Egyptian religion, typical of all its periods but very differently testified by archaeological and textual evidence, or (b) with a historical movement typical only of a particular period (viz. the Ramesside period as "the age of Personal Piety", as Breasted called it), but implying forerunners and consequences? The first position is advocated especially by J. Baines[1] and others,[2] the second one by, among others, Breasted,[3] Posener[4] and myself.[5] I think that the arguments offered by Baines should lead to a more multi-layered understanding of the phenomenon. I prefer an 'as well as' solution to an 'either-or' one, by designing a theoretical framework that allows for both structural plurality and historical changes. The conventional dichotomy between "official religion" and "personal piety" should be replaced by a tetratomy: "official religion" (state), "local religion" (nome and town), "popular religion" (house and family) and "personal religion" (individual). Within this broader framework, 'personal piety' emerges as "personal religion" in the form of a religious movement having its roots in Theban festival customs ("local religion") and spreading during the Amarna period all over Egypt, eventually changing the whole structure of Egyptian religion, mentality and world-view.

As far as the structure of the religion is concerned, I propose to interpret the change in terms of a transformation of the classical three-dimensional conception of religious experience into a four-dimensional one. The three classical dimensions are (1) the political (cult and community), (2) the cosmic and (3) the mythical (language, names and narratives). For a detailed description of these three

1 "Society, Morality, and Religious Practice", in B.E. Shafer(ed.), *Religion in Ancient Egypt. Gods, Myths and Personal Practice* (London, 1991), 123-200 and "Practical Religion and Piety", *JEA* 73 (1987), 79-98.

2 Cf. e.g. J.G. Griffiths, "Divine Impact on Human Affairs", in *Pyramid Studies and other Essays in Honour of I.E.S. Edwards*, 92-101.

3 *Development of Religion and Thought in Ancient Egypt* (1912).

4 "La piété personelle avant l'âge amarnien", in *RdE* 27, 1975.

5 *Ägypten - Theologie und Frömmigkeit*, 258-274; "State and Religion in the New Kingdom", in W.K. Simpson (ed.), *Religion and Philosophy in Ancient Egypt*, (YES 3) (1989), 55-88; *Ma'at. Gerechtigkeit und Unsterblichkeit im alten Ägypten*, 252-272.

dimensions, which underly all Egyptian religious thought and practice from the beginnings until the New Kingdom and which continue as the "implicit theology" of ritual practice until the Greco-Roman period, see *Ägypten: Theologie und Frömmigkeit einer frühen Hochkultur* (Stuttgart, 1984). "Personal piety" has to be understood as the irruption of a fourth dimension, viz. history. In the New Kingdom, and only now, historical events tend to be experienced and interpreted as "divine interventions",[6] expressions of divine will. To postulate that Egyptian religion was always and from its first beginnings "four-dimensional" and that history was never considered to be devoid of religious significance is to blur the obvious differences between the Mesopotamian, Israelite and Ramesside texts on the one hand, and the earlier Egyptian documents on the other. I prefer to respect these differences and to distinguish between a "theology of preservation" dominating earlier Egyptian thought, and a "theology of will" which emerges in the New Kingdom, becoming the dominant conception in the Ramesside period and bringing Egyptian religion nearer to Mesopotamian and even early Israelite beliefs.[7] Movements must be interpreted according to what they lead to. In the case of "personal piety" or "theology of will", this is the establishment of direct theocracy in the 21st dynasty. The will of god, expressed in oracles, takes over the affairs of earthly government after having determined the course of history in an ever increasing degree. Can it be mere accident that roughly about the same time various Palestinian tribes give themselves an even more radically theocratic constitution which leaves initiative and decision to the will of God? It seems fairly clear that we are dealing here, not with timeless basic structures valid for all periods of Egyptian history and documented for the first time only in the Ramesside period, but with fundamental historical transformations.

To deal adequately with this aspect of god in the Ramesside period would require a section larger than the previous two chapters put together. It is not to be regarded as a sort of appendage to five or six other aspects, but forms, as it were, the other side of a dual-faced god, who is both world-god and helper in time of need,[8] a god who is both cosmic and personal, the all-creating and sustaining principle and the god of the individual. This duality, which encompasses all divine forces active in the world in the two foci of the cosmic and personal god and links them to the dual unity of an all-embracing concept of god, represents the most characteristic achievement of Ramesside theology, distinguishing it from everything that went before. In a sense, it is the heir of Amarna religion. The same attempt to "focus" all divine forces was made in Amarna, but Amarna seems to have had a quite different and uncommonly selective grip on reality and, instead of developing a "dual unity", it distributed the divine powers between the king and the god.[9] This step, which proved to be too violent and too selective (because it excluded too much

6 Bertil Albrektson, *History and the Gods. An Essay on the Idea of Historical Events as Divine Manifestations* (Lund, 1967).

7 Cf. "State and Religion".

8 Cf. the pertinent remarks by F.Junge, in: W. Westendorf (ed.), *Aspekte der spätägyptischen Religion*, 95ff., concerning Isis as "Kosmosgöttin und Nothelferin", cosmic and saviour goddess.

9 *Zeit und Ewigkeit*, 54-61 and *SAK* 8 (1980),1-32. This division does not, however, mean a "division of power"; cf. §4.

that was meaningful), was a necessary historical preliminary to the integrating achievement of Ramesside theology.

## 2. Life

### *2.1 Not as cosmic element but as individual blessing*

Chapter 6 dealt exclusively with the cosmic aspect of the "life god". As such Amun is in a tradition of other life gods, who had appeared either as air (and light)[10] or as light (and air)[11] with the function of an all-life-giving force. Amun is superior to these in the sense that he is all, viz. light, air and water in one. He is superior also in that he is "life" in quite a different sense:

(1) O. Boston MFA 11.1498/Hymn of Hori the vizier to Amun-Re:[12]

| | |
|---|---|
| *twt pꜣ ꜥnḫ* | You are life, |
| *nꜣ ḥsw r ḫt=k* | the blessings of life are at your disposal: |
| *wsrw ꜥḥꜥw* | wealth and life, |
| *jmꜣḫ zmꜣ-tꜣ* | venerableness and burial |

(2) Inscription of Rome-Ray in Karnak:[13]

| | |
|---|---|
| *ꜥnḫ m-ꜥ=k* | Life is in your hand, |
| *snb ḫr=k* | health is at your disposal; |
| *šꜣjj rnnt* | Fate and fulfilment |
| *dmḏw m ḫfꜥ=k* | are united in your grip |

(3) Stela of Ramesses III in Karnak:[14]

| | |
|---|---|
| *ṯꜣw mw* | Air, water, |
| *ꜥnḫ m ḫfꜥ=k* | and life are in your grip. |
| *wḏꜣ snb ḫr=k* | Health and prosperity are at your disposal. |

The earliest example of this very common theme of the "personal life god" in Ramesside hymns comes from TT 49 (*STG* Text 59a: Ay):[15]

| | |
|---|---|
| *ꜥḥꜥw m ḫnw=k* | Life is within you, |
| *ꜣwt m ḫfꜥ=k* | Old age is in your grip. |
| *Šꜣjj Rnnt ḫr=k* | Fate and fulfilment at your disposal. |
| *wꜣḏ-wj ntj m ḥzwt=k* | How fortunate is the one who is in your favour! |

---

10 Shu as god of light: see de Buck, *Plaats en betekenis*, 33-35.
11 Re as benefactor of air: Text 52 (e); *LL*,215f.(43)-(44).
12 Ed. J. Cerny, in *JEA* 44 (1958),23 pl.X.
13 Ed. G. Lefebvre, *Les inscriptions des grands-prêtres*, 32.
14 Ed. Kitchen, *RI* V, 239; cf. *RdE* 30 (1978),42f.
15 Completed by Bankes Coll. Stela 8, Kitchen, *RI* I, 396; var. see Text 59a (m).

| | |
|---|---|
| *n pḥ.n sw ḏw nb* | No evil can overtake him. |

The final praise of the blessed[16] reveals clearly what concept of life-giving is meant here. It states that the good things of life are "in the hands of god". It is not a question of life as a cosmic omnipresent force, which is at work "permanently in all things", but rather the achievement of personal existence that will be given to the one who is "in the favour of the god".

"In the hand" and "in the grip" mean something like "at the disposal". It does not mean a blessing like light, air or water, poured indiscriminately into the world by the god and shared by everyone,[17] but rather a blessing given only to those who "act on god's water" and "put into their heart" the greatness of god.[18] The originally loyalist concept of "blessing" (*ḥzwt*) introduces a polarity and selectivity into the conception of god's life-giving and sustaining inclination towards creation that is absent from earlier and especially Amarna texts. As this selectivity implies individual recognition and evaluation, it corresponds exactly to the principle of individual religion. The partner of divine attention is not "creation" or even "mankind", but individual man or, to be more precise, the human heart as the epitome of inner man. The heart comes to be regarded as the seat of god in man.

### *2.2 The concept of the heart and of individual divine governance*

In the tomb of the Vizier Pasiara from the time of Seti I (ca. 1300 BC) a short invocation to Amun is put into the mouth of a sculptor:

> Amun the rudder
> for him who puts him into his heart.[19]

Both elements of this phrase already appear with reference to Amun 150 years earlier. On an ostracon inscribed with a prayer from the time of Amenophis II Amun is invoked as "the good rudder" (*ḥmw nfr*) and on another ostracon of the same group we read:

> I put you into my heart because of your strength. [...]
> You are my protector. Behold: my fear has vanished.[20]

The concept of "Putting god into one's heart" becomes very common in New Kingdom texts. Very often it is connected with guidance and protection. Already in

16 On the form history of the "makarismos" or beatitude cf. "Weisheit, Loyalismus und Frömmigkeit", 29ff.; the form which gives a reason for the beatitude of the blessed seems to be a creation of the Amarna Period.

17 Cf. CT spell 1130, the "apology of the creator", where god asserts that he has created "the four winds" and "the great flood" explicitly for everybody alike.

18 *jrj ḥr mw* "to act on the water of" and *rdj m jb* "to put in one's heart" are the phrases most commonly used to express piety; cf. "Weisheit", passim.

19 Assmann, Hofmann, Kampp, Seyfried, *Das Grab des Pasiara (Nr.106)*, THEBEN (in preparation), Text 173.

20 Ostr.Cairo CG 12217 recto ed. G. Posener, in "La piété personelle avant l'âge amarnien", *RdE* 27 (1975), 206f.

the time of Thutmosis III we read in a hymn already quoted in chapter 4:

> God is father and mother for him who puts him into his heart,
> He turns away from him who neglects his city, (...)
> But he whom he leads will not lose his way.[21]

In the time of Ramses II a man called Kiki, a follower of the goddess Mut who donated all his property to her temple, wrote in his tomb autobiography:

> My heart is filled with my mistress.
> I have no fear of anyone.
> I spend the night in quiet sleep,
> because I have a protector.[22]

In many prayers of the same time Amun is invoked as:

> Pilot who knows the water,
> rudder that does not lead astray,
> who gives bread to him who has none,
> who keeps alive a servant of his house.[23]

> You are Amun who comes to him, who calls unto him,
> the pilot who knows the water,
> the rudder that does not lead astray.[24]

> Pilot who knows the water,
> rudder that does not lead astray,
> sharpsighted one who knows the shoal.[25]

This idea finds its most explicit and, as it were, "classical" expression in a famous passage in the *Teaching of Amenemope*:

> Keep firm (*dns* "make heavy") your heart, steady your heart.
> Do not steer with your tongue.
> If a man's tongue is the boat's rudder,
> the Lord of All is its pilot.[26]

For classical Egyptian anthropology, there is no other place on earth to establish Maat than the heart of man. Now, instead of Maat, i.e. common sense and social reason, it is god who fills and steadies the heart. The concept of the god-directed heart seems to be shaped by individual needs: shelter from fear and anxiety, guidance in a trackless and unintelligible world, protection against persecution, human injustice, malign demons and deities, dangers of every sort,

---

21 *STG*, 228-30; *ÄHG* no.75.
22 Abd el Qader-Mohammad, in *ASAE* 59 (1960), pl. 48ff.; J.A. Wilson, in: *JNES* 29, 187-92; *ÄHG* no.173.
23 *ÄHG* no.177 pAnastasi II, 9.2
24 *ÄHG* no.188, Ostr.Wilson ed. Wilson, in: *AJSL* 49 (1932), 150-53.
25 Tabl.BM 5656 *ÄHG* no.190, 26-28.
26 *Amenemope* XX.3-6; Lichtheim (1976), 158.

including the fear of Pharaoh.[27] Typical requests for salvation refer to the injustice of the judges and to calumny: "may you rescue me from the mouth of men".[28] Not only man's inner world of passions, fears, drives and emotions but also the outer world of society and nature are now considered unsteady, irrational, subject to abrupt change:

> Do not say "Today is like tomorrow".
> How will this end?
> Come tomorrow, today has vanished,
> the deep has become the water's edge.
> Crocodiles are bared, hippopotami stranded,
> the fish crowded together.
> Jackals are sated, birds are in feast,
> the fishnets have been drained.[29]

For the Ramesside experience, the world has become unintelligible, incalculable and unstable. It no longer inspires comfort and confidence. There is nothing firm and stable within and without but god, the sole fixed point in a turning world. In order to find steadiness, man has to establish an axis between god and heart, to put god into the heart, as the phrase goes, and to surrender to god's leadership. Amenemope even goes so far as to equate the heart with "the nose of god".[30] The heart is to be smelled and breathed by god. Smelling and breathing, the sense of the nose, is the sense which establishes the closest contact. The individual is not only seen and heard, but "smelled" by god. Already in the Pyramid Texts the dead person wants to be the lotus flower at the nose of the sun-god. In a Coffin text the creator is summoned: "Kiss (or "breathe") your daughter Maat, place her at your nose!"[31] God lives from breathing human Maat: order, justice and truth. These are the ideas behind Amenemope's bold image of the heart. The heart is not to be put at the nose of god, it *is* the nose of god within man. In everything he does, says or even thinks, man cannot avoid the effect of smelling good or bad, just or unjust, to the nose of god. As offending god and offending one's own inmost self are one and the same, piety and devotion become the principle of personal identity and harmony.

27 *LÄ* "Furcht"; "Gefährdungsbewußtsein". Morenz, "Die Furcht Pharaos".

28 Tabl.BM 5656 *ÄHG* Nr.190,38-40 see p. 612 for other references. Cf. Job 5.21. Also the teaching of Amenemope promises to "save him (the disciple) from the mouth of strangers" (I.11), Lichtheim (1976), 148.

29 *Amenemope* VI.18-VII.4; Lichtheim (1976), 151.

30 I prefer this reading of the London Papyrus to that of the Turin tablet, which reads "gift". Gift is pointless because for Amenemope everything is a gift of god.

31 CT II 35c; cf. I. Shirun-Grumach, "The Goddess Maat", in: S.I. Groll (ed.), *Pharaonic Egypt, the Bible and Christianity* (Jerusalem, 1985), 173-201, 176f.

## *2.3 Theology of will: life and time in the hands of god*

Human beings are as dependent on god's blessing (*ḥzwt*)[32] as, in another sense, on the breath of life: it is the embodiment of the cosmic all-effective life energy that created and sustains them. The benefits of this blessing can be summarised abstractly as the principle of permanence: as long life (*ꜥḥꜥw qꜣ*) in the Here and Now, it will be filled with happiness, prosperity and health; in the Beyond, it means "venerableness" (*jmꜣḫjj*[33]) and "good burial" (*qrst nfrt*[34]). It is identical with the principle of Maat,[35] which until the Amarna period had been understood as the world order arranged by god at the beginning, the principle of the equitable distribution of the god-created benefits of life. Human beings are instructed to follow Maat, the just order. "Those who live by it"[36] perform justice for the creator. The close connection between "Maat" and "life" can be seen from the Shu theology in the CT, where Shu (Life) is accompanied by his sister Tefnut (Maat).[37] Maat was equally important in Amarna religion, where Aten personifies the cosmic and the king the personal aspect of the life god, the "ethical authority" that "lives from Maat".[38] One has the impression here that the "justice" of the individual turns out to consist less in following an unchangeable order than in following the instructions and will of the king: the just are those who follow the king[39]. It is this "theology of will" that characterises the Ramesside concept of a personal life god who provides not only the good things of life, the blessings of "existence", but also disposes of these things according to his own will. Success is no longer the inevitable consequence of good deeds guaranteed by the principle of Maat, but is in the gift of god alone and is entirely at his disposal.[40]

It is not necessary to examine these questions here in detail; they have been dealt with often enough before.[41] What is important in the present context is the

32 On the term *ḥzwt* see *Zeit und Ewigkeit*, 60-64; H. Tellenbach (ed.), *Das Vaterbild in Mythos und Geschichte* (1976), 26-28; "Weisheit...", 30f.,39f., 47.

33 The expression *jmꜣḫ* indicates the status of the well provided tomb owner, which was achieved in one's lifetime and survived one's death; cf. "Weisheit", 39 and note 100.

34 The value placed on a "good burial" is very clearly expressed in P.Ch.Beatty IV rto 8,6-7: *jw twn=f m qrst nfrt/n jb ḥtp ḥr mꜣꜥt* "his reward is a good burial/for a heart that is satisfied with Maat" (the whole text is quoted in §6.2). Later on (7,4) the god is addressed as follows: *mtn=k m qrst nfrt/n ḥsjj rdjw ḥs n=k/prj=f tp tꜣ m bꜣ nfr r mꜣꜣ nb nṯrw* "your reward is a good burial/for the singer who gives praise to you/that he might come forth on earth as a perfect ba to see the lord of the gods". The idea of a good burial as the ultimate benefit also occurs in Greek texts; cf. K. Preisendanz (ed.), *Papyri Graecae Magicae* XXI, 17 (ταφὴ ἀγαθή). On burial in general cf. *RdE* 30 (1978), 45-47.

35 Maat as "principle of continuation": *SAK* 8 (1980), 22f.n.110.

36 Cf. *König als Sonnenpriester*, 63f.

37 S. A. de Buck, *Plaats en betekenis*, 21f. with ns. 133-136.

38 R. Anthes, *Die Maat des Echnaton von Amarna*, *JAOS* Suppl. (1952).

39 Cf. *SAK* 8 (1980), 23 with n.111.

40 Cf. H. Brunner, "Der freie Wille Gottes in der äg. Weisheit", in *Sagesses du Proche Orient Ancien* (*CESS*) (1963), 103-117.

41 See in addition Morenz, *Die Heraufkunft des transzendenten Gottes in Ägypten* (SSAW 109.2) (1964); Otto, *Die biographischen Inschriften der ägyptischen Spätzeit* (PÄ 2) (1954), 22ff.; "Weisheit...", 12-15.

idea of the personality of god, the idea of a divine will, which in the Ramesside period is associated with the concept of a life god and is the equivalent of personal piety in human beings:

He is loved as king of the gods, lord of Karnak,
his divine face is ram-headed.
Life goes forth from him,
his is the shrine of the north wind,
the Nile is under his fingers,
it falls from the sky on the mountains at his command.
His strength is victorious, he is master of fear,
his anger is directed against the impious;
he destroys rebels.
Eating and drinking are done at his will,
heart and belly are in his grip;
there is no pleasure without him, to him belongs joy,
the one who is in his favour is jubilant.[42]

In the Ptah hymn of P. Harris both aspects of the life god, cosmic and personal, are subordinate to the higher concept of the "lord of time":

Lord of endless time, lord of endless duration,
lord of life, who enables windpipes to breathe,
who gives air to every nose,
who keeps every face alive with this nourishment.
Life, fate
and fulfilment are his to command;
his utterance makes life possible.[43]

That the Egyptians did not distinguish between "time" and "life" has already been emphatically pointed out.[44] Cosmic time, *nḥḥ* and *ḏt*, is merely the life span of the god himself. Every creature has a share of it, just as they do of the air, which is the breath of god and the breath of life in the nostrils of every human being. If, however, one begins to think of the god, not as cosmic energy, but as a person, whose forethought and "utterance" are the source of time and its contents (viz. fate and history), one's traditional orientation towards the past and the just order, fixed once and for all at the beginning, breaks down. There is a change of direction and one now begins to look towards the future, which is open and entirely at the disposal of god:[45]

| | |
|---|---|
| *nḥḥ rn=k* | endless time is your name |
| *ḏt sšm=k* | endless duration is your image |
| *k3=k ḫprw nbw* | Your ka is everything that happens.[46] |

42 P.Ch.Beatty IV rto 8,9-9,1 = *ÄHG* no.195,161-174.

43 P.Harris I,44 = *ÄHG* no.199,13-19.

44 See ch. 6 § 2.1 with ns. 145-50.

45 For a detailed discussion of this reorientation, at any rate exclusively within the framework of a theology of time, cf. *Zeit und Ewigkeit*, 61-69; here, 207ff.

46 Text 17 (= no.186), 43-45(y).

## 3. Saviour and Helper of the Oppressed[47]

| | |
|---|---|
| *jw ḥr nb ḥr ḏd Ḥn=k-jmjjḤ* | Every face says, "We belong to you", |
| *qn ḥsj m jst wʿt* | strong and weak alike; |
| *wsrw mj šwꜣw m rꜣ-wʿ* | rich and poor from one mouth, |
| *jḫt nbt m mjtt* | all things equally. |
| *bnr=k m jb=sn r-ꜣw* | Your loveliness fills their hearts, |
| *nn ẖt šwtj m nfrw=k* | no body is devoid of your beauty. |
| *jn-jw ẖꜣrt ḥr "hꜣjj.n jm=k"* | Do not the widows say, "You are our husband", |
| *kttw ḥr "jtj.n mwt.n"?*[48] | while others say,""Our father and our mother"? |
| *wsrw ḥr ʿb m nfrw=k* | The rich boast of your beauty, |
| *jw ḥr šwꜣw ḥr=k* | the poor turn their faces to you. |
| *nttw ḥr pẖr ẖr=k*[49] | Prisoners turn to you, |
| *ẖrjw ẖꜣjjt ḥr ʿš n=k* | the sick call upon you. |
| *wnn m=k r mkj-ḥʿw n wʿ nb* | Your name is an amulet for the lonely, |
| *wḏꜣ snb n ntj ḥr mw* | prosperity and health for those on the water, |
| *nḥm m-ʿ ẖntj*[50] | a saviour from the crocodile. |
| *sẖꜣ nfr m ꜣt ḥw-n-ḥr*[51] | To think of whom is good in times of distress, |
| *nḥm m-rꜣ n šmw*[52] | who rescues from the mouth of the hot-blooded. |
| *jw ḥr nb ʿnw n-ḥr=k* | Everybody turns to you |
| *r spr=sn ẖr=k* | to implore you, |
| *jw ʿnḫwj=kj wnw* | your ears are open to hear them and |
| *r sḏm sn ḥr jrt ẖrt=sn* | fulfil their wishes. |
| *pꜣjj.n Ptḥ mrjw ḥmw=f* | Our Ptah, who loves his handiwork, |
| *mjnw mrjw jdrt=f* | our shepherd, who loves his flock. |
| *jw twn=f m qrst nfrt*[53] | His reward is a "beautiful burial" |
| *n jb ḥtpw ḥr mꜣʿt* | for a heart that is satisfied with Maat.[54] |

This hymn, which may be regarded as typical,[55] deals with the existential dependence of humans on god. The consciousness of such a dependence is, certainly

47 H. Brunner, in *MDIK* 16 (1958), 5ff.; Otto, in *Tradition und Glaube* (Fs. K.G. Kuhn), 9-22.

48 This is a popular literary theme of the time; cf. Cerny-Gardiner, *Hieratic Ostraca*, pl.5,1.

49 *ntj* "to bind"; it is the opposite ofd *wḥʿ* "release". pTurin Pleyte and Rossi 73+18,1 (*JEA* 41, pl.IX,42,15f.) *wnw ntjw ntfw wḥʿw* "those bound were released and set free"; P.Ch.Beatty IX vso 2,7 (=*ÄHG* no.189,26-28): "You sweet breath for those who are in captivity/they say, 'Come to me, Amun'. When day comes, you release (*wḥʿ*) them. Similarly, pTurin Pleyte and Rossi 26,3.2: "You give air to those who are bound". The Israel Stela (ed. Kitchen, *RI* IV, 13,12): "He gives air to his subjects who are bound" The same idea is used of the kings in *ÄHG* no.241, 9-10 and Text 187(s).

50 Similarly: P.Leiden J 350 III 18-19 = *ÄHG* no.194,13-14; Zandee, *Hymnen*, 59.

51 Cf. P.Leiden J 350 III 20: *ꜣḫ rꜣ m ꜣt ḥr-n-ḥr/ṯꜣw nḏm n njsw n=f* (= *ÄHG* no.174,17ff.) "whose word is effective in the moment of panic/and sweet breath for those who call upon him".

52 Many of the prayers illustrating personal piety contain a plea for "salvation from the mouth of man": Cerny-Gardiner, *Hieratic Ostraca*, 89 vso = *ÄHG* no. 190, 38-39; ibid., 8,1; statuette Leiden D 19; Boeser, *Beschrijving* XII pl. V (22); *RT* III, 104; Bruyère, *Mert Seger*, fig. 36. Cf. Bankes Coll. stela no. 6 = *ÄHG* no. 160. It even features in the title of the *Teaching of Amenemope* (1,11) as a goal of wise instruction: "to save him from the mouth of people".

53 Cf. n.33.

54 P.Ch.Beatty IV rto 7,11-8,7.

55 *ÄHG* nos.147-200 are an attempt to present a complete collection of the longer texts. The "70th" canto of the Leiden Amun Hymn (*ÄHG* no.174) bears a striking resemblance to P.Ch.Beatty IV.

from the Old Kingdom, one of the basic elements of Egyptian cosmology.[56] However, it takes on quite a different reality and clarity if time is understood as open to the future, where human beings are entirely at the disposal of god.[57] This gives rise to a concept of total dependence on god, without whom life, directed towards an uncertain future, is impossible.

The new solar theology came very close to these views, even to the extent of using similar formulations. Compare

| | |
|---|---|
| *nn ẖt šwtj m nfrw=k* | no body is devoid of your beauty |

with *STG* text 151,15

| | |
|---|---|
| *nn bw šw m ḥḏḏwt=k* | no place is devoid of your light. |

Even the preceding sentence in P. Ch. Beatty (v.126)

| | |
|---|---|
| *jw ẖwt mḥtj m nfrw=k* | bodies are full of your beauty |

"internalises" the sentence that occurs so frequently in the new solar theology text ("when the sun god rises, he fills the Two Lands with his beauty"[58]) and changes it from mere looking at the outer light to an illumination and permeation of the whole inner person by the greatness of god.[59] Not only the eyes, but also the heart of human beings turns to god. P. Ch. Beatty continues:

| | |
|---|---|
| *jrtj gmḥ=sn jm=k* | Eyes look at you |
| *jw snḏ=k n ḥr nb* | fear of you fills everyone |
| *jb=sn pẖrw ḥr=k* | their hearts are turned to you.[60] |

The idea of the omnipresence of light elaborated in the new solar theology is here internalised with reference to human beings and extended from the phenomenon of "light dependence" of everything visible[61] to the all-embracing and existential dependence of human beings on god.

The idea of the omnipresence of light undergoes the same change of meaning also with reference to the concept of god, with only slight modification of well-established formulations. The phenomenon of light, in which the unattainably distant sun comes palpably near to earth creatures, provides the new solar theology with the idea of the simultaneous remoteness and proximity of god:

---

56 Cf. A. de Buck, "Het religieus karakter der oudste egyptische Wijsheid", in *NThT* 21 (1932), 322ff.

57 The *locus classicus* for this idea is Chapter 18 of *Amenemope* (XIX,11ff.); cf. I. Grumach, *Untersuchungen zur Lebenslehre des Amenemope*, 124-128; cf. ibid.VI,18-VII,10 Grumach,49-55; *Zeit und Ewigkeit*, 66f. with lit. in n.90.

58 Cf. ch. 3. § 2.4.

59 On *ẖt* "body" as a description of the "inner person" cf. *LL*, 196 note 2. Cf. also the examples in Text 188 (b). In P.Ch.Beatty the word also occurs in two other places, which both express an internalised idea of the omnipresence of light: v.4 "your eye is in every body" and v.250 "you are leader in every body".

60 VII, 9-10 verses 127-129.

61 Cf. supra, ch. 6, §1.4 p. 173, n. 86; ch. 3, §2.4.

| | |
|---|---|
| *wꜣjw tknw nn rḫ.tw=f* | The one who is remote and near, who cannot be known.[62] |
| *šw=f m pt*<br>*nmtt=f ḥr qꜣw (...)*<br>*ḥr tkn sḏm*<br>*jꜥ jb ḫft njs n=f* | His sun is in the sky,<br>his strides are in the heights (...)<br>(but he is) approaching and listening<br>and gladdening the heart when he is called upon.[63] |

Compare the following passage from a text of Theban Amun theology:

| | |
|---|---|
| *sḫm ꜥšꜣ rnw nn rḫ.tw=f*<br>*wꜣw pw m dgꜣ*<br>*tkn m sḏm* | Power with many names, who cannot be known<br>he is remote as a seeing one<br>and near as a hearing one.[64] |

The idea of the proximity of god arises not from the sensual experience of light, but from the transcendental idea of a divine omniscience and omnipresence, in which god is right next to the heart "that turns to him". If the "looking god" could still be identified with the sun god, the cosmic "phenomenology" of the new solar theology, with the concept of the "listening god", is transcended in the direction of a personal god, who is not equally near to all like the sunlight, but only to those who call on him. He is not, like the sunlight, "simply there". He has to be "found".[65]

(The god the individual)

> ... has eyes and ears,
> a face on all sides for those he loves.
> He hears the prayers of those who call him,
> he comes from far away[66] in a moment to those who call him.[67]
>
> He gives his hands to him who is in (his) bondage,
> who comes at the cry of the one who prays to him.[68]
>
> He looks upon human beings, and there is no one who does not know him;
> He listens to millions among them.[69]

---

62 Hymn (fragment) ed. Quibell, *Exc.at Saqq.* IV (1908-10),pl.73.3 = P.Berlin 3048 II 8-9 = *ÄHG* no.143, 17; cf. ch. 3 § 2.3.

63 P.Leiden I 344 vso IV,11-V.1; Zandee, *Amunshymnus*, 372-380.

64 P.Berlin 3049, VIII 4 (=*ÄHG* no.127B, 34-35). This formula is re-interpreted passively in the Late Period: god is seen (as the sun) in the remote distance, but heard (as the wind) in closest proximity: *wꜣw m ḥrw/ tkn m msḏrw* "far away in the faces/close to in the ears". *Edfou* I 40; *Urk* VIII 15h; *Esna* No.387.5-6, Sauneron, *Esna* III, 368; *Esna* V, 220-21; Sethe, *Amun* §§ 204, 207f.

65 The expression *gmj* "be found" indicates the revelation of god evidently experienced by the writers of the personal piety texts; cf. *ÄHG*,597 on no.148,39; Posener, Fs Ricke, 60 n.6: "le verbe s'emploie, à l'époque, en parlant de l'intervention divine". Posener refers to the Qadesh poem, to some Deir el Medina stelae and to pAnastasi IV,10, 3+5.

66 *Idem* Berlin 20377 = *ÄHG* no.148B, 24; Graffito in TT 139 = *ÄHG* no.147,32.

67 P.Leiden J 350 III 16-17 = *ÄHG* no.194; Zandee, *Hymnen*, 57f.

68 P.Leiden I 344 vso, v, 1-2, Zandee, *Amunshymnus*, 380ff.

69 Stela of the exiles, *ÄHG* p.71.

You are the one who hears with his ears,
you look upon the millions in the lands.[70]

With many eyes and large ears.[71]
he leads millions with his illumination.[72]
The lord of life, who gives as he wishes,
the globe is under his care[73].

## 4. Judge[74]

Not only does the mercy of god, which is near the oppressed and listens to the petitioner, express itself in the omnipresence and omniscience of god, but also the justice of god, which proceeds against evil. These two aspects of the saviour and judge, mercy and justice, can scarcely be separated.[75] Justice (Maat) in this context means salvation: the liberation of the oppressed from the hands of his oppressor. In his aspect of "lord of Maat", god is typically invoked as the helper of the widow and the orphan, the poor and helpless.[76]

Who saves the miserable from the hand of the violent,
who rescues the child who has no father and mother,
(...)
His abomination is fraud,
the just one who annihilates injustice
in his name "lord of Maat".[77]

The local law-court (*qnbt*) seems to play a special role in the various situations where the god is invoked for assistance and appears as a saviour. Evil manifests itself in human affairs principally as injustice, and the appeal of the distressed for help is principally an appeal for justice. God saves by punishing evil:

---

70 BD of Hunefer, *ÄHG* no.42A,40f.

71 Cf. P.Mag.Harris VII,6: "one who has 77 eyes and 77 ears" and *Hibis* 32,31 (=*Urk* VI,75): "The secret ba with ram-shaped face/with four faces on one neck/with 777 ears/with millions and millions of eyes".

72 Sim. *Edfou* II 69, III 67: *wr jrtj ˁšꜣ ˁnḫwj/sšm ḥḥw m psḏ=f* "with great eyes and many ears, who leads millions by his shining", see Otto, *Gott und Mensch*, 30 and 113.

73 Neschons 22-24 = *ÄHG* no.131,56-59.

74 Cf. Posener, "Amon juge de pauvre", in *Fs Ricke* (1971), 59ff.; Zandee, *Amunshymnus*, 380-402.

75 Cf.B. Janowski, *Rettungsgewißheit und Epiphanie des Heils. Das Motiv der Hilfe Gottes »am Morgen« im Alten Orient und im Alten Testament* (Neukirchen I,1989), with reference to the whole background of Mesopotamian, Egyptian and Biblical cultures.

76 Cf. F.Ch. Fensham, "Widow, Orphan, and the Poor in Ancient Near Eastern Legal and Wisdom Literature", in *JNES* 21 (1962), 129-139; H.K. Havice, *The Concern for the Widow and the Fatherless in the Ancient Near East. A Case Study in O.T. Ethics* (Ph.D.thesis, Yale University, 1978).

77 P.Leiden I 344 vso, v, 3-4.

The petitioners assemble around you,
who reveal the truth,
great god, leader of the gate.[78]

Who turns to those who implore him.
When the earth is bright, he has punished enemies;
the greedy are in a state of non-existence,
but the just are assigned to the land of god.[79]

*STG* Text 212 praises him in similar terms:

Who judges the guilty one and the just,
who assigns the just to the west,
to the land of those who practised justice.
Who sets the fraudulent on the way of (...)
in order to keep him from mingling with the lords of truth.[80]

Here we find not only the human tribunal, where god is being implored to help the poor (who see themselves as being at the mercy of corruptible judges), but also the divinely organised tribunal that decides about justice and injustice. In this divine tribunal post-mortem fate is decided. Only those who successfully negotiate this tribunal are directed to the west and receive a good burial.[81] Here too we come across Amun, the lord of burial,[82] who unites in himself the ideas of the Final Judgement. In fact, the concept of god as "ethical authority" for the Egyptians is almost inseparable from the idea of the Final Judgement. In this respect, the spheres of activity of both Osiris and Re merged with each other at an early date. Those who do not pass the test of divine justice die a 'second death'. Death in this case does not mean physical death, which the Egyptians regarded merely as an opportunity for the just to make the transition to life on a different plane of existence, but rather the absolute end, non-existence (*tm-wnn*). This is the ultimate divine weapon against evil. God controls not only life, but also death.[83] This shows how far and in what direction he differs from the traditional Egyptian concept of a life god:

The air is in his nostrils, the wind in his heart,
life and death are his to command.
It is he who enables blocked windpipes to breathe
and also causes windpipes to contract, as he wishes.
There is no life without him,
we have all come forth from his eye.[84]

---

78 This means the institution of judging at the gate; s. *LL*, 82(6).
79 P.Ch.Beatty IV rto 11, 4-5 = *ÄHG* no.195, 261-267.
80 *STG* p.290-93 with note (l).
81 See n.33.
82 "Amun, lord of burial, who gives a (good) age" is a name of Amun in an inscription in TT 57 from the period of Amenophis III (*Mém.Miss*.I, 129).
83 Cf. E. Otto, "Zur Geschichte einer religiösen Formel", in *ZÄS* 87 (1962), 150-154.
84 Ostr.Cairo 25208 = *ÄHG* no.193,17-22.

In the context of the theme "god as judge", the question arises of the problem of evil. Amarna religion excluded it completely, and to some extent this is true also of the new solar theology.[85] At any rate, the icon of the solar enemy, used by traditional solar theology to express the "evil - justice" complex with its characteristic method of 'analogical imagination' is avoided, as are all other icons.[86] In contrast, P. Cairo 58038 represents the personal aspect of god as the "god of the individual" and "ethical authority" in precisely those two aspects that are also the most important in Ramesside texts: the listening saviour and the just judge.[87] This stanza, however, shows the personal aspect of god still in the mild light of the beneficent philanthropist typical of this early phase of Amun-Re theology, for whom the problem of evil is not immediate.

In contrast, the problem of evil emerges very clearly in the Ramesside picture of the personality of god. The text that devotes most space to this is *STG* text 156, from the tomb of Tjanefer (3rd prophet of Amun under Ramesses III).

> This knife, this sceptre, it slays your enemy,
> you seize your sceptre and strike their heads.
> It (the sceptre) has become Geb,
> your son, your [protector],
> he has taken it and is now wreaking bloody destruction among them.
> The ames-sceptre is in your fist, its limits are unattainable;
> its nature is a secret,
> it is invisible, nobody knows what it is.
> It has power over the powers,
> it roams about, seeking to cause havoc,
> it deals blows to those who will attack it.
> You have overthrown all your enemies,
> whether they are divine, human, transfigured or dead.[88]

The Ramesside Amun-Re is a god who becomes angry with evil and proceeds against it with implacable fury.

> Who can withstand your anger or deflect the fury of your might?[89]

This god, who holds life and death in his hands, has a double face: he operates as one who gives life and brings death, preserves and destroys:

85 Cf. perhaps *STG*, Text 151(m).

86 S. "State and Religion"; *Ma'at*, 231-36; "Theology of Light and Time", 149f.; on the "abolition of icons" in the context of new solar and Amarna theology see ch. 3.

87 See ch. 4 §3.

88 *STG* p.203-209.

89 Hymn on the Stela of the Exiles, *ÄHG* p.71.

Great of punishment,[90] mightier than Sakhmet
like a raging fire
sublime in mercy, caring for those who praise him,
who turns (from his wrath) to heal the suffering.[91]

This image of god has an earlier history that requires some explanation.

## 5. "Division of power" and "representation"

It will not have escaped those familiar with this material how close many of the formulations and ideas dealt with in this section are to the Middle Kingdom theology of the king. This is true for the "duality of power", the control over life and death, expressed in a Middle Kingdom royal hymn as follows:

He is Bastet who protects the Two Lands
Those who worship him are protected by his arm
He is Sakhmet towards those who transgress against his orders
Those who incur his displeasure are forced into exile.[92]

Life is for those who praise him
but his enemies become (non-existent?)[93]

Ramesside hymns treat the subject of god as "ethical authority" using a phraseology familiar from royal texts and, to some extent, non-royal inscriptions of the First Intermediate Period and Middle Kingdom. This is the case with topoi such as "the good shepherd"[94] and "the patron",[95] the "husband of the widow"[96] and the "father-mother of the orphan",[97] "the saviour of the poor and weak from the rich and strong",[98] "the ferryman of the impecunious", "the rudder",[99] the "refuge" (*jbw*),[100]

90 *B3w* in the meaning of "anger": Posener, *RdE* 27, 201 n.9; E. Wente, *Late Ramesside Letters*, 46(g); Gardiner, *JEA* 48, 62 n.3.

91 *ÄHG*, p.71; "State and Religion", 76f.

92 *Enseignement Loyaliste* ed. Posener, §5.11-14.

93 Ibid., 4.7-8.

94 D. Müller, "Der Gute Hirte", in *ZÄS* 86 (1961), 126-144. Cf. for this and the following also the important study by E. Blumenthal, *Untersuchungen zum Königtum des Mittleren Reiches I* (1970), esp. 323f.; cf. "State and Religion", 62f. with note 21; Zandee, Amunshymnus, 94ff.; 323f.

95 On the term "patron" see "Das Vaterbild...", 16-20.

96 "Father of the orphan, husband of the widow": Hannover 11,4, Janssen, *De traditionele Egyptische autobiografie vóór het Nieuwe Rijk* (Leiden, 1946), IV,3.

97 "Father of the orphan": Janssen, loc. cit. IV H1, H2, 3 etc.; "father of the orphan, leader of the oppressed, mother of the fearful": *Urk* IV *Urk* IV 971f. Cf. *Eloquent Peasant*, B 1, 62-64 (new 93-95): "For you are the father of the orphan, the husband of the widow, the brother of the divorced, the apron of the motherless" (R.B. Parkinson, *The Tale of the Eloquent Peasant* (Oxford, 1991), 18).

98 This statement occurs in biographical inscriptions from the OK (e.g. *Urk* I, 200.17) through the MK (Janssen, loc.cit., I, 72; II, 106) until the NK (e.g. *Urk* IV 1445, 2.3; 1082, 12-13; 1077f.).

99 Cf. *STG*,Text 187(t); ch. 4, p.126 with note 147.

100 "Asylum of the oppressed, protector of the suffering": *Urk* IV 971f.

"the incorruptible judge", and so forth.[101] Only the "helper in need" in the real sense seems to be the most idiosyncratic characteristic of god: only he listens to those weeping and comes from afar to those who call on him.[102] He seems to share all other aspects of his personality with the king and even to a large degree with the commoner. In terms of historical development, it even looks as if god "inherited" these activities from the patron/nomarch/king, as if he had penetrated all areas previously regarded as royal or generally human.

This interpretation is not too wide of the mark. The Teaching for Merikare, which praises the well-appointedness of the world and regards creation and the course of the sun as having been made for the sake of human beings, mentions the "listening god", who is at hand in his "hidden chapel"[103] for those who need him, but then goes on to say:[104]

> He created for them rulers "in the egg"
> and commanders to strengthen the back of the weak.

This implies that god has, as it were, delegated the proper distribution of the good things of life created by him and the implementation of a just world order in human-social terms to the king and his officials. This view also occurs in the Cult-Theological Treatise and certainly belongs to the basic concepts of Egyptian royal theology.[105] It is the duty of the king to provide his people with justice and the gods with offerings, to realise Maat and destroy Isfet. CT 1130 also contains a similar self-justification of god, by expressly emphasising that the creator created the good things of life for all people equally, "but their hearts transgressed against what I ordained".[106] Evil was not a part of creation. It arose from the will ("heart") of those who wished to distance themselves from this order. This might indicate that the god, who bears no responsibility for evil, leaves human beings to combat it themselves, since they brought it into the world. Indeed, this is precisely the accusation levelled at the gods in those texts that "reproach god".[107] But the CT go on to say:

> I judge the weak and the poor
> I proceed vigorously against those who break the law
> Life belongs to me, I am its lord
> no one can remove the sceptre of rule from my hand.

A clear statement of the judicial function of god: he has forbidden wrongdoing[108]

101 On the function of imagery in the texts illustrating personal piety cf. *LÄ* I, 430 n.8.

102 "Weisheit,...", 48ff.

103 P.Cairo 58038 IV.1 cf. ch. § ...

104 *Merikare* P 135-136.

105 S. *König als Sonnenpriester*, 58-65; cf. *Ma'at*, chapter 7; "State and Religion".

106 *CT* VII 463f-464b; cf. Otto, *Gott und Mensch*, 38.

107 E. Otto, "Der Vorwurf an Gott" (Vorträge Marburg, 1950). G. Fecht, *Der "Vorwurf an Gott" in den Mahnworten des Ipuwer*, (AHAW 1972.1), cf. the review of Junge, in *WdO* 7 (1973/4), 267-73.

108 This is what is meant when the Egyptian says something like: "I have not ordered you to do wrong": "not order" means "forbid", just as "not cause" means "prevent". Thus, human wrongdoing means transgression of a specific prohibition and not merely, as in the usual interpretation of this passage, acting outside the order or responsibility of god. Understood in this way "wrongdoing" seems to consist in destroying the divinely created equality of all people, that is, in oppression of the weak

and does not allow it to exist. Everyone has to answer to the god.

We must not think of the relationship between god and earthly rulers in terms of a "division of power", as if it were the king who dispensed justice on earth and god in heaven, but rather as one of "representation", where the king in his earthly dispensation of justice manifests the judicial function of god. It seems likely that this same structure of representation is present whenever the subject is one of the just and beneficent exercise of power. Those who act as the husband and widow, refuge of the oppressed, ferryman of the boatless are acting as the image of god.[109] In the light of the idea that man is the image of god, this whole phraseology already acquires theological meaning long before it appears in the hymns. It points to the ways in which human beings can realise Maat. By imitation, human beings can thus share in the goodness and justice of a god who sustains and administers his creation as judge and shepherd, nourisher and support.

The idea that acts realising Maat are quasi-divine is often expressed in the texts:

| | |
|---|---|
| *wꜣḥ-jb ḥr sḏmt mdw* | Patient in listening to statements |
| *mj nṯr m wnwt=f* | like a god in his hour.[110] |

This also explains the rather curious custom of adorning oneself with divine names that embody qualities or actions, e.g. Mentuhotep is not only the "son of (the corn god) Nepre" and "husband of the (weaving goddess) Tayet", but also "Mesekhenet and Khnum the creator of human beings".[111] Rudj-ahau calls himself "Anubis" and "Thoth in his tribunal".[112] Ankhtify of Mo'alla cites himself as

Apis, lord of cattle
Seshat-Hor, lady of goats
Nepre, lord of corn
Tayet, lady of garments.[113]

In this respect, the image of man in the First Intermediate Period and Middle Kingdom reflects the same concept of god that is envisaged by the Teaching for Merikare, CT 1130 and (probably) Admonitions. The difference between human and divine action is that the gods personify these qualities at all times and with regard to the world as a whole, whereas human beings do so only in their spatially, socially and temporally limited sphere.

The distinction between "division of power" and "representation" now makes it

---

(poor) by the strong (rich) Compare the paradigmatic meaning of "greed" in wisdom literature from Ptahhotep to Amenemope. Cf. *Ma'at*, ch.7; "State and Religion". Zandee, *Amunshymnus*, 387-394 gives a rich collection of passages concerning god as a judge and a saviour of the poor.

109 E. Hornung, "Der Mensch als Bild Gottes in Ägypten", in O. Loretz, *Die Gottebenbildlichkeit des Menschen* (1970), 151; Brunner, in *LÄ* I, 306 w.n.29; Otto, "Der Mensch als Geschöpf und Bild Gottes in Ägypten", in *Fs G. v.Rad* (1971), 335-348.

110 J.M.A. Janssen, *De traditioneele egyptische autobiografie vóór het Nieuwe Rijk* (1946) I, 12 No.17; Cairo CG 20539; *Urk* IV 49; TT 27 staircase, right side: *OA* 12 (1973), 32. On the godliness of listening cf. *Anii* X, 8f.

111 Stela London 14333 ed. Goedicke, *JEA* 48 (1962), 25ff. Cf. Schenkel, *JEA* 50 (1964), 6ff.

112 BM 159, ed. Faulkner, *JEA* 37, 49; M. Lichtheim, *Ancient Egyptian Autobiographies Chiefly of the Middle Kingdom* (OBO 84) (1988), 71 Nr.29.

113 Vandier, *Mo<sup>c</sup>alla*, 242ff.; Posener, *Littérature et politique*, 77.

possible to obtain a more detailed picture of the relationship between god and the king, both of which are foci summarising all the manifestations of the divine. Here too one must be wary of interpreting this duality of god and king, cosmic life god and personal god of the individual, as a division of power; this would in no way correspond to the self-understanding of the religion. Here too the king does not dispute the rank of the god when he appears as "fate and life-giver",[114] but simply carries on divine activity in the human world. The problem of identical predicates attached to god and the king in the matter of fate and "ethical authority" is solved by representation, whereby the king is a mirror-image of the god. These ideas are much clearer in Amarna religion because there the whole intermediate sphere of "specific function" deities such as Thoth, Khnum, Bastet, Sachmet, Shay, Meskhenet, Renenet, Nepre, Tayit, Sekhat-Hor, Apis etc. is discarded,leaving only one god and the king as his only possible representative; this makes it impossible for the individual to take on divine qualities in his actions.[115]

After Amarna all the topoi of "ethical authority" (good shepherd, asylum of the oppressed, ferryman of the boatless, pilot, vizier of the poor etc.) are related to god. God is now praised precisely in those aspects of his nature which it is not only possible, but indeed obligatory for human beings to "imitate". The spiritual change expressed in these shifts can now be understood as follows: god now appears directly and no longer through a representative in institutions created by himself and courts appointed by himself. God translates his nature into action and controls creation and order. The idea that god exercises direct control and is entirely free to make decisions is expressed in phrases that speak of being "in the hand of god" or "in the grip of god" with respect to those principles which relate not only to the creation, but above all to the distribution of the good things of life.

This spiritual change is not a phenomenon of Amun theology, not even of religion as a whole. It embraces the whole of Egyptian reality and permeates all levels of the living world. Compare, for example, a simple epistolographic formula of the 19th dynasty: "I am fine today. What I will be like tomorrow I do not know" with one of the 20th dynasty: "I am fine today. Tomorrow lies in the hand of god".[116] That too, which we have defined as the replacement of Maat by divine favour (*ḥzwt*), corresponds exactly to what has recently been established as the difference between wisdom literature of the later period (Amenemope etc.) and that of the

114 Corresponding predicates occur in the Amarna-texts with reference to the god and the king; cf. *Zeit und Ewigkeit*,58 n.47.

115 Being the representative of the "sun" and "state" god (an unfortunate designation, which I have tried to interpret in "Primat und Transzendenz", 18-26) had always been the prerogative of the king. The individual was able to copy only individual aspects of the divine, as they were manifested in forms of the polytheistic divine world. An interesting question, which can be mentioned here only *en passant*, is whether the relationship of the gods to each other should not be understood as "representation" rather than "division of power". The judicial function of Thoth is a classic example: in this capacity he represents the sun god, but does not dispute his rank, any more than the vizier disputes the rank of the king on earth. The same observations may be made on a more general level and throw some light on the problem of both Egyptian "syncretism" and "Ramesside "pantheism", which explains the plurality of gods as representation of the one. In comparison, the structure of Greek polytheism (at least in its archaic form) is one of "division of power"; cf. H. Blumenberg, *Arbeit am Mythos* (1979).

116 Cf. *Zeit und Ewigkeit*, 66 with notes 87-88.

earlier period.[117] The following model will make it clearer, using "C" as a symbol for "causation":[118]

older conception ("indirect causation") — later conception ("direct causation")[119]

C C

C C

C

God Maat action consequence — God action consequence

In the later conception Maat has disappeared from her intermediate position and been absorbed directly into the divine will.[120] Human beings no longer represent god by realising Maat in the sense that they fit into a divinely based order. Rather, they follow the will of god, obey his commands, "put his greatness into their hearts" and "act on his water". In this connection, the question of how god reveals his will to human beings arises, and the answer seems to be oracles and dream-revelations.[121] However, I believe that the problem must be examined more radically. It seems to me entirely questionable whether Egyptians ever thought that the will of god could be known.[122] This question will have to be left to one side. But I do believe that many elements of Ramesside thought can be explained by this estrangement from the principle of Maat.

This is not the place to examine in detail this revolutionary change. But two points may be made in conclusion.

117 E. Otto, *Die biographischen Inschriften* (1954), 22ff.; Brunner, in *Sagesses du Proche Orient Ancien* (*CESS*) (1963), 103-117; I. Grumach, *Untersuchungen zur Lebenslehre des Amenemope*, (MÄS 23) (1972); *Ma'at*, ch. 8.

118 "Weisheit, Loyalismus und Frömmigkeit", 14. In the diagram "C" indicates the causal function: god causes Maat, which in turn causes good deeds, which lead to success (older concept)/god causes success (later concept; the theme of *Amenemope* ch.18).

119 On the distinction of "indirect" and "direct causation" cf. "State and religion", 63-68.

120 On the disappearance of Maat see *Ma'at*, 252-272. This statement has to be taken *cum grano salis*. There are contexts in which Maat does not disappear at all, quite the contrary. The most conspicuous example are the temples of the Graeco-Roman period, where the scenes of the offering of Maat appear in their hundreds. It is only in those genres where the new theology of will is central that the classical concept of Maat is fading.

121 Morenz, *Ägyptische Religion*, 63ff.

122 It seems to me not entirely impossible that a certain élite lived by the norms of social and religious behaviour which are codified in the 125th chapter of the Book of the Dead, the "laws of the hall of the double Maat", as Beki calls them, cf. *Ma'at*, 154-56 and generally 136-159. Beki in fact states in his biography that he not only "rejoiced in saying Maat", but also "put god in his heart, knowing his wrath (*bȝw*)", thus combining the new concepts of individual religiosity and fear of god with the classical idea of a life based on the social norms of Maat.

1. The term *jzft* (wrongdoing) acquires the character of "sin", i.e. transgression against god, only in terms of this later concept. Those who offend against the commandments of Maat will fail. But those who offend against the will of god sin, i.e. they disturb or even destroy a direct relationship between themselves and god. However, they are dealing with a god who can forgive, and this enables them to rectify their error by a positive act of reparation. This is the background to those sacral institutions that have provided us with inscriptional evidence of "personal piety".

2. The earlier concept is a denial of history. It sees the meaning of human actions in the realisation of eternal order. "Maat is great and lasting. She has never been destroyed since the time of her creator".[123] Progressive time is stopped by continued regressive commitment to the origin. The later concept opens up an entirely new idea concerning the historicity of human existence and the transience of life.[124] The will of god is fulfilled in the passage of time. His favour is decided in the fortunes of battle. If he turns from the Egyptians, they fall into the hands of internal or external enemies. If he turns back to the Egyptians, they become powerful and successful and justice prospers.[125] In former times, *ḫprwt*, "the flow of events", was apprehended as sheer contingency. The Teaching for Merikare even states that god has equipped man with magic as a weapon to shield off "the blow of what will happen (*ḫprwt*)".[126] In this view, the notion of *ḫprwt* seems bare of any religious significance. It is not conceived of as a realm of divine intention and intervention. In the New Kingdom, however, we find this realm qualified as the proper domain of god's planning and "ordering".[127] Whatever happens does so on god's order. "What you have ordered is what happens",[128] "everything happens on his order",[129] "you are the one, and all this is under your command"[130] The historical theology of the Ramesside period is influenced by the same concept of god that is sung in the hymns, viz. as the lord of history and fate.

123 *Ptahhotep* 88-89 (P.London 2). pPrisse reads instead of *jrjw-sj "wsjr"* "Osiris"; s. Westendorf, *MIO* 2 (1954), 165ff.; U. Luft, *Studia Aegyptiaca* IV, 158f.

124 Cf. the topic of transience of life in harpers-songs, hymns of Osiris, lamentations for the dead etc.; cf. *Gs Otto* (1977), 68ff.; *Zeit und Ewigkeit*, 15-18, esp.67.

125 The older concept allows for the possibility that Maat may break down, but equally that it may be restored. Both can be determined by human beings. If Maat does break down, the gods turn away from Egypt (Neferti, Tutankhamun). The later theology of history takes the opposite view: if the gods or god (Re-Amun-Re) turn away from Egypt, Maat too will disappear. Cf. Morenz, *Heraufkunft*, 43-46 and my article "Königsdogma und Heilserwartung" (in *Stein und Zeit*, 259-287).

126 *Merikare* P 136-37.

127 On this process and its interpretation as "semiotisation" cf. my article "Guilt and Remembrance. On the Theologization of History in the Ancient Near East", in *History and Memory* 2.1 (1990), 5-33.

128 Hittite Marriage, Kitchen, *RI* II, 249.10

129 *Edfou* I, 400.1.

130 P.Leiden I 344 vso x, 7-8; Zandee, *Amunshymnus*, 964-971.

The following sentences, which are very similar to a hymn inscribed in the tombs, come from a historical inscription of Ramesses II:

> His name is endless time
> His image is endless duration
> What happens comes from his will.[131]

131 Kitchen, *RI* II, 346.8.

# BIBLIOGRAPHY

W.F. Albright, "The Egyptian Correspondence of Abumilki, King of Tyre", in: *JEA* 23(1937), 190-203.

J.P.Allen, *Genesis in Egypt. The Philosophy of Ancient Egyptian Creation Accounts* (Yale Egyptological Studies 2) (New Haven, 1988)

. - "The Natural Philosophy of Akhenaten", in W.K.Simpson (ed.), *Religion and Philosophy in Ancient Egypt* (Yale Egyptological Studies 3) (New Haven, 1989), 89-102.

Th.G.Allen "Some Egyptian Sun Hymns", *JNES* 8(1949), 349-356.

- *The Egyptian Book of the Dead. Documents in the Oriental Institut Museum at the University of Chicago* (Chicago, 1960).

H.Altenmüller "'Messersee','gewundener Wasserlauf' und 'Flammensee'. Eine Untersuchung zur Lesung und Gleichsetzung der drei Bereiche, *ZÄS* 92(1966), 86-95.

R.Anthes "Sonnenboote in den Pyramidentexten", *ZÄS* 82(1957), 77-89.

J.Assmann *Liturgische Lieder an den Sonnengott. Untersuchungen zur ägyptischen Hymnik* I (MÄS 19) (Berlin, 1969).

- *Der König als Sonnenpriester.Ein kosmographischer Begleittext zur kultischen Sonnenhymnik in thebanischen Tempeln und Gräbern* (ADAIK 7) (Glückstadt, 1970.

- "Zwei Sonnenhymnen der späten XVIII.Dyn.in thebanischen Gräbern der Saitenzeit", *MDIK* 27.1(1971), 1-33.

- "Die 'Häresie'des Echnaton.Aspekte der Amarna-Religion", *Saeculum* 23(1972), 109-126.

- "Eulogie, Königs-", *LÄ* II (1975), 40-46.

- *Zeit und Ewigkeit im alten Ägypten. Ein Beitrag zur Geschichte der Ewigkeit* (AHAW) (Heidelberg, 1975).

- *Ägyptische Hymnen und Gebete* (Zürich, 1975).

- "Das Bild des Vaters im alten Ägypten", in H.Tellenbach (ed.), *Das Vaterbild in Mythos und Geschichte* (Stuttgart, 1976), 12-49 = *Stein und Zeit*, 96-137.

- "Gott", *LÄ* II (1976), 756-786.

- "Fest des Augenblicks, Verheissung der Dauer.Die Kontroverse der ägyptischen Harfnerlieder", in *Fs E.Otto*, (Wiesbaden, 1977), 55-84.

- "Weisheit, Loyalismus und Frömmigkeit", in E.Hornung, O.Keel (eds.), *Studien zu altägyptischen Lebenslehren*, (OBO 28) (Fribourg, 1979), 11-72.

- "Primat und Transzendenz. Struktur und Genese der ägyptischen Vorstellung eines 'Höchsten Wesens'", in W.Westendorf (ed.), *Aspekte der spätägyptischen Religion* (GOF IV.9) (Wiesbaden, 1979), 7-40.

- "Die 'Loyalistische Lehre'des Echnaton", *SAK* 8 (1980), 1-32.

- "Die Zeugung des Sohnes.Spiel, Bild, Erzählung und das Problem des ägyptischen Mythos", in id., W.Burkert, F.Stolz, *Funktionen und Leistungen des Mythos. Drei altorientalische Beispiele* (OBO 48) (Fribourg, 1982), 13-61.

"Königsdogma und Heilserwartung.Politische und kultische Chaosbeschreibungen in ägyptischen Texten", in D.Hellholm (ed.), *Apocalypticism in the Mediterranean World and the Near East* (Tübingen, 1983), 345-77 = *Stein und Zeit*, 259-87.

- *Sonnenhymnen in thebanischen Gräbern* (Theben I) (Mainz, 1983).

- *Ägypten - Theologie und Frömmigkeit einer frühen Hochkultur* (Stuttgart, 1984).

. - "State and Religion in the New Kingdom", in W.K.Simpson (ed.), *Religion and Philosophy in Ancient Egypt* (Yale Egyptological Studies 3) (New Haven, 1989), 55-88.

- *Ma'at. Gerechtigkeit und Unsterblichkeit im alten Ägypten* (Munich, 1990).

- *Stein und Zeit. Mensch und Gesellschaft im alten Ägypten* (Munich, 1991).

- "Akhanyati's Theology of Light and Time", *Proceedings of the Israel Academy of Sciences and Humanities*, VII 4 (Jerusalem 1992), 143-176.

- *Monotheismus und Kosmotheismus. Ägyptische Formen eines "Denkens des Einen" und ihre europäische Rezeptionsgeschichte* (SHAW) (Heidelberg, 1993).

P.Auffret, *Hymnes d'Egypte et d'Israel* (OBO 34) (Fribourg, 1981).

J. Baines, "Practical Religion and Piety", in: *JEA* 73(1987), 79-98.

J. Baines, "Society, Morality and Religious Practice", in: B.E.Shafer (Hrsg.), *Religion in Ancient Egypt* (London-Ithaca 1991), 123-200.

P.Barguet, *Le temple d'Amon-Re á Karnak. Essai d'exegése* (Cairo, 1962).

A.Barucq, *L'expression de la louange divine et de la priére dans la bible et en Egypte* (BE 33) (Cairo, 1962).

A.Barucq,F.Daumas, *Hymnes et priéres de l'Egypte ancienne* (Paris, 1980).

J.v.Beckerath, "Die 'Stele der Verbannten'im Museum des Louvre", *RdE* 20(1968), 7-36.

J.Bergman, *Ich bin Isis. Studien zum memphitischen Hintergrund der griechischen Isisaretalogien* (Uppsala, 1968).

U.Berner, "Überlegungen zur Übertragbarkeit des Komplementaritäts-begriffes auf ägyptische Gottesvorstellungen, *GM* 20(1976), 59-71.

M. C. Betrò, *I Testi solari del Portale di Pascerientaisu (BN2)* (Università degli Studi di Pisa, Missioni Archeologiche in Egitto, Saqqara III) (Pisa 1990).

H.Blumenberg, *Arbeit am Mythos* (Frankfort, 1979).

E.Blumenthal, *Untersuchungen zum Königtum des Mittleren Reiches I. Die Phraseologie* (ASAW 61.1) (Berlin, 1970).

E.Blumenthal, "Die Lehre für König Merikare", in: *Zeitschrift für Ägyptische Sprache* 107(1980), 5-41.

J.F.Borghouts, *Ancient Egyptian Magical Texts* (NISABA 9) (Leiden, 1978).

- "The Evil Eye of Apopis", in: *JEA* 59(1973), 114-150.

- , "Divine Intervention in Ancient Egypt and its Manifestation", in: R.J.Demarée, J.J.Janssen, *Gleanings from Deir el-Medina*, Leiden 1982, 1-70.

P.du Bourguet, "Esquisse de théologie égyptienne des temps pharao-niques", in Ch. Kannengiesser et Y.Marchasson (eds.), *Humanisme et foi chrétienne, Mélanges scientifiques du centenaire de l'institut catholique de Paris* (Paris, 1976), 437-449.

J.H.Breasted, *Development of Religion and Thought in Ancient Egypt* (1912, repr. Philadelphia, 1972).

H.Brunner, "Eine Dankstele an Upuaut", *MDIK* 16(1958), 5-19.

- "Die religiöse Wertung der Armut im alten Ägypten" *Saeculum* 12(1961), 319-344.

- "Echnaton und sein Versuch einer religiösen Reform", *Universitas* 17(1962), 149-162.

- "Der freie Wille Gottes in der ägyptischen Weisheit", in *Sagesses du Proche Orient ancien* (CESS)(Paris, 1963), 103-117.

- *Die Geburt des Gottkönigs* (ÄA 10) (Wiesbaden, 1964).

- *Die südlichen Räume des Tempels von Luxor* (AV 18) (Mainz, 1977).

- "Persönliche Frömmigkeit", in *LÄ* IV (1982), 951-963.

E.Brunner-Traut, *Gelebte Mythen. Beiträge zum altägyptischen Mythos* (Darmstadt, 1981).

A.de Buck, *De zegepraal van het licht* (Amsterdam, 1930).

- *The Egyptian Coffin Texts*, 7 Vols. (Chicago, 1935-61).

- *Plaats en betekenis van Sjoe in de egyptische theologie* (Mede-deelingen en verhandelingen der koninklijke akademie van we-tenschappen, afd.letterkunde, N.R.10.9) (Leiden, 1947).

W.Burkert, *Structure and History in Greek Mythology and Ritual* (Berkeley, 1979).

J.Cerny, *Egyptian Stelae in the Bankes Collection* (Oxford, 1958).

J.Cerny, A.H.Gardiner, *Hieratic Ostraca I* (Oxford, 1957).

M. Dahood, *Psalms III 101-150* (The Anchor Bible), (New York 1970).

N.de Garis Davies, *The MMA Expedition: the Temple of Hibis III, the Decoration* (New York, 1950).

Ph.Derchain, "Perpetuum mobile", *Orientalia Lovanensia Periodica* 6/7 (1975/76), 153-161.

- *Le papyrus Salt 825 (BM 10051). Rituel pour la conservation de la vie en Egypte* (Brussels, 1965).

E.Dondelinger, *Die Treibtafel des Herodot am Bug des ägyptischen Nilschiffes* (Graz, 1976).

Edfou: M.de Chalvet, marquis de Rochemonteix, E.Chassinat, *Le Temple d'Edfou*, 14 Vols. (Cairo, 1892-1934).

G.Fecht, "Zur Frühform der Amarna-Theologie. Neubearbeitung der Stele der Architekten Suti und Hor", *ZÄS* 94(1967), 25-50.

E.Feucht-Putz, *Die königlichen Pektorale. Motive, Sinngehalt und Zweck* (Bamberg, 1967).

R.B.Finnestad, "Ptah, creator of the gods. Reconsideration of the Ptah Section of the Denkmal", *Numen* 23(1976), 81-113.

O.Firchow, "Königsschiff und Sonnenbarke", *WZKM* 54(1957), 34-42.

H.Frankfort, *Kingship and the Gods.A Study of Ancient Near Eastern Religion as the Integration of Society and Nature* (Chicago, 1947).

J.Ste.Fare Garnot, *L'hommage aux dieux sous l'ancien empire d'apres les textes des pyramides* (Paris, 1953).

C. Garve, "Northwest Semitic sapanu in a Brak-up of an Egyptian Stereotype Phrase in *EA* 147", in: *Orientalia* NS 51(1982), 161-182.

A. Gasse, "Litanie des douze noms de Re-Harakhty", *BIFAO* 84(1984), 190-227

S.Hassan, *Hymnes religieux du Moyen Empire* (1930).

S. Hodjash and O. Berlev, *The Egyptian Reliefs and Stelae in the Pushkin Museum of Fine Arts* (Moscow-Leningrad, 1982).

E.Hornung, "Chaotische Bereiche in der geordneten 'Welt'", *ZÄS* 81(1956), 28-32.

- *Das Amduat. Die Schrift des verborgenen Raumes* 3 Vols, (ÄA 8 and 13) (Wiesbaden, 1963/1967).

- "Der Mensch als Bild Gottes in Ägypten", in O.Loretz, *Die Gottebenbildlichkeit des Menschen* (Munich, 1967), 123-156.

- *Der Eine und die Vielen. Altägyptische Gottesvorstellungen* (Darmstadt, 1971).

- *Das Grab des Haremhab im Tal der Könige* (Bern, 1971).

- Altägyptische Unterweltsbücher (1972).

- Das Buch der Anbetung des Re im Westen (Basel, 1975).

- "Monotheismus im pharaonischen Ägypten", in O.Keel (ed.), *Monotheismus im Alten Israel und seiner Umwelt* (Bibl.Beitr.14) (Stuttgart, 1980), 83-97.

- "Die Tragweite der Bilder", *Eranos* Jb.1979 (1981), 183-237.

- *Der ägyptische Mythos von der Himmelskuh. Eine Ätiologie des Unvollkommenen* (OBO 46) (Fribourg 1982).

- "Verfall und Regeneration der Schöpfung", in: *Eranos Jb.* 46(1977), 411-449.

- *Die Nachtfahrt der Sonne* (Zürich 1990).

T.G.H.James, *Corpus of Hieroglyphic Inscriptions in the Brooklyn Museum* (New York, 1974).

B. Janowski, *Rettungsgewißheit und Epiphanie des Heils. Das Motiv der Hilfe Gottes "am Morgen" im Alten Orient und im Alten Testament*, vol. I: Alter Orient (Neukirchen, 1989).

F.Junge, "Wirklichkeit und Abbild.Zum innerägyptischen Synkretismus und zur Weltsicht der Hymnen des Neuen Reiches", in G.Wiessner (ed.), *Synkretismusforschung. Theorie und Praxis* (GOF 1) (Wiesbaden 1978), 87-108.

- "Isis und die ägyptischen Mysterien", in W.Westendorf (ed.), *Aspekte der spätägyptischen Religion* (GOF IV.9) (Wiesbaden 1979), 93-115.

H.Junker, *Die Götterlehre von Memphis* (APAW 1939 Nr.23) (Berlin 1940).

L.Kakosy, *Selected Papers* (Stud.Aeg. VII) (Budapest 1981).

J.Karkowski, "Studies on the Decoration of the Eastern Wall of the Vestibule of Re-Horakhty in Hatshepsut's Temple at Deir el-Bahari", *Etudes et Travaux* IX(1976), 68-78.

- "Deir el-Bahari 1974-75", *Et.et Trav.*XI (1979), 217-220.

O.Keel (ed.), *Monotheismus im Alten Israel und seiner Umwelt* (Bibl.Beitr.14) (Stuttgart 1980).

K.A.Kitchen, *Ramesside Inscriptions, Historical and Biographical*, 7 Vols. (Oxford 1968ff.)

A.Klasens, *A Magical Statue Base (Socle Behague) in the Museum of Antiquities at Leiden* (OMRO 33) (Leiden, 1952).

W.B.Kristensen, *The Meaning of Religion* (Leiden, 1960).

C.Lalouette, *Fideles du soleil* (Faculté des lettres et sciences humaines de Paris, groupe d'études égyptologiques I) (Paris 1963).

J.Leclant, *Recherches sur les monuments thébains de la XXV.dynastie dite "éthiopienne"* (BE 36) (Cairo, 1965).

G.Lefebvre, *Le tombeau de Petosiris* II, Les textes (Cairo, 1923).

L.H.Lesko, "Ancient Egyptian Cosmogonies and Cosmology", in: B.E.Shafer (Hrsg.), *Religion in Ancient Egypt*, 1991, 88-122.

U.Luft, *Beiträge zur Historisierung der Götterwelt und der Mythen-schreibung* (Stud.Aeg.IV) (Budapest, 1978).

Medinet Habu VI: *Medinet Habu VI, The Temple proper II* (OIP 84) Chicago, 1963.

R. Merkelbach, M. Totti (eds.), *Abrasax. Ausgewählte Papyri religiösen und magischen Inhalts* vol.2 (Opladen, 1991).

E.Meyer, *Gottesstaat, Militärherrschaft und Ständewesen in Ägypten* (SPAW 1928) (Berlin, 1928).

J. de Moor, *The Rise of Yahwism* (Leuven 1990).

W.L. Moran, *Les lettres d'El-Amarna* (Paris 1987).

S.Morenz, *Ägyptische Religion* (Stuttgart, 1960).

- "Eine Naturlehre in den Sargtexten" *WZKM* 54(1957), 119-129.

- *Die Heraufkunft des transzendenten Gottes in Ägypten* (SSAW 109.2) (Berlin, 1964).

- *Gott und Mensch im Alten Ägypten* (Leipzig, 1965).

D.Müller, *Ägypten und die griechischen Isisaretalogien* (ASAW 53.1) (Berlin, 1961).

K.Mysliwiec, *Studien zum Gott Atum II: Name, Epitheta, Ikonographie* (HÄB 8) (Hildesheim, 1979).

Marquis of Northampton et alii, *Theban Necropolis, Report on some Excavations* (London, 1908).

E.Otto, "Die Lehre von den beiden Ländern in der ägyptischen Religionsgeschichte", *Stud.Aeg.*I (Rom, 1938), 10ff.

- *Die biographischen Inschriften der ägyptischen Spätzeit* (PÄ 2) (Leiden, 1954).

- "Monotheistische Tendenzen in der ägyptischen Religion", *WdO* 2(1955), 99-110.

- *Das ägyptische Mundöffnungsritual*, 2 Vols. (ÄA 3) (Wiesbaden, 1960).

- "Zum Gottesbegriff der ägyptischen Spätzeit", *FuF* 35.9(1961), 277-280.

- "Zur Geschichte einer religiösen Formel", *ZÄS* 87(1962), 150-154.

- "Altägyptischer Polytheismus.Eine Beschreibung", *Saeculum* 14(1963), 249-285.

- *Gott und Mensch nach den Tempelinschriften der griechisch-römischen Zeit. Eine Untersuchung zur Phraseologie der Tempelinschriften* (AHAW) (Heidelberg, 1964).

- *Wesen und Wandel der ägyptischen Kultur* (Heidelberg, New York, 1969).

- "Der Mensch als Geschöpf und Bild Gottes in Ägypten", in H.W.Wolff (ed.), *Probleme biblischer Theologie* Fs. von Rad (Munich 1971), 335-348.

- "Gott als Retter in Ägypten", H.Stegemann et al. (eds.) *Tradition und Glaube*, Fs. K.G. Kuhn (Göttingen, 1971), 9-22.

R.A.Parker et alii, *The Edifice of Taharqa by the Sacred Lake at Karnak* (Providence, 1979).

A.Piankoff, *Le livre du jour et de la nuit* (BE 13) (Cairo 1942).

G.Posener, *Littérature et politique dans l'Egypte de la XII.e dynastie* (Paris, 1956).

- "Amon, juge du pauvre", in Fs.Ricke (Beiträge Bf 12) (Wiesbaden 1971), 59-63.

- *L'enseignement loyaliste. Sagesse egyptienne du Moyen Empire* (Geneva, 1976).

J.E.Quibell, *Excavations at Saqqara* IV (Cairo, 1908-10).

D.B.Redford, *Akhenaten, the Heretic King*, Princeton 1984.

A.Roccati, "I libro dei morti di Sesonq", *OrAnt* 15(1976), 233-250.

A.Rupp, *Vergehen und Bleiben. Religionsgeschichtliche Studien zum Personverständnis in Ägypten und im Alten Testament* (Saarbrücken, 1976).

M.Sandman, *Texts from the time of Akhenaten* (BiblAeg VIII) (Brussels, 1938).

S.Sauneron, *Esna V. Les fetes religieuses d'Esna aux derniers siecles du paganisme*

(Cairo, 1962).

S.Sauneron, J.Yoyotte, "La naissance du monde selon l'Egypte ancienne", (Sources Orientales I) (Paris, 1959), 17-91.

H.Schäfer, *Ägyptische und heutige Kunst und Weltgebäude der alten Ägypter* (Leipzig, 1928).

- "Altägyptische Bilder der auf- und untergehenden Sonne", *ZÄS* 71(1935), 15-38.

H.A.Schlögl, *Der Sonnengott auf der Blüte* (AH 2) (Basel, 1977)

- *Der Gott Tatenen* (OBO 29) (Fribourg, 1980).

- *Echnaton - Tutenchamun. Fakten und Texte*, (Wiesbaden ²1985).

S.Schott, *Mythe und Mythenbildung im Alten Ägypten* (UGAÄ 15) (Leipzig, 1945).

- "Altägyptische Vorstellungen vom Weltende", *Analecta Biblica* 12(1959), 319-330.

K.C.Seele, *The Tomb of Tjanefer at Thebes* (Chicago, 1959).

P.Seibert, *Die Charakteristik. Untersuchung zu einer ägyptischen Sprechsitte und ihren Ausprägungen in der Folklore und Literatur* (ÄA 17) (Wiesbaden, 1967).

K.Sethe, *Amun und die acht Urgötter von Hermopolis* (APAW) (Berlin, 1929).

K.J.Seyfried, *Das Grab des Paenkhemenu (TT 68) und die Anlage TT 227* (THEBEN VI) (Mainz, 1991).

A.W.Shorter, *Catalogue of Egyptian Religious Papyri in the British Museum. Copies of the Book Pr(t)-m-hrw* I (London, 1935).

H.M.Stewart, "Some Pre-Amarnah Sun Hymns", *JEA* 46(1960), 83-90.

- "Egyptian Funerary Statuettes and the Solar Cult", *Bull. Inst.Arch.*4(1964), 165-170.

- "Traditional Egyptian Sun Hymns of the New Kingdom", *Bull.Inst.Arch.*6(1967), 29-74.

- "Stelophorous Statuettes in the British Museum", *JEA* 53(1967), 34-38.

E.Thomas, "Solar Barks from Prow to Prow", *JEA* 42(1956), 65-79.

Chr.Uehlinger, "Leviathan und die Schiffe in Ps. 104, 25-26", in: *Biblica* 71(1990), 499-526.

J.Vandier, *Le papyrus Jumilhac* (Paris, 1960).

P.Vernus "Le dieu personnel dans l'Egypte pharaonique", *Centre interdisciplinaire d'Etude de l'évolution des idées, des sciences et techniques, Colloques de la soc. Ernest Renan* (Paris, 1977), 143-157.

G.Vittmann, "Die Hymne des Ostrakons Wien 6155 + Kairo CG 25214", *WZKM* 72(1980), 1-6.

W.Westendorf, *Altägyptische Darstellungen des Sonnenlaufs auf der abschüssigen Himmelsbahn* (MÄS 10) (Berlin, 1966).

- "Ursprung und Wesen der Maat", in *Fs Walter Will* (Cologne etc.,1966), 201-225.

L.V.Zabkar, *A Study of the Ba Concept in Ancient Egyptian Texts* (SAOC 34) (Chicago, 1968).

- "A Hymn to Osiris Pantokrator at Philae", *ZÄS* 108(1981), 141-171.

- *Hymns to Isis in Her Temple at Philae* (Hanover and London, 1988)

J.Zandee, *De hymnen aan Amon van Papyrus Leiden I 350* (OMRO 28) (Leiden, 1947).

- "Prayers to the Sun God from Theban Tombs", *JEOL* 16(1959/60), 48-71.

- "Hymnical Sayings addressed to the Sun God by the High Priest of Amun Nebwenenef, from his Tomb in Thebes", *JEOL* 18(1964), 253-265.

- *Der Amunshymnus des Papyrus Leiden I 344, Verso*, 3 Vols. (Leiden 1992).

Abbreviations

Abbreviations are in accordance with the convention of the "Lexikon der Ägyptologie" except the following.

ÄHG Assmann, Ägyptische Hymnen und Gebete

KaS Id., Der König als Sonnenpriester

LL Id., Liturgische Lieder an den Sonnengott

STG Id., Sonnenhymnen in thebanischen Gräbern

## GENERAL INDEX

## SOURCES IN QUOTATION

PERIODICALS